W9-BJZ-299

LINUX APPLIANCE DESIGN

LINUX APPLIANCE DESIGN

A Hands-On Guide to Building Linux Appliances

by Bob Smith, John Hardin,
Graham Phillips, and Bill Pierce

**NO STARCH
PRESS**

San Francisco

SIENA COLLEGE LIBRARY

LINUX APPLIANCE DESIGN. Copyright © 2007 by Bob Smith, John Hardin, Graham Phillips, and Bill Pierce.

All "Tux's Workshop" illustrations © 2006 by Jon Colton.

All rights reserved. No part of this work may be reproduced or transmitted in any form or by any means, electronic or mechanical, including photocopying, recording, or by any information storage or retrieval system, without the prior written permission of the copyright owner and the publisher.

Printed on recycled paper in the United States of America

11 10 09 08 07   1 2 3 4 5 6 7 8 9

ISBN-10: 1-59327-140-9
ISBN-13: 978-1-59327-140-4

Publisher: William Pollock
Production Editor: Elizabeth Campbell
Cover and Interior Design: Octopod Studios
Developmental Editor: William Pollock
Technical Reviewer: Bob Lynch
Copyeditor: Megan Dunchak
Compositor: Riley Hoffman
Proofreader: Publication Services, Inc.
Indexer: Publication Services, Inc.

For information on book distributors or translations, please contact No Starch Press, Inc. directly:

No Starch Press, Inc.
555 De Haro Street, Suite 250, San Francisco, CA 94107
phone: 415.863.9900; fax: 415.863.9950; info@nostarch.com; www.nostarch.com

Library of Congress Cataloging-in-Publication Data

```
Linux appliance design : a hands-on guide to building linux appliances / Bob Smith ... [et al.].
      p. cm.
  Includes index.
  ISBN-13: 978-1-59327-140-4
  ISBN-10: 1-59327-140-9
  1. Linux. 2. Application software--Development. 3. Electric apparatus and appliances--Design and
construction. I. Smith, Robert W. (Robert William), 1952-
QA76.76.O63L545115 2007
005.3--dc22
```

                                                        2006020778

No Starch Press and the No Starch Press logo are registered trademarks of No Starch Press, Inc. Other product and company names mentioned herein may be the trademarks of their respective owners. Rather than use a trademark symbol with every occurrence of a trademarked name, we are using the names only in an editorial fashion and to the benefit of the trademark owner, with no intention of infringement of the trademark.

The information in this book is distributed on an "As Is" basis, without warranty. While every precaution has been taken in the preparation of this work, neither the author nor No Starch Press, Inc. shall have any liability to any person or entity with respect to any loss or damage caused or alleged to be caused directly or indirectly by the information contained in it.

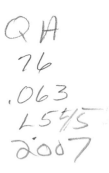

QA
76
.O63
L545
2007

BRIEF CONTENTS

CONTENTS IN DETAIL

4
BUILDING AND SECURING DAEMONS   43

5
THE LADDIE ALARM SYSTEM: A SAMPLE APPLIANCE   61

9
DESIGNING A COMMAND LINE INTERFACE 135

13
HANDS-ON INTRODUCTION TO SNMP
223

14
DESIGNING AN SNMP MIB
243

C
INSTALLING A FRAMEBUFFER DEVICE DRIVER   325

D
A DB-TO-FILE UTILITY   331

E
THE LADDIE APPLIANCE BOOTABLE CD   337

INDEX   345

ACKNOWLEDGMENTS

As authors of the book we would like to thank Peter Enemark, Chris Sommers, and Keith Garrett for their unconditional support of this project and for their contributions to the technology presented.

As readers of the book, you should thank our technical editor, Bob Lynch, for finding many, many errors in the text and on the CD. You should also thank Elizabeth Campbell, Riley Hoffman, and Megan Dunchak for changing some of our technically correct but completely incomprehensible sentences into something both readable and correct.

Our thanks also go to Jon Colton, the artist responsible for the Tux's Workshop series.

INTRODUCTION

Toasters, ovens, and dishwashers are a few of the appliances found in our everyday lives. Though we are quite familiar with their use, few of us stop to think about how an appliance works under the hood, or even what makes an appliance, well, an appliance. This book defines an *appliance* as a device designed to primarily perform a single function. If you think about the appliances just mentioned, you'll see that this definition holds true—toasters toast, ovens bake, and dishwashers wash dishes. Compared to a PC, which is capable of performing thousands of diverse functions depending on the hardware and software installed, traditional appliances are boring and simple.

What does this have to do with Linux? For starters, traditional appliances are no longer so simple. What used to be electrified but still mechanical devices, such as a vacuum cleaners, are now not only electronic, but include processors, circuit boards, and sophisticated user interfaces. With these changes comes the need to run an operating system on the appliance to manage the new features. Linux is a natural fit for this because it is low cost (in most cases, it is free to use) and open source (which means you can modify it to better suit your needs). However, the real place where Linux fits in is with the new types of appliances that are being designed. Digital video recorders (DVRs) were unheard of just a few years ago, but the first and most popular DVR appliance, the TiVo, runs on Linux, as do many other home networking and entertainment appliances.

If you were to build the next great robotic house-cleaning system, you'd want to avoid designing it completely from scratch. You'd reuse as many parts as possible from your earlier robots, and you'd use off-the-shelf components wherever possible. The same *reuse* mentality applies to Linux appliances, and that's where this book can help.

What This Book Is About

This book shows you how to build a Linux appliance, and it includes a prototype appliance that you can use as the basis for your appliance, if you wish. We divide an appliance into daemons and user interfaces and show how to create and manage daemons, as well as how to build five different types of user interfaces.

We cover the following topics:

- Appliance architectures
- How to talk to running daemons
- How to build and secure a daemon
- Laddie, our sample appliance
- Logging and event handling
- Web-based user interfaces
- Command line interfaces (CLIs)
- Front panel interfaces
- Framebuffer interfaces, including infrared remote control
- SNMP interfaces including tools, MIBs, and agents

Most of the chapters have the same basic layout. We define and explain why the feature is necessary, we describe the feature's challenges and common approaches, and we describe how we implemented the feature in our sample appliance.

What This Book Is Not About

This book does not cover C programming, the Linux operating system, or the main application that defines a particular Linux appliance. Furthermore, this book is not about embedded Linux. We believe you will find the following books on embedded Linux useful:

- *Embedded Linux*, by John Lombardo (SAMS/New Riders, 2001)
- *Embedded Linux: Hardware, Software, and Interfacing*, by Craig Hollabaugh (Addison-Wesley, 2002)

- *Linux for Embedded and Real-Time Applications, Second Edition*, by Doug Abbott (Newnes, 2006)
- *Embedded Linux System Design and Development*, by P. Raghavan, Amol Lad, and Sriram Neelakandan (Auerbach Publications, 2005)

Who Should Read This Book

This book is for Linux programmers who want to build a custom Linux appliance and support multiple user interfaces, build secure daemons, or provide logging and event management. The book may also be of value to any developer who wants to minimize the effort needed to port a daemon's user interface to different operating systems or a different programming language. Our only major assumption is that the reader is comfortable programming in C on the Linux platform.

Why Use Linux?

Before diving into the common architecture found on most Linux appliances, we should answer the question, "Why use Linux on an appliance?" While the specific arguments vary, we've found the following to be true for appliances that we've built.

Availability of Source Code

The availability of source code makes it possible to customize the operating system for a particular appliance's needs. Such customization is not possible when using a proprietary, closed source operating system.

Range of Hardware Supported

The Linux kernel supports a wide range of processors, from low-end embedded processors used in consumer electronics to high-end 64-bit processors used in super-computers. For example, Linux runs on Marvell's ARM-based XScale processors (used in Palm handheld computers), Texas Instruments' ARM-based OMAP processors (used in E28 smart phones), IBM's PowerPC (used in the TiVo and the PlayStation 3), Hitachi's H8/300 processors, as well Compaq Alpha AXP, Sun SPARC, IBM S/390, MIPS, HP PA-RISC, Intel IA-64, and AMD *x*86-64 processors.

Availability of Linux Developers

Linux, C, and C++ form the core competence of many computer science graduates in the United States, and indeed, worldwide. Exact estimates vary, but the consensus is that that there are several million Linux-capable developers worldwide.

Reliability

Linux is sufficiently reliable to be widely used in data centers. Uptimes measured in years are not uncommon for Linux, and the Blue Screen of Death has never been a problem.

Quality Compilers

The GNU Compiler Collection is a comprehensive set of compilers, assemblers, linkers, and debuggers that support multiple languages on multiple platforms. It is the compiler of choice for C and C++ development on Linux. Furthermore, it is free. See http://gcc.gnu.org for more information.

Good Documentation

A great deal of documentation about Linux is available on the Internet. One site that serves as a good starting point for documentation is the Linux Documentation Project (see http://en.tldp.org). This site includes subject-specific HOWTOs, FAQs, and in-depth guides.

Existing Software Packages

There are thousands of software packages available to help you develop an appliance on Linux. For example, there is Net-SNMP for Simple Network Management Protocol (SNMP) support, lm_sensors for monitoring the appliance's hardware environment, and lighttpd for web support.

Low Development Cost

Linux appliance programmers can typically use their desktop machines for most software development because appliance user interfaces and services seldom need to be developed on the target hardware. Therefore, software development can proceed in parallel, with one team developing embedded Linux for the appliance and another team developing the main application and user interfaces.

No Licensing Fees for Deployment

Appliance manufacturers can generally build Linux-based appliances without incurring costs for licensing fees to distribute the appliance's software, although there are some exceptions. For example, the Qt library from Trolltech and the MySQL database have licenses that may require payment for commercial use.

Security

Linux appliance developers use packages such as grsecurity and systrace to tighten security to levels undreamed of by Windows developers. Appliances have the additional advantage that a multi-purpose desktop or server can never be as secure as a well-hardened, single-purpose device.

Linux Appliance Design

We've tried to write this book and the accompanying CD to be used as a type of "parts box" that you can pull from as you assemble your appliance. A nice overview of the components in our parts box is given in the first chapter, which presents a high-level view of the architecture common to most Linux appliances.

1

APPLIANCE ARCHITECTURE

We'll begin our adventure with a high-level look at the architecture of a Linux appliance. We'll then drop a little lower in altitude and look at a Linux appliance from the perspective of processes. As you'll soon see, the view from this lower altitude matches the organization and chapters used throughout this book.

In this chapter, we will cover the following:

- UIs and daemons
- The architecture of the Laddie appliance

We have worked on Linux appliances that range from small, handheld devices to large, multi-gigabyte, multi-processor network servers. Most of these appliances have a strikingly similar software architecture.

Figure 1-1 shows the software stack we typically see in a Linux appliance. At the bottom of this stack is an embedded Linux kernel. Above the kernel are the various user interfaces and common services such as network management and logging, and at the top is the particular function that defines the appliance.

Where appliances are concerned, the term *user interface (UI)* refers to an interface through which the user manages the appliance configuration and views its status and statistics. The lack of a screen and keyboard are hallmarks of an appliance, but do not let that fool you—all appliances have UIs. To be sure, the more invisible the UI the better the appliance, but the UI is always there nonetheless. Also, network appliances often have web, SNMP, and command line interfaces, while consumer appliances have framebuffers and small, alphanumeric LCD interfaces.

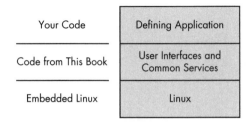

A Linux Appliance

Figure 1-1: Linux appliance software stack

UIs and Daemons

Assuming that our Linux appliance will have multiple, simultaneous UIs, when we look at the appliance from the point of view of running processes we get an architecture something like that shown in Figure 1-2. The UI programs interact with the users to accept commands and configuration and to display status and statistics. Daemons, on the other hand, interact with the hardware, other daemons, and the UIs to provide the appliance's defining service as well as status and statistics.

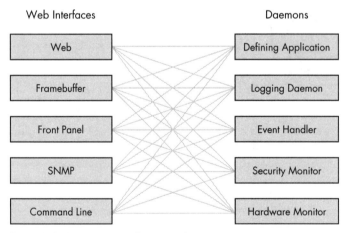

Figure 1-2: A common appliance architecture

Daemons

Daemons are background programs that are most often started just after booting Linux. Daemons distinguish themselves in that they don't have a controlling terminal like programs started from the bash command line. Let's look at the kinds of daemons found on a typical appliance.

Defining Application

The *defining application* in the diagram refers to the daemon that provides the unique function offered by the appliance. For example, the defining application for an advanced telephone answering machine is the daemon that actually answers the phone and records the call.

Logging Daemon

The *logging daemon* shown in Figure 1-2 collects log messages and either saves them to disk or routes them to another host on the network. The syslog daemon is the default logging daemon on most Linux systems.

Event Handler

The *event handler* provides a local, active response to events. Often the logging daemon and the event-handling daemon are one in the same, as they are in the logmuxd daemon that runs on our sample appliance.

Security Monitor

The *security monitor* controls access to critical configuration or resources, such as identification and authentication credentials. The security monitor should also respond to Mandatory Access Control (MAC) violations.

Hardware Monitor

The *hardware monitor* watches for temperature alarms and disk drive problems. Most PC-based Linux appliances will use the lm_sensors package to monitor CPU and motherboard sensors and the smartd daemon to monitor the temperature and error statistics on hard disks. A hardware monitor might combine the information from these and other sources into a comprehensive report of the health of the appliance.

User Interfaces

When we first started building Linux appliances we thought that the nature of the appliance defined the type of UI it would have. Boy, were we wrong. Customers always ask for more than one way to manage the device. Smartphones need a framebuffer interface *and* a web interface over Bluetooth. Network appliances need a web interface *and* an SNMP interface. When you look at Figure 1-2, don't think "Which one?" Think "How many?"

The UIs depicted in Figure 1-2 are not the only possible choices. For example, you might want an interface that runs natively on a Windows PC, or if you're building a network appliance, you may want to add interfaces to an LDAP or RADIUS authentication server or to the network's billing system and database. Figure 1-2 shows the most common UIs and the ones described in the book.

Web Interface

A *web interface* is mandatory if your appliance has a network interface. You'll have a lot to decide here: Do you use JavaScript or not? Is the back end written in Perl, PHP, C, or Java? Which do you use? Do you presume that all browsers support cascading style sheets? Chapter 8 on web UIs will help you evaluate the trade-offs for all these issues.

Framebuffer Interface

Framebuffer interfaces are popular for television set-top boxes, such as TiVo or a PVR, stand-alone kiosks, and some handheld devices. The hardware in a framebuffer gives you direct control over each pixel on the screen. This gives you great flexibility in what your interface looks like, but at the cost of burdening you with *managing* every pixel on the screen. Some libraries and graphics toolsets, such as the Simple DirectMedia Layer (SDL) can help. The art in building a framebuffer interface is in choosing the right toolset.

Front Panel

Front panel interfaces, whether simple or complex, appear on almost all Linux appliances. A simple front panel might have only a few lights and buttons, while a more complex one might have an alphanumeric liquid crystal display (LCD) or a vacuum florescent display. Even a simple front panel may require a deep understanding of the underlying hardware.

SNMP Interface

We have heard it said that an *SNMP interface* makes the difference between a commercially viable network appliance and a hobby. From our experience we'd have to agree. SNMP is not too difficult if you break it into pieces. First, you need to familiarize yourself with the concepts used in SNMP and with the SNMP commands available in Linux. Then, you need to design a Management Information Base (MIB), or schema, for the data made visible by your SNMP interface. Finally, you need to write the software that makes the MIB available to the SNMP commands.

Command Line Interfaces

Command line interfaces (CLIs) are often used as the control interface of last resort for network appliances. A CLI on a serial port remains available even when the entire network is down. CLIs also find use as an appliance-specific scripting language.

Interprocess Communication

Finally, you may have noticed the full-mesh interconnect of lines in Figure 1-2. Don't let it intimidate you. Our point is that any UI should be able to connect to any daemon. This requirement dictates a lot of the features to look for in the interprocess communication (IPC) mechanism used between the UIs and the daemons. (We'll have more to say about this in Chapter 2.)

The Architecture of the Laddie Appliance

This book's sample appliance is an alarm system that uses the input pins on a parallel port for input from the alarm sensors. The UIs include web, command line, LCD with a keypad, framebuffer with IR remote control, and SNMP.

The daemons on our appliance include the alarm system daemon and one to respond to appliance events. We chose not to implement all of the daemons shown in Figure 1-2 so that we could focus on describing how to build and secure daemons in general.

Of course, our sample appliance includes ladd (the defining application), an event handler, and a utility to make common Linux configuration files visible using a protocol common to all the UIs.

Figure 1-3 shows the architecture of the Laddie appliance and maps the UI, feature, or daemon to a chapter number or appendix so that you can see how things will come together throughout the book.

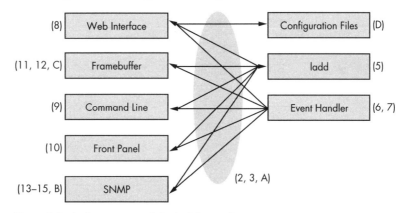

Figure 1-3: A chapter map of the Laddie appliance

We've limited the functionality of our UIs to make them more useful as tutorials. Only the web interface is full featured and representative of what a real appliance might have.

Summary

Most Linux appliances have a common architecture: Linux on the bottom, the defining application on top, and common services and UIs in the middle. We discussed some of the reasons to include various daemons and UIs and mapped this book's chapters into an architecture diagram.

The next chapter looks at the API between the UIs and daemons, since the chosen API impacts both UIs and daemons.

2

MANAGING DAEMONS

 At their core, most appliances have an application or daemon that performs the defining function of the appliance, with one or more user interfaces managing the core application or daemon. Figure 2-1 shows a typical appliance architecture that might already be similar to what you have in mind for your appliance.

In the same way that the defining application is managed by user interfaces (UIs), the common services, such as a webserver or system logger, need to be managed as well. Because the main application and most common services are implemented as daemons, the problem of management comes down to the problem of managing daemons. The focus of this chapter is how best to manage daemons.

In this chapter, we'll cover the following:

- Common approaches to managing daemons
- Control and status protocol

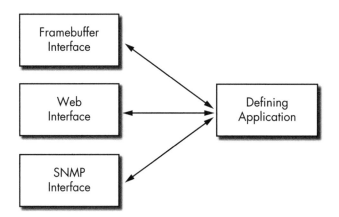

Figure 2-1: Typical user interfaces to an application

Common Approaches to Managing Daemons

By *managing* a daemon, we mean configuring the daemon, collecting statistics from it, and being able to view its current status. Most Linux daemons use ASCII text files for such communication, but there are other options for you to consider when building your daemon. The next few sections will describe various daemon-management methods and their pros and cons.

File-Based Management

Daemons are commonly managed or monitored through a few configuration files that control their run-time parameters, status, and logging. For example, the DHCP daemon, dhcpd, is controlled by the /etc/dhcpd.conf configuration file; its status is displayed in /var/state/dhcp/dhcpd.leases; its start-up script is in /etc/rc.d/init.d/dhcpd; and its logs are in /var/log/messages. There is little uniformity, however, in how a daemon's configuration is stored or how its status is made available. Status and other state changes are often logged using syslog(), but many applications use custom routines for logging and store their log files in a non-standard format. Figure 2-2 shows the typical flow of a daemon that uses files for configuration and management.

A file-based approach has the following limitations for appliances:

- There is no good way to get status or statistics from most running applications. While an application could write status and statistics to files, to do so in real time (or anything close to real time) would probably be too heavy a load on the CPU and filesystem.

- You need to be able to edit the configuration file, which is not always easy on an appliance.

- To apply new settings, you usually have to restart a running daemon, which may disrupt service and cause problems for users.

Current Unix Model

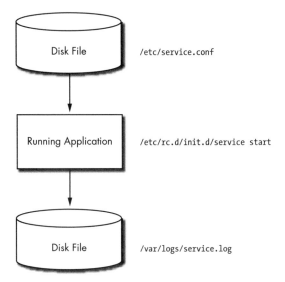

Figure 2-2: The most common way to manage a daemon

Despite the limitations of file-based interfaces, many applications use them for Unix system administration, and they will probably remain popular. If you are building a new application and you've chosen to use file-based application management, consider using libini or an XML parsing library. Also, applications like Webmin can help by offering a web front end that allows you to display and edit many configuration files.

Keep in mind that very simple applications (including some daemons) may never need run-time access to status, statistics, and configuration. There might not be any reason to switch from the traditional .conf and .log file approach of Unix. It is up to you to decide which approach is best for your particular application.

A Daemon-Based Web Interface

Another common approach to daemon management is to offer a web interface directly from the daemon. For example, cupsd, the daemon for the print spooler CUPS, provides its own web interface on TCP port 631. This approach is viable for simple daemons, but it has two problems:

- You will need to maintain code in your daemon to support the HTTP implementations in many different browsers.
- It can be difficult to add additional interfaces when they are required.

Case in point, we needed run-time access to status and configuration for one of our projects, so we added a built-in web interface. What a coding nightmare! It seemed to take forever to get all of the details of HTTP right and to make the resulting code compatible with all of the major web browsers. If you decide to build a web interface directly into your daemon, do yourself a favor and use an HTTP library like libhttpd from Hughes Technologies. Because other coders, experts in HTTP, keep it up to date regarding the quirks of various browsers, your maintenance will be much easier.

This same project also highlights the second problem. Once the web interface was working, the customer requested we add an SNMP interface. The fastest way to do this was to add SNMP directly to the daemon as we did with the web interface. This addition put us well on the path to what we call an "all-in-one" approach, which is described in the next section.

An All-in-One Approach

If you know that your users need to interact with your daemon while it is running, and if your running daemon needs more than one type of interface, you might be tempted to add the necessary interfaces directly to the daemon. Figure 2-3 shows a daemon that is not only trying to perform its real task but is also trying to support multiple, simultaneous user interfaces.

All-in-One Approach

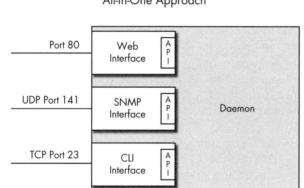

Figure 2-3: Adding all the user interfaces directly to the daemon

We used a bundling approach like this in one of our early designs, but we found that it created a lot of problems. Because only a few developers could work on the appliance at a time, development became serial, so developers had to code both the main daemon and all of the user interfaces. The tight coupling between UI and daemon made it more difficult to isolate changes to one section of code. We were afraid that even simple user interface changes might have side effects, so we made every change wait for the full regression testing of a major release. The whole development and release cycle became much slower.

Another problem with the all-in-one approach is performance. If all the user interfaces run directly from the daemon, the daemon may spend all of its CPU cycles in some possibly unimportant interface request while ignoring the real work it needs to do.

Control and Status Protocols

One way to overcome the limitations of the approaches described above is to use a protocol for control and status to separate the daemon from the user interfaces. Figure 2-4 illustrates a daemon offering a single application programming interface (API) to be used by all of the clients and user interfaces.

One Protocol for Control and Status

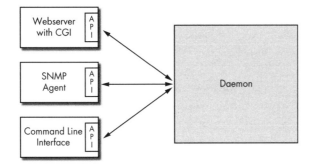

Figure 2-4: Using one protocol between the daemon and user interfaces

A control and status protocol has several advantages over the alternatives:

Reduced complexity for multiple user interfaces
A control and status protocol simplifies the user interface logic in the daemon, since the daemon only needs to implement that protocol. The user interfaces can be implemented independently using the languages and tools appropriate to the interface. For example, a web interface could be built with Apache and PHP, while an SNMP interface could be built with Net-SNMP and C.

Access to the daemon while it is running
Users want access to an application while it is running in order to get status, statistics, and run-time debugging information. A control and status protocol can give you a competitive advantage over applications that are limited to configuration file access only at startup and SIGHUP. You might note that Microsoft users do not configure a daemon by editing a file; they configure the daemon through the daemon itself. Therefore, designing your daemon to be configured in this way can make it easier for Microsoft users to migrate to your software.

Remote network access
Remote access can speed development and testing, since you can work on the appliance from almost any networked workstation. Remote access is useful to your customers who manage a large number of appliances from a central operations management center. Furthermore, good remote access will be required by your technical support staff to help diagnose problems in the field.

Parallel development

Decoupling the management user interfaces from the daemon means that you can have two teams working on the project in parallel. Staffing is easier because you can hire people with just the skills needed to develop a specific piece of the project. Separating user interface developers and daemon developers has another advantage: It forces you to think through and define your daemon's interface early in the development, when changes are easiest to make.

Easy test scaffolding

Because the user interface is separate from the daemon, building a test scaffold around each piece of code is a clean and easy process. Once you build a scaffold, you can test even if all the pieces aren't in place.

Improved security

Using a control and status protocol for your daemon can increase the security of your appliance in two ways. First, the user interfaces need not run with the same special privileges as the daemon, which means that less code with special privileges is running at any given time. Second, using a tightly defined protocol lets you focus on securing the protocol and its API. This is much easier than securing, say, an all-in-one approach.

A control and status protocol can use a serial connection, a Unix or TCP socket, or file reads and writes, or it might be hidden in a library call. These techniques are described later in this chapter. As a preview, consider the following examples, which set a single bit called *cntl_pt*.

```
AT commands    ATS301=1
XML    <rpc><cntl_pt><value>1</value></cntl_pt></rpc>
Library call    ret = set_cntl_pt(1);
/proc    echo 1 > /proc/sys/mydev/cntl_pt
SQL    UPDATE my_table SET cntl_pt = 1
```

Requirements for a Control and Status Protocol

If you design your own control and status protocol, you should judge your design on the following criteria: its data model on client and daemon, its re-use of existing protocols and software, the constraints it places on clients and daemons, and the ease with which you can discover its system:

The data model

The control and status protocol should allow the client and daemon to have the same data model. That is, if the daemon uses variables, structures, lists, and arrays, then the client on the other side of the control and status protocol should also support variables, structures, lists, and arrays. Having the same data models on both sides of the protocol can make it easier to re-use code, and it helps programmers maintain a consistent view of the problem they're trying to solve.

Use existing standards and code

The control and status protocol should use existing software and standards whenever possible. You may be able to find developers who already know the protocols and software, and existing protocols and software are likely to have good documentation for the developers who need to learn them. Using existing code is almost always a good idea, since less new code means fewer new bugs.

Few constraints on the daemon and clients

Ideally, the protocol would place few constraints on how you design your daemon and wouldn't increase the daemon's size. You should be able to add the control and status protocol to your program with few changes to the main source files. When retrofitting old programs with the control and status protocol, you should be able to put the bulk of the new code in separate source files, instead of interweaving the changes into the main code base. Client binding for your protocol should be available for all the major programming languages: at least Java and PHP for web interfaces, and C and C++ for compiled code.

Discovery mechanism

We want to discover the information that is available from the appliance without relying on documentation. For example, the ls command discovers which files are available in a Unix filesystem; the get-next operator discovers what is in a SNMP MIB; and the system tables in a database describe the database itself. In a similar way, we want a mechanism whereby a user can discover what can be configured on an appliance and what information is available from the appliance.

Common Control and Status Protocols

In our work we have developed several control and status protocols, which we will describe in this section. As you're reading, try to judge them in terms of the four criteria presented in the previous section.

AT Commands

In our first control and status protocol, we used a variation of the Hayes AT command set. The appliance we were working with was a radio modem, so most of our customers were already familiar with that command set, making it a logical choice. Our daemon listened for incoming TCP connections and offered an AT command interpreter to accepted connections. Using TCP gave us remote access for diagnostics and configuration.

We stored the system configuration as a list of AT commands. At system startup the daemon would read the configuration file and run it through the AT command interpreter. This approach meant that we did not need to add code to process a different format for the configuration files. While XML and INI are the standards in storing configuration, we did not want to add code and complexity if we could easily avoid it.

The AT command protocol had two limitations. First, we could not conveniently access data arrays using the standard AT S-register syntax. Second, client-side programmers had to write a lot of code to generate the AT commands and parse the replies.

Extensible Markup Language

We used Extensible Markup Language (XML) as the control and status format in a project to manage Juniper routers. Examples of XML protocols include XML-RPC, SOAP, and JUNOScript. JUNOScript manages Juniper routers through a telnet or SSH connection. It enables you to encode commands in XML, and the router then replies with XML responses. For example, a request for the running configuration looks like this:

```
<rpc>
<get-configuration/>
</rpc>
```

Prior to the availability of JUNOScript Juniper routers were configured via a command-line interface (CLI). The advantages of XML over CLI become apparent when you manage routers with a program rather than by hand (especially if you have to write that program). It is easier to write code for parsing XML responses than for parsing CLI responses. Other advantages of XML include its flexibility in representing rich data and the availability of software libraries for processing XML formats.

Exchanging XML data between a client and server requires the addition of a transport protocol. You could use telnet or SSH, like JUNOScript does, or you could use HTTP, as specified by the SOAP and XML-RPC standards.

Typically, you would use a library to parse the XML on the server side, and then marshal the parsed XML elements into the server's internal data structures. The code to map the XML to the internal data structures can be complex and error prone, since the XML structure seldom maps directly onto the data model used in the daemon.

If you build your control and status protocol using XML, you should consider using the Simple API for XML (SAX). SAX uses an event-driven model for processing the XML, and it is a better fit for the kinds of dialogs found in a control and status protocol.

Library Calls

For another project, we used the popular technique of hiding the protocol from the developer by wrapping it in the subroutines of an API. In this case, the daemon and client programmers included shared object libraries in their code, and neither dealt with the protocol directly. The library routines in the API *became* the protocol as far as the developers were concerned. So ubiquitous is this approach that many programmers cannot imagine an alternative. They start a project with the assumption that they'll build a daemon and a library, and clients of the daemon must include the library in order to talk to the daemon.

Our advice is to let other programmers write libraries and to avoid it yourself. Most of the reasons for saying this distill down to minimizing the number of lines of code you have to write and maintain. Hiding the protocol in a library API does not remove the need to code the protocol and library. You still need to think about which IPC to use and the actual protocol to use over that IPC. Perhaps the biggest burden is writing and maintaining the client-side libraries for all of the programming languages of interest—gone are the days when you could write a C library and be done. You'll want the library available in Java and PHP for web interfaces, and in Perl and as a shell command for scripts and testing. Few companies have all the experts on staff that are needed to write and document these libraries, and fewer still have the time to properly maintain and update the libraries after each revision change.

We've gone the route of trying to write libraries for our daemons, and one of the things we found was that we kept reinventing the wheel. Every library, no matter how similar to the previous, was written for the daemon at hand, so we had to write a different library for every daemon. While we tried to re-use code, this process fell far short of ideal. How nice it would have been to have just one library (and one underlying protocol) that we could have used for all of our daemons.

Having one library per daemon is particularly problematic for embedded systems, in that you may have to give up a lot of system RAM in order to load all the libraries needed.

Structured Query Language

In an attempt to have just one control and status protocol for all of our daemons, we tried Structured Query Language (SQL) text commands over TCP and modeled the data in our daemon as tables in a database. The daemon accepted a TCP connection and presented an SQL command line interpreter to the client. This protocol allowed us to represent arrays (and lists) in the control and status protocol, thus solving one of the limitations of the AT command protocol. Figure 2-5 illustrates the basic idea.

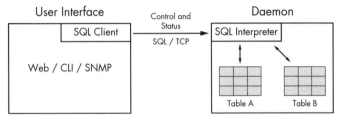

Figure 2-5: SQL as a control and status protocol

For example, a typical command over the TCP connection might be the string:

```
SELECT Column_A FROM Table_A
```

The command interpreter was then responsible for parsing the SQL string and accessing the appropriate "table." Table is in quotations because the data in the daemon could be represented by arbitrary data structures, and it was the responsibility of the SQL interpreter to make these arbitrary data structures appear as tables to the client.

Similar to the AT control and status protocol, our configuration files were stored as text files with SQL commands; this eliminated the need for libraries to parse XML or INI files.

The best part of this approach was that the data in the daemon was already stored as arrays of structs, so the shift to a "table" paradigm was trivially easy for the programmers. The limitation of this protocol was the amount of code that had to be developed on the user interface or client side. Because the protocol was text based, we had to write client-side code to format and send the request and to parse the response. This code had to be rewritten for each programming language that the particular client was written in. In our case, there was significant effort required because we developed a Windows C++ client, a Java client, a Mac OS 9 C client, and a Linux C client.

PostgreSQL

Our final control and status protocol overcomes the limitations of the previous one. It is similar to our SQL protocol in that it models the daemon's data as tables in a database and it uses TCP or Unix sockets between the daemon and the client. The difference is that instead of a proprietary text-based protocol, it uses the PostgreSQL protocol. Using PostgreSQL means we can use the client-side PostgreSQL binding for C, Java, PHP, bash, and many others.

All of the hard work of offering up a daemon's internal data structures as database tables is handled by a library called *Run-Time Access (RTA)*. We link our daemons with the RTA library, and after the daemons tell RTA about our tables, it offers them up as PostgreSQL database tables.

Although RTA uses PostgreSQL as the control and status protocol, it is *not* a database. Rather, it uses a subset of the PostgreSQL protocol and client-side bindings as a means of reading and writing memory variables in a running daemon.

PostgreSQL and RTA have several advantages as a control and status protocol. As mentioned, there are a number of PostgreSQL bindings already available in various languages, including C, C++, Java, Perl, Tcl, and Python. The availability of these bindings means that you will have less code to develop on the UI or client, so you are less constrained in how you write your UI clients. PostgreSQL has a liberal license and is exceptionally well documented, and the system tables in RTA can be used as a way to browse the data offered to the UI programs.

Security can be enhanced by using a Unix socket and setting the ownership and read/write permissions carefully. Use SELinux and the Linux Security Module for even more precise control over which programs can connect to RTA on the daemon. Consider using Stunnel or SSH with port forwarding for secure remote access.

While XML is popular, RTA and PostgreSQL have a few advantages over it. PostgreSQL offers both a data exchange format and a transport protocol. With RTA, you don't need to marshal code to map the tree structure of XML into the daemon's internal data structures, so the RTA approach requires less development than XML-based approaches. With RTA, the client can look directly at the daemon's internal memory variables, and this functionality requires no additional development.

RTA is presented in greater detail in the next chapter, but a simple example might show how RTA works as seen from the UI client. Suppose that the daemon has an array of the following structures:

```
struct Zone {
  char  zname[Z_NAME_LEN]; /* user edited string */
  int   zenabled;      /* user edited value */
  int   zcount;        /* transition count */
};
```

After telling RTA about the array (with rta_add_table()) you can use any PostgreSQL-enabled client to read and write data in the array. If you use psql, a PostgreSQL shell program, you can read the Zone table with the following SELECT command:

```
psql -h localhost -p 8889
# SELECT zname, zenabled FROM Zone;
  zname   | zenabled
-----------+--------------------
 Garage    | 1
 Front Door | 1
 (2 rows)
```

This example shows a simple way to read variables from a running daemon.

There are some disadvantages to RTA. One is that the RTA library is written in C, which means that you can't use RTA if your server process is written in another language—say, Java. Another disadvantage is that if your appliance is composed of multiple daemons, you'll need to develop a management process to manage these daemons, while exposing only a *single* management point to the clients. To be fair, this last disadvantage is true of all control and status protocols.

Summary

In this chapter we discussed various ways to manage daemons. Simple daemons can use files for all management, but we believe that for Linux appliances with multiple user interfaces, a control and status protocol is best. We described the reasons to use a control and status protocol and presented some guidelines to follow if you decide to build your own.

In the next chapter we'll show you how to incorporate RTA into a daemon so that the client has access to the daemon's status, configuration, and statistics.

All of the examples used in the remainder of the book use PostgreSQL and the RTA library as the management protocol between daemons and user interfaces. Don't be concerned if you choose not to use RTA, though. The book is more about appliance *design* than using particular libraries.

3

USING RUN-TIME ACCESS

This chapter gives you a practical introduction to developing Linux appliances with the RTA library. Consider this your "Hello, world!" example. In this chapter, we'll discuss the following:

- RTA appliance architecture
- RTA daemon architecture
- Telling RTA about your columns and tables
- Building your first RTA program
- A little SQL
- An introduction to RTA's built-in tables
- The RTA table editor

RTA Appliance Architecture

You may recall from the last chapter that there were several reasons to put a well-defined protocol between the UI programs and the daemon. A protocol offers reduced complexity in both the UI and the daemon, gives access to the daemon while it is running, lets you work on and test the UIs and daemon independently, and helps improve security. The important requirements for the protocol are that the protocol's data model matches your view of the data, that you don't have to define or write the protocol yourself, and that the protocol will be available for most UI programming languages.

The data model we use in this book is that of a database. Because we view our arrays of structures as tables of data, the UI programs (or *clients*) see the data in the daemon as data in a database. While the UI programs think they are dealing with a PostgreSQL database, they are, in fact, talking to the daemon. This arrangement results in an appliance architecture similar to that shown in Figure 3-1, in which a framebuffer UI uses the PostgreSQL C language binding in libpq.so; the web UI uses the PostgreSQL PHP binding in pgsql.so; and the test and debug UI uses the command line program psql.

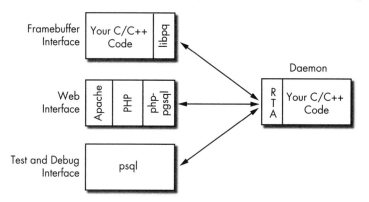

Figure 3-1: A sample appliance using RTA

After connecting to the daemon over a Unix or TCP socket, the UIs shown in Figure 3-1 can display the configuration, status, and statistics available in the daemon. The librtadb.so library presents the daemon's data as if it were coming from a PostgreSQL database. This figure shows the PostgreSQL client-side binding that we use in this book, but many more language bindings are available including Java, Python, Tcl, Perl, and Microsoft C++.

Figure 3-1 offers a global view of the appliance. Now let's look at how RTA works inside the daemon.

RTA Daemon Architecture

Adding RTA to your daemon is fairly straightforward, since it usually involves using only two routines from the library. The first routine, rta_add_table(), makes one of your daemon's tables visible to the clients. The second routine, dbcommand(), handles the protocol and SQL commands from the clients. Figure 3-2 illustrates a daemon offering RTA access to two UI-visible tables.

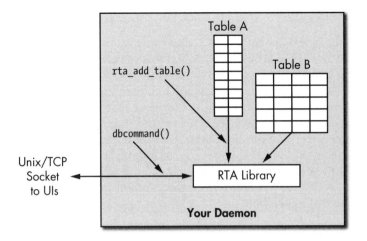

Figure 3-2: A daemon using RTA

The dbcommand() routine does not communicate directly with the client. Your program must create a listening TCP or Unix socket and must be able to accept and manage connections from the UI or other clients. Once a connection is established, all data from the connection should be passed to RTA with a call to dbcommand(). The dbcommand() routine parses the SQL command in the request from the client; if the request is valid, it executes the SQL command and returns a buffer with any data to be sent back to the client.

RTA would be of limited usefulness if all it could do was read and write values in your tables. Its real power lies in its ability to call a routine whenever a UI reads or writes a value into one of your tables. These read and write *callbacks* are similar to traditional database triggers. Callbacks are tied to the column definition and are specified separately for reads and writes. (We describe callbacks in the more detail in the next section.)

Telling RTA About Your Columns and Tables

A table is an array or linked list of data structures. Each member of your data structure is considered to be a column in a table, and each instance of the data structure is considered to be a row. From this point on, when you see the term *column*, think *member of my data structure*. In order to make a table visible to clients, you need to describe the table in a way that RTA can understand. This means describing the table as a whole and then describing each column in the table.

A TBLDEF structure describes the table as a whole; it contains a pointer to an array of column definitions with a COLDEF structure to define each column in your data table. At first you may find the process of creating COLDEFs and TBLDEFs painstaking and tedious, but once you have a little experience, you'll find it simple and mechanical.

Columns

One big advantage of RTA is that you don't need to marshal the data into and out of the protocol. RTA uses your data as it already exists in your program. Of course, you have to describe your data so that RTA can access it intelligently. A table is made up of columns, and we need to describe each column in the table. This is the purpose of RTA's COLDEF data structure.

You can also have members in your data structure that are not defined by a COLDEF. Such hidden columns might include information that you do not want to be visible to the UIs, or binary data that would have no meaning if it was displayed to the user.

A COLDEF contains nine pieces of information about each of your structure's members.

```
typedef struct {
  char    *table;         // name of column's table
  char    *name;          // name of column for SQL requests
  int      type;          // data type of column
  int      length;        // width of column in bytes
  int      offset;        // number of bytes from start of row
  int      flags;         // flags for read-only and save-to-file
  void    (*readcb) ();   // routine to call before reading column
  int     (*writecb) ();  // routine to call after writing column
  char    *help;          // description of the column
} COLDEF;
```

table

The table field specifies the name of the table as seen from the UI programs.

name

The name field specifies the name of the column. Use this name when selecting or updating this column.

type

The type of the column is used for syntax checking and for SQL SELECT output formatting. The currently defined types include:

```
RTA_STR                  // string,  (char *)
RTA_PTR                  // generic pointer  (void *)
RTA_INT                  // integer  (compiler native int)
RTA_LONG                 // long  (actually a gcc 'long long')
RTA_FLOAT                // floating point number
RTA_PSTR                 // pointer to string
RTA_PINT                 // pointer to integer
RTA_PLONG                // pointer to long
RTA_PFLOAT               // pointer to float
```

length

RTA uses the native compiler data types in order to match the data types you use in your structures. The `length` member is ignored for integers, longs, floats, and their associated pointer types, but it has meaning for strings and pointers to strings, both of which should report the number of bytes in the string (including the terminating null).

offset

The `offset` is the number of bytes from the start of the data structure to the structure member being described. For example, a table using a data structure with an int, a 20-character string, and a long would have the offset to the long set to 24 (assuming it was a 4-byte int).

Computing the offset of a structure member is painstaking and error prone. The gcc compiler suite provides the `offsetof()` macro to automatically compute the offset of the structure member.

flags

A column has two binary attributes that are specified by the `flags` member. The first attribute specifies whether the column can be overwritten or if it is read-only. Statistics are often marked as read-only. An error is generated if a column marked as read-only is the subject in an UPDATE statement. The #define for this attribute is `RTA_READONLY`.

The second attribute specifies whether or not values written to this column should be saved in a configuration file associated with the table. Values that should persist from one invocation of the program to the next should be marked with the #define `RTA_DISKSAVE` attribute.

The flags field is the bitwise `OR` of `RTA_DISKSAVE` and `RTA_READONLY`.

readcb()

If defined, the *read callback* routine, `readcb()`, is called every time the column's value is used. This is handy for values that take lots of CPU cycles to compute but that are used infrequently. A read callback is invoked each time the column is referenced—if your SQL statement uses the column name twice, the read callback is called twice.

The read callback is passed five parameters: the table name, the column name, the text of the SQL request, a pointer to the row affected, and the zero-indexed row number. A function prototype for a read callback is shown below.

```
int readcb(char *tbl, char *col, char *sql, void *pr, int rowid);
```

A read callback returns zero on success and an error code if an error occurred in the callback. (See Appendix A for a list of the error codes and more details on callbacks.) Check the return value in your clients in order to enhance reliability and security.

writecb()

Write callbacks can be the real engine driving your application. If defined, the write callback, writecb(), is called after all columns in an UPDATE have been changed. Consider the following SQL command:

```
UPDATE ifcfg SET addr="192.168.1.1", mask = "255.255.255.0";
```

If there is a write callback on addr, it will be called after both addr and mask have been updated. RTA does the write callback after all the fields have updated in order to help maintain consistency.

Write callbacks are passed six parameters: the table name, the column name, the text of the UPDATE statement, a pointer to the row affected, the zero-indexed row number, and a pointer to a copy of the row before any changes were made. (This last parameter is useful when you want to know both the old and new values for the row.) The copy of the old row is in dynamically allocated memory, which is freed after the write callback returns. A function prototype for a write callback is shown below.

```
int writecb(char *tbl, char *col, char *sql, void *pr, int rowid, void *poldrow);
```

The write callback returns zero on success and nonzero on failure. On failure, the row is restored to its initial value and an SQL error, TRIGGERED ACTION EXCEPTION, is returned to the client. Write callbacks allow you to enforce consistency and can provide security checks for your system.

help

Your help text for the column should include a description of how the column is used, any limits or constraints on the column, and the side effects caused by any read or write callbacks. (Give yourself and your fellow developers meaningful help text for your columns to make it easier to maintain and troubleshoot your code.)

Tables

You tell RTA about each of your tables with a call to the RTA routine rta_add_table(). The single parameter to rta_add_table() is a pointer to a TBLDEF structure that describes the table.

The TBLDEF structure uses 10 pieces of information to describe your table. The most critical of these are the name of the table, the start address of the array of structures, the width of each structure (that is, the width of each row), the number of rows, and a pointer to an array of COLDEF structures that describe the columns in the table. Most of the fields in the TBLDEF structure should be self-explanatory.

```
typedef struct {
  char    *name;        // the SQL name of the table
  void    *address;     // location in memory of the table
```

```
int     rowlen;      // number of bytes in each row
int     nrows;       // number of rows
void    *(*iterator) (void *cur_row, void *it_info, int rowid);
void    *it_info;    // transparent data for the iterator call
COLDEF  *cols;       // an array of column definitions
int     ncol;        // number of columns
char    *savefile;   // save table in this file
char    *help;       // a description of the table
} TBLDEF;
```

savefile

The need to save configuration data from one boot of the appliance to the next is so common that the authors of RTA included the ability to automatically save table data in a file when the data is updated. There is one file per table, and the name of the file is specified in the TBLDEF structure as the savefile string. You can mark the columns to save by adding the RTA_DISKSAVE flag to the column definition.

The save file contains a list of UPDATE statements, one for each row in the table. The save file is read from the disk and applied to the table when you initialize the table with the rta_add_table() call. The combination of RTA_DISKSAVE on a column and a savefile for the table eliminates the need to parse XML or INI files to get initial or saved configuration values. Of course, you can use XML or INI if you prefer to—just set the savefile pointer to a null.

iterator

An *iterator* is a subroutine in your code that steps through a linked list or other arrangement of the rows in your table. The iterator lets you treat a linked list, a B-tree, or just about any other scheme for organizing data as if the data was in a table.

The iterator function is called with three parameters: a pointer to the current row, the void pointer it_info from the TBLDEF, and the zero-indexed row number. The function returns a pointer to the next row. When RTA asks for the first row, the current row pointer is NULL, and the desired row index is zero. The function should return a NULL when RTA asks for the row after the last row in the list. If an iterator is defined, the address and nrows members in the TBLDEF are ignored. Here is its function prototype.

```
void    iterator(void *cur_row, void *it_info, int rowid);
```

There is one caveat when using iterator functions: Loading a save file may fail if you have not already allocated all the links in the linked list. (Remember, the save file is a list of UPDATE statements and expects the rows to already exist.) Fortunately, there is a simple way around this problem. Always keep one unused row available, and when that row is written by an UPDATE statement, have a write callback allocate another row so that you can stay one step ahead of the UPDATEs. The logmuxd program presented in Chapter 7 uses this technique.

Building Your First RTA Program

Now we'll look at how to use RTA to expose a table inside a running program. The five basic steps for doing so are:

1. Defining the problem.
2. Reviewing the code.
3. Installing RTA.
4. Building and linking.
5. Testing.

Defining the Problem

We want to expose the UI program to an array of structures that contain a user-editable string and two integers. One of the integers, *zalarm*, is set by the user. The other, *zcount*, is incremented on each transition of zalarm from one to zero or from zero to one. We print a message to the console each time a transition occurs. The string, *zname*, is considered a configuration value and is saved in a disk file whenever it is updated. Since zcount is a statistic, we mark it as read-only. This sample problem is a precursor to the actual Laddie appliance application presented in Chapter 5. The code presented below is also available in the file myapp.c on this book's companion CD.

Reviewing the Code

This code walk-through should give you an idea of what to expect in RTA-enabled programs.

Includes, Defines, and Memory Allocation

First, we'll look at the code:

```
/* A simple application to demonstrate the RTA package. */
/* Build with 'gcc myapp.c -lrtadb' */
#include <stdio.h>
#include <stdlib.h>
#include <stddef.h>              /* for 'offsetof' */
#include <unistd.h>              /* for 'read/write/close' */
#include <sys/socket.h>
#include <netinet/in.h>
#include "/usr/local/include/rta.h"ludes string.h.

    /* Forward references */
❶ int   zedgedetect(char *tbl, char *col, char *sql, void *pr,
                    int rowid, void *poldrow);
❷ #define INSZ      500
  #define OUTSZ     5000
  #define Z_NAME_LEN    20
❸ struct  ZData {
      char    zname[Z_NAME_LEN]; /* user-edited string */
      int     zalarm;            /* user-edited value */
```

```
      int    zcount;              /* transition count of zalarm */
};
❹ #define ROW_COUNT  5
   struct ZData zdata[ROW_COUNT];
```

The transitions of zalarm are detected in a write callback. Here, ❶ is the forward reference for it.

We need to allocate buffers for the text of the SQL command from the client and for the response returned to the client. At ❷ we are using 500 and 5,000 bytes, respectively. These values are chosen to hold the largest possible SQL statement we expect to use and the largest possible result we expect to get back.

The structure definition at ❸ is the heart of the application's data. Each instance of this data structure looks like a row in a database to the various UIs and clients.

We see at ❹ that our table has five rows in it.

Column Definitions

Here is the array of COLDEFs that define the columns in our table. The information in the COLDEFs is derived from the data structure we want to make visible and from our problem statement.

```
COLDEF zcols[] = {
  {
    "ztable",             /* the table name */
    "zname",              /* the column name */
    RTA_STR,              /* it is a string */
    Z_NAME_LEN,           /* number of bytes */
    offsetof(struct ZData, zname), /* location in struct */
    RTA_DISKSAVE,         /* flags: configuration data */
    (int (*)() 0,         /* called before read */
    (int (*)() 0,         /* called after write */
    "User assigned name for this row. The names are "
    "saved to a disk file since they are part of the "
    "configuration. Note that the maximum name length "
    "is 20 characters, including the terminating NULL. "
  },
  {
    "ztable",             /* the table name */
    "zalarm",             /* the column name */
    RTA_INT,              /* it is an integer */
    sizeof(int),          /* number of bytes */
    offsetof(struct ZData, zalarm), /* location in struct */
    0,                    /* no flags */
    (int (*)() 0,         /* called before read */
❶  zedgedetect,          /* called after write */
    "A user read/write value. Print a message on all transitions "
    "from high-to-low or from low-to-high. Do not display anything "
    "if a write does not cause a transition. A write callback "
    "translates all nonzero values to a value of one."
  },
```

Note ❶ the definition of the zedgedetect write callback in the COLDEF above. We do the transition detection of zalarm in this callback.

```
  {
    "ztable",           /* the table name */
    "zcount",           /* the column name */
    RTA_INT,            /* it is an integer */
    sizeof(int),        /* number of bytes */
    offsetof(struct ZData, zcount), /* location in struct */
    RTA_READONLY,       /* flags: a statistic */
    (int (*)()) 0,      /* called before read */
    (int (*)()) 0,      /* called after write */
    "The number of transitions of zalarm. This is a"
    "read-only statistic."
  },
};
```

Table Definition

In the TBLDEF we give the name of the table, its start address, the size of each row, the number of rows, a pointer to the table of COLDEFs for this table, and the number of columns in the table. The save file, /tmp/zsave.sql, will be used to save the RTA_DISKSAVE columns, which, in this case, is only the name column.

```
TBLDEF ztbl = {
    "ztable",           /* table name */
    zdata,              /* address of table */
    sizeof(struct ZData), /* length of each row */
    ROW_COUNT,          /* number of rows */
    (void *) NULL,      /* linear array; no need for an iterator */
    (void *) NULL,      /* no iterator callback data either */
    zcols,              /* array of column defs */
    sizeof(zcols) / sizeof(COLDEF),
                        /* the number of columns */
    "/tmp/zsave.sql",   /* Save config in /tmp directory */
    "A sample table showing the use of column flags and write callbacks"
};
```

main() Routine

This is pretty standard code. We allocate our socket structures and other local variables, then we initialize the table values and use rta_add_table() to tell RTA about our table.

```
int main()
{
    int   i;                    /* a loop counter */
    int   srvfd;                /* File Descriptor for our server socket */
    int   connfd;               /* File Descriptor for conn to client */
    struct sockaddr_in srvskt;  /* server listen socket */
    struct sockaddr_in cliskt;  /* socket to the UI/DB client */
```

```
        socklen_t adrlen;
        char   inbuf[INSZ];        /* Buffer for incoming SQL commands */
        char   outbuf[OUTSZ];      /* response back to the client */
        int    incnt;              /* SQL command input count */
        int    outcnt;             /* SQL command output count */
        int    dbret;              /* return value from SQL command */


        /* init zdata */
        for (i=0; i<ROW_COUNT; i++) {
            zdata[i].zname[0] = (char) 0;
            zdata[i].zalarm   = 0;
            zdata[i].zcount   = 0;
        }

        /* tell RTA it about zdata */
        if (rta_add_table(&ztbl) != RTA_SUCCESS) {
            fprintf(stderr, "Table definition error!\n");
            exit(1);
        }
```

Setting Up a Listening Socket

Remember that each UI program treats our application as if it were a
PostgreSQL database, and we have to accept either Unix or TCP connections
from these clients. Therefore, as the final piece of initialization, we set up the
socket to listen for incoming client connections. Our program is listening on
TCP port 8888, so we need to tell our PostgreSQL clients to use this port.

NOTE   *The following code has some serious shortcomings (i.e., blocking I/O, ignoring error
conditions, and making optimistic assumptions about socket I/O). Our goal, however,
is to make the code understandable by keeping it as short as possible.*

```
/* We now need to open a socket to listen for incoming
 * client connections. */
adrlen = sizeof (struct sockaddr_in);
(void) memset ((void *) &srvskt, 0, (size_t) adrlen);
srvskt.sin_family = AF_INET;
srvskt.sin_addr.s_addr = INADDR_ANY;
srvskt.sin_port = htons (8888);
srvfd = socket(AF_INET, SOCK_STREAM, 0); /* no error checks! */
bind(srvfd, (struct sockaddr *) &srvskt, adrlen);
listen (srvfd, 1);

/* Loop forever accepting client connections */
while (1) {
    connfd = accept(srvfd, (struct sockaddr *) &cliskt, &adrlen);
    if (connfd < 0) {
        fprintf(stderr, "Error on socket/bind/listen/accept\n");
        exit(1);
    }
    incnt = 0;
    while (connfd >= 0) {
```

❶

```
        incnt = read(connfd, &inbuf[incnt], INSZ-incnt);
        if (incnt <= 0) {
            close(connfd);
            connfd = -1;
        }
        outcnt = OUTSZ;drlen from int to socklen_t.
```

The ❶ read() call above uses blocking I/O. In a real application we would want to accept the connection and use a select() or poll() to multiplex for us. However, in this example we are trying keep the line count low.

dbcommand() Call

The following call is where the real work of RTA occurs. We pass the SQL command read from the client into the RTA library which parses it, verifies it, executes it, and fills outbuf with the result. We switch on the result of the dbcommand() call to see if we should send the result back to the client or close the connections. Under normal circumstances, the PostgreSQL client will do an orderly close and the dbcommand() call will return RTA_CLOSE.

```
        dbret = dbcommand(inbuf, &incnt, outbuf, &outcnt);
        switch (dbret) {
            case RTA_SUCCESS:
                write(connfd, outbuf, (OUTSZ - outcnt));
                incnt = 0;
                break;
            case RTA_NOCMD:
                break;
            case RTA_CLOSE:
                close(connfd);
                connfd = -1;
                break;
            default:
                break;
        }
    }
  }
}
```

Write Callback

Here is the subroutine that is called after a UI/client program has set the zalarm column. A typical SQL command for this update would be UPDATE ztable SET zalarm = 0.

NOTE *When first learning to use callbacks, you might want to add a print statement to the callback to display the table, column, input SQL, and row number.*

```
/* zedgedetect(), a write callback to print a message when
 * the alarm structure member is set from zero to one or
 * from one to zero. We also normalize zalarm to 0 or 1. */
```

```
int zedgedetect(char *tbl, char *col, char *sql, void *pr,
                int rowid, void *poldrow)
{
    /* We detect an edge by seeing if the old value of
     * zalarm is different from the new value. */
    int oldalarm;
    int newalarm;

    /* normalize nonzero values to 1 */
    if (((struct ZData *) pr)->zalarm != 0) {
        ((struct ZData *) pr)->zalarm = 1;
    }

    oldalarm = ((struct ZData *) poldrow)->zalarm;
    newalarm = ((struct ZData *) pr)->zalarm;
    if (oldalarm != newalarm) {
        zdata[rowid].zcount++;   /* increment counter */

        printf("Transition from %d to %d in row %d\n",
               oldalarm, newalarm, rowid);
    }
```

A transition is detected by comparing the old value of zalarm with the new value. Both old and new values of the row are passed into the routine as parameters. We always return success in this example.

```
    return(0);  /* always succeeds */
}
```

NOTE   *As a reminder, if the write callback returns a nonzero value, the row affected is restored to its old value and the client program receives an error result from the SQL command that it sent.*

Installing RTA

You can find a copy of the RTA package on this book's companion CD and on the RTA project website (http://www.linuxappliancedesign.com). Check the website for the latest version. The SQL parser in RTA is written using yacc and lex, so your development system will need to have both installed if you build RTA from its source code.

The default installation of RTA puts the .a and .so libraries into the /usr/local/lib directory. If you do not want to use /usr/local/lib, you can edit the makefile before performing the install.

Once you have downloaded the RTA package, extract the files and build the library. The sample code below shows you how.

```
# tar -xzf rta-X.Y.Z.tgz
# cd rta-X.Y.Z
# cd src
# make librtadb.so.2
# make install
```

Building and Linking

Now create a test directory under rta-X.Y.Z and copy myapp.c to it. Next, build the application with this command:

```
# gcc myapp.c -o myapp -L/usr/local/lib -lrtadb
```

To compile and run the application, we tell the system where to find the RTA libraries at runtime. You can edit /etc/ld.so.conf and run `ldconfig` or export the `LD_LIBRARY_PATH` environment variable. If the compile succeeded, you should be able to run the application with these commands:

```
# export LD_LIBRARY_PATH=/usr/local/lib
# ./myapp
```

That's it! Your sample application should be up and running and ready to respond to PostgreSQL requests.

Testing

In this section we assume you have installed PostgreSQL from your Linux distribution or from the version included on this book's companion CD, and that the psql command is somewhere on your path. If all has gone well, you should now have an application running which pretends to be a PostgreSQL database server. Instead of a database, however, our sample application is offering up its internal table for use by various PostgreSQL clients. The client we will be using first is the command line tool, psql.

Assuming everything is in order, open another terminal window and start psql, specifying the host and port of the database server as follows. (Remember that we told our application to listen on port 8888.)

```
# psql -h localhost -p 8888
```

PostgreSQL should respond with something like this:

```
Welcome to psql 8.1.5, the PostgreSQL interactive terminal.

Type:  \copyright for distribution terms
       \h for help with SQL commands
       \? for help on internal slash commands
       \g or terminate with semicolon to execute query
       \q to quit
```

Let's give psql a simple SQL command:

```
# SELECT * FROM ztable;
 zname | zalarm | zcount
-------+--------+--------
       | 0      | 0
       | 0      | 0
       | 0      | 0
       | 0      | 0
       | 0      | 0
(5 rows)
```

If your SQL command did not display the above table, you need to debug the RTA installation. The most common problem is a version mismatch in the PostgreSQL protocol between the client and RTA. The psql client may give a warning, but it is fairly forgiving of using a newer client with an older server. This may be the case if you are using the very latest psql client.

Check the RTA website to see if your version of RTA is compatible with your version of PostgreSQL. If there is a mismatch, update either RTA or PostgreSQL. This book's companion CD contains versions of the RTA and PostgreSQL libraries that are known to be compatible. You can also do a `netstat -natp` to verify that the application is really listening on port 8888.

Before dropping into the tutorial on SQL, let's try a couple of commands just to see how the application responds.

```
# UPDATE ztable SET zalarm = 1;
UPDATE 5
#
```

This should cause a *transition* message to be printed on the console where you started myapp. (Note that psql responds with the number of rows changed, and because we did not specify which row to change, all five rows were updated.)

Now issue the same command a second time.

```
# UPDATE ztable SET zalarm = 1;
UPDATE 5
#
```

There should be no message printed to the console, since this time there was no transition.

Setting zalarm back to zero should cause a transition, and the count of transitions should now be 2.

```
# UPDATE ztable SET zalarm = 0;
UPDATE 5
# SELECT * FROM ztable;
 zname | zalarm | zcount
-------+--------+--------
       | 0      | 2
       | 0      | 2
       | 0      | 2
       | 0      | 2
       | 0      | 2
(5 rows)
```

When you first started ./myapp, the saved table configuration file, /tmp/zsave.sql, did not exist. Create it by doing an update on a column that is marked as RTA_DISKSAVE.

```
# UPDATE ztable SET zname = "row name";
UPDATE 5
#
```

You can verify the above by doing a cat on /tmp/zsave.sql. You should see the following:

```
UPDATE ztable SET zname = "row name" LIMIT 1 OFFSET 0
UPDATE ztable SET zname = "row name" LIMIT 1 OFFSET 1
UPDATE ztable SET zname = "row name" LIMIT 1 OFFSET 2
UPDATE ztable SET zname = "row name" LIMIT 1 OFFSET 3
UPDATE ztable SET zname = "row name" LIMIT 1 OFFSET 4
```

To conclude this section on RTA, let's generate some errors and look at the corresponding error messages.

```
# UPDATE ztable SET zcount = 0;
ERROR:  Can not update read-only column 'zcount'
#  UPDATE ztable SET zname = "abcdefghijklmnopqrstuvwxyz";
ERROR:  String too long for 'zname'
#
```

A Little SQL

Structured Query Language is a standard way to manipulate data in a database. RTA uses only two SQL commands: SELECT, to get data from a table, and UPDATE, to write data to a table. The RTA syntax for SELECT and UPDATE is a limited subset of the standard SQL syntax, with one minor extension.

SELECT

The SELECT statement reads values out of a table. The syntax for the RTA SELECT statement is:

```
SELECT column_list FROM table [where_clause] [limit_clause]
```

The column_list is a comma-separated list of column names or a single asterisk (*) to retrieve all columns. The variable table is the name of the table you wish to examine. The where_clause specifies which rows to return, and the limit_clause tells how many rows to return. Here are some simple examples.

```
SELECT * FROM ztable
select * from ztable
SELECT zcount, zname FROM ztable
```

You can specify the columns in any order, and you can ask for the same column more than once.

NOTE *The SQL parser recognizes the SQL reserved words in both upper- and lowercase letters. We use uppercase in our examples to make the reserved words more visible.*

Also, SQL does not require a semicolon at the end of the line, but the psql command line tool does.

UPDATE

The UPDATE statement writes values into a table. The syntax for the RTA UPDATE statement is:

```
UPDATE table SET update_list [where_clause] [limit_clause]
```

The update_list is a comma-separated list of value assignments in the following format:

```
column_name = value[, column_name = value...]
```

In the example above, value is a literal value. Let's look at some more examples.

```
UPDATE ztable SET zalarm = 44
UPDATE ztable SET zalarm = 0, zname = Terminator
UPDATE ztable SET zalarm = 1, zname = "Mr. Terminator"
```

Strings with spaces must be enclosed in either single or double quotes. One kind of quote can be enclosed in the other kind of quote.

```
UPDATE ztable SET zname = "Baker's Pride"
UPDATE ztable SET zname = 'Just say "no"'
```

WHERE

A WHERE clause specifies which rows to select or update, based on the data in the rows. WHERE might be the single biggest reason to use SQL. The form of the WHERE clause is:

```
col_name rel_op value [AND col_name rel_op value ...]
```

The supported comparison operators are equality, inequality, greater than, less than, greater than or equal to, and less than or equal to. Only logical AND is available to link column comparisons, and value must refer to a literal value. For example:

```
SELECT * FROM ztable WHERE zalarm != 0
UPDATE ztable SET zalarm = 1 WHERE zname = "Front Door"
```

LIMIT

The LIMIT clause can limit the number of rows selected to limit rows, and can specify that the first OFFSET rows be ignored. The form of the LIMIT clause is:

```
[LIMIT limit [OFFSET offset]]
```

Normal SQL does not support the idea of "give me only the third row," but this functionality is important if you're trying to manage an embedded application. The LIMIT and OFFSET clauses let you specify exactly how many rows should be returned and how many candidate rows to ignore before starting the read or write. If there is a WHERE clause, the offset and limit apply only to the rows that match the WHERE conditions. For example:

```
UPDATE ztable SET zname = "Front Door" LIMIT 2
UPDATE ztable SET zname = "Back Door" LIMIT 3 OFFSET 2
UPDATE ztable SET zalarm = 1 LIMIT 2 OFFSET 1
SELECT zname FROM ztable LIMIT 4
UPDATE ztable SET zname = "Garage" LIMIT 1 OFFSET 2
SELECT * FROM ztable WHERE zalarm = 1 LIMIT 1
```

NOTE   *A great way to step through a table one row at a time is to set LIMIT to 1 and increment OFFSET from 0 up to one less than the number of rows.*

You may remember that we said that we stored RTA_DISKSAVE columns in the save file given in the table definition, and that we wanted to store the configuration as SQL commands so that we could run it through the SQL parser. You can see a good example of the LIMIT clause and of save files by looking at /tmp/zsave.sql.

```
# cat /tmp/zsave.sql
UPDATE ztable SET zname = "Front Door" LIMIT 1 OFFSET 0
UPDATE ztable SET zname = "Front Door" LIMIT 1 OFFSET 1
UPDATE ztable SET zname = "Garage" LIMIT 1 OFFSET 2
UPDATE ztable SET zname = "Back Door" LIMIT 1 OFFSET 3
UPDATE ztable SET zname = "Back Door" LIMIT 1 OFFSET 4
```

Real SQL purists reading this are probably pounding the table with their shoe and shouting, "Where's ORDER_BY and INSERT and DELETE . . . and . . . and . . . ?" They are not there. Remember, RTA is *not* a database—it is an interface. We only need SELECT and UPDATE.

Introduction to RTA's Built-in Tables

The RTA library has several built-in tables. Appendix A has the full details, so we will introduce them here. The first table has only one row.

rta_dbg

The rta_dbg table lets you control how and what is logged. You can turn on tracing of all SQL by setting trace to 1, and you can direct log messages to neither, syslog, stderr, or both by setting target to 0, 1, 2, or 3, respectively. You can also specify the priority, facility, and ident values for syslog(). From psql we get:

```
# select * from rta_dbg;
 syserr | rtaerr | sqlerr | trace | target | priority | facility | ident
--------+--------+--------+-------+--------+----------+----------+-------
 1      | 1      | 1      | 0     | 1      | 3        | 8        | rta
(1 row)
```

rta_stat

The rta_stat table holds statistics related to the calls into RTA. It contains counts of the different types of errors, how many connections have been opened into RTA, and the number of SELECTs and UPDATEs.

```
# select * from rta_stat;
 nsyserr | nrtaerr | nsqlerr | nauth | nselect | nupdate
---------+---------+---------+-------+---------+---------
 0       | 0       | 1       | 3     | 6       | 7
(1 row)
```

rta_tables

The rta_tables metatable is a collection of table definition structures. In order to add a table into RTA, you had to fill in a data structure with a description of your table. The collection of table definition structures is itself a table in RTA. This is one of the RTA metatables.

```
# select name, address, rowlen, nrows, ncol from rta_tables;
    name     |   address   | rowlen | nrows | ncol
-------------+-------------+--------+-------+------
 rta_tables  | 0           | 40     | 5     | 10
 rta_columns | 0           | 36     | 36    | 9
 rta_dbg     | 1073986432  | 48     | 1     | 8
 rta_stat    | 1073988768  | 48     | 1     | 6
 ztable      | 134517280   | 28     | 5     | 3
(5 rows)
```

The two RTA metatables have zero in the address field because they are actually an array of pointers, so they use an iterator function. All of the columns in the metatables are marked read-only, since all of the values are set from the rta_add_table() call.

rta_columns

The rta_columns metatable is a collection of column definitions. All of the column definitions from all of the tables are collected into the rta_columns table. (The table actually holds pointers to the COLDEF structures.) We can see what columns are in a table using the metatables and a WHERE clause.

```
# SELECT table, name FROM rta_columns WHERE table = ztable;
 table  | name
--------+--------
 ztable | zname
 ztable | zalarm
 ztable | zcount
(3 rows)
```

What do you suppose we would get if we combined the RTA metatables with PHP? Read on.

The RTA Table Editor

The RTA package has a web/PHP-based utility called a *table editor* that reads the RTA metatables and lets you view and edit any table in the system. Figure 3-3 shows the screen that lets you choose which table to view or edit. The screenshots in Figures 3-3, 3-4, and 3-5 were taken from our development system while we were working on the myapp.c application. You can see a similar screen by booting this book's companion CD and using the browser on another PC to view http://192.168.1.11/rta/rta_tables.php?port=8885.

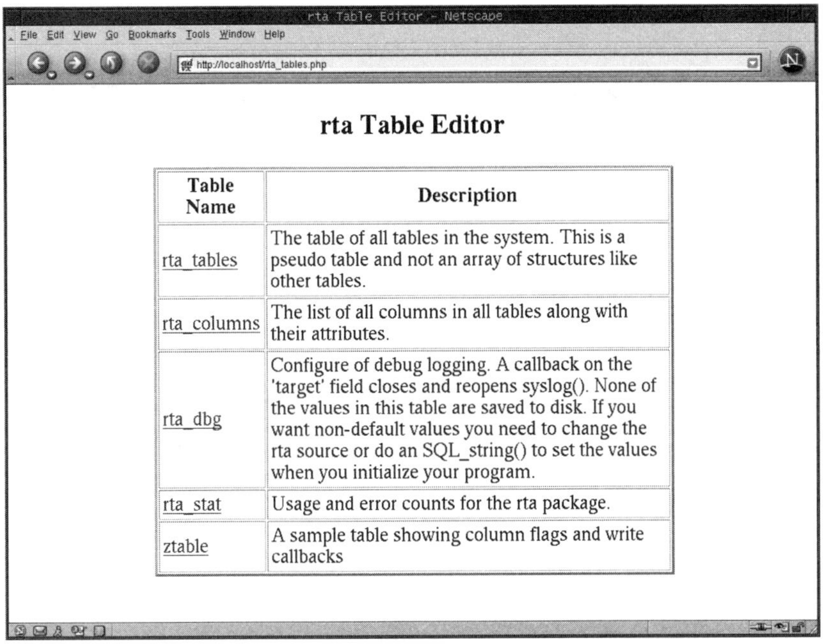

Figure 3-3: The RTA Table Editor

Selecting a table from the top screen opens a web page with the contents of the selected table. Figure 3-4 shows a display of the example program's ztable.

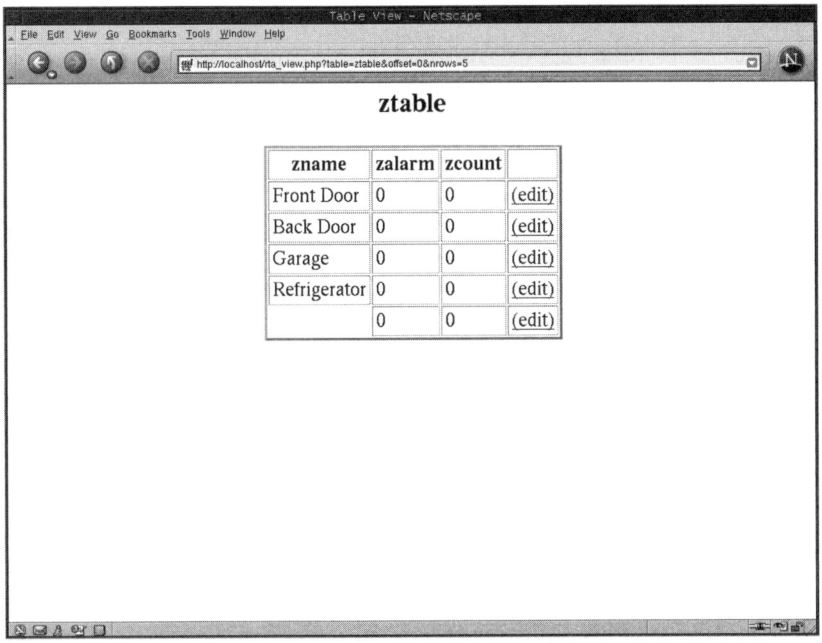

Figure 3-4: A sample table display

SIENA COLLEGE LIBRARY

You can select a row to edit from the table display. Figure 3-5 shows the view after selecting row number 3.

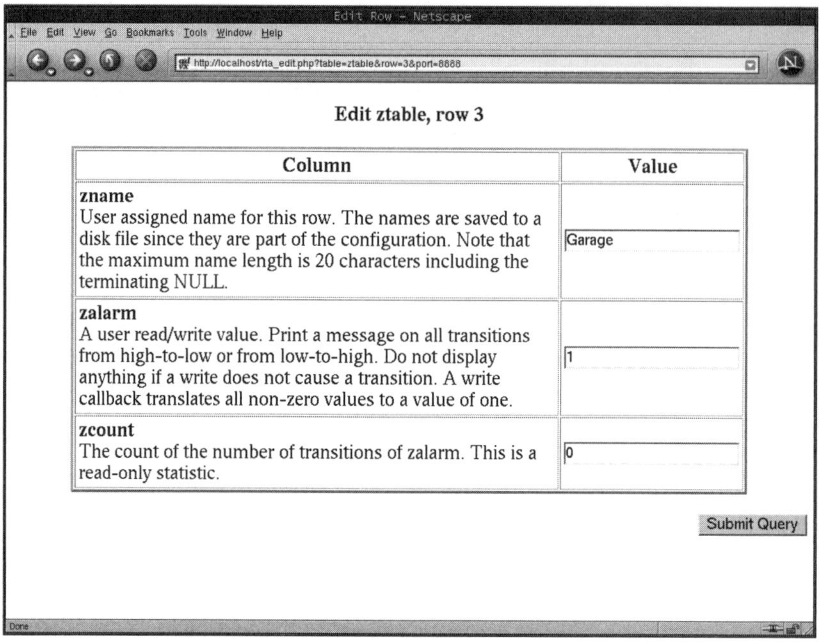

Figure 3-5: A sample row edit screen

The RTA table editor has one HTML file and four PHP files that can be put on any PHP-enabled webserver. In fact, the webserver does not even need to run on the same machine as the application.

The HTML file contains a list of the RTA port numbers in use. You will have a different port number for each RTA-enabled application that you run. On our development machine, we have an HTML table with port numbers and RTA application names that looks like this:

```
<table border=3 cellpadding=4 align=center width=60%>
<tr><th>App Name</th><th>Port Number</th></tr>
<tr><td><a href=rta_tables.php?port=8884>network</a></td>
    <td>8884</td></tr>
<tr><td><a href=rta_tables.php?port=8885>rta2filed</a></td>
    <td>8885</td></tr>
<tr><td><a href=rta_tables.php?port=8886>LCD</a></td>
    <td>8886</td></tr>
<tr><td><a href=rta_tables.php?port=8887>Logmuxd</a></td>
    <td>8887</td></tr>
<tr><td><a href=rta_tables.php?port=8888>LAD-D</a></td>
    <td>8888</td></tr>
<tr><td><a href=rta_tables.php?port=8889>empd</a></td>
    <td>8889</td></tr>
</table>
```

Summary

This chapter has presented the details of how to build your application using RTA so that several different types of UI programs can manage it. You've seen that you need to tell RTA about the data structures you want to make visible by describing them with TBLDEFs and COLDEFs.

While all this may seem a little overwhelming at first, stick with it. After just a little practice, you'll find that writing TBLDEFs and COLDEFs is straightforward and mostly mechanical. The extra effort to add RTA to your daemon is more than compensated by having run-time access to configuration, status, and statistics.

4

BUILDING AND SECURING DAEMONS

 At the heart of almost all Linux appliances is one or more daemons, the background programs that provide a network or system service. You can get an idea of the daemons available on your Linux system by looking in the /etc/rc.d/init.d directory or by using the ps ax command to show the daemons you have running on your system.

The term *daemon* refers to a program that runs in the background without a controlling terminal. Daemons also run in their own process group in order to avoid inadvertently receiving signals meant for other processes. A daemon usually redirects standard input, output, and error to /dev/null or to a log file. Many daemons use a Process ID file (or pidfile) to enforce mutual exclusion to a resource; this prevents more than one copy of the daemon from running at the same time.

This chapter shows you how to build and secure the daemons you'll be using in your appliances. It's divided into three main sections.

- How to Build a Daemon
- How to Secure a Daemon
- A Prototype Daemon

How to Build a Daemon

This section shows you how to build a daemon and offers a brief explanation of why each step is needed. Your application may not require all of the steps listed, and you may need to do them in a different order to meet your needs, but this will give you a general idea, nonetheless.

1. Load the configuration.
2. Go into the background.
3. Become the process and session leader.
4. Set the working directory.
5. Redirect stdin, stdout, and stderr.
6. Set up logging.
7. Set group IDs and user IDs.
8. Check for a pidfile.
9. Set the umask.
10. Set up signal handlers.

NOTE   *The sample daemon presented later in this chapter includes code for each of these steps. Some of the following sections use code taken from the sample daemon.*

Load the Daemon's Configuration

When a daemon starts, it needs to load a set of parameters that govern its operation. This usually means parsing options on the command line and reading settings from a configuration file.

The command line used to start the daemon often contains entries such as the location of the configuration file, the user and group IDs to use while running, and whether or not the program should become a daemon or stay as a foreground process. Some daemons let you specify the daemon's working directory as well as whether or not to do a chroot() before starting.

There is a precedence to the configuration information. Specifically, compiled-in values are always loaded first, since they are loaded when the program starts. Next, the configuration values from the configuration file are loaded, overwriting the compiled-in values. Finally, the values from the command line are loaded, overwriting the values from the configuration file.

Compiled-in values should focus more on security than functionality, since an attacker might delete or modify the configuration file as part of a break in. As a security precaution, some daemons refuse to run if they cannot open and load a configuration file.

Since the configuration file is often specified on the command line, your program may need to make two passes through it: once to get the configuration file and a second time to parse the command line again after the configuration file has been loaded. Parameters on the command line are often used while debugging, so their values normally override those in the configuration file.

NOTE *Make sure your program does a sanity check by verifying the consistency of the configuration and that it reports errors or exits if any problems are found.*

Go into the Background

Once the configuration is loaded, the next step is for the process to (optionally) go into the background, where it can detach itself from the controlling terminal. This is achieved by calling the fork() function to create a child process. The parent process should exit after the fork.

In order to go into the background, the child process closes the file descriptors of the controlling terminal. The result is that we have a *background process* that is not attached to a controlling terminal.

Your code might look like this example in which the parent process forks and exits, leaving the child process to continue setting up the daemon:

```
pid_t   dpid;          //daemon PID

dpid = fork();
if (dpid <0)       // Error ?
     exit(-1);
if (dpid > 0)      // Parent?
     exit(0);
// we are the child and continue setting up the daemon
```

There are two times when you should not send your process into the background: when debugging (since you want your terminal to remain the controlling terminal for the program so that you see any diagnostic messages and can kill the program if you need to), and when you want to automatically respawn your program if it dies. In the latter case, the daemon should remain in the foreground so that the parent process will receive control when the daemon exits (whether gracefully or due to some error).

The following example shell script shows how you can automatically respawn a daemon.

```
#!/bin/sh
while true
do
     mydaemon
     logger "Restarting mydaemon"
done
```

Two common alternatives to a shell script monitor are to add your daemon to /etc/inittab and let the init process respawn it, or to write a custom monitor program to respawn the various daemons on the appliance. The /etc/inittab approach might save memory and a few entries in the process table, and you don't need to write any new software. The script to respawn mydaemon could be replaced with a single line in /etc/inittab. If the default runlevel is 3, the line might appear as:

```
ap:3:respawn:/usr/local/bin/mydaemon
```

The word *respawn* tells the init program to restart mydaemon if it dies.

Become the Process and Session Leader

The Linux kernel assigns each process to a process group and to a session, both of which are used in the distribution of signals. In a *session*, all the processes are typically started from an xterm window or from a virtual console login. In a *process group*, all the processes are started in a command-line pipe. Each session has only one process group that receives input from the controlling terminal; that process group is called the *foreground process group*.

For example, open an xterm or log in to a virtual console, and enter these commands:

```
cat | sort | uniq | tr a d &
cat | sort | uniq | tr a d
```

From another xterm or console, the output of ps xj might appear as:

	PPID	PID	PGID	SID	TTY	TPGID	STAT	UID	TIME	COMMAND
	2501	2504	2504	2504	pts/2	5331	S	501	0:00	bash
❶	2504	**5327**	5327	2504	pts/2	5331	T	501	0:00	cat
	2504	5328	5327	2504	pts/2	5331	S	501	0:00	sort
	2504	5329	5327	2504	pts/2	5331	S	501	0:00	uniq
	2504	5330	5327	2504	pts/2	5331	S	501	0:00	tr a d
❷	2504	**5331**	5331	2504	pts/2	5331	S	501	0:00	cat
	2504	5332	5331	2504	pts/2	5331	S	501	0:00	sort
	2504	5333	5331	2504	pts/2	5331	S	501	0:00	uniq
	2504	5334	5331	2504	pts/2	5331	S	501	0:00	tr a d

All of the processes from the first command line will appear in a process group with ❶ the cat process (PID 5327 in the above example) as the process leader.

Now look at the Process Group ID (PGID) column in the output of ps xj. All of the programs on each command line have the PGID set to the PID of the cat command that starts the command line. All the commands for the first line have a PGID of 5327, and all the commands for the second line have a PGID of 5331. The second command (❷), the one you did not put into the background, is the foreground process group for the session, so its PID (5331) is the Session Group ID (TPGID) for all of the processes running in the xterm session. Recall that the session leader (5331 in this example) is the process that gets standard input from the terminal (hence the term Terminal Process Group ID, TPGID).

The reason for having separate IDs for the process group and session is that if you kill a process group, you want the kernel to send the TERM signal to all of the processes in the group. The same is true if you want to kill the processes in a session.

We don't want a daemon to receive signals that were not meant for it, and so we want the daemon to be in its own session and its own process group. Here is code that shows how to use setsid() to make your daemon a session and process group leader:

```
pid_t  dpid;       // setsid() return our PID or a -1

dpid = setsid();  // Be session & process group leader
if (dpid <0)
    exit(1);       // Should not happen
```

As an exercise, you might try typing the ps jax command and examining the sessions, process groups, and foreground process groups for the daemons running on your system. You should be able to tell which processes belong to the different session and process groups.

NOTE   *As a security precaution, do another fork() after calling setsid() and have the parent exit immediately, leaving the child to continue as the daemon. This removes the session leader status of the daemon in such a way that it can never regain a controlling terminal.*

Set the Working Directory

Daemons traditionally use the root directory, /, as the working directory. This allows the daemon to continue working even if most other filesystems are unmounted. Using the root directory also makes it easier to put your daemon into a chroot jail for added security. (Chroot jails are described in "Chroot if Possible" on page 59.)

Some daemons let you specify the working directory in the configuration file or on the command line. Whether you use the root directory, the /tmp directory, or a value from the configuration file, you should be deliberate in specifying the working directory of your daemon.

Use chdir() to set the working directory of your daemon.

Redirect stdin, stdout, and stderr

To remove itself from the controlling terminal, a daemon redirects the stdin, stdout, and stderr file descriptors by closing and then reopening them (usually to the /dev/null device). A daemon inherits all of the open file descriptors of the parent. For this reason, many daemons loop through all possible file descriptors and close each one. You can get the maximum number of file descriptors from OPEN_MAX at compile time or from mx = getdtablesize(); at run time.

Once you've closed all open files, it is good practice to reopen stdin, stdout, and stderr; some libraries write to stderr, and therefore stderr should be initialized with a valid file descriptor. Instead of using /dev/null, some daemons open a log file as stderr.

The following code redirects these three file descriptors by closing them and then reopening them to the /dev/null device. The code also closes all file descriptors up to the maximum returned from getdtablesize().

```
int mx;                    // maximum file descriptor
int i;                     // loop index
int fd0, fd1, fd2;         // New FDs for STDIN, OUT and ERR

if (!debug_mode) {         // Close IN,OUT,ERR if not in debug
    close(0);
    close(1);
    close(2);
    // Reopen them pointing to /dev/null.
    fd0 = open("/dev/null", (O_RDONLY | O_NOCTTY | O_NOFOLLOW));
    fd1 = open("/dev/null", (O_WRONLY | O_NOCTTY | O_NOFOLLOW));
    fd2 = open("/dev/null", (O_WRONLY | O_NOCTTY | O_NOFOLLOW));
    if (fd0 != 0 || fd1 != 1 || fd2 != 2) {
        LOG(LOG_ERR, CF, E_NoSTDIO);
        exit(-1);    // die on errors
    }
}
mx = getdtablesize();      // get max # open files
for (i=3; i<mx; i++) {
    close(i);              // Make sure inherited FDs are closed
}
```

Set Up Logging

Your daemon should report errors and other events of interest. While you are working on the daemon, you will want to see debugging information, and you may want to record your daemon's activity when it is in operation. Logging can fill all of these needs.

The three common destinations for log messages are syslog, stderr, and a log file. It is fairly common to see debugging information directed to stderr, errors directed to syslog, and activity logs put into files.

NOTE   *If you save log files to a local disk, you should probably run* crond *and have* logrotate *delete old log files. Be sure to add any custom log files to* logrotate*'s configuration.*

If you're building a network appliance, you may want to send both errors and usage logs to syslog, then configure syslog to send log messages to a log host on the network instead of saving them in local disk files. This helps minimize your appliance's disk requirements and, since all log message are saved on one host, makes it easier to analyze the messages.

Many daemons let you set the verbosity of debug logging with a parameter on the command line. For example, typing -d 5 might turn on debugging output with a verbosity level of 5.

There is no standard meaning for the debug levels in Linux. Some daemons have a simple on/off option, while others use a level between 0 and 9. Some daemons let you turn debugging on and off while the program is running by sending it SIGUSR1 and SIGUSR2 signals, and some daemons read the debug level from the configuration file.

On a large project with several developers, you may want to have separate debug levels for different parts of the code so that each developer can independently control the logging in his or her code. It is also nice if you can set the debug levels while the program is running. (Chapter 6 covers logging in greater detail, and shows how we use RTA to modify debug levels at run time.)

Set Group and User IDs

Many daemons start from inittab or from the rc scripts at boot time; others are started by cron. Thus, most daemons start with a root user ID, which presents a security risk if the program is ever compromised.

To limit possible damage if the program is compromised, many daemons drop root privileges as soon as possible. For example, a webserver might drop root privileges as soon as it has bound to TCP port 80.

Likewise, your daemon should drop root privileges if at all possible. But if not root, which user IDs and group IDs should you use? Many applications create their own users and groups. (A quick look at /etc/passwd and /etc/group confirms this.) If you decide to create a user for your daemon, try to keep the user shell as /bin/nologin. Your daemon can get the user IDs and group IDs from the configuration file or from the command line.

You can drop root privileges and become another user by using the setuid() system call. Other routines that can change the user ID include seteuid() and setreuid(), which set both the real and effective user IDs. Your needs should dictate which of these to use.

The following code from our sample daemon ❶ gets the user ID (UID) name from Config[], a global configuration table, and calls ❷ getpwnam() to convert the name to a numeric UID. A call to ❸ setuid() sets the UID for the daemon. Our routine to set the group ID (GID) is similar, using setgid() instead of setuid(). (The LOG macro is explained later.)

```
void do_set_uid(){
    struct passwd *ppw;    // pointer to passwd struct
    int           uid;     // UID as an integer

    /* The UID in the Config table is a string and may contain
       either a number or a user name. We test for a numeric
       value by trying a to-int conversion. If that fails we
       do a passwd file look up on the name. */
❶   if (sscanf(Config[ED_WORKING].uid, "%d", &uid) != 1) {
❷       ppw = getpwnam(Config[ED_WORKING].uid);
```

```
    if (!ppw) {
      LOG(LOG_ERR, CF, E_NoUser, Config[ED_WORKING].uid);
      exit(-1);    // die on errors
    }
    uid = ppw->pw_uid;
  }

  /* Got a numeric UID. Set it */
❸  if (setuid(uid) != 0) {
    LOG(LOG_ERR, CF, E_Bad_uid, Config[ED_WORKING].uid);
    // There was a problem setting the UID. Die on errors, so ...
    exit(-1);
  }
}
```

Check for a pidfile

Many daemons require exclusive access to the computer's resources, such as
a TCP port or a printer. In these cases, there should not be two instances of
the daemon running, as both instances cannot have exclusive access to a
resource. The most common way to reserve access is through the use of a
pidfile.

The *pidfile* is a text file containing the process ID (PID) of the running
daemon and is usually located at /var/run/*xxx*.pid, where *xxx* is the name of
the daemon. For example, you might see the following in /var/run:

```
$ ls /var/run/*.pid
/var/run/apmd.pid            /var/run/ntpd.pid
/var/run/atd.pid             /var/run/rpc.statd.pid
/var/run/crond.pid           /var/run/sendmail.pid
/var/run/dhclient-eth0.pid   /var/run/sm-client.pid
/var/run/gdm.pid             /var/run/sshd.pid
/var/run/gpm.pid             /var/run/syslogd.pid
/var/run/klogd.pid           /var/run/xfs.pid
/var/run/messagebus.pid      /var/run/xinetd.pid
```

When a daemon starts, it checks to see if a pidfile exists. If the file does
not exist, the daemon creates it and writes its own PID there. If the file does
exist, the daemon checks to see if the process specified in the file is still
running. Then it reads the PID from the file and calls kill(0) to send a signal
to the process (this is just a test, kill(0) won't actually terminate a running
process). If the kill() succeeds, it means that the process specified in the file
was running and able to accept the signal, so the new daemon can simply exit
(optionally logging the event). There is no way to atomically check for and
create a pidfile, so you have to use a Linux file lock to be sure another instance
of the daemon does not also create a pidfile. The code given later in this
section illustrates how to use a file lock.

As a security precaution, you may want to configure your appliance so
that one process is not allowed to kill() another. To do so, check for the

existence of the daemon by looking for its PID in the /proc directory. If the PID specified in the pidfile is not running, the new daemon overwrites the pidfile with its PID and continues. (Your daemon should also verify that a process with a matching PID is an instance of your daemon and not some other program that happens to have a PID matching the one in the pidfile.)

Stale pidfiles are a nuisance, so when your daemon exits, it should remove its pidfile. Write a subroutine that deletes the pidfile and use atexit() to register the subroutine for execution at program termination. You may also want to modify your rc.sysinit or other initialization scripts to delete all of the old pidfiles from /var/run.

NOTE *Be sure to delete stale pidfiles early in the boot sequence before the daemon is started so that your system initialization does not inadvertently remove active pidfiles.*

The name and location of the pidfile is often in the configuration file; if it is not there, it can be passed in from the command line. Being able to specify the pidfile in the configuration file or on the command line makes it easier to run multiple instances of the daemon should the need arise (during debugging, for instance).

The code below is taken from our sample daemon and presents one approach to the voluntary mutual exclusion of a pidfile. We ❶ get the name of the pidfile and try to open it. If the open succeeds, we read the PID from the file and ❷ try to send a signal to the process. If the kill() call succeeds, it means the process specified in the pidfile is still running and this instance should exit. If the pidfile exists, but the process it specifies is not running, the pidfile is stale and should be ❸ removed. If this instance of the daemon is the valid one, it ❹ creates a pidfile, ❺ locks it, and ❻ writes the PID into it.

```
    void do_pidfile() {
      FILE *pf;        // We use a FILE to use fscanf
      int   fd;        // File descriptor for pidfile
      int   fpid;      // PID found in existing pidfile
      int   opid;      // Our PID

❶    pf = fopen(Config[ED_WORKING].pidfile, "r");
      if (pf) {
        if (fscanf(pf, "%d", &fpid)) {
          /* We've gotten a PID out of the file. Is it running? */
❷        if (!(kill(fpid, 0) == -1 &&  errno == ESRCH)) {
            /* Looks like another daemon is running. Exit. */
            (void) fclose(pf);
            LOG(LOG_ERR, CF, E_Not_Alone,fpid);
            exit(-1);
          }
        }
        /* stale pidfile. remove it */
        (void) fclose(pf);
❸      if (unlink(Config[ED_WORKING].pidfile) != 0) {
          /* Could not remove pidfile. Exit. */
          LOG(LOG_ERR, CF, E_Pid_File, Config[ED_WORKING].pidfile);
          exit(-1);
```

```
        }
    }

    /* No pidfile or a stale one's been removed. Write a new one. */
❹  fd = creat(Config[ED_WORKING].pidfile, 0644);
    if (fd < 0) {
        LOG(LOG_ERR, CF, E_Pid_File, Config[ED_WORKING].pidfile);
        exit(-1);
    }

    /* get a file lock or die trying */
❺  if (flock(fd, LOCK_EX | LOCK_NB) < 0) {
        LOG(LOG_ERR, CF, E_Pid_File, Config[ED_WORKING].pidfile);
        exit(-1);
    }

    opid = getpid();        // get our pid

    /* Get a FILE pointer so we can use fprintf */
    pf = fdopen(fd, "w");
    if (!pf) {
        LOG(LOG_ERR, CF, E_Pid_File, Config[ED_WORKING].pidfile);
        exit(-1);
    }

❻  (void) fprintf(pf, "%d\n", opid);
    fflush(pf);

    (void) flock(fd, LOCK_UN);

    (void) close(fd);
}
```

Set the umask

The umask command sets the default read/write permissions for files created in the current shell. It is generally good practice to set the umask of your daemon to 0, which forces you to explicitly set the permissions of any files you create.

Because there is no need to save the old value of the umask, we cast the return value to void:

```
(void) umask((mode_t) 000);
```

Set Up Signal Handlers

A *signal handler* is a function that is compiled with the rest of your application. Instead of directly invoking the function, you use signal or sigaction to tell the operating system to call the function when a signal arrives.

The last step in setting up a daemon is to configure the signal handlers. The requirements for your application dictate which signals to catch and how to handle them. Running the `man 7 signal` command will give you an idea of the signals you might want to catch. Some of the most common signals and actions are:

SIGHUP   Reread the configuration file and reinitialize as appropriate. Close and reopen any log files to give `logrotate` a chance to work.

SIGTERM, **SIGQUIT**   Do a graceful shutdown of the daemon and exit.

SIGUSR1   Toggle debug mode on or off.

SIGCHLD   Handle the death of any child processes.

You should consult both the man page for `sigaction()` and your favorite Linux programming book before implementing your signal handler, but this simple example might help you get started:

```
struct sigaction sa;
volatile int Got_HUP = 0;    // Clear global flag

sa.sa_handler = handle_hangup;
sa.sa_flags   = 0;   // no flags in this example
if (sigaction(SIGHUP, &sa, NULL)) {
    LOG(LOG_ERR, E_No_Signals);   // report problem and die
    exit(-1);
}
```

The routine that will handle the signal is passed an integer with the signal number. The routine should be of type void.

```
void handle_hangup(int recv_sig)
{
    Got_HUP = 1;      // Set global flag
}
```

NOTE   *The code in a signal handler is not executed in the main execution path of your program, and since a signal can occur while the signal handler itself is running, signal handlers must be reentrant.*

Writing reentrant code can be a little tricky, and you might want to consider just setting a volatile flag and having your main loop examine the flag periodically, leaving the real work to be done in the main loop. The flag has to be volatile so that the compiler does not optimize away tests for it in the main loop. If you decide to do more than set a flag in your signal handler, make sure that all the glibc and system calls in your signal handler are reentrant safe.

How to Secure a Daemon

This section will give you some general guidelines to help you write more secure programs. However, because your daemon's security is much too important to use this document as the sole source of your security information, we urge you to read the books listed in the bibliography at the end of this chapter. The information here is really just an overview of the points you need to consider. Furthermore, this section does not tell you how to secure the Linux kernel or your appliance in general.

We'll break the topic of daemon security into three sections:

- Designing a secure daemon
- Writing a secure daemon
- Limiting damage in case of a breach

Designing a Secure Daemon

Securing your daemon starts when you begin thinking about its specification, architecture, and design. You have the greatest ability to make your application secure when you lay out your daemon's foundation.

By secure, we mean that the daemon should respond to errors and malicious attacks in a predictable way. This implies that we must first detect errors (and attacks) and then handle them appropriately. One way to think about this is to always have a plan for each possible error condition and attack.

Always Have an Escape Plan

Many buildings post escape plans next to elevators and stairwells. The escape plan is a map showing the best route to take in case of an emergency. As you design your daemon, think about how you will recover or escape from each possible error condition. Laying the foundation for a good escape plan early makes it less burdensome for you to add the code after your daemon has been developed.

An exit may mean a core dump and program termination, or it may mean aborting a single request, closing a network connection, or performing some other error recovery. Program termination may be appropriate if you detect an error during startup or during a configuration change, or if for any reason you think security has been breached. For example, if your daemon is a network server handling client requests, it may be appropriate to close a network connection if the daemon receives a badly formed request.

In practice, having an error escape plan usually means that all of your subroutines return an error code. No matter how deeply nested your subroutine calls are, you should be able to pass an error indicator up the chain of subroutine returns. An event-driven or state-machine-driven program can use a flag or separate state to indicate an error.

Your escape should always begin with a log message describing the location of the error and the inputs that generated it. You can have two log messages, one to detect the error, and another, at a higher level, to report how you've decided to handle the error.

Be Restrictive

When designing a daemon from scratch, you can specify its operation in detail. Your specification and the resulting code should allow only the simplest subset of requests and configuration data. Setting a tight standard will make your daemon more secure and may help eliminate subtle bugs.

For example, let's consider restrictions you could place on configuration or other internal filenames. Type the following at a bash prompt (noting the placement of single and double quotes):

```
date > \
 "cd ..; cd ..; cd ..; cd etc; echo 'nameserver1.2.3.4' >resolv.conf"
ls -1 cd*
```

Amazing, isn't it? The above command works. The string, `cd ..; cd ..; cd ..; cd etc; echo 'nameserver 1.2.3.4'>resolv.conf` is a perfectly valid Linux filename. While bash must honor this as a valid filename, you do not need to. Consider stating in your specification that filenames are limited to the characters [_a-zA-Z/.] but the sequences .. and // are invalid. In addition, the maximum length of a Linux path and filename is `PATH_MAX` in `limits.h` and is usually set to 4096 characters. You might want to restrict filename lengths to the minimum that your daemon needs.

Filenames are just one example. Give some thought to other ways in which you can tighten your daemon's specification.

Write a Secure Daemon

Security is only as good as the weakest link in its chain. Designing a secure daemon is not enough. You must also *write* a secure daemon.

Validate Input

Many of the recent Linux vulnerabilities stem from buffer overruns that allow an intruder to place executable code on the stack. The most effective defense against this kind of attack is to validate all input from a user or from any non-secure source. Verify string lengths and make sure strings do not contain any illegal characters. Verify that integers are reasonable, relative to their uses, and that counting integers are always positive.

Perform as much application-specific checking as possible before committing other resources. For example, make sure that HTTP requests are well formed and that SQL statements are valid. Checking early helps prevent the problem of trying to back out of a request once you've allocated buffers, sockets, or other resources for the request.

Do not let any malformed input into your daemon. Remember: If it's only 99 percent right, then it's still wrong.

Check All Return Codes

One of the best things you can do to enhance security is to check all return codes, especially from system calls. Normally, this would seem like a burden, but if you've laid out your design with an error escape plan, you'll find that it does not take a lot of thought or effort to test every return code.

Avoid Buffer Overrun Attacks

Some library functions are considered unsafe because they do not limit how much memory they will overwrite. For example, the strcpy() function is considered unsafe, while the strncpy() function is considered safe.

Nevertheless, we are not convinced that the strn routines are all that safe, since they do not guarantee that the resulting string is null terminated. The best thing to do is to check the length of the string before doing a copy. Let's look at some examples.

```
VERY BAD:     strcpy(dest, src);
```

This is an invitation to a buffer overrun attack if src has not been previously checked.

```
BAD:     strncpy(dest, src, MAXN);
```

This call does not guarantee that dest is null terminated.

```
BETTER:     strncpy(dest, src, MAXN);
    dest[MAXN -1] = (char) 0;   //truncation ==> still bad
```

The above code protects the program in that it prevents a buffer overrun and guarantees that dest is null terminated, but it could quietly truncate the source string.

```
BEST:     if (strlen(src) >= MAXN) {
        LOG("String error at %s:%d\n", __FILE__, __LINE__);
        return(ERROR_STR_LEN);
    }
    strncpy(dest, src, MAXN);
```

While it uses more code, the above protects the program and reports source strings that might be part of an attack on your program.

Several other function families are considered unsafe. Specifically, these include strcat(), sprintf(), gets(), and scanf().

Other Security Software

Even if you follow the best coding practices, you may want the added protection of the following software:

IBM's ProPolice   GNU Compiler Collection (GCC) patch to help prevent buffer overruns

StackGuard   GCC patch to help prevent buffer overruns

Libsafe   Alternate library for strcpy() and other unsafe functions

grsecurity   Kernel patch that can (among other things) make the stack non-executable

Systrace   Kernel patch that can limit which system calls your daemon can make

We strongly recommend using grsecurity and configuring your system so that code is never executed from the stack. This feature uses the hardware in the memory management unit and will not affect your program's performance.

Limit Damage in Case of a Breach

Almost every major Linux application has, at one time or another, been found to be vulnerable. Since the same may happen to your daemon at some point, you want to limit the amount of risk a compromised daemon might present to the appliance.

Prevent Library and Path Attacks

If an attacker gains access to your appliance, he might be able to run your daemon having first set LD_LIBRARY_PATH or PATH to point to compromised libraries and commands. If your program is Set User ID (SUID) root, your attacker has just gained complete root control over your appliance. Don't despair. There are a few things you can do to limit disaster in the event that your daemon is compromised.

First, do not run your application with an SUID of root. This is easier on an appliance than on a multi-user system where programs like passwd and the X server must be SUID root. It is better to drop root privileges or to run as a non-privileged user. (You'll learn a few more details about this in the next section.)

The second defense is to do a static build of your daemon using -static as an option to your gcc invocation. A statically linked executable might not increase the size of your executable as much as you'd imagine, and if you are using chroot jails, it might actually save disk space. Statically linked executables usually load faster, too.

Another way to prevent a library or path attack is to ignore the environment variables that tell your program where to look for shared object libraries and system commands. If you are really security conscious, use the glibc clearenv() function to undefine all environment variables. You will need to give the full path to any commands you run with system(), but this is probably a good idea anyway.

Avoid Root Privileges

Attackers want root privileges so they can take control of your appliance. If you run your daemon as root, you make your daemon a target for their attacks. Avoid root privileges if at all possible. Create a new user (with the login shell set to /bin/nologin) and use setuid() and setgid() to change to that user. This technique is used by most web- and database servers.

Another approach is to modify your rc initialization scripts to launch your daemon with sudo to change to the appropriate user. For example, your rc script might start your webui daemon as user *wuser* with the command:

```
sudo -l wuser webui
```

Drop Root Privileges and Set Capabilities

If you must have root privileges to open network ports below 1024 or to write to root-owned files, try to drop as many root privileges as possible. The 2.2 and later kernels make this possible with capabilities. *Capabilities* are separate permissions that perform very specific operations. Your SUID root program may drop individual capabilities and keep others.

The kernel keeps track of three sets of capabilities for each program:

Effective   What is currently allowed

Permitted   Maximum capabilities the process can use

Inherited   What to transfer across an execve()

The system call to set capabilities is capset(). You might also be able to use cap_set_proc(), which is more portable.

Capabilities are seeing a lot of active development in Linux. Here is a sample of the more than 25 capabilities that your daemon should relinquish if possible. A list of all of the capabilities is available from the output of man capabilities.

CAP_CHOWN	Allow arbitrary changes to file UIDs and GIDs. Drop this capability to disallow changes to UIDs and GIDs.
CAP_KILL	Bypass permission checks for sending signals.
CAP_MKNOD	Allow creation of special files using mknod(2). Some devices, such as /dev/mem and /dev/kmem, are particularly attractive to attackers. Once your system is up and running, you should probably drop this capability. You might want to remove both /dev/mem and /dev/kmem if you can verify that none of your appliance's programs require them.
CAP_NET_ADMIN	Allow various network-related operations—for example, setting privileged socket options, enabling multicasting, interface configuration, and modifying routing tables.
CAP_NET_BIND_SERVICE	Allow binding to Internet domain–reserved socket ports (port numbers less than 1024).
CAP_NET_RAW	Permit use of RAW and PACKET sockets.
CAP_SYS_CHROOT	Permit calls to chroot(2).
CAP_SYS_MODULE	Allow loading and unloading of kernel modules.
CAP_SETPCAP	Allow modifications to capability sets. After you've made your system more secure by dropping unneeded capabilities, you may want to drop all ability to change the system capabilities. Once system CAP_SETPCAP is dropped, even full root access can't regain the dropped capabilities.

The kernel itself honors a set of capabilities, and as the last step in your boot process, you might want to limit what the kernel can do. For example, if your kernel uses modules, at the end of system bootup, you may want to completely remove the kernel's ability to load or remove modules.

NOTE   *A full description of capabilities is beyond the scope of what we can present here. A good place to start is man capabilities on your Linux system.*

Chroot if Possible

One of the oldest and most trusted techniques to limit damage in case of a breech is to run a daemon in a chroot jail. The idea is to put all of the files that your daemon will need in a directory subtree and to then tell your daemon that the top of the subtree is the "root" of the filesystem. The system call is chroot(), and it is a good way to make the rest of the real filesystem invisible in case your daemon is breeched.

It is fairly easy for a process owned by root to break out of a chroot jail, so be sure to drop root privileges after the chroot() call. A typical sequence of calls to build a chroot jail looks like this:

```
chdir("/var/app_jail");
chroot("/var/app_jail");
setuid(500);
```

Following the chroot() call, the application will be able to see only the files and directories under the directory specified in the chroot() call. You will need to close file descriptors to directories outside of the chroot jail, since they can provide a means to break out of the jail.

The trick in building a successful chroot jail is in limiting the number of files and devices in the jail. Of course you will need all of your daemon's working files, but do not include the startup configuration directory if it contains, for example, where to locate the chroot jail. If your program is dynamically linked, you will need to include a /lib directory and whatever shared object libraries your program uses. Consider doing a static build of your application to avoid the necessity of adding the /lib directory.

The standard library logging routine, syslog(), assumes access to a Unix socket at /dev/log. Create a /dev directory in your jail and tell the system logging daemon, syslogd, to listen on an additional socket using the -a command line option. Here's an example of how to start syslogd so that it listens on an additional socket:

```
syslogd -a /var/app_jail/dev/log
```

A common alternative to a chroot jail is a virtual machine. Programs such as VMware, VServer, and User-mode Linux all provide more isolation than a chroot jail but at the cost of higher memory or CPU requirements.

A Prototype Daemon

This book includes a bootable CD that turns a PC into a Linux-based appliance. The programming effort for the book's sample appliance was divided among the authors, with each of us writing some of the programs. To make the appliance code easier for you to read (and easier for us to write), we decided to start by building a common core for each of our programs.

The code for the empty daemon is available as part of the code for our appliance, and you can get it from the CD or from the book's website. We've tried to build the empty daemon to reflect all of the lessons learned in the sections above, and you are welcome to copy our empty daemon code and use it as you see fit.

Summary

In this chapter we have demonstrated the initialization steps a typical daemon takes—for example, redirecting stdin, stdout, and stderr, and going into the background. We've also introduced some concepts and techniques that you might use to make your daemons more secure.

Further Reading

We've found the following books useful in determining how to secure a daemon.

- *Secure Programming for Linux and Unix HOWTO* by David A. Wheeler (http://www.dwheeler.com/secure-programs, 2003)
- *Real World Linux Security* by Bob Toxen (Prentice Hall, 2000)
- *Network Security Hacks* by Andrew Lockart (O'Reilly, 2004)
- *SSH, The Secure Shell: The Definitive Guide* by Daniel J. Barrett and Richard E. Silverman (O'Reilly, 2001)
- *Linux Security* by Shadab Siddiqui (Premier Press, 2002)

5

THE LADDIE ALARM SYSTEM: A SAMPLE APPLIANCE

 Previous chapters covered how to build and secure a daemon and how to communicate with the daemon while it is running. We'll tie these topics together in this chapter by building *Laddie*, a Linux-based alarm system.[1]

Laddie uses the five status inputs on a standard PC parallel port as sensor inputs to the alarm system. The heart of the Laddie appliance is the *ladd* (pronounced *lad-dee*) daemon that polls the status lines and reports input transitions using syslog(). An alarm system is a good choice for a sample application since most readers will have some familiarity with alarm systems and because an alarm system application is simple to write, understand, and modify.

This chapter includes the following five sections:

- Introduction to alarm systems
- A functional specification for Laddie

---

[1] Laddie is a sample appliance used to illustrate the techniques and software presented in this book. Laddie is *not* a commercially viable alarm system and should never be used in place of a real alarm system.

- Laddie hardware design
- Laddie software design
- Building and testing Laddie

As you read this chapter, keep in mind that the alarm system itself is not as important as the techniques used to build it. Don't let the implementation details overshadow the design principles being taught.

Introduction to Alarm Systems

This section presents the concepts and definitions used to describe alarm systems in general and Laddie in particular.

Sensors

An alarm *sensor* is a small device or switch that detects movement in a room or activity in an area. An *alarm system* monitors several alarm sensors and reports any unexpected activity they pick up. The area that a sensor protects is called a *zone*. Zones are given *names* that usually describe the area protected; typical zone names might include *Garage*, *Second Floor Windows*, and *Refrigerator*.

Figure 5-1 shows an example arrangement of sensors and zones for a small business. There are door sensors on the front and back doors and a motion detector that looks for movement near the office and storeroom.

Small Business with Three Zones

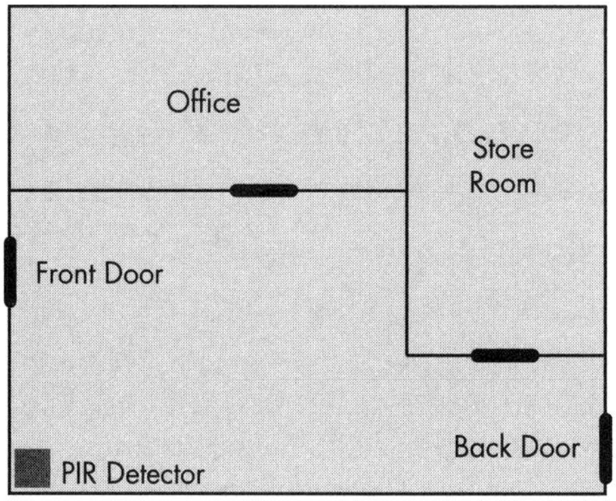

Figure 5-1: An example alarm system

Types of Sensors

Since an alarm system can only report what its sensors detect, it is important to choose sensors carefully. Let's consider the types of sensors that are available.

Magnetic reed switches

These are most often used to monitor doors; they are placed with the switch on the doorframe and the magnet on the door.

PIR motion detectors

Passive Infrared (PIR) motion detectors detect minute changes in the movement of infrared (heat) sources. A person or animal can set off a PIR motion detector, but, for example, a baseball cannot.

Acoustic sensors

Acoustic sensors detect specific sounds. They are often used to detect the sound of breaking glass, and are so sensitive that a single acoustic sensor can protect all of the windows in a room.

Floor mat sensors

Floor mat sensors have switches that can detect the weight of a person. They are very thin and are usually placed under carpet at entryways.

Vibration sensors

Vibration sensors can detect very slight physical motion. They are often used to protect cars.

Smoke and carbon monoxide detectors

These sensors are used to detect potential fires.

Temperature sensors

Thermostats and other temperature sensors trip at a certain temperature or simply report the current temperature in the zone. They are often used to protect temperature-sensitive equipment and supplies.

Sensor Contact Type

To the alarm system, most sensors look like switches. The switch contacts can be either open when not in alarm (called *normally open* or *NO* sensors), or closed when not in alarm (*normally closed* or *NC* sensors). When you install a sensor, you have to tell the alarm system the *contact type* of the sensor—that is, whether the contacts are normally open or normally closed. Most sensors are normally closed. A normally closed sensor has the desirable property of triggering an alarm if the wires to the sensor are cut.

Another helpful feature of the sensor-and-zone setup is that it is possible to cascade sensors within a zone, as long as the cascaded sensors are all of the same contact type. Figure 5-2 shows how to cascade normally open sensors and Figure 5-3 shows how to cascade normally closed sensors.

Cascading NO Sensors

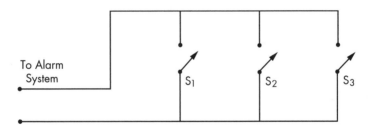

Figure 5-2: How to cascade normally open sensors

Cascading NC Sensors

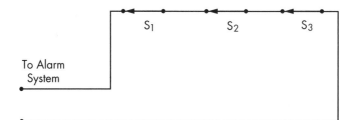

Figure 5-3: How to cascade normally closed sensors

Logically, the alarm system sees just one sensor in each zone, even if there are actually several cascaded sensors there.

Latching a Sensor

Most sensors return to the non-alarm or normal state when the detected condition is removed—for example, when someone closes a door or steps off of a floor mat. You usually want to configure the alarm system to latch alarms detected by these sensors. *Latched* alarms remain in alarm, even if the detected condition is removed, until they are manually cleared by a user.

However, you might not want to latch every sensor. For example, you might want to automatically remove an alarm when the temperature in a thermostat-protected room returns to normal.

Think about the type of sensor you're using and your specific needs when you set alarms in a zone to be latching or non-latching.

Enabling a Zone

Mark zones as *enabled* if the sensors in the zone are working and you want to monitor the zone. Unused inputs can be ignored by disabling the zone. Also, you may find it convenient to temporarily disable zones when you want to leave a door or window open.

A Functional Specification for Laddie

The Laddie alarm system monitors up to five zones and raises an alarm when a change occurs in one of the monitored zones. Alarms are reported to Laddie's five different user interfaces. In addition to being able to view the status of the zones that Laddie monitors, the user interfaces allow you to test and clear alarms, view logs, and configure zones. Configuration parameters include the following:

- Zone name
- Contact type
- Latching or non-latching
- Enabled or disabled

Laddie's functional specification is divided into two parts: one that allows users to access alarm configuration and status and another that allows Laddie to handle alarms.

NOTE *As a reminder,* Laddie *refers to the whole appliance, and* ladd *refers just to the daemon that monitors the five input pins on the parallel port. It's easy to confuse the two, since they are pronounced the same.*

ladd's Configuration and Status

ladd has one configuration and status table, called *Zone*, that is visible to all of the user interfaces as an RTA table. The Zone table has five rows, with each row defined by the following data structure:

```
/* The structure to hold the definition, configuration, and status
   of each alarm pin on the parallel port */
typedef struct {
  int     id;          // ID number of alarm [1-5]
  char    name[ZONE_NAME_LEN]; // the zone name
  int     enabled;     // ==1 if enabled
  int     edge;        // ==1 if alarm on low to high transition
  int     latching;    // ==1 if we should latch the alarm
  int     input;       // is the latest raw input from the alarm pin
  int     alarm;       // ==1 if in alarm
  int     count;       // count of alarms on this pin
} ZONE;
```

Let's consider each of these fields in turn.

id (Configuration)

Zones are identified by a number between one and five. The id field is initialized when ladd starts, and users cannot edit it. You can use the id field in user interface programs to uniquely identify a particular zone.

name (Configuration)

This field stores the brief mnemonic or name that the user assigns to the zone.

enabled (Configuration)

Only zones marked *enabled* cause the system to enter an alarm state. Zones marked *disabled* do not generate log messages or cause alarm states. This field holds an integer instead of a boolean, since RTA does not support a boolean data type.

edge (Configuration)

For the hardware described in the next section, a normally closed sensor triggers an alarm on a zero-to-one edge on the input pin. Normally open sensors on Laddie trigger an alarm on a one-to-zero edge. "Laddie's Hardware Design" on page 68 describes open and closed sensors in more detail.

latching (Configuration)

The user sets this field to 1 to have an alarm persist even after the sensor pin returns to its normal state. The user must manually clear latched alarms.

input (Status)

This field shows the most recent raw value of the input pin. This is a status field, and the user is not able to edit it.

alarm (Status)

Each zone is said to be in either an *alarm* condition or in a *safe* condition. This field is set by the ladd daemon in response to detected edges on the input pin. A write callback on this field lets a user test a zone by writing a 1 to it. An alarm is cleared when the user sets this field to 0.

count (Status)

This field contains the number of input edges that have caused an alarm. This field is incremented only when the zone is marked *enabled*; it is not incremented by user-initiated tests of the zone. This is a read-only, statistic field that is set to zero when ladd starts.

You may recall that the advantage of RTA is that it gives all of the user interfaces the same API for daemon configuration, status, and statistics. The API defined by RTA is that of a PostgreSQL database. The advantages of PostgreSQL are that SQL is widely used and understood and there are many bindings for PostgreSQL, including C, PHP, Java, and Perl. Figure 5-4 illustrates Laddie's use of RTA to allow five different UIs to get status and set configuration using only one daemon-side protocol.

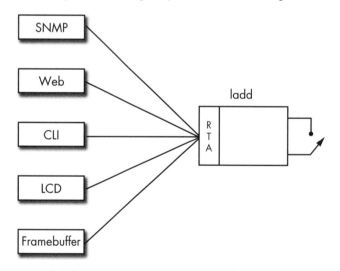

Figure 5-4: One daemon with many user interfaces

Let's look at the SQL for some typical Laddie configuration changes and queries.

To disable zone 2, type:

```
UPDATE Zone SET enabled = 0 WHERE id = 2
```

To find out how many times zone 4 has gone into alarm, type:

```
SELECT count FROM Zone WHERE id = 4
```

To clear all alarms in the system, type:

```
UPDATE Zone SET alarm = 0
```

Any program that can issue commands like these can function as a user interface for Laddie. Watch for commands like these later in the book as we go through the five user interfaces currently available for Laddie.

ladd's Alarm Handling

ladd responds to an alarm by sending a log message using syslog(). The text of the log message depends on whether the alarm was detected by the hardware or was a test alarm issued by a user. The text also depends on whether the alarm was set or cleared. For a zone with ID *n* and the name *zone_name*, the four log messages are:

- Alarm set on zone *n, zone_name*
- Alarm cleared on zone *n, zone_name*
- User set alarm on zone *n, zone_name*
- User cleared alarm on zone *n, zone_name*

Some users do not care *which* zone is in alarm; they just want to know if *any* zone is in alarm. To address this need, ladd provides two other log messages:

- Alarm system status: alarm
- Alarm system status: safe

These messages are sent when the first zone goes into alarm and after the last zone is cleared. Laddie also sets all four control pins on the parallel port to 1 (see Table 5-1) to indicate any alarm in the system. It sets the control pins low when all alarms are cleared.

One nice aspect of our overall architecture for Laddie is that ladd itself does not need to send signals to the UI, send email, or send SNMP traps. We leave all of this to a separate process, greatly simplifying the design and implementation of the ladd daemon. (The event processor is described in the next chapter.) Syslog-as-output not only simplifies ladd, it makes debug and test easier too since we can easily examine the log files for the messages we expect and we can use the logger command to generate test events for the event processor. The data flow for an alarm response is depicted in Figure 5-5.

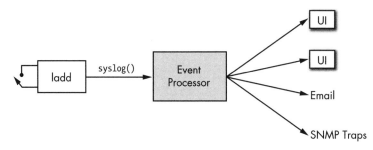

Figure 5-5: Processing alarm events in Laddie

Laddie's Hardware Design

This section presents the hardware needed to use Laddie as a real alarm system. You can skip over this section if you are uncomfortable with electronic circuits or if you aren't interested in seeing how the hardware works.

The pins on the parallel port are divided into three main groups: data lines, control lines, and status lines. Each group is controlled using a register, which is available at a particular I/O address. The data lines are at the base address of the parallel port, the status lines are at the base address plus one, and the control lines are at the base address plus two. Table 5-1 shows how the pins on a 25-pin parallel port connector relate to the printer port names, to the port registers, and to the alarm system.

Table 5-1: Laddie's Use of the PC Parallel Port

Pin	Name	Register	Bit	Alarm input
1	STB	Control	0	
2	D0	Data	0	
3	D1	Data	1	
4	D2	Data	2	
5	D3	Data	3	
6	D4	Data	4	
7	D5	Data	5	
8	D6	Data	6	
9	D7	Data	7	
10	ACK	Status	6	Zone 4
11	BSY	Status	7	Zone 5
12	PAP	Status	5	Zone 3
13	OFON	Status	4	Zone 2
14	ALF	Control	1	
15	FEH	Status	3	Zone 1
16	INI	Control	2	
17	DSL	Control	3	
18–25	Ground			

The alarm daemon uses the data lines as output and the status lines as input. Figure 5-6 shows a schematic for one alarm sensor. The daemon initializes the parallel port by setting the output pins to 0xFF, making pin 2 a high level. When the sensor S1 is open, no current flows through the 2K ohm resistor R1, and the voltage at pin 15 is pulled high. When the sensor is closed, pin 15 is shorted to ground through pin 21.

In other words, pin 15 is biased high when the alarm sensor is open and pulled low when the sensor is closed. By reading the status lines, which includes pin 15, the daemon can detect whether the sensor is open or closed. This description applies to all five of the status inputs on the parallel port.

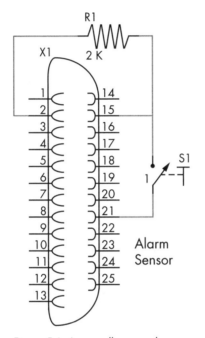

Figure 5-6: A normally open alarm sensor from Laddie

Laddie's Software Design

We used the empty daemon introduced in Chapter 4 to build the ladd daemon. But whether we used the empty daemon, wrote a select()-based program, or wrote a threads-based program, there would still be three main subroutines:

appInit()   Initialize hardware. Start timer. Register the Zone table with RTA.

poll_timeout()   Read the status lines. Log relevant changes.

user_update()   Send logs for user changes to the alarm status.

These routines are described in more detail in the next few sections.

The appInit() Callback Subroutine

The appInit() subroutine is the first callback subroutine the empty daemon invokes. This callback subroutine is responsible for performing any application-specific initialization, setting up any timer callback subroutines, and registering any RTA tables. In ladd, the appInit() subroutine initializes the Zone array of ZONE structures, calls rta_add_table() to register the Zone table with RTA, initializes the parallel port, and starts a periodic 100-millisecond timer with poll_timeout() as its callback subroutine. Note that once the appInit() subroutine returns, the daemon is ready to accept connections from the user interfaces.

Although the COLDEFs or TBLDEF for the Zone array are not shown, Table 5-2 should give you an idea of what they contain.

Table 5-2: The Columns in Laddie's Zone Table

Column name	Type	Read-only	Save-to-disk
id	int	yes	no
name	char	no	yes
enabled	int	no	yes
edge	int	no	yes
latching	int	no	yes
input	int	yes	no
alarm	int	no	no
count	int	yes	no

All of the initialization code for ladd is in the appInit() routine given below.

```
/*************************************************************
 * appInit():   - Initialize all internal variables and tables.
 *                Set and read control lines as needed.
 *
 * Input:  int argc, char *argv[] --- command line parameters
 * Return: None
 *************************************************************/
void    appInit(int argc, char *argv[])
{
  int    value;    /* input value from parallel port */
  int    i;        /* a loop index */

  /* Initialize the zone ids */
  for (i = 0; i < NUM_INPUTS; i++) {
    Zone[i].id = i+1;
  }

  /* Add the table of single bit alarm inputs */
  rta_add_table(&ZoneTable);

  /* Give us control of the parallel port and set data pins high */
```

```
if (ioperm(PORT,3,1)) {
  fprintf(stderr, "Cannot open parallel port at %x\n", PORT);
  exit(1);
}
outb((unsigned char)0x00FF, PORT);

/* Now read the input pins to get initial states */
value = inb(PORT+1);
for (i = 0; i < NUM_INPUTS; i++) {
  Zone[i].input = (value & (8<<i)) ? 1 : 0;
}

/* Set the output pins on the control port low since we start
 * in a "no-alarm" state. Set global alarm to match. */
outb((unsigned char)0x0000, PORT+2);
GlobalAlarm = 0;

/* Setup poll timer */
if (!add_timer(ED_PERIODIC, 100, poll_timeout, (void *)__LINE__)) {
  fprintf(stderr, "Can not set up periodic timer. Exiting ....\n");
  exit(1);
}
}
```

The poll_timeout() Callback Subroutine

The poll_timeout() subroutine performs the bulk of the alarm daemon's functions. This subroutine reads the parallel port, processes the input pins, and modifies the state of the appropriate ZONE data structure. This subroutine is invoked every 100 milliseconds, as specified by the call to add_timer(). Note the following salient features of the poll_timeout() subroutine.

- The main responsibility of poll_timeout() is to set the alarm field for each zone in the Zone table. As mentioned above, the alarm field shows whether or not a particular zone is in an alarm condition.

- The subroutine treats each zone independently of the other zones. That is, one zone can be in alarm condition while another is in the safe condition.

- The alarm field for a particular zone is modified only if the enabled field is nonzero. This feature allows a user to disable a zone in cases where there is either no sensor or where the user wishes to ignore a sensor.

- When poll_timeout() detects that the zone has entered the alarm condition, it sets the alarm field to 1 and sends a syslog message. In a later chapter, we'll show you how to convert syslog messages into email and SNMP traps.

- Similarly, when this subroutine detects that the input pin transitions back to the normal state, it clears the alarm variable, and, if the latching field is set to zero, it sends a syslog message. This mechanism allows the user to configure a zone so that once it enters the alarm condition, it must be cleared manually.

- The poll_alarm() subroutine also maintains a global alarm variable, GlobalAlarm, which is set to one if any zone is in alarm condition and is set to zero if all zones are safe. The subroutine tracks when this GlobalAlarm variable changes states. When the GlobalAlarm variable is set, the control pins of the parallel port are set high. When the GlobalAlarm variable changes state, then an appropriate syslog message is sent.

All of the polling for new alarms is done in the poll_timeout() routine given below.

```
/****************************************************************
 * poll_timeout():  - The background routine to read the status
 *                    lines and to set (or clear) alarms if needed.
 *
 * Input:  None
 * Return: None
 ****************************************************************/
void poll_timeout(void *handle, void *cbd)
{
  int   value;    /* input value from parallel port */
  int   i;        /* a loop variable */
  int   new;      /* new state of pin */

  /* Read the input pins from the parallel port */
  value = inb(PORT+1);

  for (i = 0; i < NUM_INPUTS; i++) {
    new = (value & (8<<i)) ? 1 : 0;
    if ((new != Zone[i].input) && (Zone[i].enabled)) {
      /* We have a change of state of an enabled input pin */
      /* Look for a new alarm */
      if ((new == 1 && Zone[i].edge == 1 && Zone[i].alarm != 1) ||
          (new == 0 && Zone[i].edge == 0 && Zone[i].alarm != 1)) {
        Zone[i].alarm = 1;
        Zone[i].count++;
        syslog(LOG_ALERT, "Alarm set on zone %d, %s", Zone[i].id,
               Zone[i].name);
      }
      /* Look for a cleared alarm */
      if ((Zone[i].alarm == 1) && (Zone[i].latching == 0) &&
          ((new == 0 && Zone[i].edge == 1) ||
           (new == 1 && Zone[i].edge == 0))) {
        /* We can remove an alarm */
        Zone[i].alarm = 0;
        syslog(LOG_ALERT, "Alarm cleared on zone %d, %s", Zone[i].id,
               Zone[i].name);
      }
    }
    Zone[i].input = new;
  }

  /* All inputs have been processed. Set or clear the global alarm
   * status and control pins. Note that we use this code to process
   * manually set or cleared alarms too.  */
```

```
    for (i = 0; i < NUM_INPUTS; i++) {
      if (Zone[i].alarm == 1) {
        if (GlobalAlarm == 0) {
          /* A new alarm. Log it and set control bits (low three) high. */
          syslog(LOG_ALERT, "Alarm system status: alarm");
          outb((unsigned char)0x0007, PORT+2);
          GlobalAlarm = 1;
        }
        return;  // in alarm, no need to check the other zones
      }
    }
    /* If we get here, there are no alarms */
    if (GlobalAlarm == 1) {
      /* Clear alarm. Log it and set control bits (low three) low. */
      syslog(LOG_ALERT, "Alarm system status: safe");
      outb((unsigned char)0x0000, PORT+2);
      GlobalAlarm = 0;
    }
}
```

The user_update() Callback Subroutine

The user_update() callback subroutine is invoked whenever the user manually modifies the alarm field in a ZONE data structure. This callback subroutine is responsible for sending a syslog message whenever the user manually clears the alarm condition (for latched zones) or manually sets the alarm condition. In Chapter 7, we'll show you how to use the syslog message to update the user interfaces.

This callback subroutine is included in the RTA COLDEF structure for our alarm daemon. Take a look at the snippet of source code below, and you'll see that the user_update subroutine is included in the write callback entry. The user_update subroutine is invoked whenever the user writes to the alarm variable in a ZONE data structure.

```
COLDEF   ZoneColumns[] = {
  {
      "Zone",                    // the table name
      "alarm",                   // the column name
      RTA_INT,                   // data type
      sizeof(int),               // number of bytes
      offsetof(ZONE, alarm),     // location in struct
      0,                         // flags
      (int (*)()) 0,             // called before read
      user_update,               // called after write
      "Alarm state.  The (possibly latched) state of the "
      "alarm for this input. Just equals InputState for "
      "non-latching alarms. The user clears this to reset "
      "a latched alarm. A write callback on this column "
      "logs the user action if the alarm value changes."
  }
```

The user_update() subroutine shown below checks to see if a user has set the alarm variable and caused it to change. If the alarm variable has changed, the user_update() subroutine writes a syslog message.

```
/**************************************************************
 * user_update():  - A write callback on the alarm column. We
 *                   do a little sanity checking and send a syslog
 *                   message if the user changed the alarm value.
 *
 * Input:  None
 * Return: 0 on success, -1 on error
 **************************************************************/
int user_update(char *tbl, char *col, char *sql, void *pr, int rowid,
                void *poldrow)
{
  /* Make sure we are looking at a valid row */
  if (rowid >= NUM_INPUTS) {
    return(-1);     // An error return
  }

  /* Check for a change */
  if (((ZONE *)pr)->alarm != ((ZONE *)poldrow)->alarm) {
    if (((ZONE *)pr)->alarm) {
      syslog(LOG_ALERT, "User set alarm on zone %d, %s",
             Zone[rowid].id, Zone[rowid].name);
    }
    else {
      syslog(LOG_ALERT, "User cleared alarm on zone %d, %s",
             Zone[rowid].id, Zone[rowid].name);
    }
  }
  return(0);  // Success
}
```

In the last two sections, we showed you the alarm daemon source code and explained how the source code works. Did you notice how easy it was to implement the alarm daemon? The next section shows you how to build and test the alarm daemon.

Building and Testing ladd

You don't need to install a whole set of alarm sensors to run this daemon—all you need is a standard PC with a parallel port. Before running the daemon, you must create the directory /opt/laddie/ladd/, because the alarm daemon creates a PID file in this directory. Use these commands to create this directory as root:

```
mkdir /opt/laddie/ladd
```

The source code for ladd is on the companion CD in /Code/src/ladd. Compile the alarm daemon and then run the daemon as root, as shown in the following commands:

```
cd /Code/src/ladd
make
su
./ladd
```

To make sure that the alarm daemon is running and responding to user requests, invoke the psql SQL command shown below, and verify that the Zone table is displayed.

```
psql -h localhost -p 8888
SELECT * FROM Zone;
 id | name | enabled | edge | latching | input | alarm | count
----+------+---------+------+----------+-------+-------+-------
 1  |      | 0       | 0    | 0        | 0     | 0     | 0
 2  |      | 0       | 0    | 0        | 0     | 0     | 0
 3  |      | 0       | 0    | 0        | 0     | 0     | 0
 4  |      | 0       | 0    | 0        | 0     | 0     | 0
 5  |      | 0       | 0    | 0        | 0     | 0     | 0
(5 rows)
```

Typically, you would add hardware sensors to your alarm appliance, but you can simulate an alarm without the hardware sensors.

Consider zone 1. Our approach is to invoke the alarm write callback using this command:

```
UPDATE Zone SET name = "BackDoor", enabled=1, edge=0, WHERE id=1;
```

Next, we'll simulate an alarm on the input of zone 1 with the following command:

```
UPDATE Zone SET alarm=1 WHERE id=1;
```

Verify that ladd generated a log saying *User set alarm on zone 1*. Then manually clear the alarm, as such:

```
UPDATE Zone SET alarm=0 WHERE id=1;
```

Again verify that ladd generates a message for syslog. We'll show you how to build more accessible user interfaces to the alarm daemon in future chapters.

Summary

This chapter tied the previous chapters together by showing you how to build ladd, a simple alarm daemon, using RTA and the empty daemon. You saw the design of ladd's RTA table, the control point by which the user interfaces manage the alarm daemon. You also saw the alarm daemon's source code, including the three subroutines used by the empty daemon to implement the alarm daemon's run-time behavior. Finally, you saw how to configure the alarm daemon and how to manually set and clear an alarm from the command line.

The next chapter continues to develop Laddie's design by showing you how to handle events on an appliance, including events such as ladd sending messages to syslog.

LOGGING

A *log message* is an asynchronous report of an event of interest. This chapter discusses logging in general and then looks in some detail at syslog, the default logging system on Linux. We also describe how to control logging thresholds while a daemon is running.

We've organized this chapter into the following sections:

- Do You Need Logging?
- Architecture of a Logging System
- syslog
- On-Demand Logging

Do You Need Logging?

Before getting into the mechanics of logging, let's discuss why you might want logging on your appliance.

Uptime

The number one reason for logging is to increase the system availability of your appliance. Proper routing and displaying of log messages like *CPU fan speed below 1000 RPM* can help your end users keep their systems up and running. A regression or trend analysis of the system's collected log messages can help identify problems before they interrupt service. Trend analysis is particularly useful in spotting problems with fans, disks, and power supplies.

Security

If your appliance is on a network, it will almost certainly come under attack at some point. You can use log messages to trigger changes in the firewall rules or to notify the system operator or the end user that the system is under attack.

Debug

The first step in fixing a bug is recognizing that a bug exists. Log messages that report any inconsistency in input or output of a subroutine are invaluable for finding bugs. You can use the on-demand logging described later in this chapter to trace program execution and to record subroutine inputs and outputs when a bug is detected.

Integral to the application

Laddie is a good example of an application with integrated logging and event processing. It simplified our design of the ladd daemon to have it report all alarm transitions using only a log message.

You may be unable to use logging on some deeply embedded Linux systems with limited connectivity and limited disk space. But for most systems, logging will be a real asset for your appliance.

Architecture of a Logging System

This section describes the architecture and properties of an "ideal" logging system. The next section describes syslog and compares it to the ideal presented below.

A logging system can be divided into three major sections: one to collect log messages, one to route them, and one to deliver them (or to start other actions). Figure 6-1 illustrates the architecture of a logging system.

Let's consider each of these three sections in more detail.

Message Sources

The ideal logging system is a clearing house for messages from anywhere on the appliance, and it should be able to accept messages from many sources, including Unix sockets, UDP and TCP sockets, named pipes, and from following a file (the output of tail -f).

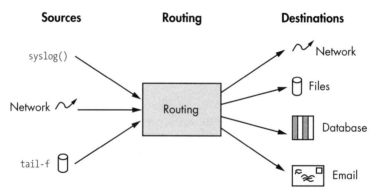

Figure 6-1: Log message flow in an appliance

The source code of the logging system should be well documented and modular to make it easy to add new types of message sources. The configuration of the system should make it easy to add new sources while the system is running.

Let's discuss three common message sources in a little more detail.

Unix sockets

Syslog, the most popular logging system on Linux, uses a Unix socket as its message collection point. Stream-oriented communication channels, such as a Unix socket, must have a delimiter to separate the messages. The two most common delimiters are a null character, which syslog uses, and a carriage return.

Network sockets

Network messages might arrive in a UDP datagram or over a TCP connection. Some applications accept TCP connections and broadcast their log messages to all connected sockets. The logging system should be able to accept TCP connections as well as initiate them. If the log messages are going to traverse an insecure network link, the system should encrypt them in transit using either Stunnel or SSH with port forwarding.

Following a file

Many applications write log messages directly to a file. If you want to capture the events reported in these log messages, you must watch the file for new messages. The `tail -f` command does this. Most often, you'll see this as the command string:

```
tail -f app_log_file | logger
```

It seems a waste to create two processes just to capture an application's log messages, and a good logging system should handle following a file as part of its core functionality.

Message Routing

The routing section identifies the appropriate destinations for each message. The routing criteria vary from one system to another, but most systems include the ability to route based on event importance and source programs (such as mail, cron, kernel, and authentication). Some systems include filters that recognize and route based on the text in the log message.

In this chapter, we define a *filter* as a set of routing rules and the destination associated with each rule. The routing rules and their associated destinations are stored in a configuration file (or, in the case of Laddie, in an RTA table). Filters only make sense if the system supports (and you use) multiple message destinations.

Message Destinations

A logging system finishes processing a message by sending it to a destination. Common destinations are discussed below. While the following list of message destinations may seem quite long, there are in fact many possible destinations not described.

Files

Files are the most common destination for log messages. Log files are the accepted norm, perhaps because they are so easy to access for periodic post-processing analysis. Unfortunately, files pose a problem for many embedded systems that do not have hard disks: RAM is volatile, and flash memory is too expensive to use for archiving log messages. Your choices for a diskless appliance are to filter messages heavily and only save a few to flash, to send them to a server on the network, or to just not save log messages.

If you save log messages to a file, you can use logrotate to periodically remove the oldest file, rotate the newest file into a numbered archive, and send a SIGHUP signal to the process that is the source of the messages. A SIGHUP should cause the application to open a new log file.

Named pipes

Named pipes are an easy way to pass your filtered log messages to another program. A helper application opens the named pipe for reading and then blocks while waiting for log messages to arrive. When the logging system has a message to send, it writes the message to the named pipe, unblocking the helper application. Make sure your helper application can handle "broken pipe" errors, since they can occur if the logging system is restarted.

Named pipes and helper applications are very useful for destinations that are too big or too complex for inclusion in the logging daemon itself. A named pipe is a great way to tie the logging system to a custom application that is specific to your appliance.

One alternative to a named pipe is a *fanout* device, a kernel module and associated /dev entries that act as a one-to-many multiplexer. Unlike named pipes, fanout devices let many readers get the same message (hence the name *fanout*). This book's website hosts the fanout project, including source files and more detailed documentation. Please visit http://www.linuxappliancedesign.com for more information.

Remote UDP/syslog host

If your appliance is a network appliance designed for a large data center, be sure to include the ability to forward log messages to another host in the network. The syslogd logging daemon can receive and/or forward log messages to other hosts using UDP.

TCP multiplexer

If you want to route some reports to other programs, you can define a listening TCP socket that accepts connections. When a message arrives at the multiplexer, it is replicated and sent down each open TCP connection on the socket.

For example, in our Laddie appliance we have a command line interface (CLI) that can show Laddie alarm messages.[1] When a CLI user gives the command set logs on, the CLI opens a TCP connection to logmuxd, Laddie's logging daemon, and log messages are sent down each accepted TCP connection to the CLI at the other end. (logmuxd is described in the next chapter.)

Email

It is nice to have significant events reported to you via email, since email is ubiquitous, if not timely. Also, email is often used as a gateway to pagers and cell phones (so that really important disasters can find you no matter where you hide).

Console

Output to /dev/console or to a serial port is a must for debugging. Some large network centers still prefer to collect log messages over a physically secure and non-shared channel like an RS-232 cable.

Database

Some messages require an immediate response, but most of the time you are interested more in trends or changes in the pattern of a system's events. A relational database is an ideal repository for log messages, since it has a wide range of tools to sort and count log messages. Since databases can use a lot of CPU cycles while they are sorting and counting, you might want to put the DB somewhere else on the network instead of on your appliance.

SNMP traps

Most large networks have one or more dedicated network-management workstations that run an SNMP manager. The operators of these networks often insist that all network equipment use SNMP for status, configuration, and error reporting.

---

[1] *Log messages* give a report of an event. An *alarm* is a system state of failure or reduced availability. Log messages are used to report the transitions in to and out of an alarm state, and the two terms are sometimes confused.

`system()`

A system() call to run a utility is another common destination. While simple and flexible, this approach uses more memory and CPU cycles than the other destinations and is not appropriate for processing large numbers of log messages.

The use of system() is almost always considered a security risk. We mention system() for completeness, but discourage its use. If you must run an external command, try to use popen() in place of system(). We solve this problem on Laddie by using the RTA-to-file utility described in Appendix D.

We do not have space here to describe all of the many possible destinations. For example, we did not discuss pagers, voice mail, or instant messaging.

syslog

A logging system needs a standard way to report events, a *lingua franca* for log messages. That standard, for most of us, is syslog. There are several advantages to syslog. It is the primary event-reporting mechanism used by all legacy Linux applications, and it is well known and understood. In conjunction with the kernel logging daemon, klogd, syslog captures kernel and other system log messages that you may want to make visible to the appliance user.

This section describes how syslog works, how to use it in your applications, and how to configure its message filters. We give enough detail that you should have no trouble using syslog as the basis for your logging system.

syslog Architecture

Messages from syslog are generated in your program by a call to the glibc C-library routine syslog(). Then, glibc formats the message and tries to write it to /dev/log, a Unix socket that is opened when syslogd starts. syslogd reads the message from /dev/log and handles it according to filters defined in /etc/syslog.conf, the syslogd configuration file. Figure 6-2 shows the overall architecture and message flow of syslog.

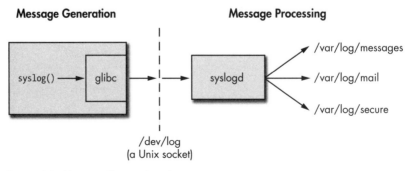

Figure 6-2: Message flow with syslog

Using syslog

Almost all Linux programming languages have a routine to send a syslog message. The C-library prototype shown below is fairly typical of most languages.

```
void syslog(int priority, const char *format, ...);
```

Priority is combination of the log level, the importance or severity of the event, and the *facility*, the type of program that generated the message.[2] Most programmers specify only the log level when using the syslog routine. There are eight log levels, ranging in importance from emergency to debug. This excerpt from syslog.h shows the eight levels available.

```
#define LOG_EMERG    0    /* system is unusable */
#define LOG_ALERT    1    /* action must be taken immediately */
#define LOG_CRIT     2    /* critical conditions */
#define LOG_ERR      3    /* error conditions */
#define LOG_WARNING  4    /* warning conditions */
#define LOG_NOTICE   5    /* normal but significant condition */
#define LOG_INFO     6    /* informational */
#define LOG_DEBUG    7    /* debug-level messages */
```

The syslog() routine uses a printf style format string that can have a variable number of arguments. The text in the format string should form a clear, unambiguous description of the event, and any arguments to the format string should give further details of the event.

When we build appliances, a big part of what we deliver is documentation, and a big part of our documentation is a list of all the appliance log messages and their meanings. This list is easy to generate using grep on the source code. A list of log messages will be exceptionally valuable to your customers, and generating it requires only a little discipline on your part.

NOTE   *Generate a list of all log messages in your appliance as part of your appliance's documentation.*

You have more control over what is sent to syslogd than just the priority and text of the message. In particular, you can also use the optional openlog() routine to control the syslog facility, the message prefix, and whether or not to include the process ID with the log message. The openlog() calling syntax is:

```
void openlog(const char *ident, int option, int facility);
```

The ident is a short string that syslog prepends to each log message. If you do not specify one, ident defaults to the name of the program that called

---

[2] Unfortunately, the documentation for syslog and syslog.conf are not in full agreement. One defines *priority* as the bitwise OR of facility and log level, and the other defines *priority* as what we call log level. While this book is self-consistent, you should use care when reading other syslog documentation.

syslog(). The option parameter lets you control things such as what to do if /dev/log is not available and whether or not to include the PID of the calling program. The option is the bitwise OR of zero or more of the following:

- LOG_CONS—write log to console on failure to write to /dev/log
- LOG_NDELAY—open socket to /dev/log immediately
- LOG_ODELAY—wait until first message to open socket to /dev/log
- LOG_PERROR—write log to standard error as well as /dev/log
- LOG_PID—include PID with each message

The facility is meant to correspond to the type of program sending the log message. It defaults to LOG_USER if openlog() is not called. There are 24 standard facilities defined in syslog.h; the following excerpt shows the definitions for the most common ones. Note that the values are shifted up by three bits to keep the lower three bits reserved for the log level.

```
/* facility codes */
#define LOG_KERN       (0<<3)  /* kernel messages */
#define LOG_USER       (1<<3)  /* random user-level messages */
#define LOG_MAIL       (2<<3)  /* mail system */
#define LOG_DAEMON     (3<<3)  /* system daemons */
#define LOG_AUTH       (4<<3)  /* security/authorization messages */
#define LOG_SYSLOG     (5<<3)  /* messages generated by syslogd */
#define LOG_LPR        (6<<3)  /* line printer subsystem */
#define LOG_NEWS       (7<<3)  /* network news subsystem */
#define LOG_UUCP       (8<<3)  /* UUCP subsystem */
#define LOG_CRON       (9<<3)  /* clock daemon */
#define LOG_AUTHPRIV  (10<<3)  /* security messages (private) */
#define LOG_FTP       (11<<3)  /* ftp daemon */
```

While the priority and facility are used by syslogd for routing, their values are not part of the saved text; however, you can infer the priority and facility of saved log messages by setting up syslogd to save messages with different priority and facility values to different files.

The syslog Protocol

Before going into a description of how to set up syslogd, let's examine the protocol used to send syslog messages. As mentioned earlier, syslogd opens a Unix datagram socket on /dev/log and blocks while waiting for messages to arrive on the socket. The information passed from the application to the syslogd daemon includes a facility, a log level, and the message itself. The daemon uses the facility and level as its sole filtering criteria.

The original authors of syslog combined the priority and facility into a 32-bit integer, with the priority using the low three bits for the log level. The combined facility/level is ASCII encoded and placed between angle brackets before being written to /dev/log.

For example, say your program sets the facility to LOG_USER and sends an INFO log message with the following code.

```
#include <syslog.h>

main() {
  openlog("my_prog", 0, LOG_USER);  //LOG_USER = 0x0008
  syslog(LOG_INFO, "abc=%d", 2);    //LOG_INFO = 0x0006
}
```

If we looked at the message just after syslogd reads it from its Unix
socket, we would see:

```
<14>Aug  2 13:18:31 my_prog: abc=2
```

Notice how LOG_USER (8) and LOG_INFO (6) are combined into <14>. A
newline or other termination character is not needed, since syslog() adds a
null character before writing the message to the /dev/log socket. If you
don't include a newline, syslogd will append one before writing the message
to the log file.

Using the syslogd Daemon

The syslog daemon reads the messages from the /dev/log Unix socket and
routes the messages based on their facility and log level. The destinations for
a syslog message are called *actions* and include files, named pipes, the system
console (or other TTY port), other syslogd systems on the network, and
users.

The filters and actions for syslogd are defined in /etc/syslog.conf. The
configuration file usually has one line per destination, with a list of as many
facilities and levels as needed for that destination. The facilities in the action
are separated by commas, followed by a dot and then a log level. An asterisk
can be used to represent all facilities or levels, and specifying a log level
implies including that level and all the levels more severe than it. For
example:

```
*.*             all log messages
mail,lpr.*      all messages from the mail and printer daemons
*.crit          all messages with a critical log level or higher
```

The most common destinations for syslog messages include files, pipes,
and other log daemons on the network. Pipes are specified by giving a pipe
symbol, |, at the start of the destination. A network destination starts with an
at symbol, @. The man page for syslog.conf gives a more complete description
on how to specify which facility and priorities are routed to which actions.
The lines of syslog.conf that route all mail logs to /var/log/mail and all
critical or higher print spooler and FTP logs to a network log server are:

```
mail.*                      /var/log/mail
lpr,ftp.crit                @loghost.myintranet.com
```

Recall that the facility is part of the priority integer passed from syslog() to syslogd, and that you can define your own facilities. This lets you build a private logging system on top of syslog. You could add the new facility integer and name to syslog.h, then rebuild glibc and syslogd. However, it is probably easier to use an explicit integer for the new facility. There are 24 predefined facilities, so choose a number much larger, say 1,000. The code that sends an INFO log with this facility might look like the following:

```
syslog((1000<<3) | LOG_INFO, "an event occurred");
```

We've shown the shift and OR explicitly to illustrate what is happening. We suggest that you use the equivalent LOG_MAKEPRI(*facility, level*) macro.

To continue with this example, say you have a program listening for your new log messages on the named pipe /usr/local/private_pipe. You could configure syslogd to deliver all logs with the new facility by adding the following line to syslog.conf and restarting syslogd.

```
1000.*                    |/usr/local/private_pipe
```

Desktop developers might cringe at the thought of using syslog for event processing. But then again, Linux desktop systems typically have more RAM and CPU resources than an appliance, so they can afford the (relatively) high disk, memory, and CPU overhead of D-Bus. We recommend syslog for its simplicity, availability in almost all programming languages, and its small memory and CPU overhead.

Limitations, Advantages, and Alternatives to syslogd

There are a few limitations with the default syslogd daemon. As mentioned previously, it does not save the message level or facility (although you can get them indirectly by routing based on them). Syslogd can not route based on regular expressions, it only accepts messages from Unix sockets, and it has a somewhat limited set of actions. Some programmers find the limited numbers of levels a problem when setting up debug and trace mechanisms. On the plus side, syslogd is universally accepted and is thoroughly debugged, tested, and secure.

The logger utility (which we saw briefly in the beginning of this chapter) lets you work around the limited set of message sources for syslogd. Logger sends log messages to syslogd, getting the log messages from either its command line or from each line of its standard input. If you wish, you can specify level, facility, and a prefix string. See the logger man page for more details. You can also combine netcat (a simple utility to read and write from network connections) and a logger to accept log messages from a single accepted TCP connection using a command similar to the one shown below.

```
nc -l -p 2250 | logger
```

The logger utility lets you "watch" other log files. For example, say you want to have each line that is added to /usr/www/error.log to also be sent to syslog. The following command line does this.

```
tail -f /usr/www/error.log | logger
```

One other logging helper program worth mentioning is klogd. Since the Linux kernel does not use glibc, it cannot use syslog() to send kernel log messages. Instead, kernel log messages are made available either with the system call sys_syslog() or from the circular buffer visible in /proc/kmsg. The daemon klogd translates kernel log messages from either source into syslog messages. In addition, klogd translates the hex addresses in the kernel log messages into their equivalent symbolic names. To get the symbol from a hex address, klogd reads the memory map in the System.map file. If you load or unload kernel modules after starting klogd, be sure to tell klogd to reload its symbol table using the command klogd -i.

Popular alternatives to syslogd include nsyslog, which supports TCP using SSL; minirsyslogd, which is a minimalist logger that can handle a very high volume of traffic; and syslog-ng, which can filter on regular expressions, does message rewriting, and supports TCP sources and destinations. The evlog package is one of the best in terms of recognizing and responding to log messages. The latest information on these alternatives can be found with a web search on the package name.

On-Demand Logging

Wouldn't it be nice if you could dynamically control how verbose the logging is in your program? Sure, you can use a -v switch on the command line when starting the program, but that's not exactly dynamic. Also, it would be nice if you could independently control the log level in different parts of your program. That way, you could zoom in to study a particular piece of code. This section describes how you use an RTA table called Logit and code from the Laddie appliance to independently control the log thresholds in different parts of your code, while your program is running. Figure 6-3 illustrates the idea of giving different parts of a program different thresholds for logging.

Here is the definition for a row in the Logit table:

```
typedef struct
{
  char     sect[LOGIT_NAME_LEN]; /* the section name */
  int      thres;      /* log threshold.  0-6=normal 7-15=debug */
  int      output;     /* 0=none,1=stderr,2=syslog,3=both */
  char     comment[LOGIT_COMMENT_LEN]; /* description of section */
} LOGIT;
```

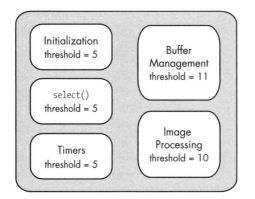

Figure 6-3: Independent control of logging in each
program section

The idea is to have a separate logging threshold for each section of code, and to send a log message only if the message's level is numerically below the log threshold for that section. Our implementation of Logit has 12 rows, the first five of which are used internally by the Laddie prototype daemon. You can easily change LOGIT_NROWS in logit.c to add more rows if you wish.

Let's work through an example. Say you want to add on-demand logging control to two different sections of code, image processing (IM) and buffer management (BM). During its initialization your program must create its entries in the Logit table. You can do this directly, or you can use the wrapper function logitSetEntry(). The code below shows both methods.

```
#include "empd.h"      /* defines for the prototype daemon */
#define IM  5
#define BM  6

/* Initialize on-demand logging for the image-processing section */
strncpy(Logit[IM].sect, "img proc", LOGIT_NAME_LEN-1);
Logit[IM].thres = LOG_DEBUG;
Logit[IM].output = 2;    /* output to syslog() */
strncpy(Logit[IM].comment, "IM, image process",LOGIT_COMMENT_LEN-1);

/* Initialize on-demand logging for buffer management */
logitSetEntry(BM, "buf_mgmt", LOG_DEBUG, 2, "BM, buffer management");
```

With the above initialization in place, you can now add log messages that you can control by raising or lowering the threshold in the Logit table.

The LOG() macro defined in the Laddie empty daemon header file, empd.h, will send a message to syslog() or send a standard error if the threshold set in the LOG call is numerically lower than the threshold in Logit for that section of code. For example, to selectively trace the operation of the image-processing and buffer-management code, you might have a few lines like the following.

```
LOG(LOG_DEBUG,  IM, "Deep into image processing");
LOG(DBG_2, BM, "Freeing buffer ID=%d", buf_id);
```

The file empd.h defines five additional log levels (DBG_0 to DBG_4) below LOG_DEBUG to give you more precise control over the verbosity of debug messages.

With all of the above in place, you can enable and disable log messages in individual sections of your program. For example, the SQL commands to disable all logging except for the IM section might be:

```
UPDATE Logit SET thres = 0
UPDATE Logit SET thres = 10 WHERE sect = "IM"
```

Summary

Logging is a valuable addition to almost all appliances, even those with limited disk, memory, and CPU power. An ideal logging system has many sources and destinations for log messages and allows for the addition of new sources and destinations.

There are two components to syslog, the default logging system on Linux: a library routine to send log messages, and a daemon to process them. The syslog() library routine is available in every major programming language available on Linux. The syslog daemon, syslogd, routes messages based on the source of the message (the facility) and on the severity of the event reported (the log level). In this chapter, you learned how to add your own facility to syslog in order to route log messages specific to your appliance.

On-demand logging gives us the ability to dynamically control the verbosity of logging in different parts of our application. While RTA makes on-demand logging easier, it is not required for on-demand logging.

This chapter reviewed logging and the collection and archiving of log messages. The next chapter describes a logging system that can recognize specific text in log messages and then rewrite and route the messages on a case-by-case basis.

7

LADDIE EVENT HANDLING

Your appliance needs to respond when alarms or other critical events occur. Whether it's CPU temperature, battery level, low disk space, or paper level, something is going to occur that requires action from your appliance.

The idea of having a general purpose event-handling system is, surprisingly, not common in Linux. Too often the need for event handling is not apparent until near the end of system testing of the appliance, so it is usually addressed as an afterthought—with ad hoc and poorly integrated code.

The authors have built enough Linux appliances to know that we should build event handling into the core of our design for Laddie. As part of the Laddie project, we built our own event-handling system that uses logging to capture the events of interest. Our event-handling daemon is called logmuxd, and this chapter explains why we built it, describes its features, presents its major tables, and gives complete examples of its use. This chapter may be of value even if you choose not to use logmuxd, since it shows the kinds of processing needed for any event-aware appliance.

This chapter discusses event handling in the context of logging, but bear in mind that the goal is event handling, and logging is just the mechanism used to reach that goal.

We've organized this chapter into the following sections:

- Rationale for a New Event-Handling System
- Features and Capabilities of logmuxd
- Configuring logmuxd
- Examples Using logmuxd

Rationale for a New Event-Handling System

We've found that the only code we've ever delivered on time and bug free was code that we did not write. That is, our most successful projects were the ones in which we were most able to avoid writing new code. New code always has bugs, and new code is always late. Why, then, did we decide to write a logging daemon to do event handling? There are really two parts to the answer: why we chose to use logging as the mechanism, and why we chose not to use an existing logging system.

Chapter 6 explains why we think logging is the right mechanism for event reporting. All events that are of interest to us are already captured by, or can easily be captured by, syslog messages. There are syslog libraries for almost every programming language, and syslog is well understood, fairly secure, and is both CPU and memory efficient.

A distant second to syslog for event handling is D-Bus, an open source package often used to distribute desktop events. D-Bus offers libraries and an API that allows processes to exchange messages, provided that both processes are D-Bus aware. (Because of this, legacy applications that use syslog must be rewritten to add D-Bus support.) However, D-Bus does not offer the same breadth of languages that syslog offers, and D-Bus usually requires two running daemons, which makes it relatively RAM and CPU intensive (compared to syslog).

NOTE   *D-Bus comes standard on most Linux desktops, but it's probably inappropriate for event handling on most Linux appliances.*

If syslog is the event reporting mechanism, then why not use the syslog daemon for event handling? The major feature that we found missing from the currently available logging systems was the ability to easily duplicate log messages and broadcast them on accepted TCP connections.

The Laddie Alarm System needs to have Laddie alarm messages routed to several running programs and UIs. Figure 7-1 illustrates a typical case. When an alarm occurs, ladd sends a log message to report the event. We need to send a copy of the resulting log message to every CLI that has logging enabled and to every web page that is looking at the system status. The problem is that we don't know beforehand how many of each of these interfaces are open.

Our new logging daemon, logmuxd, solves this problem by allowing us to route messages to many destinations, even if those destinations are transitory. No other logging system supports multiple, transitory destinations. When ladd detects an alarm, it sends a log using syslog(); then logmuxd captures the event, rewrites it if needed, and multiplexes it out to each of the accepted TCP connections.

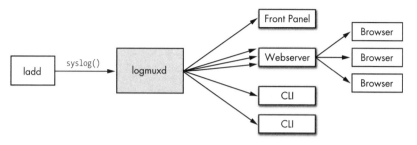

Figure 7-1: The need for a multiplexing log daemon

We decided to invest the time to build a new logging system for event handling because we wanted the ability to capture, rewrite, and route event reports from all applications and daemons on the appliance. As an appliance designer, you may find that your appliance needs to capture event reports from many sources and route the messages to many destinations. If so, you should consider using logmuxd in your appliance.

Features and Capabilities of logmuxd

We want logmuxd to work either with an existing syslogd installation or as a replacement for it. That is, we need to be able to read and write messages in the syslog style of angle brackets surrounding an integer. We want our logging daemon to support many types of input and many types of destinations, to be able to route based on a regex, and to be able to rewrite a log message before forwarding it on to its destination.

Each destination has its own set of routing and rewriting rules. This is similar to syslogd and means that you may have otherwise identical filters with the output of each filter going to a different destination.

Filters use the regex() library for pattern matching and for extracting relevant fields from the log messages. Messages can optionally be rewritten using the fields extracted from the regex pattern.

Figure 7-2 presents the overall architecture of logmuxd. In the next section we discuss each of the blocks in this diagram.

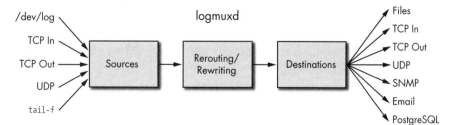

Figure 7-2: Architecture of logmuxd

The use of logmuxd might be easier to understand if we start with a list of its configuration tables[1] grouped according to the three processing blocks shown in Figure 7-2. Table 7-1 doesn't describe all of the tables in detail, so you might want to use the RTA table editor to examine them more closely.

Table 7-1: Configuration Tables Grouped According to Processing Block

Section	Table	Contents
Source	MuxIn, Rawlog, Accpt	Descriptions of all input sources, last 10 raw log messages, and accepted input TCP connections
Routing	Filters	Patterns to match, rewriting rules, and destinations
Destinations	FileDest, NetDest, AccptDest, SnmpDest, PgdbDest, MailDest, TblDest	Destinations existing in a filesystem, TCP and UDP destinations on the network, accepted output TCP connections, SNMP trap destinations, RTA and PostgreSQL DB destinations, email destinations, and a local table with the last 20 Laddie log messages

logmuxd has several limitations. It does not have any flood filtering (for example, syslog's "Last message repeated 10 billion times"). It uses regex, which gives it a lot of power and flexibility, but at the expense of CPU cycles. Finally, it is a relatively new logging daemon and is still in flux to a certain degree, as new features are added and as bugs are found and fixed.

You can overcome most of the limitations of logmuxd by pairing it with syslogd. Configure syslogd to output all messages to a FIFO, and configure logmuxd to read from the FIFO and to filter and rewrite only those few messages that you want to capture for further processing.

Configuring logmuxd

RTA tables store the configuration and statistics for logmuxd. The following discussion describes the tables, and the examples in the next section give the SQL for using them.

logmuxd Sources

You tell logmuxd about your event sources by describing them in the four editable fields in logmuxd's MuxIn table. These fields are source, port, type, and term.

The *source* field contains the filename if the source is a file, pipe, or Unix socket, or the IP address if the source is a UDP or TCP socket.

The *port* field contains the port number for UDP and TCP sockets and is ignored for sources with an entry from a filesystem.

The *type* field specifies one of the six possible types for the source. Table 7-2 describes the six source types.

---

[1] Other programming books might give configuration as a file format or set of subroutine calls. Instead, we present logmuxd configuration in terms of its RTA table interface. You should now think of all status and configuration information in terms of how it would appear in an RTA table.

Table 7-2: Six Possible Source Types

Type	Meaning
1	The read end of a named FIFO
2	The "tail" of the specified file
3	A UDP socket
4	A TCP connection that logmuxd opens to the specified address and port
5	A TCP connection that logmuxd accepts on the specified listen address and port
6	A Unix datagram socket

The *term* field specifies how the source terminates log messages. A zero indicates that log messages are terminated with a null character. Messages from syslog use a null terminator. A one indicates that each read() on the source will receive a complete message. This termination is used on UDP sockets, for example. A two indicates that a newline terminates the message. Newline termination is used for tail -f types of sources.

The MuxIn table also has read-only fields that hold usage statistics, error statistics, and the file descriptor for the source. For more information on these fields, use the RTA table editor to examine them on a running Laddie appliance.

Two other logmuxd tables are associated with message input processing. The Rawlog table acts as a FIFO to hold the 10 most recent messages. This is useful when debugging filters or monitoring the raw input to the logger. The Accpt table holds the file descriptor and other information needed by accepted TCP connections and by open Unix sockets. There are no configurable fields in either Rawlog or Accpt.

logmuxd Filters and Rewriting

One of the main reasons to use logmuxd is that it rewrites messages and forwards them on to another process. For example, when a user sets a test alarm in a zone, ladd sends the log message "User set alarm on zone *n*, *zone_name*" (where *n* and *zone_name* are replaced by the zone number and user-assigned name). We want this log message to appear on the front panel LCD display, but the LCD display can only display 16 characters, so we use the rewriting capability of logmuxd to rewrite the message to fit on the LCD display. The original message is rewritten from this:

```
Aug 12 22:28:31 ladd[3820]: User set alarm on zone 5, Refrigerator
```

to this:

```
22:28 Usr set 5
```

All of the configuration data to recognize and rewrite a log message is contained in the Filters table. This table contains the type and name of the destination, the regular expression to match, and an snprintf() format string for the rewritten message. Let's look at each of these fields in turn.

Two fields are used to specify the destination: *desttype* and *destname*. There is a separate table for each type of destination. This is necessary because, for example, an email destination needs different configuration information than an SNMP trap destination does. The type of the destination and its destination table are set by the desttype field. There are nine valid destination types. The types for 1 and 2 are not included in Table 7-3, since they are strictly source types.

Table 7-3: The Nine Valid Destination Types

desttype	Destination Table	Meaning
0	None	No destination (useful for collecting statistics)
3	NetDest	Accepted TCP connections
4	NetDest	Outgoing TCP connections
5	NetDest	UDP socket destinations
7	FileDest	File (includes both FIFOs and regular files)
8	PgdbDest	PostgreSQL DB (or an RTA table)
9	SnmpDest	SNMP trap destinations
10	MailDest	Email destinations
11	TblDest	logmuxd's internal table for output messages

There can be several distinct destinations described in each of the destination tables. Each destination has its own unique name (a destname) in one of the destination tables. For example, if you have two different SNMP destinations, you may call one of them *allsnmp* and the other *laddiesnmp*. By giving them different names, you can define different routing and rewriting rules for them. To link a filter in the Filters table to a specific destination, you need to specify both the destination type and destination name.

Logmuxd routes messages based on the message's facility, log level, and on a text pattern match. These three corresponding fields in the Filters table are *facility*, *level*, and *regex*. The facilities and log levels are the same as those defined for syslogd. The regex pattern is a regular expression used for both pattern matching and subpattern extraction.

The regex library is a good choice for pattern matching and extraction, since the patterns can be precompiled to improve the speed of the pattern match, and regex lets you easily extract subpatterns from the search pattern. In our use of logmuxd, we've found that we don't really need to know too much about regex patterns. The following example illustrates most of what you need to know.

Say that you are processing the event of a train's arrival at a station, and the log message is *Train from San Jose arriving on Track number 15*. To rewrite this message as *San Jose : 15*, you need to extract both the city and the track number. The regex pattern to capture the city is *[A-Za-z -]+*. This pattern matches any combination of at least one upper- or lowercase alphabetic character, a space, or a dash. The pattern for the track number is just *[0-9]+*. Here's the trick: If you put parentheses around a pattern, regex makes that pattern available separately in the regex output. The following is a regex pattern to match the message and extract the city and train number.

```
Train from ([A-Za-z -]+) arriving on Track number ([0-9]+)
```

The Filter table's *rewrite* field contains the snprintf() format string used to rewrite the log message. The format string contains text of your choosing and can contain the strings extracted from the regex pattern. The matches to the regex patterns are available as explicit parameters to the snprintf(). Table 7-4 lists the parameters available to you.

Table 7-4: Available Parameters to the snprintf()

Parameter	Meaning
%1$s to %9$s	Up to nine regex subpatterns
%10$s	The entire match to the full regex pattern
%11$s	The date and time per the time_fmt field
%12$s	A newline character

Continuing the example above, you can get the message *San Jose : 15* with a rewrite format string of *%1$s : %2$s*.

You can add a date and time to your rewritten message by including *%11$s* in your rewrite string. The format of the date and time is set by the *time_fmt* field, which is passed to strftime() for the conversion. Common examples of time_fmt include *%F %T*, which gives a date and time display of *YYYY-MM-DD hh:mm:ss*, and *%R*, which displays only the time as *hh:mm.*

The explicit parameter for a newline is handy, since it can be difficult to get a newline character into an RTA table. Remember, to PostgreSQL, a \n is a two-character string with a backslash and the letter *n*.

We'll show more examples of regex pattern matching and message rewriting in the section "Examples Using logmuxd" on page 98.

logmuxd Destinations

Each type of destination has a table to hold the parameters unique to that type. You can easily figure out most of the tables and their content by browsing them with the RTA table editor, but three destination tables deserve some additional comments.

The *MailDest* table has a *subject* field that contains the subject of the email message to send. The *to_list* field is a space-separated list of recipients of the email. For security reasons, the only characters allowed in to_list are alphanumerics, periods, underscores, at signs (@), and spaces. If you are going to use email as a destination, be sure to run Sendmail, Postfix, or another mail transfer agent on your appliance.

The *SnmpDest* table contains the name of the destination, the IP address of the SNMP trap daemon, the community string for the SNMP daemon, the port number, and the type of trap to send (version 2 trap or version 2 inform). The values in these fields are passed as parameters to the snmptrap command, which actually sends the trap.

The *TblDest* table holds 20 log messages, with the most recent message always at the top of the table. In Laddie we use this table to hold the log messages that we make visible to the end user.

Examples Using logmuxd

Let's go over a few examples to help clarify how to use logmuxd.

Example 1: A logmuxd Demonstration

In the previous sections, you saw that one of the nice features of the Laddie Alarm System is that when an alarm occurs, all of the UIs are updated to reflect the new alarm and the new system status. This demonstration shows how to see the log messages that are distributed to all of the UIs.

1. Boot the Laddie CD. After the system is up, verify that you can see Laddie's web interface on the web browser of another PC.

2. On Laddie, logmuxd is configured to broadcast alarm system events down all accepted TCP connections to port 4444. Open a terminal window and telnet to port 4444 on the Laddie PC. For example:

```
telnet 192.168.1.11 4444
```

3. Use the web interface to test a few zones, and then clear all the alarms. Your telnet session should display log messages similar to the ones below.

```
2007-10-07 12:03:35 User set alarm on zone 2, Back Door
2007-10-07 12:03:35 Alarm system status: alarm
2007-10-07 12:03:37 User set alarm on zone 3, Garage
2007-10-07 12:03:38 User cleared alarm on zone 2, Back Door
2007-10-07 12:03:40 User cleared alarm on zone 3, Garage
2007-10-07 12:03:40 Alarm system status: safe
```

As simple as this example is, it shows logmuxd's ability to multiplex log messages.

Example 2: logmuxd and Accepted TCP Connections

Our rationale for building a new logger was that we wanted the ability to open a TCP connection to the logging daemon and have log messages delivered to us over that connection. The last example showed us this ability in action, and in this example we see how to configure logmuxd to accept TCP connections. We use logmuxd to replace syslogd, the logger command to generate a "train arriving" message, and a telnet connection to logmuxd to view the rewritten log messages. In this example we are going to rewrite log messages of the form "Train arriving from *city_name* on track *track_number*" to the form "*city_name* : *track_number*".

You can copy the source from the CD and build logmuxd on your development system, or you can boot the Laddie CD and use its running version of logmuxd. Don't worry about changing the logmuxd tables on Laddie, a reboot will restore them to their original state. We are going to use psql for the table updates, but you can also use the table editor, if you wish. Figure 7-3 illustrates the data flow in this example.

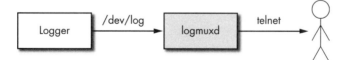

Figure 7-3: A logmuxd example using telnet

The basic steps in the configuration are:

1. Configure logmuxd to accept syslog messages from /dev/log. Verify the setup.
2. Configure logmuxd to recognize and rewrite "train arriving" messages.
3. Configure logmuxd to accept TCP connections on port 3333.
4. Use `logger` and telnet to verify that messages are distributed to connections to TCP port 3333.

We start by clearing the configuration in all of the tables that we are going to use. Using the console or telnet, log in on the PC that is running logmuxd (the PC booted from the book's CD). The RTA interface on logmuxd listens on port 8887; you can start the SQL session and clear the tables with these commands:

```
psql -h localhost -p 8887
UPDATE MuxIn SET source = "", type =0;
UPDATE Filters SET desttype = 0, destname = "", regex = "",
  rewrite = "", time_fmt = "";
UPDATE NetDest SET destname = "", dest = "", port = 0;
```

MuxIn

We want logmuxd to replace syslogd in this example, so we need to configure it to listen at the Unix socket /dev/log and to read log messages in the syslog style. We specify the source as /dev/log, the type as 6 (syslog format), and the log message terminator as 0 (null character between messages).

```
UPDATE MuxIn SET source = "/dev/log", type = 6, term = 0 LIMIT 1;
```

If everything is working at this point, the above command opened a Unix socket on /dev/log, and a display of the MuxIn table should show a valid file descriptor for our source. (A `netstat` command should also show the /dev/log socket.)

```
SELECT source, fd FROM MuxIn;
```

If we are now listening on /dev/log, we should be able to see log messages sent with `logger`. Open another terminal window and telnet into the PC running logmuxd a second time. Issue the following command in the new window:

```
logger "Hello, world!"
```

Verify that logmuxd received the message by looking at the Rawlog table.

```
SELECT source, log FROM Rawlog;
```

Filters

Continuing with the example, we are going to use the first row in Filters, but we are going to update it one or two columns at a time so that we can better explain just those columns.

desttype

You may recall that the desttype is an integer that implicitly selects which of the destination tables this filter will use as its destination. A desttype of 3 is used for accepted TCP connections.

destname

There may be multiple, independent destinations within a destination table. We need some way to distinguish one destination from another, so we give each destination a name. The destype in the Filter table selects which destination table to use, and the destname selects which row in that table to use. For this example we will assign a name of *example_2*.

```
UPDATE Filters SET desttype = 3, destname = "example_2" LIMIT 1;
```

regex

If we combine the regex pattern we built when we first looked at the train arrival example with some simple SQL, we get the command to set the regex pattern in our filter.

```
UPDATE Filters SET regex =
  "Train from ([A-Za-z -]+) arriving on Track number ([0-9]+)"
  LIMIT 1;
```

level and facility

The logmuxd daemon routes based on the level and facility of the incoming log message. In this example we do not care which level and facility were used to send the message, so we set the level to a high value, and we clear the facility mask.

```
UPDATE Filters SET level = 15, facility = 0 LIMIT 1;
```

At this point in our example, we can test the pattern-matching ability of our regex pattern. Use the terminal with the bash prompt to issue the following command.

```
logger "Train from Phoenix arriving on Track number 22"
```

Verify that the count of matches in our filter has gone up by one.

```
SELECT * FROM Filters LIMIT 1;
```

Repeat the above two steps a few times using different city names and track numbers. Issue a few logger commands where the pattern does not quite match, and verify that the count does not increment.

rewrite

You may recall that the magic of regex patterns is that you can extract a subpattern by placing parenthesis around it. Here, we are extracting the city name and the track number and rewriting them as *city_name* : *track_number*. The regex subpatterns are available to the rewriting string as *%1$s to %9$s*. We want the first two patterns, and we want to add a newline to the output, so we set the rewrite string with the command:

```
UPDATE Filters SET rewrite = "%1$s : %2$s %12$s" LIMIT 1;
```

We are done with the Filters table and can now finish the configuration by editing the NetDest table.

NetDest

We want to set up a TCP socket listening on port 3333. Let's give everyone on the network access to the port by binding to 0.0.0.0. The name of this network destination should be example_2, and the type of this network destination should be an accepted TCP connection, which is type 3:

```
UPDATE NetDest SET destname = "example_2", dest = "0.0.0.0",
    port = 3333, type = 3 LIMIT 1;
```

If all has gone well, there should be a listening socket on port 3333. Use netstat -nat to verify that the port is open and bound to the right address. Use the following SQL to see the file descriptor of the socket.

```
SELECT * FROM NetDest LIMIT 1;
```

We can now verify the whole system. Open a third terminal window and connect to port 3333. Your command might look something like this:

```
telnet 192.168.1.99 3333
```

You should now be able to verify that logmuxd has accepted your telnet connection. Enter the following on the terminal, still at the psql prompt:

```
SELECT * FROM AccptDest;
```

It should all be working. Enter the following on a terminal with the bash prompt:

```
logger "Train from Phoenix arriving on Track number 22"
logger "Train from San Jose arriving on Track number 15"
logger "Train from San Francisco arriving on Track number 9"
```

Verify that the city and track number are extracted and displayed on the connection to port 3333. Your output should appear as:

```
Phoenix : 22
San Jose : 15
San Francisco : 9
```

This has been a long example, but it has illustrated both how to configure logmuxd and how to debug that configuration.

Example 3: logmuxd and SNMP Traps

The *Simple Network Management Protocol (SNMP)* is an Internet standard that is used to manage network devices such as routers. The protocol has commands to read and write values (GET and SET) as well as *traps*, which are its equivalent to log messages. Network appliances are often required to send SNMP traps when specific events occur. This example shows how to use logmuxd to translate syslog-style log messages into SNMP traps. (SNMP and traps are covered in detail in later chapters, and you might want to delay going through this example until after reading those chapters.)

The Laddie Alarm System sends SNMP trap messages when the system enters or leaves an alarm state. To send the SNMP traps, logmuxd uses a helper application, snmptrap. The snmptrap command sends SNMP traps in the same manner that logger sends syslog messages.

You may recall that ladd uses syslog to send logs similar to the following when a zone goes into alarm.

```
Alarm set on zone 2, Back Door
User set alarm on zone 3, Garage
```

The snmptrap commands corresponding to the above two log messages are shown below.

```
snmptrap -v2c -c public snmp_mgr:162 '' ladAlarm ladTrapZoneId \
        i 2 ladTrapZoneName s "Back Door"
snmptrap -v2c -c public snmp_mgr:162 '' ladTestAlarm ladTrapZoneId \
        i 3 ladTrapZoneName s "Garage"
```

In the above lines, *public* is the community name, and it comes from the SnmpDest table since it is specific to the destination. The same is true for *snmp_mgr:162*, which is the destination name (or IP address) and the port number used by snmptrapd. If the type field of SnmpDest is set to 3, a -Ci is added to the command, making it an SNMP version 2 *inform*. The SnmpDest fields for destination name, port, community string, and type of trap to send should all appear in your UI, since the end user must configure these with values that match the end user's installation.

You can use the name of the trap if your MIB[2] is installed and accessible to the snmptrap command. If the MIB is not installed, you need to put the full, numeric object ID (OID) of the trap on the command line. The two single quotes in the command line tell the snmptrap command to send the current uptime in the trap. Be sure to read the man page for snmptrap to learn more about the command and its options. The SNMP chapters in this book will answer many of your questions regarding SNMP and its event notification system, traps.

Information about the SNMP trap server comes from user information entered into the SnmpDest table. Some information for the traps must be extracted from the log messages. For example, to send our SNMP traps, we need to translate these:

```
Alarm set on zone 2, Back Door
User set alarm on zone 3, Garage
```

into these:

```
ladAlarm ladTrapZoneId i 2 ladTrapZoneName s "Back Door"
ladTestAlarm ladTrapZoneId i 3 ladTrapZoneName s "Garage"
```

This is where regex pattern matching and rewriting come into play. Using the regex patterns given in the train station example above, you have everything you need to fill in the tables.

The destination type 9 indicates an SNMP destination, and the name we've given this destination is snmp_monitor. We need two rows from the Filters table, one row for the "User set" message that is sent when a user tests a zone, and another row for the "Alarm set" messages generated by real alarms. We use Filters rows 1 and 2 so that we don't overwrite row 0, which was used in the previous example. We show the configuration here using SQL, but the table editor would work just as well.

```
UPDATE Filters SET desttype = 9 LIMIT 1 OFFSET 1;
UPDATE Filters SET destname = "snmp_monitor" LIMIT 1 OFFSET 1;
UPDATE Filters SET regex = "User set alarm on zone ([1-5]), (.*)"
    LIMIT 1 OFFSET 1;
UPDATE Filters SET rewrite = "ladTestAlarm ladTrapZoneId i %1$s
    ladTrapZoneName s '%2$s'" LIMIT 1 OFFSET 1;
```

---

[2] If the SNMP GET and SET commands correspond to the SQL SELECT and UPDATE commands, then the SNMP Management Information Base (MIB) corresponds to a database table.

```
UPDATE Filters SET desttype = 9 LIMIT 1 OFFSET 2;
UPDATE Filters SET destname = "snmp_monitor" LIMIT 1 OFFSET 2;
UPDATE Filters SET regex = "Alarm set on zone ([1-5]), (.*)"
    LIMIT 1 OFFSET 2;
UPDATE Filters SET rewrite = "ladAlarm ladTrapZoneId i %1$s
    ladTrapZoneName s '%2$s'" LIMIT 1 OFFSET 2;
```

The values in the SnmpDest table are specific to the network computer that is configured to receive the traps, so you should provide user access to these values from one or more of your UIs. (The Laddie web interface lets you specify where to send Laddie's SNMP traps.) In this example we set the values manually using SQL. Let's assume that the trap destination is on a network host named snmp_host.

```
UPDATE SnmpDest SET destname = "snmp_monitor" LIMIT 1;
UPDATE SnmpDest SET dest = "snmp_host" LIMIT 1;
UPDATE SnmpDest SET community = "public", port = 162 LIMIT 1;
UPDATE SnmpDest SET version = 2 LIMIT 1;
```

You can test this configuration by running snmptrapd on one of your network hosts. (See Chapter 13 for details.)

Summary

Traditional logging handles an event by putting the report of the event (the log message) into one or more files on disk. A better approach is to examine each event individually and then decide how best to handle it. Making your appliance aware of events and able to respond to those events is one of the best things you can do for your customers.

In earlier chapters we showed you how to use the PostgreSQL protocol and API for control and status of your appliance. But control and status is only half of the solution—in this chapter we presented event handling, the other half of a successful appliance design.

8

DESIGNING A WEB INTERFACE

The web browser has become the user interface of choice for configuring networked appliances, particularly home-based routers from companies like Linksys and Netgear. The driving force behind the popularity of web interfaces is that they are easy to use and don't require specialized client software. Customers now expect to be able to access web interfaces for their devices, and so it is no surprise that leading manufacturers of home-based networked appliances provide them.

This is the first of several chapters devoted to user interface (UI) design. This chapter covers web UIs in general, and the development of Laddie's web UI in particular. In the chapters that follow, we'll look at Laddie's other UIs: the CLI interface in Chapter 9, the front panel LCD interface in Chapter 10, the framebuffer interface in Chapter 11, and the infrared remote control interface in Chapter 12. All of these UIs communicate with the back-end daemons via the PostgreSQL protocol.

This chapter covers the following topics:

- An overview of web technology
- Establishing requirements for your appliance's web interface
- Choosing a webserver
- Designing the look and feel of the web interface
- Highlights of our implementation
- Lessons learned and future improvements

Web Basics

Web browsers communicate with webservers using the *HyperText Transfer Protocol (HTTP)*, a client-server protocol. The communication is initiated from the web browser (the client) when it requests a web page via a particular Uniform Resource Locator (URL), for example, http://www.google.com. When the webserver receives this request, it checks that the requested page is available, and if it is, it sends the page to the web browser.

Because the HTTP protocol is text based, you can use telnet to imitate the browser request as follows:

```
telnet www.google.com 80
```

Once the telnet session has connected, enter the following:

```
GET / HTTP/1.0
```

Then press ENTER twice (the empty line created by the second ENTER causes the webserver to respond to the GET request). The page returned is formatted using HTML; an example page appears below. (Obviously, this page would look different if you opened it in a browser, because the browser would interpret the HTML markup and present it in a human-readable way.) Note that the middle portion of the page has been replaced by ellipses (. . .) to reduce its size.

```
HTTP/1.0 200 OK
Cache-Control: private
Content-Type: text/html
Set-Cookie:
PREF=ID=9dad60d4761f019c:TM=1156611888:LM=1156611888:S=p7NO7cVNpUMK6vxX;
expires=Sun, 17-Jan-2038 19:14:07 GMT; path=/; domain=.google.com
Server: GWS/2.1
Date: Sat, 26 Aug 2006 17:04:48 GMT
<html><head><meta http-equiv="content-type" content="text/html;
...
<a href=/intl/en/about.html>About Google</a></font><p><font size=-2>&copy;2006
Google</font></p></center></body></html>
```

DNS and TCP

The network protocols DNS (Domain Name System) and TCP (Transmission Control Protocol) make this client-server exchange possible. Given the URL (e.g., http://www.google.com), the client uses DNS to determine the IP address of the server. HTTP uses TCP for error-free data transmission between client and server.

These protocols are defined by the Internet Engineering Task Force (IETF), the authoritative Internet standards body. (For more information on IETF standards, see http://www.ietf.org; for more information on TCP/IP, see *The TCP/IP Guide* by Charles M. Kozierok, No Starch Press, 2005.)

The Webserver

The webserver finds and returns the web page for the given URL. This page may reside in the server's filesystem or in memory, or it may be generated dynamically at the time of the request.

CGI

The *Common Gateway Interface (CGI)* emerged as a way for a webserver to communicate with a purpose-built program, which would in turn generate the web page on behalf of the webserver. In the Unix world, the early CGI programs were written in languages like bash, Perl, and C. Today, web-specific scripting languages like PHP are more common. Furthermore, modern webservers like Apache can be configured to run PHP scripts within the same process as the Apache webserver, thereby avoiding the CGI communication mechanism.

JavaScript

JavaScript has become accepted as the client-side programming language for web pages. JavaScript code is embedded in the HTML page, and tags in the web page tell the web browser when to execute the JavaScript functions.

One of JavaScript's main advantages is that it provides a more responsive user experience. One of JavaScript's main disadvantages is that not all browsers support it, and those that do don't necessarily support it in a standard way.

Evolving Technologies

Coupled with developments on the client side and server side, the HTML protocol has undergone many revisions and has expanded to include XHTML, CSS, XSL, and XPath.

The bottom line is that web technology is still evolving. This evolution introduces challenges for developers striving for interoperability and longevity for their web pages. Therefore, as a web developer, it is prudent to plan ahead for changes in web technology.

Establishing Requirements

Before developing a web UI for the Laddie alarm appliance, we established the following requirements to guide us with its design:

- The web interface should be easy to use.
- The web interface should support a wide variety of browsers, including text-based ones.
- The web pages should update automatically as the state on the appliance changes.
- The web pages should adhere to Internet standards, avoiding proprietary features.
- The implementation should work with various webservers so that the appliance webserver can be replaced should a better one become available.
- The implementation should be simple so that it can be easily maintained.

Choosing a Webserver

Which webserver should you use when building your appliance? In this section we'll review several webservers suitable for Linux appliances.

Choices

Webservers come in several different flavors. Many support the CGI interface, which allows the webserver to spawn an arbitrary process to generate the web page content on behalf of the webserver.

- The Apache webserver can be compiled with a PHP interpreter so that PHP scripts are interpreted within the Apache process. This approach reduces inter-process communication and improves response time.
- The lighttpd webserver supports the FastCGI interface. The FastCGI mechanism spawns multiple PHP interpreters and load balances requests for PHP web pages between them. For more information, see http://www.fastcgi.com.
- The GoAhead webserver allows the webserver and all web pages to be packaged into a single executable, which allows the webserver to run without a filesystem.
- The webserver in the Linksys WRT54G wireless router is written entirely in C and includes handcrafted functions for each web page.
- The TUX webserver runs in the Linux kernel.

Perhaps the first thing to consider when choosing a webserver is the license. If you don't want to release your source code modifications, then you should avoid webservers with GPL and Apache licenses. On the other hand, if you do select a mature webserver like Apache, it is unlikely that you will have to modify it, and consequently, you won't have to worry about having to release source code.

We suggest that you resist developing your own webserver. It is cheaper to select an existing one and to develop the web pages in a server-agnostic way. The advantage to this approach is that you don't have to spend your development resources maintaining a webserver, and you can replace the webserver should a better one become available.

Use PHP

We suggest using PHP as the language to generate dynamic web pages. Though you can write smaller CGI programs in C, if you use a compiled language and need to modify a web page once the appliance has been deployed, you will need a compile environment, which would typically not be available on the deployed appliance.

When you use an interpreted language like PHP, you can easily modify and test the web pages on the deployed appliance.

PHP is a good language for generating web content because it is popular, mature, has an active developer community, and is well integrated into open source webservers such as Apache, thttpd, and lighttpd. Even for webservers that don't support PHP, you can still write CGI programs *using* PHP. Thus, you can use PHP with just about any webserver. It is for these reasons that we selected PHP to develop the Laddie web UI.

Case Study: Linksys WRT54G Wireless Router

Let's examine the approach taken by the Linksys WRT54G wireless router. The webserver in this router is a handcrafted combination of both the micro_httpd and mini_httpd webservers, enhanced with specialized C functions that generate the dynamic content of the web pages. The code is GPL licensed and is available from http://www.linksys.com under the GPL Code Center. (Both micro_httpd and mini_httpd were written by Jef Poskanzer and are available at http://www.acme.com.)

The specialized C functions are responsible for generating dynamic content for the web pages. Because these functions are compiled into the webserver, there is no need for a script interpreter like PHP.

For example, the C function `dump_route_table()` is invoked from a web page by placing the function name between a matching pair of tags, as follows:

```
<% dump_route_table(""); %>
```

This tag mechanism is similar to the approach taken by PHP, except that here, the function is implemented in C and compiled into the webserver.

The advantage of this approach is that it has smaller memory requirements. However, as mentioned earlier, the problem with this approach is that the development cycle is extended because any change to a specialized C function requires a recompile.

Case Study: The TUX Webserver

Unlike most other webservers, which run in user space, the TUX webserver runs in the Linux kernel. Running in kernel space allows TUX to avoid communication between kernel space and user space; therefore, TUX offers better server response time than other webservers.

TUX supports both static and dynamic web page content, but for it to support dynamic content, another webserver must be running in user space. TUX operates by responding to requests for static web pages itself and forwarding requests for dynamic content to a user space webserver like Apache. As you might imagine, TUX doesn't offer speed advantages when it comes to support for dynamic web pages. Thus, for websites that have mostly dynamically generated content, the extra TUX configuration might not be worth the trouble.

Comparison of Webservers

In the previous section, we listed a range of webservers from Apache to TUX. In this section, we'll narrow our focus to comparing only webservers that support PHP as the scripting language. For space reasons, we've limited the set of webservers to Apache, Boa, BusyBox's httpd, Cherokee, GoAhead, lighttpd, and thttpd. These webservers have been selected because they are either used in commercial products or they are tailored for embedded applications.

Possible criteria for comparing webservers include:

- Memory footprint
- Size of executable file
- Performance
- Security support
- Ongoing maintenance and development
- Debugging support
- Documentation
- Cost

Regardless of how you weigh the different criteria, choosing a webserver will require a compromise. For example, the memory footprint may be critical for some appliances, but not for others.

Rather than advocating one webserver for your appliance, we've compiled Table 8-1, which shows how the various webservers in our limited set compare in each area. You can use this table as a starting point when selecting a webserver.

You can use different webservers for different stages of development. For example, you could use one webserver that has good debugging support in the development phase, and then switch to another one with a small memory footprint during testing and deployment. If you choose to use different webservers, plan ahead to ensure that you use features supported by all of them.

Table 8-1: Comparison of Various Webservers

	Apache 2	thttpd	lighttpd	Cherokee	BusyBox	Boa	GoAhead
Version tested	2.2.3	2.21b	1.4.13	0.5.5	1.2.1	0.94.14rc21	2.1.8
Virtual memory (KB)	4276	3152	972	1224	396	732	640
Executable size (KB)	439	1663	134	5	22	68	100
Response time (ms)	23.9	8.4	19.8	21.5	86.9	32.0	583.8
Supports CGI?	Yes	Yes	Yes	Yes	Yes	Yes	Yes
Supports FastCGI?	Yes	No	Yes	Yes	No	No	No
Supports in-process scripting?	Yes, PHP	Yes, PHP	No	No	No	No	Yes, Active Server Pages
Server API used	Apache	Apache	FastCGI	FastCGI	CGI	CGI	CGI
Last release	July 2006	December 2003	October 2006	September 2006	July 2006	February 2006	December 2003
Debugging	Yes, Zend	No	No	No	No	No	No
Documentation	Good	Poor	Good	Poor	Poor	Poor	Poor
Cost	Free	Free	Free	Free	Free	Free	Free
Security	chroot, Unix file permissions & config file	chroot & Unix file permissions	chroot & Unix file permissions	chroot & Unix file permissions	Unix file permissions	Unix file permissions	Minimal
License	Apache	BSD-like	BSD	GPL	GPL	GPL	GoAhead

About the Tabular Data

Let's look at Table 8-1 in more detail.

Version tested   This is the software version of the webserver that we tested.

Virtual memory   This is the virtual memory (in kilobytes) that the running webserver consumed. The virtual memory was measured using the Unix top command, which displays virtual memory under the SIZE column. For webservers that spawn multiple processes, we recorded the maximum value. In each case, the virtual memory was recorded during the performance test. (See *Response time* on the next page.)

Executable size   This is the size (in kilobytes) of the executable file after compiling it with mostly default options and then manually stripping it with the strip command. This metric is not as good of an indication of required memory as virtual memory is because libraries are sometimes linked dynamically and sometimes linked statically.

When programs are linked dynamically, much of the code can be in dynamically linked libraries. When you view the size of the executable, the code in these libraries will not be factored in. So the size of a dynamically linked executable is not a good indication of how much memory will be required when the executable is run (when all the libraries are linked-in at load-time). Typically, what's important is how much memory a program requires to run, because memory is the precious resource.

Response time   This is the average response time (in milliseconds) to access Laddie's status.php page, as recorded by the httperf utility (available at http://www.hpl.hp.com/research/linux/httperf). The motivation for this performance test is to measure how quickly the web-server responds to requests for the status web page. The following steps were taken for each webserver:

a. The webserver's software was compiled with default options, except for those options necessary to make it work correctly. Detailed instructions on how each webserver was configured is available in /Code/src/web/INSTALL_WEB_SERVER.txt on this book's companion CD. We used PHP version 5.0.3.

b. The resulting webserver executable was stripped with the `strip` command.

c. The back-end Laddie process, ladd, was run.

d. The following command was used to measure the response time:

```
httperf --hog --server 192.168.1.11 --uri=/cgi-bin/status.php --num-conn 200 --rate 1
```

The resultant dynamically generated status.php page was 4546 bytes. The server we used for testing consisted of an Intel Celeron 2.4 GHz processor running Linux Red Hat 9 with otherwise idle processes. The client consisted of an AMD Duron 1 GHz processor running Linux Red Hat 9. The server and client had 10 MHz NICs with a Linksys switch/router between them.

Supports CGI   This denotes whether or not the webserver supports the Common Gateway Interface (CGI).

Supports FastCGI   This denotes whether or not the webserver supports FastCGI, a performance enhancement to CGI. Documentation about FastCGI may be found at http://www.fastcgi.com.

Supports in-process scripting   This denotes whether the webserver supports a built-in PHP interpreter (or some other script interpreter). This functionality provides faster performance because it avoids interprocess-communication in the CGI interface.

Server API used   This is the Server API interface used during the response time performance test. The Server API is the communication mechanism between the webserver and the scripts, for example, Apache, CGI, and FastCGI. As you can see from the table, some webservers support only one Server API, while others support more than one.

Last release   This is the last time the software was released at the time of writing. This value is an indication of whether the software is actively maintained. In most cases, the version we tested was the last version released. However, there is one exception—the last version of thttpd released as of this writing was 2.25b, but we tested version 2.21b, because 2.21b was the last version that supported in-process scripting.

Debugging   This denotes whether or not you can debug scripts with the webserver. In the case of Apache and PHP, there is a commercial development environment called Zend Studio that allows you to debug PHP scripts using Internet Explorer. Using Zend, you can step though PHP scripts one line at a time and view PHP variables.

Documentation   This is a rough measure of whether or not the documentation specifies clearly which features the webserver supports and whether it provides instructions on how to use each feature.

Cost   This is the monetary cost of distributing the webserver in an appliance. Note that we have not included any webservers for which there is a monetary cost.

Security   These are the security features that prevent users from accessing files that they shouldn't be able to access. The most secure webservers are those that enforce access through a configuration file.

License   This is the type of software license the webserver has. The Apache, BSD, and GPL licenses are well known. The GoAhead license requires that you notify GoAhead prior to shipping your product and that you display a GoAhead logo on your initial web page.

Considering Memory Requirements

If memory is not a factor in your appliance, the Apache webserver would be a good choice. The advantage of Apache is its mature feature set, good development tools (like Zend Studio), and an active development community.

If memory is at a premium, then the BusyBox webserver might be a good choice; it has the smallest virtual memory requirements of the webservers we tested. The GoAhead webserver has the next smallest memory requirements; however, the disadvantage of GoAhead is that it uses Active Server Pages, a Microsoft technology, rather than PHP, an open source technology. (You can still run PHP scripts in GoAhead using the CGI mechanism, but it isn't as seamless as using a webserver with a built-in PHP interpreter.)

Considering Response Time

The top three webservers in terms of response time are thttpd, Apache, and lighttpd. Both thttpd and Apache get their speed from running PHP scripts in the same process as the webserver itself, which avoids the inter-process communication used by the other webservers. The thttpd webserver has the disadvantage that it only services one request at a time, so it will block subsequent requests until previous requests have been completed. This behavior may be fine for some web pages, but it will be a problem if the web page is written to block requests for a certain length of time, or to block until a state change. One of the Laddie web pages does block for a state change, and so this web page behavior rules out using thttpd webserver for the Laddie appliance. (We'll discuss this particular web page in the section "Asynchronous Updates Using Ajax" on page 125.)

Our Choice

When we were developing Laddie, we used the Apache webserver because of its debugging support, while for the production appliance, we selected lighttpd because of its smaller memory requirement and its speed. We chose which webserver to use in the production appliance rather late in the development cycle. We were able to make this decision later because we had written our PHP scripts to work under Apache, CGI, and FastCGI.

In his book about embedded Linux, Yaghmour advises against using Apache because it is difficult to cross-compile (*Building Embedded Linux Systems,* by Karim Yaghmour, O'Reilly, 2003). There was no need to cross-compile for our appliance, but if your appliance's CPU differs from your development machine's CPU, you should keep this in mind.

UI Design

In this section, we'll review various approaches to designing the UI look and feel, and the trade-offs they require. We will weigh these trade-offs when making implementation decisions in the "Implementation" section on page 118.

Menu System

One of the most important functions of a menu system is that it allows users to quickly grasp the system's capabilities. A menu with lots of top-level options can make it difficult for the user to choose an action, because there are so many choices. On the other hand, a menu with lots of nesting, though reducing the crowding on the top-level menu, tends to increase the time it takes to find an action.

Menu systems can be divided into those in which the top-level menu runs vertically down the left side of the window (see Figure 8-1), and those in which the top-level menu runs horizontally, near the top of the window (see Figure 8-2). While the vertical menu can be useful, it can quickly become difficult to navigate as the number of menu items increases (note the scroll-bars in Figure 8-1). The horizontal menu is usually superior because it can be more compact because the second-level menus share the same real estate.

Figure 8-1: A vertical menu

Figure 8-2: A horizontal menu

One disadvantage to the vertical MyFaces menu in Figure 8-2 is that it is not visually clear that the second-level menus (e.g., *Tomahawk, Documentation,* and *Components*) are not selectable; they look like the third-level menus, but they behave differently. The MyFaces menu could be improved by making the non-selectable menu items more distinct. For example, see the menus shown in Figure 8-3.

Essentials	**Jetspeed-2 Overview**
Overview	
Getting Started	Jetspeed-2 is the next-generation enterprise portal at Apache. Jetspe
Localization	and improvements over Jetspeed 1.0. First, Jetspeed-2 is conforman
User Attributes	standard mechanism for the deployment of portlets. Second, Jetspee
Sub Projects	featuring multi-threaded functionality. Third, Jetspeed-2 is decoupled
Maven Plugin	Jetspeed-2 is based on a component architecture.
Documentation	
Security	
Security Overview	

Figure 8-3: A menu with distinct non-selectable items

Dialog Boxes

Our advice on dialog boxes is simple: Avoid them. Dialog boxes halt proceedings because the user cannot continue until he or she clicks a button to close the box. Alan Cooper argues against dialog boxes because they break the flow of the user experience and don't move users closer to their goal (*About Face 2.0: The Essentials of User Interaction Design* by Alan Cooper and Robert Reimann, Wiley, 2003).

An alternative to dialog boxes is to place informational messages into the web page itself. We'll demonstrate this in the next section.

Error Messages

Good error messages can greatly improve the usability of your web UI. Experts generally agree on the following guidelines:

- If possible, make the program smarter to either avoid the particular error condition or recover from it.

- If an unrecoverable error has been detected, provide an explicit error message—that is, don't suppress the error.

- The error message should be human readable.
- The error message should be detailed.
- The error message should advise how to fix the problem.
- The error message should be close to the field with the error.
- The fields with errors should be clearly identified.

Some error conditions are caused by the user (when the user enters a bad value in a web form), while others are caused by external events (when the appliance disk becomes full). When designing your appliance's web pages, think about how these different errors will be handled.

One way to present error messages is to use dialog boxes (see Figure 8-4), but as we mentioned before, we discourage this approach. A second approach is to insert the error message into the refreshed web page (see Figure 8-5). The salient feature with this approach is that the error message is displayed in the form field, so that users can immediately re-enter their data.

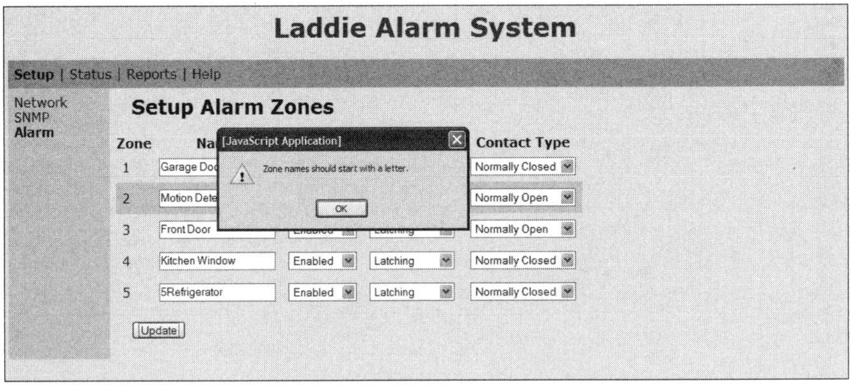

Figure 8-4: An error dialog box

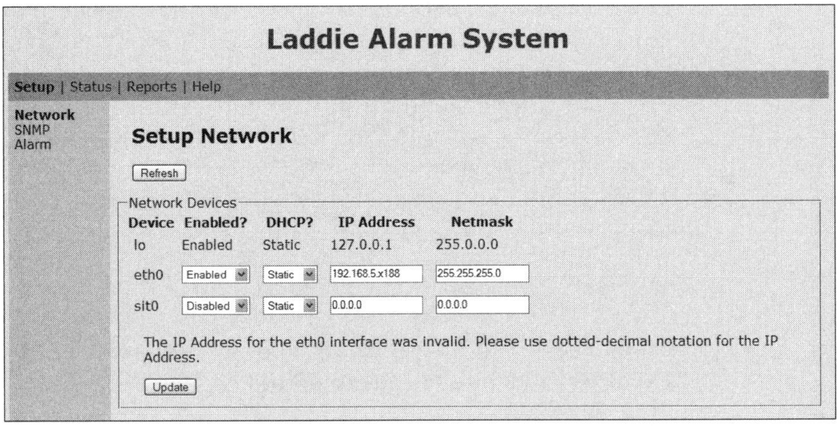

Figure 8-5: An in-line error message

A third approach is to annotate the labels where an error has occurred, as shown in Figure 8-6. In this example, errors are shown by displaying the labels in another color. In this figure, all of the field labels are in black, except for *Lan IP* and *Control IP*, which are in red (they're circled here because they appear gray); this tells you that there is a problem with those fields. One problem with this approach is that it fails to provide a detailed message. While some systems provide a tooltip with a message, such a mechanism is usually not explicit enough, and the user must mouse over the label to see more detail, which makes the user do unnecessary work.

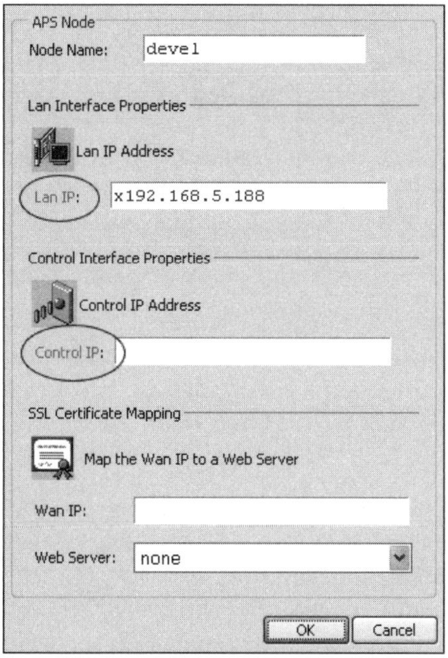

Figure 8-6: An annotated error message

Improving Responsiveness with Ajax

Ajax (Asynchronous JavaScript and XML) is a set of technologies that enables partial updates of web pages. Because only parts of a web page are refreshed, the update occurs more quickly than it would if the entire web page was refreshed. Furthermore, the partial update may be triggered by user events like mouse clicks and key presses. This behavior makes the UI more responsive than that of a traditional web page.

For example, Gmail, Google's email service, uses Ajax. When you compose an email and start typing the name of a contact, the browser responds to every key, reducing the list of matches as you type. The responsiveness is impressive.

Figure 8-7 shows an example of how the Ajax communication mechanism works. The exchange in this figure is initiated when the user mouses over an active element on the web page at event ①. An onmouseover action is triggered and JavaScript code is executed in the web browser at event ②. The JavaScript code creates an XMLHttpRequest object with the URL of the server-side script and a JavaScript callback function, and the web browser then sends the XMLHttpRequest object to the server at event ③. On the server side, the particular script identified by the URL responds with XML data at event ④.

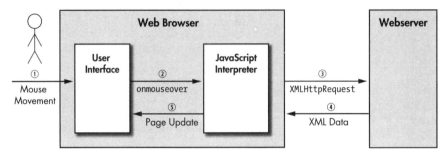

Figure 8-7: Typical Ajax sequence.

NOTE   *The format of the XML is known by the client and the server, so that when the server sends the XML data, the client understands its format. Typically, the XML data will contain the updated information to be displayed on some portion of the web page in the browser.*

Back on the client side, the web browser receives the XML data and invokes the JavaScript callback function. This callback function extracts the data from the XML message and modifies some portion of the web page using the XML Document Object Model (DOM) API at event ⑤.

Mouse movements are not the only events that are supported by Ajax, but they are the most popular, along with mouse button clicks, key presses, text selections, and keyboard focuses on editable fields—and more events are made available with each browser upgrade.

Implementation

In this section, we'll discuss the implementation of Laddie's web UI. We'll show some screenshots of the web UI and discuss how it works.

The web UI supports at least the following web browsers: Internet Explorer (version 5.0 and later), Netscape Navigator (version 4.72 and later), Firefox (version 1.0 and later), Safari (version 1.0 and later), Opera (version 5.0 and later), and Lynx (version 2.8.2 and later). These versions were determined through direct testing with archived browsers available from http://browsers.evolt.org.

NOTE   *Unlike the other graphical browsers, the Lynx browser is text-based.*

Interfacing with the Daemons

The Laddie web UI presents information from several running daemons. As you know, each of these daemons communicates using the PostgreSQL protocol. In this section, we'll discuss how the web UI interacts with ladd, the Laddie alarm daemon. Once you understand this interaction, you'll understand how the web UI interacts with the other daemons as well. Figure 8-8 shows a typical sequence where a user requests a web page and the web page is generated dynamically, based on the state of a daemon.

The figure shows the Linux appliance with the webserver and the ladd alarm daemon running on it. For simplicity, we've shown the PHP interpreter running in the same process as the webserver, as in the case of Apache, but it could be running as a different process if you're using CGI scripts.

As mentioned, the figure shows a typical request-response sequence for a web page. First, the user requests a particular page at event ①. The webserver locates the web page from the filesystem, and because the webserver finds PHP tags in the page, it invokes the PHP interpreter, which interprets the PHP code. In our case, the particular PHP code includes PHP functions pg_connect() and pg_exec(), which are invoked by the PHP interpreter at events ② and ③. The PHP code generates the web page at event ④, and this new page is then sent back to the browser at event ⑤.

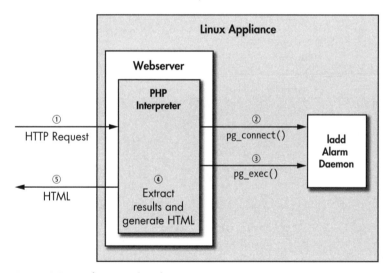

Figure 8-8: Interfacing with a daemon

Connecting to the Daemon

As you can see in the illustration, before you can read and write to the ladd daemon, you must establish a connection using the pg_connect() function, which is built into the PHP interpreter when you configure PHP with the --with-pgsql option. The pg_connect() function takes a string argument that specifies the hostname (or IP address) of the server and the port. In our case, the server is on the same machine as the webserver, and the ladd daemon is listening on port 8888. More information on pg_connect() can be found by searching for *PostgreSQL Functions* in the PHP manual at http://us2.php.net/pgsql.

The following code fragment shows how to open a connection to the daemon:

```
$connection = pg_connect("host=127.0.0.1 port=8888");
if (!$connection) {
    // some error
} else {
    // valid connection
}
```

Reading from the Daemon

Once a connection has been established, you can read from and write to the ladd daemon. We use the pg_exec() function to do this. This function requests that a given statement be executed, in our case a SELECT statement. For more details on pg_exec(), see the PostgreSQL Functions at http://us2.php.net/pgsql.

The following PHP code fragment shows how to read the alarm status:

```
$result = pg_exec($connection, "SELECT id,name,enabled,alarm FROM Zone");
if (!$result) {
    // some error
    return;
}
for ($row = 0; $row < pg_NumRows($result); $row++) {
    $id = pg_result($result, $row, 0);
    $name = pg_result($result, $row, 1);
    $enabled = pg_result($result, $row, 2);
    $alarm = pg_result($result, $row, 3);
    // do something with $id, $name, $enabled, $alarm
}
pg_freeresult($result);
```

In this example, the names id, name, enabled, and alarm in the SELECT command are the column names in the Zone RTA table in the ladd daemon. Generally, the SELECT command will have the same form for different daemons, but the number of columns and their names may differ. The value returned by the pg_exec() function is an object handle, which is then used to extract the number of rows with pg_NumRows() and each row's contents with pg_result().

NOTE *All the functions with names that start with pg are part of the PostgreSQL PHP library and are not unique to our daemon.*

Once the information has been read from the daemon, you can use this information to generate an HTML page. For example, we would use the results in $id, $name, $enabled, and $alarm to generate an HTML table.

Writing to the Daemon

To write to the ladd daemon and set alarm zone 3 into the alarm state, you could use the following code:

```
$id = 3;
$value = 1; // 1 for alarm, 0 for no alarm
$result = pg_exec($connection, "UPDATE Zone SET alarm=$value WHERE id=$id");
if (!$result) {
    // some error
    return;
}
pg_freeresult($result);
```

Note that you use the same pg_exec() function call as when reading information from the daemon; the difference is that the SQL command is UPDATE rather than SELECT. The SQL command in the preceding code snippet specifies to update the alarm column in the Zone table to the value $value, but only in the case where the id column matches $id.

In the preceding code snippet we've set the $value and $id variables to arbitrary values, but typically the $id and $value variables would be extracted from an HTML form.

The interaction between the web UI and the ladd daemon is straightforward enough. The web UI can read information from the ladd daemon and it can write information to the ladd daemon. The web UI interacts with the other daemons in the same way, so there is nothing new to learn about those interactions. (The interaction is straightforward because we are using an established protocol, PostgreSQL, and the function bindings to this protocol are readily available to PHP programs.)

Alarm Status Page

Figure 8-9 shows Laddie's alarm status page. This page allows you to view the status of each alarm zone, clear alarm conditions, and set an alarm condition (for testing purposes).

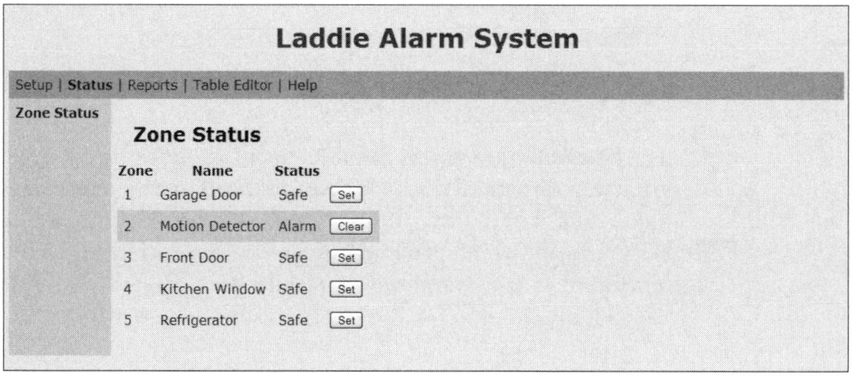

Figure 8-9: Laddie status page

An alarm condition can be shown either as a gray horizontal bar or with the label *Alarm* under the *Status* column. If you were to actually use this interface, you would probably find that the horizontal bar is much easier to read than the label because it offers a quick visual cue. When designing your web interface, think about how you might augment your interface with similar visual cues to convey information quickly.

Unlike traditional web pages, which require a user to refresh the page to update status, this status page automatically updates when an alarm condition changes. To observe this automatic update behavior, start two browsers and point them to the alarm status page. In one browser, modify the alarm condition by clicking the Clear and Set buttons. If JavaScript is enabled in your two browsers, you should see a page update on both browsers.

You can find the PHP code that generates this web page on this book's companion CD in the file /opt/laddie/htdocs/web/cgi-bin/status.php.

Alarm Setup Page

The alarm setup page, shown in Figure 8-10, allows you to configure the names of the alarm zones. When designing this page, we considered two UI design approaches: an Update button for each zone and a single Update button for all zones. We chose the single button because it reduces the navigation required to configure all the zones; you simply modify the parameters of several zones and click Update.

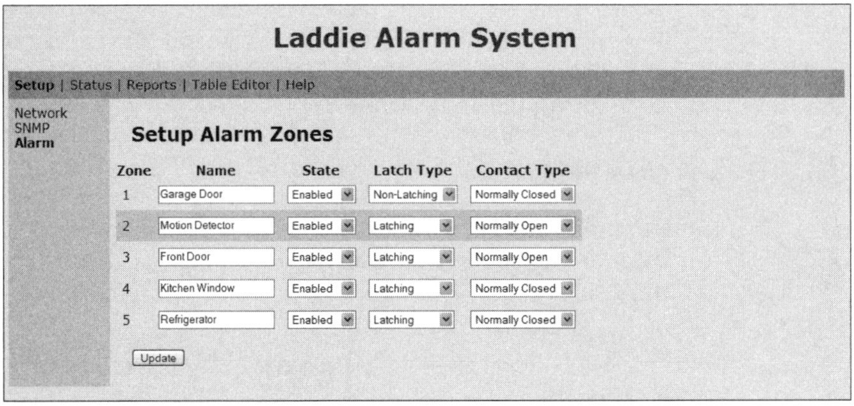

Figure 8-10: Laddie alarm setup page

This web page allows the user to enter the names of each alarm zone. We'll now describe how the web page works and in particular how to work with the tabular data shown there. On the browser side, the web page includes an HTML form, which is a mechanism for accepting input from a user and sending it to the webserver when the user presses a Submit button. If you take a look at the web page's HTML source, you will see the following line:

```
<td>  <input type=text name=Name_1 value="Garage Door" /> </td>
```

The `input` tag tells the browser to display a field for textual input. The `name` tag tells the browser how to name the field, and the `value` tag tells the browser how to populate the initial value for the field. When the user hits the Submit button, the names and values of all form fields are sent to the server. When the server receives this request, our PHP code will extract the zone names from the request and update the Laddie daemon.

PHP provides a simple mechanism to extract the field values. For example, to extract the value for the field with name *Name_1*, you would use the following PHP code:

```
$name = $_REQUEST["Name_1"];
```

The `_REQUEST` variable is a global variable that is populated by the PHP interpreter, while the *Name_1* string corresponds to the name of the field in the HMTL form. Once this statement is executed on the server, the `$name` variable will contain the text that the user entered in the browser.

For tabular forms we need to be careful about field naming because the HTML specification requires that all fields in a form must have a unique name. One common approach to naming such form fields in HTML is to append a row number to the column name. For example, we append the row number *1* to *Name* (using underscore as a separation character) to get *Name_1* for the Name column for Zone 1.

The PHP code to generate this web page can be found on this book's companion CD in the file /opt/laddie/htdocs/web/cgi-bin/setup_alarm.php. Take a look at the function `displayZoneForm`. The PHP code that handles the web form updates is in the same file.

Page Layout and Menu System

In this section, we'll describe Laddie's web page layout and menu system. This simple scheme is handled by two PHP files. The first file, layout.php, defines Laddie's two-level menu system as a two-dimensional array (see the global variable `$menu_system` on this book's companion CD in /opt/laddie/htdocs/web/cgi-bin/layout.php) and it defines the function `display_page()`. This function refreshes the page whenever the user navigates the menu. The second file, alarmstyle.css, controls color, fonts, and indentation (see /opt/laddie/htdocs/web/alarmstyle.css on the CD). Figure 8-11 shows an example web page; the PHP code that generated this web page follows.

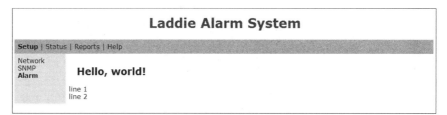

Figure 8-11: Laddie's "Hello, world!" example

```php
<?php
include_once "layout.php";
$widget = "<h2> Hello, world! </h2>";
$widget .= "line 1<br>";
$widget .= "line 2<br>";
display_page("Setup", "Alarm", $widget);
?>
```

The first two parameters in the call to display_page() are indices into the menu structure (defined by the global variable $menu_system in layout.php). The first parameter, "Setup" in this example, is the top-level index, while the second parameter is the second-level index. The third parameter is an HTML-formatted string, which is displayed in the main window. In this example, the main window consists of the heading Hello, world! and two lines. It is the main window that is different for each web page, and typically this content is generated dynamically, depending on the state of the system.

In summary, the presentation logic for page layout is encapsulated by the function display_page(). For another example of how to use display_page(), see /opt/laddie/htdocs/web/cgi-bin/help_contact_us.php on the CD.

Webserver Independence

PHP works with many different webservers, each having a slightly different way of interacting with the PHP interpreter. The API with which PHP interacts with the webserver is called the Server API. The Server API used by PHP is determined when compiling PHP, so as a developer you probably know this before writing the PHP scripts. But what if you decided to use another webserver? If you didn't plan ahead, you would have to modify a lot of code to get it to work with the new webserver.

As an aside, PHP provides the function php_sapi_name() to programmatically determine which API is currently in use. This function returns one of many possible strings, three of which are *apache*, *cgi*, and *cgi-fcgi*, corresponding to Apache, CGI, and FastCGI. There's not too much documentation on the Server API, but try searching for it on Google.

Early in the design phase, we decided to write our PHP scripts so that they would work with these three Server APIs, because the webservers that we investigated supported at least one of them. This would mean that our PHP scripts would work without modification under any webserver that supported one of these APIs. This server-independent approach offers two advantages: It avoids locking you in with a particular webserver (should a better one become available) and it allows you to develop scripts using a different webserver than the one deployed in your appliance.

Script input parameters are defined by name-value strings. For example, an input parameter might have the name *disp_id* and a value of 51. The script's input parameters are provided by the HTTP request that invokes the script; for example, the following request will set the input parameter *disp_id* for the script wait_for_status.php:

```
http://127.0.0.1/wait_for_status.php?disp_id=51
```

The trick to supporting Apache, CGI, and FastCGI lies in handling the script's input parameters the same way, regardless of which environment the script is running in. (There is no problem with the output because these three Server APIs handle output the same way.)

For CGI scripts, the script's input parameters are extracted from STDIN, whereas for Apache and FastCGI scripts, they are extracted from PHP global variables. Actually, the Apache and FastCGI cases are identical, so there are only two cases, CGI and Apache. We chose to abstract these two cases with a function called read_params(). The implementation of read_params() handles the details of both cases, but from the caller's perspective, it provides a uniform way to extract the input parameters.

The PHP code fragment below shows how the function is used:

```
include_once "php_params.php";
$params = read_params();
if (array_key_exists('disp_id', $params) {
    $disp_id = $params['disp_id'];
} else {
    // handle error; missing parameter
}
```

The read_params() function returns an array containing all the script's input parameters. The calling script can then retrieve a particular parameter value using the parameter's name (which is known at design time). Note that the function array_key_exists is a PHP built-in function that determines whether or not a given index exists in a given array.

The implementation of the read_params() function can be found in the file /opt/laddie/htdocs/web/cgi-bin/php_params.php on the CD. You'll find another example of its use in /opt/laddie/htdocs/web/cgi-bin/setup_snmp.php.

Asynchronous Updates Using Ajax

Consider the status web page shown in Figure 8-9. How should the web page react to changes in the state of an alarm?

Preferably, the web page should be updated automatically, rather than requiring the user to repeatedly click the browser's Refresh button. One approach is to poll the server at a fixed frequency, for example, using the Refresh HTML meta tag as follows:

```
<META HTTP-EQUIV="Refresh" CONTENT="5;URL=refreshed-page.html">
```

Another approach is to use Ajax so that the web page updates only when there is a state change on the server. The disadvantage with Ajax is that it requires JavaScript to be enabled in the web browser; if the user disables JavaScript, the update mechanism breaks. On the other hand, when Ajax is used, the web page updates quickly in response to state changes on the server.

In the section "Improving Responsiveness with Ajax" on page 117, we described how a typical Ajax exchange works. However, note that this typical exchange is initiated by the client, rather than the server. We need a way to modify Ajax so that the browser responds to state changes on the server.

It turns out that we can modify the Ajax exchange so that the system behaves as if the webserver initiates the exchange. The trick is twofold. First, replace the `onmouseover` event with the `onload` event, so that the `XMLHttpRequest` is sent as soon as the web page is loaded. Second, write the webserver script so that it blocks while waiting for an event. By implementing this modified Ajax exchange, the web page will update whenever the particular event occurs on the server. The experienced Ajax programmer will note that there is another mechanism that achieves a similar result, notably the *HTTP Streaming pattern* documented at http://www.ajaxpatterns.org (and in the associated book, *Ajax Design Patterns*, by Michael Mahemoff, O'Reilly, 2006). Both our approach and the HTTP Streaming pattern have the disadvantage of using a long-lived TCP connection, which may be a problem for webservers that allow only a finite number of concurrent connections. However, for our approach we can control how long the request waits for a server event, thereby limiting the number of concurrent connections.

Before we describe the details of this modified Ajax exchange, let's review the big picture. Figure 8-12 shows the sequence for a user requesting a new web page, with the first full page update and subsequent partial page updates. In terms of timing, events ① through ⑩ occur in quick succession after the user requests the particular web page. At this point, the web page is loaded with the latest alarm state. When some alarm state changes at event ⑪, it triggers events ⑫ through ⑲ in quick succession, at which point the web page is refreshed with the new alarm state. This latter sequence repeats until the user navigates away from the web page.

Browser Sends First HTTP Request

The sequence from events ① through ⑦ is the standard HTML request response exchange. In step ①, the user requests a web page, the server responds by sending the web page and, in step ⑦, the browser displays the page. These steps are performed for all web requests regardless of whether the web page includes JavaScript. The remaining sequence from event ⑧ through ⑲ is more interesting, and it is this sequence that we'll describe in more detail.

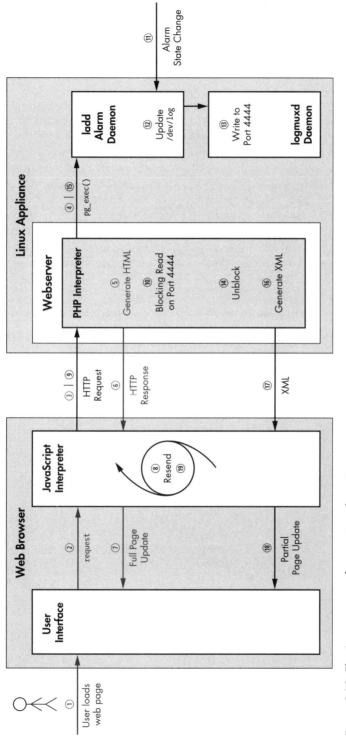

Figure 8-12: The Ajax sequence for an external event

Browser Sends Second HTTP Request

On the client side, event ⑧ is triggered as soon as the web page is loaded for the first time at event ⑦. In particular, the function GetCurrentStatus() is invoked. Take a look at the HTML source for the Zone Status web page by booting up this book's companion CD and using a browser to visit http://192.168.1.11.

The default IP address of the Laddie alarm appliance is 192.168.1.11 (and the default netmask is 255.255.0.0). When you insert this book's CD into your computer and reboot it, you will then be able to connect to the web UI by typing the URL http://192.168.1.11 in any web browser on another computer. If the default IP address conflicts with an existing node on your network, you can change the IP address for Laddie with the following steps. Quit the framebuffer interface (press Q for quit), then at the shell prompt, enter **root** for the user and press ENTER for the password (there is no password). Then enter **lynx** at the command prompt. From lynx you can navigate to the Network Setup page and modify the IP address of the network interfaces. Once you have changed the IP address with lynx, you can re-type the URL (with your new IP address) in a browser on another computer.

If you view the source for this web page, you will see the following line:

```
<body onload="GetCurrentStatus()">
```

The GetCurrentStatus() function then makes an XMLHttpRequest with the URL wait_for_status.php (at event ⑨). You'll see the following code in the file /opt/laddie/web/cgi-bin/status.php on this book's companion CD:

```
function GetCurrentStatus() {
    // The ms= portion is to make the url unique so that IE doesn't retrieve
    // a cached copy.
    url = "wait_for_status.php?disp_id=" + curr_id + "&ms=" + new
Date().getTime();


    if (window.XMLHttpRequest) {
      // branch for Firefox/Netscape XMLHttpRequest
      req_status = new XMLHttpRequest();
      if (req_status) {
        req_status.abort();
        req_status.onreadystatechange = GotStatus;
        req_status.open("GET", url, true);
        // Header necessary for lighttpd
        req_status.setRequestHeader("Accept", "*/*");
        req_status.send(null);
      }

...
}
```

This code snippet instructs the browser to send a HTTP GET request with the URL wait_for_status.php. It also instructs the browser to invoke the callback function GotStatus() when a response is received from the server.

Server Blocks Waiting for Alarm State Change

On the server side, the script wait_for_status.php is invoked. This script does a blocking read on port 4444 at event ⑩. Whenever there is a change in alarm state in the ladd daemon at event ⑪, the logmuxd daemon writes a message to port 4444 at event ⑬. The contents of what is written to the port are unimportant; what is important is that the message unblocks the PHP thread at event ⑭.

Notice in the code above that curr_id is sent with the URL. This variable prevents the browser from losing log events when the events come too quickly. This variable is passed like a token between the server and the browser, and it increases in lock-step with the number of log events. If the curr_id value from the browser does not match the number of log events on the server, the PHP thread skips blocking on port 4444. This way, if there are new log events during the time interval that the PHP thread is not blocking on port 4444, the PHP thread will continue.

Server Sends Alarm State as XML

Once the blocking read returns, the PHP script reads the alarm status from the ladd alarm daemon (at event ⑮), and combines the data into an XML document (at event ⑯). The webserver then passes this XML document to the browser (at event ⑰). An example XML document looks like this:

```
<?xml version="1.0" ?>
<laddie_status>
<zone id="1" name="Front Door" enabled="1">1</zone>
<zone id="2" name="Back Door" enabled="1">0</zone>
<zone id="3" name="Garage" enabled="1">0</zone>
<zone id="4" name="Motion Detector" enabled="0">1</zone>
<zone id="5" name="Smoke Detector" enabled="0">0</zone>
<logcount>294</logcount>
<log>2005-11-11 06:23:54  Alarm system status: safe</log>
<log>2005-11-11 06:23:54  User cleared alarm on zone 4, Motion Detector</log>
<log>2005-11-11 06:23:54  User cleared alarm on zone 1, Front Door</log>
<log>2005-10-28 09:29:11  Alarm system status: alarm</log>
<log>2005-10-28 09:29:11  Alarm set on zone 4, Motion Detector</log>
<log>2005-10-28 09:29:04  Alarm system status: safe</log>
</laddie_status>
```

Browser Updates Portion of Web Page

Back on the client side, the browser receives the XML document, and generates an HTML fragment from it; it uses this fragment to update the web page (event ⑱). The function GotStatus() in status.php has the following code.

```
var zones = req_status.responseXML.getElementsByTagName("zone");
table = generateHtmlTable(zones);
mdiv = document.getElementById('status_table');
mdiv.innerHTML = table;
```

The first line extracts the zone data from the XML response, the second line generates an HTML fragment specifically for the Laddie status page, and the last line inserts the HTML fragment into the displayed page.

Browser Repeats by Sending Another HTTP Request

The browser then invokes another XMLHttpRequest and the process repeats (at event ⑲). After a small delay, the GotStatus() function invokes GetCurrentStatus() with the following line:

```
setTimeout("GetCurrentStatus()", 2000);
```

You can see how this behavior works by opening two web browsers to the status page at http://192.168.1.11. If you change the state of an alarm zone in one of the browsers, you should see this state change on the other web browser, as well.

To summarize, we have shown a technique for using Ajax to update web pages where the update is triggered by events on the server rather than by events on the client.

Graceful Degradation Without JavaScript

When designing a web-based appliance, you must decide which web browsers you will support. Do you support non-graphical browsers like Lynx, or do you only support fully featured browsers? By reducing the level of required browser functionality, you can support a wide variety of browsers, but it will be at the expense of an increased effort in development. At the other extreme, you could dictate that a specific browser be used, with the advantage of using proprietary features, but with the risk of some customers disliking your browser selection. Customer input would be invaluable in helping you to make this decision.

We chose to support a wide variety of browsers, then sought to reduce the developmental effort by avoiding browser-specific code. That is, we avoided code that didn't work the same way on all major browsers.

Of particular concern was the ability to support browsers without JavaScript. One of the difficulties with JavaScript is that it can be disabled by the user, and even worse, the user may not know that it is disabled.

One approach for supporting browsers with and without JavaScript is to structure the website as two "universes"—one universe in which JavaScript is used and another in which it isn't. The home page is written to detect whether JavaScript is enabled on the browser and to then redirect the browser to the appropriate universe. Unfortunately, this solution does not work if the user disables JavaScript and then reloads a particular page. The work-around is for the user to turn on JavaScript and then revisit the home page.

We took another approach, one which allows the user to enable or disable JavaScript and then simply reload the particular page. This means that each web page must support a JavaScript version and a non-JavaScript version. In the past, this problem might have been tricky to solve because browsers that didn't support JavaScript were confused by JavaScript code. But this problem is easily solved today, because the majority of browsers (even those like Lynx that don't support JavaScript) understand the HTML <SCRIPT> tag. When a modern browser has JavaScript disabled, it ignores all HTML code between the pair of tags <SCRIPT> and </SCRIPT>.

Hiding JavaScript

The following pattern for hiding JavaScript content from browsers is known to work for Internet Explorer (version 5.0 and later), Netscape Navigator (version 4.72 and later), Firefox (version 1.0 and later), Safari (version 1.0 and later), Opera (version 5.0 and later), and Lynx (version 2.8.2 and later).

```
<SCRIPT TYPE="text/javascript">
<!-- hide from old browsers

// javascript code goes here

// end of script hiding -->
</SCRIPT>
```

The HTML comments <!-- and --> are included as a fail-safe mechanism for those old browsers that don't understand the <SCRIPT> tags. Similarly, you can use <NOSCRIPT> and </NOSCRIPT> tags to provide alternate content when JavaScript is not enabled.

Using these patterns, each web page can support both JavaScript and non-JavaScript versions, and consequently, the user can change the browser's JavaScript setting and reload the page. Because the user doesn't have to find and reload some site-wide redirection page, the user's experience is greatly simplified.

Improving Our Design

Having implemented the web UI, we are in a better position to review and improve our design. What are some areas that could use improvement?

One problem with the current design is that the logic for configuring network interfaces is contained in setup_network.php, and unfortunately, this logic is not available to other UIs, like the command line interface (CLI). When we first implemented the network setup page, we did not foresee how complex this configuration logic would be, and so we decided that all UIs would duplicate this "simple" logic. In hindsight, we feel that the design would be improved by subsuming the network configuration logic into a single manager, notably the networkd daemon. That way, the CLI user interface could provide the same functionality as the network setup web page, without duplicating much of the logic in setup_network.php.

We could improve the web UI's usability by clarifying the relationship between the second-level and top-level menus. This might be done using different colors for the top-level and second-level menus, as shown in Figure 8-2. Note in this figure that it is easy to see that the second-level item *Components* falls under the first-level menu *Tomahawk*.

Another improvement would be to add error-checking functionality on the client side. This improvement would be achieved by adding JavaScript functions to check the validity of form fields, resulting in a more responsive UI.

We could enhance functionality by adding a web page that would provide diagnostics functions for network connectivity and hardware health, such as temperature and fan speed. This functionality would allow management software to remotely monitor the appliance for degrading performance.

Resources

The following resources will be useful for further study of web page design, Ajax, debugging, and testing.

UI design   The book *About Face 2.0: The Essentials of User Interaction Design* by Alan Cooper and Robert Reimann (Wiley, 2003) is a good book about UI design.

JavaScript   A good reference book on JavaScript is the *JavaScript Bible, 5th Edition* by Danny Goodman and Michael Morrison (Wiley, 2004).

Ajax   The Wikipedia web page on Ajax programming is a starting point for learning about the technique and includes the history of Ajax. See http://en.wikipedia.org/wiki/Ajax_(programming).

HTML validation   The World Wide Web Consortium (W3C) provides a free HTML validation service at http://validator.w3.org. A CSS validation service is also available.

Web browsers   Older web browsers, useful for testing your web pages, are archived at http://browsers.evolt.org.

Debuggers   The Zend Studio debugger allows you to debug PHP code using Microsoft's Internet Explorer and the Apache webserver. Using this browser, you can step through PHP code that is executing under Apache. It is a commercial software package, available at http://www.zend.com.

Summary

In this chapter, we have discussed the development of web UIs for Linux-based appliances, in particular, the web UI for Laddie. It has not been our goal to discuss all of web technology—you will find entire books on that subject.

This chapter highlighted the pertinent features of Laddie's web UI:

- The web UI degrades gracefully for browsers that don't support JavaScript so that the web UI functionality is accessible to a wide variety of browsers.
- The alarm status page updates automatically whenever there is a change in the alarm state on the appliance:
  - When an alarm is triggered, each browser viewing the status web page is refreshed automatically.
  - When any browser is used to clear an alarm, the change is reflected on all other browsers.

After implementing the web UI, we looked back at our design and suggested some future improvements. In particular, we suggested that the logic for configuring network interfaces should be moved from PHP into the network daemon, networkd. This restructuring would have the advantage that other UIs, for example the CLI, could configure network interfaces without duplicating the complex logic in PHP. Other improvements include restructuring the menu system and adding JavaScript error-checking functions.

9

DESIGNING A COMMAND LINE INTERFACE

A command line interface (CLI) gives your customers a secure, low-bandwidth, easily scripted way to configure and manage your appliance. As a Linux developer, you are already familiar with bash, Linux's most popular CLI. For the same reasons that you would not want to manage a Linux box without a bash command line, your customers might not want to manage your appliance without a similarly easy-to-manage CLI.

This chapter covers the following topics:

- Why you need a CLI
- Types of CLIs
- Giving users access to a CLI
- The Laddie CLI
- Code review for the test command

Why You Need a CLI

Despite their age, CLIs are still one of the most-requested features for Linux appliances, especially network appliances that will be installed in a server room or network operations center. Let's look in turn at each of the major reasons to have a CLI on your appliance:

- Security
- Availability
- Bandwidth
- Scriptability
- Configuration backup and restore

Security

Many service providers will reject an appliance that places its control and status protocol on the same wire as user data; the setup they prefer is an entirely separate physical channel that is dedicated to management of the appliance. Historically, this separate channel has been an RS-232 interface with a CLI on it. The RS-232 lines are routed to the control center using terminal servers or port concentrators.

When an appliance has a serial port, users expect it to also have a character or command line interface. Of course, you could attach a PPP daemon to the serial port and make it a network interface, but this is seldom done. Newer network appliances feature a second (or even third) Ethernet interface to provide the separate physical channel required for appliance control and status. Separate LANs that are dedicated to secure control and status are starting to appear, but the installed base of Network Management Systems (NMS) that deal with serial ports will make CLIs and appliance serial ports standard requirements for some time to come.

Availability

Network-based UIs, such as web interfaces, require that the network be correctly configured and running before the UI becomes accessible. The problem with this is that if something goes wrong with the network configuration, you can lose all ability to fix the configuration. A serial port, on the other hand, does not need an address, so a UI running on it is always available.

There is another popular solution for unavailability due to a misconfigured network. Many appliances have a hidden or difficult-to-reach switch that will reset the appliance to its factory default configuration if it remains in the closed position while the appliance boots up. If you don't intend to use a serial port, you should consider having a hidden switch or some other mechanism to allow the user to reset the appliance's configuration.

Bandwidth

CLIs are useful when you want to access an appliance over a low-bandwidth channel. A low-bandwidth channel might be a slow radio link or an otherwise fast network that is overloaded or failing. Low bandwidth capabilities can also be advantageous if your appliances are to be dispersed geographically but managed centrally.

Scriptability

One of the biggest advantages of a CLI is that it usually allows you to collect a series of command lines into a file, or *script*, and execute the commands as if a user had interactively entered them. This can offer huge advantages over web or other graphical UIs, which are difficult to automate. Scripts are particularly useful to help automate repetitive or tedious tasks. A CLI can allow users to build their own commands, using the commands in your CLI as their primitives or base operations.

Not all CLIs are equal in their ability to be scripted. We'll have more to say about this later in the chapter.

Configuration Backup and Restore

One of the biggest problems you should anticipate as an appliance developer is your customer's need to preserve or migrate configuration data across a software upgrade. We've approached this problem several ways, and the worst of our solutions was to give users a web page where they could initiate an FTP transfer of a binary file that contained the configuration data. This was a disaster for several reasons. Customers objected to the hassle of setting up an FTP site to accept files, and they *really* objected to not being able to see the configuration.

Upgrades were a hassle, as well. We had to write and distribute programs to read the binary file and convert it to the format required by the new software. Paying attention to version numbers, finding a place to run the converter, and getting the new file back onto the appliance was a real mess. Saving the configuration as XML helped, but it didn't help that much.

The solution that really worked was providing a web page that displayed the entire configuration as a list of CLI commands. Our customers loved this. They could see the configuration at a glance, and making a backup of the configuration was as simple as visiting a web page and selecting Save As in the browser. Of course, we also had a matching web form in which users could paste the CLI commands of the saved configuration and so easily restore the original settings. Tools such as wget allow configuration backups to be automated, too. You'll see an example later in the chapter when we review the Laddie CLI command that dumps Laddie's configuration as a series of CLI commands.

This approach made upgrades easier for us as well. The CLI was fairly stable, and changes to it were almost always backward-compatible extensions. After switching to this approach, we no longer had to write and distribute programs to convert one version of a configuration file to the next version of the file.

Having the appliance configuration saved as a list of CLI commands in a script has other advantages. One of our customers wanted the master copy of all his configurations to reside in his NMS. He configured our appliances to use DHCP and set up his DHCP and NMS to use wget to send the appropriate configuration to our appliances as soon as he received an IP address from the DHCP server. In one instance, he ordered 10 new servers, and we gave him the Ethernet MAC addresses before shipment. He had the configurations for the 10 new servers ready for download before the appliances arrived, and all of the new appliances were configured and running within a few minutes of initial power on.

Types of CLIs

The default CLI on most Linux systems is bash, but bash is just one type of CLI. There are other types that might be more applicable to your needs, and your CLI may switch from one type to another, as you choose the type to match the task at hand. Let's look at the different types of CLIs: sentences, menus, and wizards, and at two CLI attributes: statefulness and whether the CLI is line- or character-oriented.

Sentences

The sentence CLI, the most common type of CLI, maps actions and objects in the appliance into verbs and nouns. Consider a simple bash command:

```
rm -f backup.sxw
```

Here, rm is the verb, -f is an adverb, and backup.sxw is the noun. The key to a successful CLI of this type is to select the verbs and nouns that map well into the customer's understanding of the appliance.

Of course, you can use other sentence structures like verb-adverb-noun, verb-noun-adjective, or noun-verb-adjective—it's up to you. The idea is to make reading the CLI line sound like a sentence. You'll know that you've gotten it right when customers, field support, and engineers all describe a configuration using the same vocabulary and syntax as that of your CLI.

Typically, you will need verbs to view status or statistics, to change the configuration, and to initiate actions. For example, the verbs in the Laddie CLI are *view*, *set*, *test*, and *clear*.

The big advantage of the sentence CLI is that it is the most easily and reliably scripted type of CLI. The major disadvantage of this CLI is that there can be a steep learning curve for it. The user has to remember a fair amount of vocabulary and syntax in order to use this type of CLI effectively. However, users who spend a lot of time in the CLI usually prefer the sentence CLI.

Wizards

A *wizard* is a type of interface that prompts the user with a series of questions, usually giving the user some descriptive text before asking the question. For example, the following might appear as part of a wizard configuration for Laddie.

```
Type of Sensor:
Alarm sensors come in two different types, normally closed (nc)
and normally open (no). The switch in a normally closed sensor
is closed, or making electrical contact, while the sensor is
not in an alarm state. A normally open sensor does not make
electrical contact when in the normal, or non-alarm, state.
Look for the sensor type on the body of the sensor or on its
packaging.
Type of Sensor:  [NO, nc, q] ?
```

If there is a reasonable default value, you should show it in the prompt for the question. The convention is to show the default in all caps. You should also give the user the ability to abort the wizard at any point in the series of questions. Common abort sequences include q and CTRL-C. At the end of the series of questions, you should display a summary of the responses and ask the user to confirm that these are the values he or she wants.

Here is a tip to help the user and yourself. Your web interface has forms with fields that the user fills in before hitting the *Submit* button. If you are building a wizard, map the same fields from the web form to the wizard. For example, if the web form for network configuration asks for host name, boot protocol, and default gateway, the network wizard should ask for host name, boot protocol, and default gateway. This helps the user by letting him or her transfer training from one interface (web) to another (CLI). It also helps you because your back-end processing only needs to deal with one type of request, regardless of the source of the request.

Wizards are a great way to help a new or infrequent user through a configuration. Wizards are also nice if you need a synchronous update of all of the fields presented in the wizard. For example, you would probably want to change a static IP address and its associated netmask with one atomic update.

Since wizards are used only to collect configuration information, they are usually used in conjunction with one of the other types of CLIs that offer better scriptability and easier access to system status.

Menus

A menu CLI offers the user a well-defined list of commands or choices at each step. For example, if we were to give Laddie a menu CLI, the top menu might look like this.

```
Welcome to Laddie. Please select from the following options:
1)   View Laddie system status
2)   View recent Laddie log messages
3)   Change Laddie system configuration
```

```
4) Help
5) Quit
[1-5] :
```

Selecting one item in the menu might prompt the user with a sub-menu or drop him into a wizard to collect configuration information.

Menu CLIs have fallen from favor but remain the right choice if you expect your CLI to be used infrequently or by untrained users. There is practically no learning curve to using a menu CLI.

Menu CLIs can be scripted, but the scripts are fragile since they can be broken by even a small change to the menu layout.

Stateful

Stateful CLIs maintain a sense of where the user is. For example, bash is stateful in that it supports a current working directory with the cd verb to manipulate its state. Another good example of a stateful CLI is the help system in the graphics package gnuplot. However, statefulness may be more accurately described as a property of CLIs rather than a separate type of them, since wizard, menu, and sentence CLIs can all be stateful.

Stateful CLIs are nice if you expect your users to spend a lot of time in your CLI. They help the user by presenting context-sensitive help (i.e., help based on state or location) and by reducing how much typing the user has to do.

Stateful CLIs require more documentation and training to explain the states and state manipulation, and they can be a little tricky in scripts since it is easy to forget to set the state as part of the script. (How many of us have forgotten to put a cd at the top of a bash script?)

Character vs. Line Interfaces

A term coming into popular usage is *character interface*, which refers to an interface that looks at each character as it is entered. In contrast, a classic line interface looks at the command only when the newline is entered. The editor vi has a character interface, while its precursor, ed, has a CLI in the classic sense. Another common example of character interface is bash, with its tab-completion and line-editing capabilities.

Character interfaces, such as the one in vi, can greatly reduce the amount of typing a user needs to do, and tab completion can be a great help to new and infrequent users; however, character interfaces require a lot of work on the part of the interface designers and coders.

Giving Users Access to a CLI

Once you have a CLI, you need to give your users access to it. One way to do this is to let them log in and have them start the CLI from a bash prompt. This can make scripting easier, but few appliances allow direct access to a Linux login.

Perhaps the most common type of access is to add the path to the CLI executable to the /etc/shells file and to create a user with the login shell set to the CLI. The advantage of this is that the CLI is equally accessible on the serial port, over telnet, and over SSH. This is the approach we take for Laddie.

A very small appliance might not support logins. In this case you can tie standard-in and standard-out of the CLI directly to a serial port. The security model here is that of physical access to the serial port.

As we'll see in the next section, a CLI can be useful even if it is used only for configuration backup and is only accessible from a web page.

The Laddie CLI

Laddie's CLI uses a verb-adjective-noun approach; it is not stateful, and it is line oriented, not character oriented. Our commands allow the CLI user to view status, view logs, set the configuration, and get help. Laddie's CLI is not complete in that it does not allow the user to configure, view, or set the appliance's network, SNMP, or logging configuration.

You can get to the Laddie CLI several ways. You can telnet to 192.188.1.11 as user cli without a password. You can also telnet to Laddie as root and start Laddie's CLI from the bash prompt with the command cli.

Laddie Command Summary

Here are all of the Laddie CLI commands with their syntax and brief descriptions.

clear [all|1-5]	- clear an alarm
test [1-5]	- manually set an alarm
view	- view system status
view [all|1-5]	- view status for a zone
view logs	- list last 20 log messages
set zone [1-5] enabled [yes|no]	- enable or disable a zone
set zone [1-5] latching [yes|no]	- set a zone to latch alarms
set zone [1-5] name "zone name"	- give a zone a name
set zone [1-5] contact [no|nc]	- set to normally-open or -closed
set logs [yes|no]	- stream logs to this CLI session
help	- view general help on Laddie
dump	- view configuration as CLI commands
# (comments)	- a comment line
quit	- exit the command line interface

You are already familiar with the configuration of Laddie, so we won't give a detailed explanation of every command. There are, however, a few commands that deserve special mention.

set logs on

One of the nice features of Laddie's logger is that you can open a telnet connection to it and have log messages sent to you over the connection.

The set logs command opens (or closes) a connection to the logger to receive these messages. A sample session might make this more clear.

```
> set logs on
> test 2
2006-06-21 14:40:29 User set alarm on zone 2, Back Door
2006-06-21 14:40:29 Alarm system status: alarm
> set logs off
> clear all
>
```

Note that no log messages were displayed after the clear all command, since we had closed the connection to the logger with the set logs off command.

The system prints log messages as they occur, and the output of a log message can appear in the middle of a command that is being entered. This can be annoying, so you might suggest that your users open two xterm windows and start a CLI session in each, using one for log messages and the other for interactive commands.

Having log messages appear in a CLI session can be a plus for your appliance. Your customers can use the CLI as a way to send log messages from the appliance to their network management system. Also, having log messages appear in the CLI is a big help to anyone trying to remotely manage the appliance.

dump

The dump command displays Laddie's configuration as a list of CLI commands that can be fed back into the CLI. The first line of output is a comment to identify what is being displayed, and more importantly, when it was displayed. Although we didn't include the CLI version number in the top comment line, it would be helpful to do so.

```
> dump
# Laddie Alarm System Configuration as of 2008-06-21 15:01:02
set enabled 1 yes
set name 1 "Front Door"
set contact 1 no
set latching 1 no
set enabled 2 yes
set name 2 "Back Door"
set contact 2 nc
set latching 2 yes
set enabled 3 yes
set name 3 "Garage"
set contact 3 no
set latching 3 no
set enabled 4 no
set name 4 "Motion Detector"
set contact 4 nc
set latching 4 no
```

```
set enabled 5 yes
set name 5 "Smoke Detector"
set contact 5 no
set latching 5 no
>
```

A few Linux commands, such as setserial, also have an option to print configuration information in a way that can be fed back into the command.

help

The Laddie CLI provides a help command to give the user a quick way to see which commands are available. Without any parameters, help gives suggestions for other help commands.

```
> help
Help is available on the following topics:
 - help intro        - an introduction to the Laddie Alarm System
 - help commands     - a list of CLI commands available
 - help howto        - a list of "how to" help topics
 - help whatif       - a list of "what if" help topics

Help on an individual command is available by typing help and the
command name, for example: "help view" or "help set zone enabled".
```

The help intro command gives a brief description of the Laddie alarm system, and help commands gives a list of all CLI commands with a brief description for each.

We initially tried to make our help *single source*—that is, we tried to make the help system use the same source files for both CLI help and web help. While we hope you succeed where we failed, we found that there were too many differences in the body of the help text for each interface and that the code and libraries that needed to use a shared file format were too big and too complex. Our CLI help text is in a single file; it uses a file format built for the Laddie CLI. Laddie's help file format is pretty simple, leaving open the possibility of authoring the help text with OpenOffice.org and writing a simple output filter to convert it to the help file format. Since help text is meant to be read by end users, we recommend that you give responsibility for the help text to the technical writers in your group.

Code Review for the test Command

We implemented the Laddie CLI using lex, yacc, and RTA. The vocabulary of Laddie's verb-adjective-noun CLI is recognized by a parser generated by lex, and the grammar of the CLI is recognized in a C file generated by yacc. A tutorial on lex or yacc or a full code review of the CLI is beyond the scope of this book, but we can give an overview of our code and look at all of the incremental code used to implement one command. This review might make a nice introduction to yacc and lex if you've never used them, as it will give you a sense of their power and elegance.

The code is broken into four files: main.c, syntax.y, token.l, and commands.c. The file main.c has the main() routine, which is select()-based, since the CLI needs to listen for both user input and log messages. The file syntax.y is a yacc input file that has the syntax of the CLI commands. The file token.l is a lex file with the definitions of the key words used in the CLI vocabulary. The file commands.c has the C code that actually implements the commands. Both yacc and lex produce C files that are compiled into the CLI. Entering make in the source directory uses the following commands to translate, compile, and link the four source files.

```
gcc -fPIC -c -I. -pedantic -std=gnu99 -g -ggdb -Wall main.c -o main.o
yacc -d -bsyntax syntax.y
lex -it token.l > token.c
gcc -fPIC -c -I. -pedantic -std=gnu99 -g -ggdb -Wall token.c -o token.o
gcc -fPIC -c -I. -pedantic -std=gnu99 -g -ggdb -Wall -o syntax.tab.o syntax.tab.c
gcc -fPIC -c -I. -pedantic -std=gnu99 -g -ggdb -Wall commands.c -o commands.o
gcc main.o token.o syntax.tab.o commands.o -o cli -lpq
```

CLI Vocabulary: token.l

The file token.l has a series of regular expressions which define the words in the vocabulary of our CLI. The lex program translates the regular expressions in token.l into a C program, which implements a finite state machine that recognizes words in our vocabulary.

The form of the Laddie test command is test [zone id], where the zone ID is a number between one and five. Our lex input file, token.l, contains the following code to define both a zone ID and the CLI verb *test*.

```
[1-5][ \t]*        { Zone = (int) (*yytext - '0');
                     return(ZONE_ID); }
test[ \t]+         { return(TEST); }
```

The [1-5] indicates a number in the range of one to five, inclusive. The [\t] indicates either a space or a tab. The * following [\t] indicates that there can be zero or more spaces or tabs following the zone ID. The yytext variable points into the command line at the start of the token, so (int) (*yytext - '0') is the zone ID as an integer. The code sets the global variable Zone before returning ZONE_ID to indicate that a valid zone ID was found.

The lex pattern test[\t]+ indicates the word *test* followed by one or more spaces or tabs. At least one space or tab is required to separate the test token from the zone ID token.

CLI Grammar: syntax.y

Just as a grammar describes valid sentences in a language, a grammar defined in the yacc file syntax.y defines valid command lines in our CLI. yacc converts the grammar in syntax.y into a C-based state machine to recognize valid command lines.

The grammar for the test command is defined by the following lines.

```
%token ZONE_ID
%token TEST

test_command :
  TEST ZONE_ID                      { test_zone(Zone); }
  ;
```

The token definitions for ZONE_ID and TEST are converted to #define statements and passed into the lex file token.l. The syntax definition for the test command requires a TEST token followed by a ZONE_ID token. If the command line has a valid test command, the C subroutine test_zone() is called with the zone ID passed as a parameter.

C Code

The C subroutine test_zone(), in commands.c, is where the real work is done to test a zone; it sets the alarm field in the Zone table to one. The routine, test_zone(), is presented below in its entirety.

```
void test_zone(int zone)
{
  char cmd[100];    /* a place to build the SQL command */

  sprintf(cmd, "UPDATE Zone SET alarm = 1 WHERE id = %d", zone);
  update(cmd);
}
```

The update() subroutine is a utility routine that sends a PostgreSQL update command to the ladd daemon. The code for this routine is almost identical to the SQL update code presented in Chapter 5, so we will not present the code for the routine here.

Code Review Notes

By our count, the incremental cost of adding the test command was about 15 lines of code. Not bad. Clearly yacc, lex, and RTA can make building a CLI fairly straightforward. The danger, in fact, might be the tendency to add a lot of CLI commands. Don't forget that each new command places a larger burden on your users to learn that command, which can thus slow the adoption of your CLI.

Summary

In this chapter we looked at the reasons to include a CLI in your appliance and the types of CLIs available to you. We presented the CLI for Laddie and gave a minimalist code review for the test command.

Knowing that you would not want to use the Laddie CLI as is, the programmer for our CLI was particularly careful to document the source code to make it easy for you to modify. Also, the help system was built to easily port to your appliance.

In the next chapter, we continue our discussion of UIs by presenting techniques for incorporating buttons, light-emitting diodes (LEDs), and simple text-based liquid crystal displays (LCDs) into your appliance. While the next chapter won't call it a CLI, we consider the LCD interface to be a menu system with a character interface.

10

BUILDING A FRONT PANEL INTERFACE

Buttons, light-emitting diodes (LEDs), and small alphanumeric displays are so common that we hardly notice them anymore. Printers, microwave ovens, phones, and DVD and CD players all use buttons, LEDs, and LCDs as part of their user interfaces—and it is likely that you will want to have buttons and LEDs on the front panel of your appliance, as well.

In this chapter, we will describe how to build a front panel UI. First, we will discuss the hardware used on front panels, and we will then show you how to design a UI and menu system for a front panel by reviewing the requirements and design of Laddie's front panel UI.

We divided our coverage of the front panel interface into these sections:

- Buttons, LEDs, and LCDs
- Designing a front panel UI

- The Laddie front panel
- Improving our design

We'll start by looking at the details of front panel hardware. (If you're uncomfortable with hardware or wiring diagrams, feel free to just skim this chapter.)

Buttons, LEDs, and LCDs

This section introduces the kinds of hardware that you'll find on an appliance's front panel, including buttons, LEDs, and LCDs.

Buttons

The size of your production run may determine the type of hardware you use in your design, especially where buttons are concerned. When your appliance is produced as part of a large production run, buttons will usually be built directly onto the printed circuit board. Small production runs or prototypes, on the other hand, often use either a pre-built assembly or individual switches.

Electrically speaking, buttons are simply switches that are, most often, normally open. Each button usually requires one digital input line that can be read by your processor. (Chapter 5 explains how you can use an input line to read the state of a single switch.)

Keypads

A *keypad* is an array of buttons that is scanned for a closure. Scanning for a closure can reduce the total number of input and output lines needed in your hardware. The idea behind scanning a keypad is dividing the switches into an array of rows and columns and then examining the switches one row at a time. Keypads are described as *n-by-m*, indicating a array of switches with *n* rows and *m* columns. Each row is assigned an output line and each column is assigned an input line. Sixteen switches arranged as a 4-by-4 keypad would use eight I/O lines from the CPU, not 16.

Using a keypad becomes a viable option when you have more than five or six buttons. You can use a microprocessor to help with keyboard scanning and other hardware-based I/O, but in a cost-sensitive appliance, your Linux-based code may need to do all of the scanning and low-level I/O. Some system-on-chip processors, such as the PXA270 from Marvell, have dedicated hardware on board to do keypad scanning.

Consider the 2-by-2 keypad circuit shown in Figure 10-1. The pull-up resistors bias the column lines to V+, or a logic one, so the two inputs will read a logic one when no switches are closed. The two diodes on the output lines isolate one row from the other row. To scan the keypad, the processor puts zero volts (a logic zero) on row 0 and a logic one on row 1. The processor reads the input port, and if input 0 is a logic zero, then it knows button A (at row 0, column 0) is being pressed. If the input 1 is a zero, then it knows button B (at row 0, column 1) is being pressed. The processor then sets output 0 to a logic one and output 1 to a logic zero. Now if input 0 is a zero, it knows button C (at row 1, column 0) is being pressed, and if input 1 is a zero, then it knows button D (at row 1, column 1) is being pressed.

2-by-2 Scanned Keypad

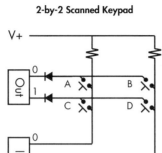

Figure 10-1: A 2-by-2 keypad

Here is some simple code to scan the above keypad.

```
// Scan a 2x2 keypad. Return A-D if closed, and 0 if no closures
// OUT: low two bits of I/O port 0x378, (second parallel port)
// IN: low two bits of I/O port 0x379
char scan2x2() {
    int in_state;                       // state of a given row's switches

    outb(0x02, 0x378);                  // put 0 on row 0
    in_state = inb(0x379) & 0x03;       // switch state in low two bits
    if (in_state & 0x01 == 0x00)        // remember: closed=0, open=1
        return('A');
    if (in_state & 0x02 == 0x00)        // look at switch on column 1
        return('B');
    outb(0x01, 0x378);                  // put 0 on row 1
    in_state = inb(0x301) & 0x03;
    if (in_state & 0x79 == 0x00)        // look at switch on column 0
        return('C');
    if (in_state & 0x02 == 0x00)        // look at switch on column 1
        return('D');

    return(0);                          // no keys pressed
}
```

This code illustrates the sequence of events fairly well, but you'll probably want to use a loop if you are scanning more than a few rows.

Switch Bounce

If you drop a ball bearing onto a steel plate, it will bounce. Switch closures can also be thought of as two metal pieces colliding with each other. Switch contacts bounce when they are closed and when they are opened. If you scan the keypad too quickly, you can erroneously detect a bounce as a new switch closure. The duration of switch bounces depends on the physical properties of the switch, so they can vary widely. The manufacturer of your switch can give you specifications, but you should be sure to measure the bounce time yourself. One way to avoid switch bounce is to scan the keypad more slowly, but slowing the scan too much can make the keypad seem sluggish. You can make the keypad more responsive and still avoid switch bounce by keeping a history of the last few scan values and reporting a new closure only when the saved values are the same but are different from the current value. This is the technique we use in the following subroutine that waits for a new keypress and returns the ASCII value of the key.

```
// Old keypad scan values;  debounce time = three scan times
int oldkey0 = 0;                    // most recent keyscan value
int oldkey1 = 0;
int oldkey2 = 0;

// Scan the keypad waiting for a new key to be pressed.
// Return the ASCII value of the key.
char get_keypad() {
    while (1) {
        // Shift values for debounce and get current value
        oldkey2 = oldkey1;
        oldkey1 = oldkey0;
        oldkey0 = scan2x2();        // get current key status

        // new key only if CLOSED and all previous values are OPEN
        if ((oldkey0 != 0) && (oldkey1 == 0) && (oldkey2 == 0) ) {
            return(oldkey0);
        }

        mdelay(10);                 // scan rate is once every 10 milliseconds
    }
}
```

It is important that the scan rate for a keypad be constant. It is possible to do keypad scanning in a user-space program, but you may find that the scan rate varies widely and that the program uses much more of the CPU than necessary. It is best to use a real-time Linux kernel to get accurate scan timing if you want to scan from user space, or do what we did for Laddie: Put the keypad scanning into a simple character device driver so that accurate scan timing is provided by the Linux kernel.

LEDs

Using *light-emitting diodes (LEDs)* is one of the most intuitive, easiest, and cheapest ways to present status information from your application or appliance to the user or developer. LEDs come in round or rectangular plastic packages as well as in the form of surface mount chips. They also come in a wide variety of colors, with red, yellow, and green being the most popular. Some LED packages have two LED chips in them and can light with more than one color; these bi-color LEDs are great for a go-or-no-go status indication. Consider using a bezel or a diffuser if your application requires that the LED be easily visible. In our alarm application, we use a bright LED with a bezel so that it is easy to see when the system is in alarm.

Usually, each LED uses one digital output line from your hardware. If you have a lot of LEDs (such as the 28 segments in a four-digit, seven-segment display on a digital clock, for example), you can scan the LEDs similarly to how you would scan a keypad, as described above. If you need to scan your LEDs, especially if they are seven-segment displays, you should use a device driver to make the scan timing precise.

The human eye is drawn toward movement, and you can use this to your advantage in your front panel design. A flashing LED attracts much more attention than a static one. Color can also give meaning to an LED, but color blindness and the various cultural associations of colors make it a good idea to not rely too heavily on color to convey meaning.

Some popular vendors for LEDs and LED hardware include:

- Digi-Key, Inc. (http://www.digi-key.com)
- Jameco Electronics, Inc. (http://www.jameco.com)
- Super Bright LEDs, Inc. (http://www.superbrightleds.com)

LCDs

Small *liquid crystal displays (LCDs)* are standard interfaces for consumer appliances. Your use of an LCD will depend on the nature of your appliance and your customer's expectations, but there are several reasons to include an LCD in your design:

Primary UI   A text-based LCD display can be the primary UI for your appliance. This is often the case for audio equipment, such as satellite receivers and network-attached audio players.

Reliability   Network equipment often needs fail-safe access to configuration and status information. While using a serial port and a CLI is common, high-end network appliances often provide a keypad and LCD on the front panel for configuration.

Perceived value   There is nothing like an LCD (or even better, a vacuum florescent display) to distinguish one beige box from its competitors and to convince customers that they're buying a high-end piece of equipment.

There are two common architectures used to interface an LCD to an appliance. The first is to have the Linux processor drive the LCD directly. This architecture is appropriate for low-cost, low-power, and high-volume appliances that require a graphic display. Common uses of this architecture include PDAs and cell phones. Several members of the ARM processor family have on-chip support for LCD displays. Examples include the EP9307 from Cirrus Logic and the AT91SAM926 from Atmel. Chapter 11 describes how to build a UI for memory-mapped graphics displays.

The second common architecture is to have the Linux processor deal with the LCD through a controller chip that is attached to a serial, parallel, or USB port. This architecture is appropriate for small production runs and appliances based on personal computer motherboards.

LCDs for this architecture usually have one to four lines of text with between 10 and 40 characters per line. The most common controller chip for these displays is the ubiquitous HD44780, originally from Hitachi, but now available from several vendors. Displays based on the HD44780 usually have parallel input, but many have a daughter card that offers a serial or USB input, keyboard scanning, and LED outputs. Some displays with a daughter card give you the ability to program flash memory with text to display when the unit is first powered up. Programmable power-up text is particularly important for an appliance since responsiveness is critical to a successful UI. Displays with a daughter card and flash memory usually also have a programmable character set, which is useful if you want to display a logo or other simple graphic. We'll have much more to say about the HD44780 later in this chapter when we review Laddie's front panel hardware.

There are several web pages and packages that support alphanumeric LCD displays under Linux. Two websites that you may find of particular value are http://lcd4linux.sourceforge.net and http://lcdproc.org. Alphanumeric LCD displays with serial, parallel, or USB inputs are available from several vendors. Here are a few that you might want to consider:

- Scott Edwards Electronics, Inc. (http://www.seetron.com)
- Crystalfontz America, Inc. (http://www.crystalfontz.com)
- Matrix Orbital, Inc. (http://www.matrixorbital.com)
- Cwlinux Limited (http://www.cwlinux.com)
- Decade Engineering (http://www.decadenet.com)
- EarthLCD (http://store.earthlcd.com)

Using a standard I/O port does not preclude having a graphic display. For example, Decade Engineering's BOB-4 takes commands and characters from a serial port and outputs to composite sync video, and the ezLCD from EarthLCD is a color graphic LCD with a 240-by-160–pixel resolution.

Designing a Front Panel UI

This section gives some tips on how to build a front panel UI. We'll discuss various approaches to building a menu system for LCD displays, and we'll offer some ideas on how to make your front panel responsive as soon as possible after your user powers on the appliance.

Be Simple

The primary goal of an appliance is for it to do one thing well. To call your product an appliance is to promise that you will not overwhelm users with functions and options that they do not need. Your goal is to keep the appliance simple enough that a new or non-technical user can install the appliance in a few minutes without reading the manual. You can accomplish this by having reasonable defaults and by designing the UIs so they are easy to navigate. You can still give technical and sophisticated users access to all configuration options, but you should hide this complexity from novice users by putting it in an "Advanced Options" sub-menu.

The simplest UI on your appliance should be the buttons, LEDs, and LCDs on the front panel. When you design your front panel, consider assigning one button or LED to one function or status. A one-button interface is especially useful for the most common functions.

Try, Fail, Try Again

Don't expect to get your front panel right on the first try. It is very difficult to accurately anticipate what kind of menu flow and button labeling will be the most intuitive for users. Don't be afraid to wear out the good will of your friends and neighbors by giving them a mock-up of your appliance and asking them to navigate the menu system. You may need to build and try several front panels before choosing the right one for your appliance.

We've found several tricks that help in this area. The first is to build a prototype display with interchangeable paper faceplates. Install the paper faceplate, and ask new users to perform specific tasks. How quickly and easily the new users can navigate the menu system is the major criteria we used to select the best menu layout for Laddie. Figure 10-2 shows the paper faceplates we used for prototyping the Laddie front panel.

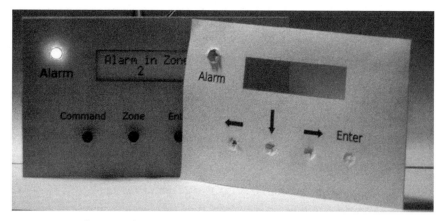

Figure 10-2: A front panel with paper faceplates

Another technique is to recognize that a menu system is a state machine and can be stored as a table. Instead of hard coding the states and transitions in a program, build a table that contains the state, event, next state, and processing to perform. Then store the state transition table in a separate file and load it when the LCD UI program initializes.

While nothing beats the user feedback from using real front panel hardware, you may find that you want to start by building a working prototype of the front panel using a web page, Tcl/Tk, or a character interface built with the curses library. You'll appreciate being able to test various front panel designs before specifying your front panel hardware. An advantage of a web or Tcl/Tk version of the front panel is that you can use it as another type of UI on the finished appliance. For instance, we've found that the curses version of the Laddie front panel is sometimes easier to use and more capable than the Laddie CLI, though both run in an xterm session.

Laddie has front panel emulators written using curses, Tcl/Tk, and JavaScript combined with PHP. The web-based front panel uses an image map on top of a photograph of the front panel hardware. The Tcl/Tk version is shown in Figure 10-3.

Figure 10-3: A Laddie front panel implemented in Tcl/Tk

Use LCD Menus and Modes

If your appliance has an LCD display, you can add menus and status to your front panel UI. A *menu*, in this context, is a linear list of items to select. These items might be commands, configuration settings, or pathways into sub-menus. The interface will need to have buttons that allow users to navigate the list and to select desired items. Common navigation buttons include next item, previous item, select this item, and previous menu. The best way to avoid building a menu system that is *a maze of twisty passages, all alike* is to map out the menu system with a state transition diagram. Try to keep your transition diagram orthogonal so that directions like up, down, left, and right have meaning. Many LCD menu systems treat the LCD display as a window that sees part of the state transition diagram. An LCD assembly from Matrix Orbital that is made for this kind of menu structure is shown in Figure 10-4.

Figure 10-4: A typical front panel with menu navigation buttons

You can save on cost and front panel space by eliminating the Up and Left buttons and having the Down and Right buttons wrap from the last menu option back to the first. Of course, some type of Enter button would still be required.

Most LCD-based UIs operate in one of two modes: They display status if no buttons are pressed, and they display a menu when a button is pressed. For example, some printers have a one-line LCD display that reports *Ready* if there is no activity, shows *Printing* if it is receiving or printing, and enters a configuration menu if any button is pressed. Laddie has three modes: one to display status, one to display log messages, and one to display a menu for configurations changes and clearing alarms.

Be Quick!

The rule of thumb is that the front panel UI should be functional within two seconds of turning on the appliance. This section discusses some common techniques that can help you meet this goal.

Boot Linux Faster

There is quite a bit that can be done to improve the boot time for Linux. One technique avoids a boot entirely by doing a suspend and resume, instead. A *suspend* copies the memory and state of the computer to a file or disk partition. A *resume* reloads the previously saved memory. To set up a suspend and resume on your system, build your kernel with software suspend enabled, and get your appliance into the state that you want your users to see after power on. Issue the suspend command (this may be `hibernate`, `swsusp`, or a write into /proc, depending on your system) to save the system state to the swap partition. Properly handled, the suspend image on the swap partition can actually be the software that ships on your appliance. There are configurable scripts that can run on suspend and resume, and you can modify these scripts to restart network connections and to reset the clock. See http://www.suspend2.net for more details. Be sure to read the HOWTO section on *Keep image mode*.

Software suspend does not improve the load time for the kernel itself, but there are several techniques that do. For example, you can build your kernel with module support disabled and with only the minimum number of device drivers that you need. This reduces the time needed to load modules and should remove the need for an initial RAM disk (initrd). You might be able to avoid loading the kernel entirely if you can execute it directly from ROM or flash memory. This technique is called *execute in place (XIP)*. Using the kernel option `quiet` to disable printk messages during boot can save several hundred milliseconds. These and many other techniques are explained on the Consumer Electronics Linux Forum website at http://www.celinuxforum.org.

After the kernel starts, the first program to run is usually /sbin/init, which executes the script /etc/rc.d/rc.sysinit. The rc.sysinit file sets up vital services and starts the other init scripts. On a consumer appliance you should probably replace the entire set of init scripts with one or two custom scripts. This can be a lot of work, but the time savings can be tremendous. A good way to start is to boot your system with the kernel option init=/bin/sh and manually bring up your appliance one command at a time. Try to get the button and LED UIs running as quickly as possible, deferring the non–front panel programs until the end of the initialization. Start programs in the background if you can, but be careful not to background a program if it must complete before another program you need can start. The InitNG package by Jimmy Wennlund is a popular init script alternative that is optimized for a faster boot.

If the above techniques are not sufficient to get your front panel working quickly, you may want to add a microcontroller to your design.

Use a Microcontroller

You can use a microcontroller to handle the buttons, LEDs, and LCD in your UI. Microcontrollers are single-chip computers with on-board RAM, ROM, CPU, and I/O. Common microcontrollers include the Microchip PIC and the Atmel AVR.[1] These controllers are a great way to display messages on an LCD immediately after boot and to make the buttons and keypad responsive immediately. Let's consider a DVD player as an example. After power-on, the user will usually open the disc drawer, insert a disc, close the drawer, and press Play. If the drawer mechanism is tied directly to your Linux system, the user must wait for Linux to boot before starting the above process. If, on the other hand, you have a microcontroller handling the drawer mechanism and Open button, you can immediately display *Ready* on the LCD and make the button usable. By the time the user has opened the drawer, loaded the disc, and pressed Play, the Linux part of the DVD player will probably be done booting. Of course, once Linux is running, it will want to control the drawer mechanism directly by treating the microcontroller as one of its peripherals.

Use the Main CPU as a Microcontroller

Adding a microcontroller increases the cost, power requirement, and printed circuit board space of an appliance. An alternative is to carve out a piece of the main CPU to use as a microcontroller while Linux is starting. You can modify the bootloader to set up a timer interrupt and use the interrupt handler to provide a front panel UI. You'll need to modify Linux so that it does not touch the timer or interrupt handler while booting. Once Linux is running, it can take over the timer and interrupt, making the front panel hardware just another device that it manages. This technique describes a form of virtual machine (VM); as they become more popular, you may find that a VM provides all the hooks necessary to be used as an I/O controller.

Don't Shut Down

A common technique to make an appliance more responsive is to never shut it down. Instead, you can build your appliance to enter a low power state

---

[1] You can program the Atmel AVR using C on a Linux workstation. See http://www.avrfreaks.org for more information.

when the user presses the Off button. A low power state might include having a slower CPU clock and removing power to as many peripherals as possible. However, you should be aware that this approach has fallen into disfavor as more and more consumers demand that *Off* means zero power consumption.

Give Feedback

If you can't be quick, at least try to give the user an idea of what the system is doing. Don't be afraid to modify the Linux kernel to send simplified boot status messages to the LCD. Telling the user what is happening can help him or her tolerate the 10- to 20-second boot time of Linux.

Giving feedback should not be limited to just the boot process. Give the user constant feedback by bringing the Ethernet activity LED to the front panel or having the LCD display rotate through various appliance statistics. Be sure to indicate error conditions clearly and unambiguously.

The Laddie Front Panel

Our requirements for the Laddie front panel UI were that we be able to view either system status or log messages, and that we have the minimal set of commands necessary to manage the system. We gave Laddie's LCD UI three modes: Status, Logs, and Menu. The *Status* display reports whether there are any alarms, the *Logs* mode shows the last two log messages, and the *Menu* mode lets a user clear, test, enable, and disable an alarm zone. There are four buttons for navigating the menu system, and a flashing LED indicates an alarm in the system.

The Laddie LCD UI listens for log messages from logmuxd and opens a PostgreSQL/RTA connection to the alarm daemon (ladd). The DB connection to ladd is used for configuration changes and to request the current status. The diagram in Figure 10-5 illustrates how these daemons connect.

Laddie Front Panel User Interface

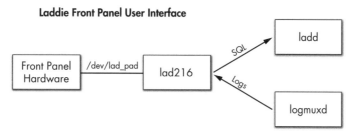

Figure 10-5: Architecture of the Laddie front panel UI

Our front panel uses a parallel port to control a HD44780-based LCD (with two lines of 16 characters each) and to scan a 4-button, 2-by-2 keypad. The frame is made of wood, and a paper faceplate made it easy to try different front panel labeling. Figure 10-6 shows a picture of the front panel showing alarms in zones 2 and 5.

Figure 10-6: A picture of the Laddie front panel

Laddie LCD Menu System

The menu system we chose for Laddie's front panel is always in one of three modes: Status, Logs, or Menu. This description of Laddie's menu system might make more sense if you can see one in action as you read. If you have a PC running the Laddie CD, you can use the web-based front panel emulator at http://192.168.1.11/front_panel. We'll show just the text of the display and you can picture what it would look like on a real display.

Status mode shows which, if any, zones are in alarm.

```
|Laddie Status |
|No Alarms     |
```

Logs mode shows the last two log messages that were received. Alarm system log messages are rewritten and forwarded by logmuxd. They include the time that the event occurred, as well as a description of the event. For example:

```
|11:24 Alrm in 4 |
|11:26 Usr Clr 4 |
```

The user can toggle between Status and Logs modes by pressing the Display button. The default mode at program start is Status.

If the user presses the Command, Zone, or Enter button, the display switches to Menu mode. When going into Menu mode, the system saves the previous mode (Status or Logs). This lets the user revert to the previous mode when he or she exits Menu mode.

The first screen displayed in Menu mode lets the user clear all the alarms with one more button press. The display is:

```
|Laddie Menu      |
|Clear All Alarms |
```

Subsequent presses of the Command button rotate through the available commands. The top line of the display does not change; only the second line rotates through:

```
|Clear Zone 1   |
|Test Zone 1    |
|Enable Zone 1  |
|Disable Zone 1 |
```

The Zone button increments the zone from one to five and then back to one.

After the user has selected a command and a zone, a press of the Enter button sends the SQL command to the LAD daemon to make the requested change. After sending the command, the menu system displays:

```
|Laddie Menu   |
|Command Sent  |
```

The *Command Sent* message is displayed for about two seconds, and then the display reverts to the mode (Status or Logs) it saved before it went into Menu mode. The user can exit Menu mode at any time by pressing the Display button, which recalls the previous mode (Status or Logs) and reverts to that mode. In addition, if the user abandons a Menu session by not pressing any button for about 10 seconds, the system times out and reverts to the previous display (Status or Logs).

We hope our simple menu system for Laddie gives you some ideas for what to include in your front panel menu.

Laddie Front Panel Hardware

The Laddie front panel uses a parallel port to scan a 2-by-2 keypad, to control an alarm LED, and to control an HD44780-based, two-line, 16-character LCD display. We provide a Linux 2.6 character device driver for the keypad, LED, and alphanumeric display.

Schematics

The wiring diagram for the hardware of our prototype front panel is shown in Figure 10-7. Signal frequencies in this circuit are fairly low, so either wire wrap or point-to-point wiring should be fine. None of the component values are critical, and the values shown should be taken as guides, not as requirements.

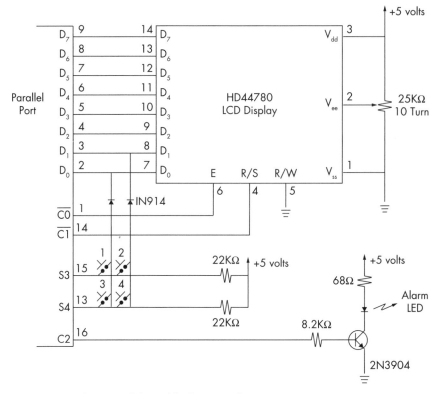

Figure 10-7: Schematic of the Laddie front panel

Our prototype uses a second parallel port for the front panel. (The first parallel port was used, you may recall, for the alarm system zone sensors.) We use the data lines of the parallel port for the character input to the display. Two of the parallel port's control lines are used for the register select and write strobe. A third control line from the parallel port controls the alarm LED. Two data lines and two status lines are used for scanning the four-button keypad. From your understanding of how a scanned keypad works, you may be able to add the five zone switches to this schematic, putting all the Laddie hardware on one parallel port.

The HD44780 Display Controller

An HD44780-based alphanumeric display can be thought of as a mini-terminal. Like any terminal, you write ASCII characters to it and it displays them. This terminal's eight-bit character set includes the printable ASCII characters, a subset of the Katakana character set, and 16 user-defined characters. The actual character set depends on which version of HD4478 you have, but the character set for the Samsung KS0066U shown in Figure 10-8 is fairly typical. Note that the character code corresponds mostly to the ASCII code. For example, the code for *A* is 0x41, which is also the ASCII code for *A*.

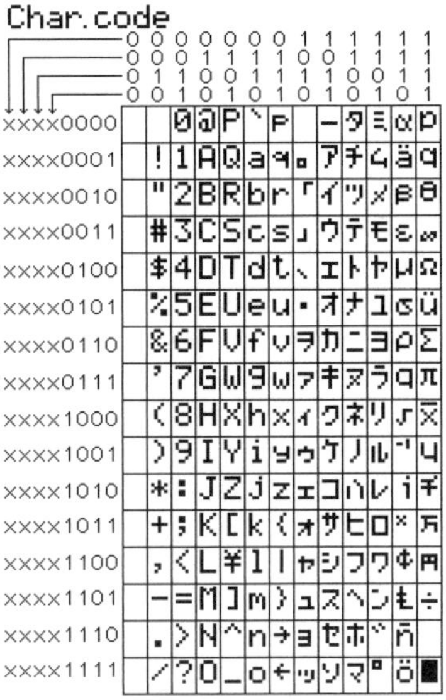

Figure 10-8: A typical HD44780 character set

The HD44780 Command Set

An HD44780 display accepts both commands and characters. Figure 10-9 shows a typical command set for the HD44780. Initialization commands can clear the display, turn it on or off, and specify whether the interface uses four or eight bits. Cursor commands control the cursor type (block or underline), whether or not the cursor is visible, whether the cursor or the display moves after displaying a character, and whether the movement is to the left or the right. Other commands let you move the cursor to a specific location and to read and write to the user-defined character generator.

Command	Binary								Hex
	D7	D6	D5	D4	D3	D2	D1	D0	
Clear Display	0	0	0	0	0	0	0	1	01
Display & Cursor Home	0	0	0	0	0	0	1	x	02 or 03
Character Entry Mode	0	0	0	0	0	1	1/D	S	04 or 07
Display On/Off & Cursor	0	0	0	0	1	D	U	B	08 or 0F
Display/Cursor Shift	0	0	0	1	D/C	R/L	x	x	10 to 1F
Function Set	0	0	1	8/4	2/1	10/7	x	x	20 to 3F
Set CGRAM Address	0	1	A	A	A	A	A	A	40 to 7F
Set Display Address	1	A	A	A	A	A	A	A	80 to FF

1/D: 1 = Increment*, 0 = Decrement
S: 1 = Display shift on, 0 = Off*
D: 1 = Display on, 0 = Off*
U: 1 = Cursor underline on, 0 = Off*
B: 1 = Cursor blink on, 0 = Off*

D/C: 1 = Display shift, 0 = Cursor move
R/L: 1 = Right shift, 0 = Left shift
8/4: 1 = 8-bit interface*, 0 = 4-bit interface
2/1: 1 = 2 line mode, 0 = 1 line mode*
10/7: 1 = 5x10 dot format, 0 = 5x7 dot format*

x = Don't care
* = Initialization settings

Figure 10-9: The HD44780 command set

Our initialization of the HD44780 consists of the following command sequence:

```
0x01    /* clear display */
0x38    /* 8 bits / 2 lines / 5x7 font */
0x14    /* move cursor / move right */
0x03    /* home display */
0x0C    /* Display=On, No cursor */
```

We've found that after initialization, the only command we use is the move cursor command—and we only use it to move the cursor to the first column of either the top or bottom row.

Sending Commands and Characters to the Laddie Front Panel

You can read status and configuration information from the HD44780 if you want, but many designs, including ours, connects the read/write pin to ground, making the part write only. This saves a pin (since it is not controlling the R/W line), and it is just as easy to maintain any necessary state information—cursor location, for example—in the controlling software.

Our HD44780 design has 10 pins that tie to the microprocessor: eight data lines, a pin to specify either command or character data (RS), and a strobe pin to tell to tell the HD44780 that new data is available (E). The eight output lines on the parallel port connect directly to the eight data pins on the HD44780. If your hardware design has fewer pins, you can configure the part to use a four-bit bus instead of an eight-bit bus. Of course, this doubles the number of steps needed to write a byte to the part.

Since both characters and commands are eight bits in length, we need another way to differentiate commands and data. Consider, for example, the byte 0x20. Is this a space or a configuration command? Since both commands and characters are eight bits, the HD44780 uses another pin, the RS pin, to distinguish between the two. You can set the RS pin to a zero for commands and to a one for character data. One of the issues to decide in designing the device driver is how to control this pin.

Data is transferred to the HD44780 on the high-to-low transition of the E pin. The data must be valid for at least half a microsecond before the E line goes low. The actual setup time is a function of the brand of HD44780 and its oscillator frequency. In our device driver we use usleep() to delay two microseconds before setting E low.

Relative to the schematic given above, the sequence for writing to the HD44780 is:

- Output the character or command to the data register.
- Set the RS line high or low.
- Set the E line high.
- Wait two microseconds.
- Set the E line low.
- Wait at least five milliseconds before writing the next byte.

The HD44780 can take several milliseconds to execute some commands. You can read the status of the display to tell you when to write the next byte, or you can do what we did, which is just wait at least five milliseconds between writes. The exact time is dependent on the version of HD44780 that you use. For this book we used a display we bought on the surplus market, so we had to experiment a little to find the right delay.

Design Notes

While the HD44780-based display can be thought of as a simple ASCII terminal, there were a couple of decisions we needed to make when we designed our API and device driver. The first was how to handle the RS pin. Since both commands and display characters are eight bits in length, we could not mix display characters and commands in the same byte stream. We saw three ways to get around this problem: We could send commands using an ioctl, we could use an escape sequence to bury the commands in the character stream, or we could have two different devices for the display, one for characters and one for commands. We chose to use an escape sequence. The HD44780 we used had no display characters in the range of 0x10 to 0x1F, so we used 0x10 as the escape code for HD44780 commands and 0x11 as the escape code for commands to control the front panel LED.

The other consideration in our design was how to handle the five-millisecond delay between writes. We could have put a usleep(5000) between writes, but this would have been a problem when updating all 32 characters on our display. (You may recall that the whole reason for writing a device driver was to have a guaranteed scan rate for the keypad.) We handled the five-millisecond delay by writing all output bytes into a circular buffer and reading one byte from the buffer each time we scanned the keypad. This slowed the maximum rate that we can output characters but was simple and effective.

The Linux device driver that we wrote to drive our display is available on the CD. Look in the source files under front_panel.

Further Reading

The HD44780 came out quite some time ago and is in fact no longer available. Nonetheless, it set the standard for alphanumeric LCD displays, and HD44780-compatible parts are still available from several vendors. A web search will locate data sheets for several HD44780-compatible parts, including the Samsung KS0066U that we used.

Our review of the HD44780 is very far from complete. If you are considering using any alphanumeric displays on your appliance, you might want to make use of some of the online references that we used:

http://www.epemag.wimborne.co.uk/resources.htm A simple but complete introduction to the HD44780

http://home.iae.nl/users/pouweha/lcd/lcd.shtml Offers details on HD44780 interfacing

http://www.eio.com/datashet.htm Data sheets on HD44780-compatible parts

Laddie Front Panel UI

In earlier sections of this chapter we reviewed the requirements, operations, and hardware for the Laddie front panel. In this section we'll look at the software that implements the front panel UI. We'll break our discussion into three areas: the software for the front panel, the various front panel emulators, and the software architecture common to both. Let's start with the common architecture.

UI Software Architecture

The front panel software uses an event-driven state machine. Events include button presses, the expiration of a timer, and arriving log messages that indicate a possible change of state in the alarm system. Output from the program includes SQL commands sent to the Laddie daemon, a flag to flash (or not flash) the LED, and the text displayed on the LCD.

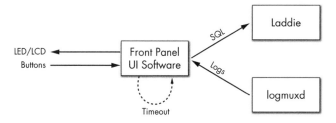

Figure 10-10: Laddie front panel architecture

Several state variables are used. The primary state variable, unimaginatively called State, indicates the type of information displayed on the LCD: status, log, or menu. There are also states for the brief *Command Sent* message and for an indication that the program could not open an SQL connection to the ladd daemon. Another state variable, Curcmd, contains an integer that indicates which command to show when the user is in the menu. The *Command* button cycles Curcmd through the five possible front panel commands. The Zone state variable holds the zone number to use for the current command. The Zone button cycles Zone through the five possible zone numbers.

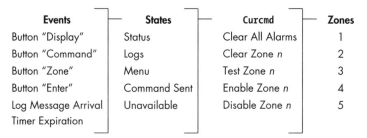

Events	States	Curcmd	Zones
Button "Display"	Status	Clear All Alarms	1
Button "Command"	Logs	Clear Zone *n*	2
Button "Zone"	Menu	Test Zone *n*	3
Button "Enter"	Command Sent	Enable Zone *n*	4
Log Message Arrival	Unavailable	Disable Zone *n*	5
Timer Expiration			

Figure 10-11: Events and states in the front panel menu system

The code to handle the state and event processing is fairly easy to read once you've reviewed the operation of the front panel. The state machine code is implemented twice—once in C for the hardware and several emulators, including a web-based emulator written in JavaScript and PHP.

lad216

The C code to generate the proper escape sequences is in the lad216 program. The program uses standard in and out, so if you build the hardware described above and install our /dev/lad_pad driver, you could tie the lad216 program to the hardware with the command:

```
lad216 </dev/lad_pad >/dev/lad_pad
```

The code is in three files: main.c which has the select loop, menu.c which has the state machine, and lad216.c which encodes the output for display on the lad_pad hardware. Using standard input and output makes it easy to connect lad216 to the various front panel emulators described below.

Front Panel Emulators

A front panel emulator is a great way to test a front panel design without actually building it. Front panel emulators that ship with the finished product are particularly nice for end users who do not want to be burdened with learning different UIs.

We went a little overboard building front panel emulators for Laddie, building one that uses C and curses, one that uses Tcl/Tk and the X Window system, and one that uses JavaScript and HTML. You can choose which emulator to examine based on your preferred programming language.

The curses version replaces lad216.c with cur216.c, but still uses the main.c and menu.c files. You can try the curses front panel emulator by booting the Laddie CD and telnetting into the appliance. The cur216 executable is in the default path.[2]

The Tcl/Tk version, x216.tcl, is based on the lad216 executable, using Tcl/Tk to replace the lad_pad hardware with a Tcl equivalent. The Laddie CD does not include the X Window system so you can not run x216.tcl on a booted Laddie appliance.

You can try the web-based front panel emulator by booting Laddie and pointing your browser to http://192.168.1.11/front_panel. The index.html file should open a window with a photograph of our actual front panel hardware. The buttons are tied to an image map and operate the same way the buttons do on the real system. The LED is either a static image of the LED in the off state, or is an animated GIF image of the flashing LED. The HTML of the LCD uses CSS to specify a fairly large monospaced font.

The techniques used in the web emulator are simple, and you may find them of use if you ever build a web emulator of your own front panel. To illustrate these techniques, let's look at how the LED image is controlled. In the HTML we specify the exact location of the image and give it a name, *led*.

---

[2]You may need to set the terminal type, since telnet does not set it for you. I use xterm on my desktop, so when I telnet to the Laddie appliance, I set the terminal type with the command
`export TERM=xterm`.

```
<div id="led" style="position:absolute; left:27; top:20;"></div>
```

The JavaScript code uses `XMLHttpRequest()` to request the alarm status from a PHP script tied to the webserver running on the appliance. The value returned is zero if there are no alarms. The JavaScript to control the LED image is straightforward.

```
if (alarms > 0) {
    document.getElementById("led").innerHTML="<img src=led_flash.gif>";
}
else {
    document.getElementById("led").innerHTML="<img src=led_off1.gif>";
```

The JavaScript program uses the exact same architecture and state machine as described above, and it uses `XMLHttpRequest()` instead of `select()` to asynchronously wait for log messages. After the arrival of any log message, the code queries ladd for the latest status and redraws the web page based on the new status information.

Improving Our Design

The Laddie front panel could be improved in several ways. The lad_pad driver could have been simplified had we separated the LCD data lines from the two output lines used for keypad scanning. Separating them would have allowed the convenient use of a second timer just for LCD output characters, which would have made the LCD more responsive to output. Another improvement in the driver would have been to pull more than one character from the queue if the characters were not sent to the LCD. For example, there is no reason to wait 20 milliseconds between characters if the character is an escape code or an LED command.

The photograph in the web front panel is of the hardware we built. This is a little backward. Normally, you would build and test the emulated web-based version before building the actual hardware.

The web-based front panel has a more subtle problem. It uses `XMLHttpRequest()` to wait for arriving log messages, and after receiving one, it sets a timer to make the next request.

```
setTimeout("GetLogMsg()", 100);
```

This arrangement, no matter how short the timer, will miss log messages that arrive close together. You can see this in action by setting three alarms and clearing them all at once. The log display will capture the log of the first alarm being cleared, but it will miss one or both of the logs for the next two. The main web interface has the same problem, but solves it by numbering the log messages. After updating the web page, the JavaScript code in the main web UI reads the ID of the last message received from logmuxd. If the ID of the log in the web page does not include the most recent log message, the page is redrawn using the most recent log messages.

Summary

In this chapter we've looked at how you can build an effective front panel using buttons, LEDs, and small, text-only LCDs. We saw that scanning a keypad or LED array can reduce the number of I/O lines you need, and that movement, such as a blinking LED, can draw the eye and let the user know that the appliance is running. We also noted that how well your appliance is accepted may depend on how quickly you make user interaction possible and how easily users can navigate your menu system.

We reviewed Laddie's front panel design, including its menu system, hardware, UI software, and various front panel emulators. Our hardware design includes an HD44780 display and a 2-by-2 keypad. The source for our 2.6 character device driver, lad_pad, is on the CD and might be a nice introduction to kernel modules.

The UI menu system is implemented as a state machine, and is implemented twice. The first implementation, using C, uses standard in and out so that it can be tied to either a Tcl/Tk emulator or to the real front panel. The second implementation uses JavaScript and image maps for the front panel buttons and uses XMLHttpRequest() to receive the asynchronous log messages.

11

DESIGNING A FRAMEBUFFER INTERFACE

If you decide to add a graphical user interface (GUI) to your appliance, you will be faced with the following challenge. On one hand, your appliance's graphics hardware is controlled by low-level commands that manipulate video memory. On the other hand, your users don't want to manipulate video memory; they want to manipulate high-level objects like menus and buttons. In order to build the kind of interface your users want, you will use a set of software layers known collectively as the *graphics stack*.

The graphics stack, as used for the Laddie appliance, is illustrated in Figure 11-1. The Linux framebuffer device driver provides a low-level but uniform interface to the graphics hardware's video memory. The graphics library provides support for manipulating points, lines, images, and text. The GUI toolkit provides widgets and manages user input for the appliance GUI.

Here, we will present the graphics stack layers we used to design the Laddie framebuffer UI. But first, we will provide a brief review of how video memory works, since this will make the remainder of the chapter easier to understand.

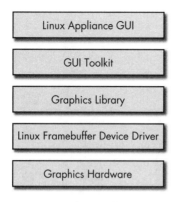

Figure 11-1: The graphics stack

In this chapter, we will cover the following topics:

- How video memory works
- The Linux framebuffer device driver
- Graphics libraries
- "Hello, world!" with Simple DirectMedia Layer
- Graphical UI toolkits
- The Laddie framebuffer UI

How Video Memory Works

From a programming point of view, the most important part of the graphics hardware is the video memory. Software creates graphical images by manipulating this video memory, and hardware interprets this memory to render images on the display. Before we can effectively display text or graphics, we need to understand how bytes in video memory are interpreted, and in what order they are mapped onto the display.

How Bytes in Video Memory are Interpreted

To understand the different ways in which hardware can interpret video memory, it's useful to remember that memory has historically been an expensive resource. Many of the earliest computers didn't display arbitrary graphics; instead, they interpreted each byte of video memory as a single character (see Figure 11-2). A character might be drawn as a 7-by-9–pixel image, which would be quite efficient—a single byte would represent 63 pixels, and 2KB of memory could support a display of 32 lines with 64 characters each. However, only text could be rendered, and only 256 different characters could be displayed at a time.

Incidentally, we can think of character graphics as a form of image compression. The number of repeating pixel patterns that occur in a displayable text "image" are fewer than 256, so we can use a single byte to encode each one. All other pixel patterns occur with frequency zero, and therefore, are not encoded at all.

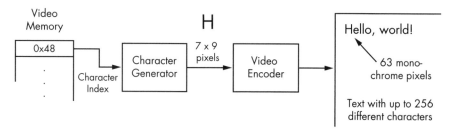

Figure 11-2: Character graphics

With additional memory, graphics cards can dedicate one bit to every pixel. This creates *monochrome* graphics, which are illustrated in Figure 11-3. Although this approach requires roughly an eight-fold increase in memory over using character graphics, it removes all limitations on the character set. It supports all typefaces, styles, and sizes, and even Kanji can be displayed as easily as Roman characters.

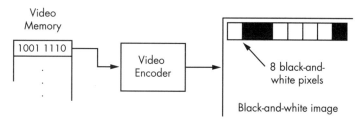

Figure 11-3: Monochrome graphics

If we dedicate an entire byte to each pixel, we have a few options. For single-color displays, the graphics hardware could be designed to produce 256 different intensity (*grayscale*) levels. This would be appropriate for rendering text with *anti-aliasing*, in which shades of gray are used to soften jagged edges.

Alternatively, we could use each pixel's byte to signify one of 256 different colors. In this approach, known as *pseudocolor*, the graphics hardware maintains a 256-entry table of colors, known as a *palette* or *colormap*. Each color in the palette is typically represented by three bytes, one each for the red, green, and blue intensity levels. This approach is illustrated in Figure 11-4. In this example, the first pixel in the displayed image is represented by the value 0x3F, which indexes a 3-byte entry with red, green, and blue intensity levels that correspond to a light blue pixel, with a touch of green.

As in the character graphics case, we can think of pseudocolor as a form of compression, driven by the need to conserve memory. To display an image in pseudocolor, we choose the 256 most important colors and represent each with one byte, neglecting all other colors.

Using even more memory, we can dedicate two or three bytes to each pixel and directly represent the red, green, and blue intensity levels, without the use of a look-up table. With two bytes (*highcolor*), we might, for example, use 5 bits for red, 6 for green, and 5 for blue. This supports over 65 thousand colors in an image, but it is still limited. For example, it only supports $2^5 = 32$ different shades of gray.

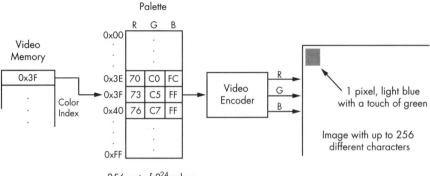

Figure 11-4: Pseudocolor graphics

The three-byte case, with one byte each for red, green, and blue, is illustrated in Figure 11-5. This is referred to as *truecolor*, since it is capable of representing images with near-photographic quality.

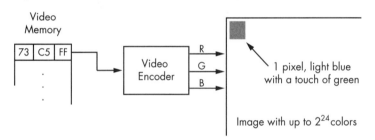

Figure 11-5: Truecolor graphics

How Video Memory Is Mapped to the Display

If the video memory provided by a graphics card is the same size (in pixels) as the display, then the mapping between video memory pixels and display pixels is straightforward: The first pixel of video memory corresponds to the pixel at the top left of the display, and the following pixels are mapped from left to right and top to bottom, the same way we read a page in English. To state this mathematically:

address of pixel at (x, y) = address of video memory + (y*xres + x)*pix_width

where *xres* (the *x* resolution) is the number of pixels in a row, and *pix_width* is the number of bytes in a pixel.

But memory is no longer the critical resource it once was, and it is now common for graphics hardware to provide more video memory than necessary to fill the display. In one approach to using this extra memory, we can think of the available video memory as corresponding to a virtual display. The visible display is too small to show us all the virtual pixels at once, but we can pan the visible display left and right or up and down in order to expose any portion of the virtual display we are interested in. This situation is illustrated in Figure 11-6. If we want to find the memory address of a pixel at position (x, y) in the visible display, we have to consider where the pixel resides in the virtual display. If the visible display is panned *xoffset* pixels to the right and *yoffset* pixels down, then the virtual position of our pixel is $(x+xoffset, y+yoffset)$. If *line_length* is the length of a virtual row, then, applying the earlier formula, we have a memory address of:

$$address\ of\ video\ memory + ((y+yoffset)*line\_length+x+xoffset)*pix\_width$$

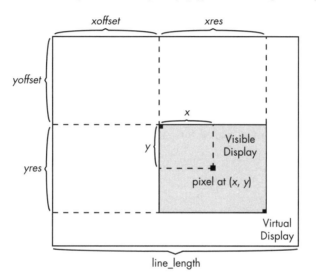

Figure 11-6: Virtual and visible displays

If we have an object that we want to render on the visible display, we can use this formula to determine which bytes to manipulate in video memory. In the remainder of the chapter, we will look at the layers that allow us to effectively manipulate video memory in software.

The Linux Framebuffer Device Driver

Linux provides access to video memory (also known as the *framebuffer*) the same way it provides access to most other devices—via a device file. The framebuffer device file is /dev/fb0, and as with other files, we can access the data in the file using the system calls open, read, write, and close. You can learn more about these system calls from their man pages (e.g., execute man 2 write). Most system calls that access files do so using a small integer called a *file descriptor*. The system call open is an exception; it returns a file descriptor using a path to a file.

Manipulating the Framebuffer with open, read, write, and close

Because of this device file interface, it is easy to exercise the framebuffer with some simple Unix commands. At this point, we recommend you boot the Laddie CD and try these commands yourself. (You could also try these examples on your own system. See Appendix C if you need help setting up your framebuffer.)

Once you've booted the Laddie CD, wait for the framebuffer UI to load, then press ESC to get a login prompt. Log in as root with an empty password. Now execute the following commands:

```
laddie:~# cat /dev/fb0 > /tmp/screen
laddie:~# clear
laddie:~# cat /tmp/screen > /dev/fb0
```

The cat command, as used in the first line, invokes the open, read, and close system calls to make a copy of the framebuffer in a separate file. The second line clears the console display. In the third line, the redirection invokes the open, write, and close system calls to replace the contents of the console display with what was originally there. The result may be confusing, since the cursor position will no longer match the display (you can clean up the display with another clear command). However, this experiment illustrates that, to the cat command, the framebuffer is just another file.

If your graphics adapter has a large amount of video memory, the first cat command may take a while (and produce a large file in /tmp). If the first command (cat /dev/fb0 > /tmp/screen) returns immediately with

```
cat: /dev/fb0: No such file or directory
```

you need to use mknod to create the /dev/fb0 device file. Do so by running:

```
laddie:~# mknod /dev/fb0 c 29 0
```

If the command cat /dev/fb0 > /tmp/screen produces the error

```
cat: /dev/fb0: No such device
```

the framebuffer device driver has not been loaded successfully. Again, see Appendix C if you need help setting up the framebuffer device.

NOTE *For the remainder of this chapter, we will assume that you have a working framebuffer.*

To experiment with the relationship between pixel data and what is displayed on the screen, try any of the following commands:

```
laddie:~# yes | cat > /dev/fb0
laddie:~# while [ 1 ]; do echo 01234567; done | cat > /dev/fb0
laddie:~# cat /dev/urandom > /dev/fb0
```

On successful completion of each command (which may take a while for large framebuffers) you should see the error:

```
cat: write error: No space left on device
```

You see this error because you are attempting to cat an infinite supply of bits into a finite supply of memory. After each experiment, type the command clear to restore the console.

Configuring the Framebuffer with the ioctl Command

In our experiments so far, we have manipulated video memory without any regard to the way pixel data is interpreted. The way that graphics hardware interprets video memory is determined by the framebuffer configuration data, which also includes the physical address of video memory, the screen resolution (virtual and visible), the placement of the visible screen relative to the virtual one, as well as timing and other information that is outside the scope of this chapter. To access the video mode, we need an additional system call, ioctl, which allows us to access or modify parameters for devices.

The ioctl system call takes a file descriptor for a device and an integer representing a request (see the ioctl man page for details). In the case of the framebuffer, the possible ioctl commands are listed in the /usr/include/linux/fb.h header file and include the following:

```
#define FBIOGET_VSCREENINFO    0x4600
#define FBIOPUT_VSCREENINFO    0x4601
#define FBIOGET_FSCREENINFO    0x4602
```

The first two ioctl requests allow us to retrieve or update variable framebuffer parameters, and the third allows us to retrieve fixed framebuffer parameters. The variable parameters are summarized in the following data structure (with some fields omitted), taken from fb.h:

```
struct fb_var_screeninfo {
    __u32 xres;                  /* visible resolution */
    __u32 yres;
    __u32 xres_virtual;          /* virtual resolution */
    __u32 yres_virtual;
    __u32 xoffset;               /* offset from virtual to visible */
    __u32 yoffset;               /* resolution */

    __u32 bits_per_pixel;        /* guess what */
    __u32 grayscale;             /* != 0 Graylevels instead of colors */

    struct fb_bitfield red;      /* bitfield in fb mem if true color, */
    struct fb_bitfield green;    /* else only length is significant */
    struct fb_bitfield blue;
    ...
};
```

For the most part, it should be clear from the identifiers how the fields in this data structure correspond to the notions we discussed in the section "How Video Memory Works" on page 170. The fb_bitfield structs characterize the way pixel bits are interpreted when they are used to specify color intensities directly (as in truecolor mode).

For the Laddie appliance, we had no need to modify the variable framebuffer data. In fact, the VESA framebuffer driver that we used does not easily support modification after system startup. If you are using a non-VESA framebuffer and you need to modify its configuration at run time, consult the documentation for the fbset utility.

The fixed framebuffer configuration parameters are provided by the following data structure (with some fields omitted), also in fb.h:

```
struct fb_fix_screeninfo {
    char id[16];                /* identification string eg "TT Builtin" */
    unsigned long smem_start;   /* Start of frame buffer mem */
                                /* (physical address) */
    __u32 smem_len;             /* Length of frame buffer mem */
    __u32 type;                 /* see FB_TYPE_*        */
    __u32 visual;               /* see FB_VISUAL_*      */
    __u32 line_length;          /* length of a line in bytes    */
    ...
};
```

The main fields we will use here are visual, which specifies how pixels are interpreted (e.g., monochromatic, pseudocolor, or truecolor), and line_length, which we need when computing the mapping between video memory and the display.

Finally, the following ioctl requests allow us to retrieve or update the palette (colormap) for video modes that use one.

```
#define FBIOGETCMAP       0x4604
#define FBIOPUTCMAP       0x4605
```

We will show an example of how to update colormaps in the next section.

At this point, we can determine the way pixel data is interpreted, so we can also update framebuffer memory in a meaningful way. We could use the write system call, just as the cat utility does, but making system calls with every framebuffer update is too expensive. A better approach is provided by a different system call: mmap. The mmap system call takes the file descriptor for our framebuffer, maps the framebuffer memory into the virtual address space of our process, and returns a pointer to the beginning of that memory. With this mapping in place, updating the framebuffer becomes as simple as writing to memory.

In summary, to efficiently manipulate the framebuffer, we open the appropriate device file, use ioctl commands to establish the graphics hardware configuration, use mmap to provide simple access to pixel data, and write the appropriate pixel data for our application.

A Simple Graphics Program for the Framebuffer

In the remainder of this section, we'll illustrate the Linux framebuffer interface by writing a simple graphics program. Our program, hazy_moon, will display a disk, 240 pixels in diameter, that fades from bright cyan at the top to a hazy red at the bottom. The picture we have in mind, rendered in grayscale, is shown in Figure 11-7. Our program will illustrate the use of a colormap and will provide a quick, visual indication of whether or not we have configured the framebuffer correctly.

Figure 11-7: A hazy moon

The complete source for this program is on the Laddie CD in the directory /Code/src/examples/hazy_moon. Before working through the rest of this section, we recommend building and running the program. After booting the CD and logging in, change to the program's directory, type **make**, and then type **./hazy_moon**. You should see the disk in the middle and a thin cyan border around the visible screen. If you don't see all of the border lines, try adjusting the width and height of the image on your monitor. To return to the original virtual terminal, use CTRL-ALT-F1. If the dimensions of the graphics virtual terminal are not what you expected, try the command deallocvt at the bash prompt to deallocate resources for the unused terminals, and then run the test program again.

NOTE   *When using the Laddie CD, you can view source files using vim or less. Use the commands* man vim *or* vimtutor *if you're not familiar with the vim editor.*

Now we'll discuss the details of the hazy_moon program. The first detail requires a little working knowledge of virtual terminals.

A Virtual Terminal for Graphics

One of the advantages and challenges of Linux is that it uses framebuffers for text consoles. This use of framebuffers is an advantage because it supports colored text and a wide range of fonts and character sets. However, using framebuffers in this way also presents a challenge, because while developing a framebuffer application, it's easy to trip over Linux's machinery for managing consoles.

For example, a program that prints a one-line message to the console can modify the position of the visible display relative to the virtual display; the result is that a displayed graphic is misplaced by the width of that line. Or, if the graphics hardware is configured to use a palette, and if a program modifies the colors used to display text in the console, printed messages may become hard to read or even invisible.

For these reasons, it's best to use a separate virtual terminal for graphical displays. We accomplish this in the hazy_moon program with the following lines.

```
#include <fcntl.h>
#include <linux/vt.h>

console_fd = open("/dev/tty", O_RDWR);
ioctl(console_fd, VT_ACTIVATE, 7);
ioctl(console_fd, VT_WAITACTIVE, 7);
```

Note that we're using the familiar open and ioctl system calls, though in this case, it's not with the framebuffer. The first call (console_fd = open("/dev/tty", O_RDWR);) opens the console device; the second (ioctl(console_fd, VT_ACTIVATE, 7);) requests a switch to virtual terminal 7; and the third (ioctl(console_fd, VT_WAITACTIVE, 7);) waits until the switch is complete. (We chose virtual terminal 7 because our system uses terminals 1 through 6 for consoles.)

open

Now we use the open system call on the framebuffer device file, specifying the device file as read/write.

```
fb_fd = open("/dev/fb0", O_RDWR);
```

The function open returns −1 on error; otherwise, it returns an integer file descriptor that we will use in making subsequent system calls for this device.

NOTE   *The* open *system call returns an error value that should be handled. We won't discuss error handling here, but you can see how we handled errors by looking at the full source in the hazy_moon.c file.*

ioctl

Using the framebuffer's file descriptor, we can make the ioctl calls to retrieve the fixed and variable configuration data for a framebuffer.

```
#include <linux/fb.h>

struct fb_fix_screeninfo fixed_info;
struct fb_var_screeninfo var_info;

ioctl(fb_fd, FBIOGET_FSCREENINFO, &fixed_info);
ioctl(fb_fd, FBIOGET_VSCREENINFO, &var_info);
```

Before updating the display, hazy_moon calls two helper routines to display the fixed and variable data. This information can be useful when you're trying to debug—or simply understand—a framebuffer application.

```
display_fb_fixed_info(&fixed_info);
display_fb_var_info(&var_info);
```

If you ran the program earlier, you saw this output after returning to the virtual terminal from which you launched the program. The output would have shown, in particular, that our display screen is 640 by 480, that we have 8 bits per pixel, and that our visual type is pseudocolor.

The following code first ❶ creates a new colormap using a helper function new_fb_cmap. This function is defined in the accompanying file colormap.c. The program then ❷ copies the current values from the framebuffer using an ioctl call and ❸ updates the entries to provide a gradient from cyan to dark red. Finally, the program ❹ updates the framebuffer with the new colormap using a second ioctl call.

```
#include "colormap.h"        /* for new_fb_cmap() */

struct fb_cmap *new_cmap;
int entry;

❶ new_cmap = new_fb_cmap(256);              /* Create a new, empty colormap */
                                            /* with 256 entries. */
❷ ioctl(fb_fd, FBIOGETCMAP, new_cmap);      /* Copy the current colormap. */

  /* Fill in the new colormap with a gradient. */
  /* We'll leave the first 16 colors intact for the linux console. */
  if(new_cmap->len >= 256){
❸     for(entry=16; entry < 256; entry++){
          /* Fade from bright cyan to dark red. Color values are 16 bit. */
          new_cmap->red[entry]   = 64*256;
          new_cmap->green[entry] = entry * 256 +255;
          new_cmap->blue[entry]  = entry * 256 +255;
      }
  }

❹ ioctl(fb_handle, FBIOPUTCMAP, new_cmap);
```

mmap

We now use the mmap() system call to map the framebuffer into our program's address space.

```
#include <sys/mman.h>          /* For mmap. */

unsigned char *frame;

frame = mmap(0, fixed_info.smem_len, PROT_READ|PROT_WRITE, MAP_SHARED, fb_fd, 0);
```

The first argument to mmap is 0, indicating that mmap will choose where the framebuffer is mapped. The value fixed_info.smem_len is the length of the framebuffer. We specify that the framebuffer can be read or written with PROT_READ|PROT_WRITE, and we use MAP_SHARED to indicate that changes to this memory region will propagate to the actual framebuffer. The file descriptor for the opened framebuffer device is fb_fd, and we specify an offset of 0, since we want to map the entire framebuffer.

If this call succeeds (again, see the source on the CD for error handling), frame will point to the start of framebuffer memory.

Writing Pixel Data

Now that we have a colormap and a way to place pixels on the screen, we can write a simple graphics program. The following code will create the promised 240-by-240–pixel hazy moon, as well as the single-pixel border around the perimeter of the display.

```
/* Compute offset of visible frame */
❶ visible_frame = frame + var_info.yoffset*fixed_info.line_length + var_info.xoffset;

/* Paint the top and bottom borders of the visible display. */
for(col=0; col<var_info.xres; col++){
  visible_frame[col] = 255;
❷  visible_frame[(var_info.yres-1)*fixed_info.line_length + col] = 255;
}

/* Paint the left and right borders of the visible display. */
for(row=0; row<var_info.yres; row++){
❷  visible_frame[row*fixed_info.line_length] = 255;
❷  visible_frame[row*fixed_info.line_length + var_info.xres - 1] = 255;
}

/* Compute the offset for a 240x240 square in the middle of the screen. */
❷ img_off = ((var_info.yres-240)*fixed_info.line_length + (var_info.xres-240))/2;

/* Paint a 240x240 disk in the center of the visible screen. */
for(row = 0; row < 240; row++){
  for(col = 0; col < 240; col++){
    /* Only display points that lie within a circle. */
    if((row-120)*(row-120) + (col-120)*(col-120) <= 120*120){
❷      visible_frame[img_off + row*fixed_info.line_length + col] = 255 - row;
    }
  }
}
```

As we illustrated in Figure 11-6, the visible display might be a subset of the available framebuffer memory. We first find the beginning of displayed memory, ❶ visible_frame, using the xoffset, yoffset, and line_length values from the framebuffer device's variable information. In the rest of this code, we compute memory offsets relative to visible_frame, and therefore have no further need for xoffset or yoffset. However, we have to use ❷ line_length consistently whenever we compute an offset for a number of rows.

Cleaning Up

At this point, we can clean up and exit the program.

```
munmap(frame, fixed_info.smem_len);
free_fb_cmap(new_cmap);
```

This program is meant to be a simple demonstration; to build a useful framebuffer interface would require a good deal more work. For example, we haven't discussed displaying text or responding to keyboard input, and we haven't written code to recover the screen after blanking out or to get rid of the cursor in the upper-left corner. We could write code to address these problems, but in fact, they have already been solved by graphics libraries that work on top of the framebuffer interface. In the next section, we'll consider two choices for graphics libraries and work through an example with one of them, the Simple DirectMedia Library. If you would still like to spend more time mastering the framebuffer interface, see the header file /usr/src/linux/include/linux/fb.h and the documentation files in the directory /usr/src/linux/Documentation/fb.

Graphics Libraries

Using the Linux framebuffer interface, we have reduced the problem of manipulating pixels on the display to the problem of writing bytes to memory. But think of some of the ways in which we would like to manipulate display pixels: drawing lines of a specified thickness, drawing windows with rounded edges and a three-dimensional look, transferring images, or drawing text with a given font and size. These are nontrivial problems; that's why we need a graphics library. With an appropriate graphics library, we can write programs that manipulate lines, windows, images, and text, and let the underlying library decide what to do with the pixels.

The most common library for manipulating graphics objects in Linux is Xlib. Xlib is actually more than a graphics library; it is the interface by which clients access an X Window display server. In particular, it also manages user input events. Because of its popularity, building a Linux appliance on top of X can be a good choice. Xlib is cumbersome to program directly, but with an X system, a UI developer can choose among several competing GUI toolkits (for example, Qt, which is used by the KDE desktop, or GTK+, which is used by the Gnome desktop). Alternatively, UI developers can include an X-based web browser on the appliance and provide the UI as a set of web pages. In any of these cases, UI development for the appliance would be little different from UI development on a Linux desktop.

On the other hand, the X Window system is complex and provides features that will often not be needed on an appliance. Because X is network-oriented, it involves an additional network layer between Xlib and the Xserver. X incorporates support for multiscreen displays and multiple clients, and it also provides for window management that is not controlled by the client application. These are nice features for a distributed networking environment, but their complexity makes X an expensive option for appliances with tight memory and storage budgets. If you have resource constraints but would still like to use X, you may want to investigate TinyX, described at http://XFree86.org as "a family of X servers designed to be particularly small." For more information on Xlib, see the *Xlib Programming Manual* by Adrian Nye, (O'Reilly, 1994). There are also several articles about X on Wikipedia, such as http://en.wikipedia.org/wiki/Xlib.

Another option for a graphics library is the *Simple DirectMedia Layer (SDL)*, a multimedia library originally designed for developing and porting games. Like Xlib, SDL is cross-platform and manages user input as well as graphics. Unlike Xlib, SDL provides only minimal support for managing windows. It has a small footprint; the libraries for SDL (including SDL_ttf for TrueType fonts) take up about 330KB, stripped.

Because of its simplicity (we didn't need windowing support), we chose SDL as the graphics library for the Laddie appliance, and we will demonstrate this library with a simple example in the next section. For more details on SDL, especially on multimedia support, see *Programming Linux Games* by John R. Hall, (No Starch Press, 2001). The SDL website (http://www.libsdl.org) also provides good documentation on the SDL API. We used the SDL_ttf library as a wrapper for TrueType fonts, which in turn required the FreeType package from http://www.freetype.org. See http://www.libsdl.org/projects/SDL_ttf for links to documentation.

"Hello, world!" with SDL

To introduce SDL, let's work through a simple program to display *Hello, world!*, monitor the keyboard, and exit gracefully when the spacebar is pressed (see Figure 11-8).

This program is on the Laddie CD; before looking at the details, we recommend building and running the program. Boot the Laddie CD and, after the framebuffer UI loads, exit by pressing ESC.

Figure 11-8: "Hello, world!" with SDL

NOTE   *It's important that the framebuffer isn't running, because it would interfere with our current example. Incidentally, if the framebuffer UI didn't start automatically when you booted the CD, you may have problems with your framebuffer. In this case, see Appendix C for help. The framebuffer UI display is shown in Figure 11-10.*

Log in as root with an empty password, change to the sdl_hello directory, then build and run the program.

```
laddie:~# cd /Code/src/examples/sdl_hello
laddie:~# make
laddie:~# ./sdl_hello
```

You should see the display shown in Figure 11-8. When you press the spacebar, the display will disappear and you will be back at the command prompt. In the remainder of this section we'll show how we implemented the sdl_hello program.

Our program uses a single main function and includes five steps: initialize the libraries, initialize the framebuffer, create a *surface* (SDL's term for a rectangular area of pixels), display the surface, and handle events. As in our earlier example, we will not show error handling here. Please see the source for the sdl_hello program on the CD in the /Code/src/examples/sdl_hello directory for example error-handling code.

Initialize the Libraries

The following lines from our example program initialize the SDL and SDL_ttf libraries.

```
#include "SDL.h"
#include "SDL_ttf.h"

❶ SDL_Init(SDL_INIT_VIDEO);
❷ TTF_Init();

❸ atexit(SDL_Quit);
  atexit(TTF_Quit);
```

SDL supports several subsystems, including TIMER, AUDIO, VIDEO, CDROM, and JOYSTICK, and we ❶ select these when calling SDL_Init(). (We will only use the VIDEO subsystem in this chapter.) In order to display text, we ❷ initialize SDL's support for TrueType fonts. The calls to ❸ atexit() provide functions (SDL_Quit and TTF_Quit) to be invoked at program exit; they ensure that SDL quits cleanly at the end of the program.

Initialize the Framebuffer

To configure the framebuffer's resolution and bits per pixel, we use the function SDL_SetVideoMode.

```
SDL_Surface* Screen;

❶ Screen = SDL_SetVideoMode(640, 480, 8, 0);
❷ SDL_ShowCursor(SDL_DISABLE);
```

When a desired video mode is unavailable, SDL will emulate it; however, we will keep things simple and choose a mode that works natively with most graphics adapters: 640 by 480, with 8 bits per pixel. The final argument to SDL_SetVideoMode provides flags for features such as whether to use video memory or system memory, whether to support double buffering, and whether to support OpenGL. For our purposes, the defaults are fine. The return value, ❶ Screen, has type SDL_Surface. These surfaces represent rectangular collections of pixels and are characterized by height, width, pixel format, scanline length, a clipping rectangle, and, of course, the actual pixel data. The Screen surface is special, since it corresponds directly to the displayed memory. But surfaces can also represent any graphical object, such as an image or a piece of text. For the examples in this chapter, we will create graphical objects from bitmaps or by rendering text, but it is also possible to create an empty surface and then manipulate its pixel data directly.

After setting the video mode, we ❷ call the function SDL_ShowCursor to hide the cursor, since we are not using a mouse for input.

Create a Surface

To create a text object, we need to open a font and then render the text to create a surface.

```
    TTF_Font    *helloFont;
    SDL_Surface *helloSurface;
❶   SDL_Color    helloColor = {128,128,255,0}; /* light blue */

❷   helloFont = TTF_OpenFont("/usr/local/share/fonts/bitstream/VeraBI.ttf", 42);
❸   helloSurface = TTF_RenderText_Solid(helloFont, "Hello, world!", helloColor);
```

The ❷ TTF_OpenFont() function requires a pathname to a TrueType font file and a font size. The ❸ TTF_RenderText_Solid() function uses a font, a string of text, and a color to create a surface. An ❶ SDL color consists of four 16-bit values for red, green, blue, and an alpha channel. The alpha channel value is used for blending translucent surfaces and is not practical when using pseudo-color graphics; we won't consider it further in this chapter.

Since fonts are subject to copyright, you will need to put some thought into the fonts you choose for your application. For the Laddie CD, we chose the liberally licensed Bitstream Vera fonts, associated with the GNOME foundation (available from http://www.gnome.org/fonts). These include monospace and proportionally spaced fonts, serif and sans-serif, normal, italicized, bold, and bold-italicized. These may already be installed on your system in /usr/X11R6/lib/X11/fonts/truetype.

Display the Surface

Displaying rendered text is no different than displaying any other object in SDL: We just blit (transfer) the surface onto the screen (i.e., the Screen surface).

```
SDL_Rect helloRect  = {150,100,0,0};    /* {x, y, width, height} */

❶ SDL_BlitSurface(helloSurface, NULL, Screen, &helloRect);
❷ SDL_UpdateRects(Screen, 1, &helloRect);
```

The ❶ SDL_BlitSurface function takes a source surface, a rectangle specifying a subset of this surface (NULL for the entire surface), a destination surface, and a rectangle whose *x* and *y* values indicate the position where the source is to be placed. The SDL_BlitSurface function fills out the width and height values for the destination rectangle based on the portion of the destination that was updated. We use this rectangle to update the Screen surface with ❷ the SDL_UpdateRects function.

Handle Events

At this point, we have displayed the *Hello, world!* message. Now we need to monitor the keyboard and exit when the spacebar is pressed.

```
    enableQuit = 0;
    while(!enableQuit){
❶      SDL_WaitEvent(&event);
        switch(event.type){
        case SDL_KEYDOWN:
❷          switch(event.key.keysym.sym){
❸          case SDLK_SPACE:
              enableQuit = 1;
              break;
          }
          break;
        }
    }
```

This code could be simplified for the "Hello, world!" application, but in this form it represents a general approach to event handling with SDL. The ❶ SDL_WaitEvent function suspends the main thread until an event occurs. The event variable has a union type corresponding to more than a dozen SDL events, including keyboard, mouse, and user-defined events. SDL also distinguishes keypresses from key releases. In the case of a keyboard event, we can check the particular key using ❷ the event.key.keysym.sym field, which can take on values such as ❸ SDLK_SPACE, SDL_TAB, SDLK_0, SDLK_a, and so on.

Graphical UI Toolkits

While the SDL API is easier to use than the framebuffer interface, it is not, in itself, a convenient library for developing a GUI. SDL supports event handling and graphics, but the two are only loosely coupled. When building a GUI, we use objects for which the display and the input mechanism are inherently connected. Examples include scroll bars, drop-down menus, and text-entry forms. GUI toolkits support GUI development by providing a collection of these objects (*widgets*). Figure 11-9 illustrates the relationships between a widget, a user, and the underlying application.

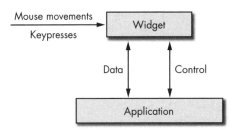

Figure 11-9: A typical, full-featured widget

User input events (e.g., mouse movements or keypresses), update the widget and control the underlying application by initiating callbacks. The application can control the widget or exchange data with it by calling the widget's functions.

In addition to providing widgets, a GUI toolkit also provides a framework for managing them. The framework is typically built on top of a window manager. It routes events, determines which widget has focus, and ensures that overlapping widgets are displayed appropriately.

The two most popular GUI toolkits for Linux are GTK+ (http:// www.gtk.org) and Qt (http://www.trolltech.com); if you choose one of these, your decision will probably come down to cost and licensing. GTK+ is released under the more liberal LGPL license, allowing you to link your proprietary software to GTK+ libraries. Qt may be licensed under the GPL, but this requires that your GUI application also be released under the GPL. To build a proprietary application on top of Qt, you will need to pay Trolltech for the commercial license.

If your application will be licensed under GPL or if money is not an object, there are other differences to consider. GTK+ is written in C, though it does have many object-oriented features. Qt is written in C++. Both have a broad user base: GTK+ is the basis for the Gnome desktop, and Qt is the basis for the KDE desktop.

In case you are not using X on your appliance, Qt also has support for the Linux framebuffer. Some work has been done on a framebuffer back end for GTK+ using DirectFB, which is also released under the LGPL. See http://www.directfb.org/wiki/index.php/Projects:GTK_on_DirectFB for more information.

The Fast Light Toolkit (FLTK; http://www.fltk.org) is a promising choice for a free GUI toolkit if you would like a smaller footprint than GTK+ but are still willing to adopt X. FLTK is designed for tight, statically linked applications, and its modified LGPL license allows static linking in proprietary applications. It is written in C++ and supports Windows in addition to Linux.

We won't discuss the popular GUI toolkits any further here; they are documented well elsewhere.[1] In fact, for the Laddie appliance, we found that these toolkits provided a good deal of functionality that we didn't need, and, because of their orientation toward the mouse and keyboard, they didn't cleanly match our approach of using a simple, handheld remote control. In the remainder of this section, we will describe STBmenu, a thin layer built on SDL that we developed with set-top box interfaces in mind.

Building Simple UIs with STBmenu

Besides having a framework that functioned naturally with remotes, we saw two other advantages of writing our own GUI toolkit. We thought it would be useful for illustrating how GUI toolkits work (at about 1,300 lines including comments, it doesn't take long to read), and, in keeping with the philosophy of this book, we wanted to see how clean a separation we could make between the UI and the underlying application.

At this point, we recommend taking a quick tour of the Laddie framebuffer UI in order to see the kind of GUI STBmenu can support. As we noted in the section "'Hello, world!' with SDL" on page 182, when you boot the Laddie CD, it will attempt to launch the Laddie framebuffer UI automatically. (If it doesn't, see Appendix C for help on setting up your framebuffer.) If you are already running the CD and have a command prompt, start the framebuffer UI with the `fbmenuctl start` command. If the UI is already running, but isn't visible, use CTRL-ALT-F7 to switch to the appropriate virtual terminal.

The Laddie framebuffer UI consists of two pages, as illustrated in Figure 11-10. We will discuss remote control in the next chapter; for now, use the arrow keys to navigate the UI and the ENTER key to activate a selection. Use the Setup and Status buttons to switch between pages. As you make changes, use CTRL-ALT-F1 to switch to a command prompt and check the results with the cli utility described in Chapter 9. Make changes using the cli utility, and confirm these by returning to the framebuffer UI with CTRL-ALT-F7. (Alternatively, you could use another machine on the network to check results using the web interface described in Chapter 8.)

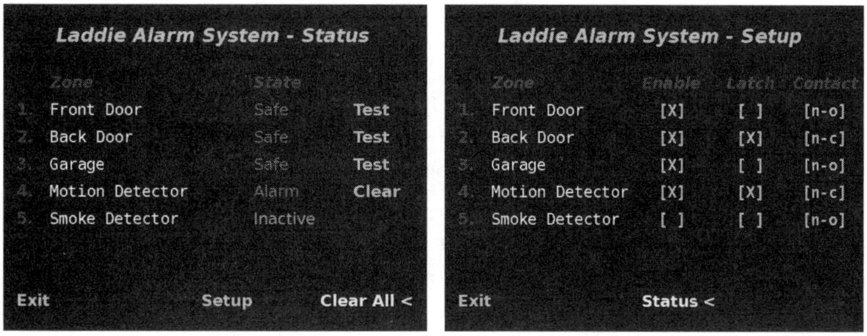

Figure 11-10: The Laddie framebuffer UI

---

[1] For example, *Beginning Linux Programming*, 3rd ed., by Richard Stones, Neil Matthew, and Alan Cox (Wrox, 2004) includes one chapter each on GTK+ and Qt.

The STBmenu Framework

Having experimented a bit with the Laddie framebuffer UI, you will have noticed some differences between it and a fully featured GUI. The Laddie framebuffer UI does not have windows that can be moved around the screen; it consists, instead, of a series of full-screen pages. There is no free-floating cursor that can select any point on the screen; instead, it is the two-dimensional geometry of the input widgets that determines how the arrow keys shift focus. And finally, the input options for widgets are minimal: There is only one, and it corresponds with pressing ENTER.

NOTE   *When experimenting with DVD interfaces, we've been surprised that pressing arrow keys to get to the icon you want can be like solving a puzzle. One attribute of the STBmenu framework is that each of the arrow keys is guaranteed to traverse all input widgets. It may seem like a trivial point, but when you're trying to disable a home alarm that is unnecessarily waking up the neighbors, you don't want to be tripped up by a challenging UI.*

The STBmenu Widgets

The Status page, shown on the left of Figure 11-10, contains 25 visible widgets. Eight of these are static displays (the title, the column headings, and the zone numbers); five present variable text (the zone descriptions); five display the state of the alarm; and the remaining seven are buttons. (The background screen is not a widget.) Figure 11-11 illustrates the relationships between an STBmenu widget, a user, and the underlying application.

Two Events

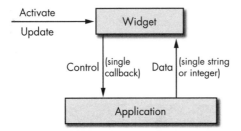

Figure 11-11: An STBmenu widget

Comparing the STBmenu widget to the full-featured widget of Figure 11-9, we notice several simplifications. The STBmenu widget responds to only two kinds of events: Activate, and Update. The *Activate* event invokes the widget's single callback, and the *Update* event tells the widget to redraw itself, since the data it represents may have changed. With full-featured widgets, the application can call functions to configure the widget (e.g., change its size or position) and retrieve its input data (e.g., its entered text or its scrollbar position). However, STBmenu widgets are fully configured when they are constructed, and data is only passed to the application when the Activate callback is invoked. With full-featured widgets, the application can call functions to change the widget's output data (e.g., status text or meter position), but STBmenu widgets use static pointers into application data structures to retrieve the data they display. Finally, the type of data displayed by STBmenu widgets is limited to integers and strings.

Because there are no functions for configuring STBmenu widgets or setting their displayed data, the developers of the underlying application don't have to be familiar with the toolkit. All they are required to do is expose the displayed application data and provide appropriate callbacks for user input.

We summarize the STBmenu API below. Class constructors are in bold, and methods are in italics.

> **Menu(nPages, width, height, bpp);**
>> *AttachPage(n, page);*
>> *SetCursor(page,row,col);*
>> *DisplayCurrentPage();*
>> *CursorLeft();*
>> *CursorRight();*
>> *CursorUp();*
>> *CursorDown();*
>> *Activate();*
>> *Update();*
>
> **Page(nRows, nCols, background);**
>> *AttachWidget(row, col, xPos, yPos, widget);*
>
> **Font(fontPath, fontSize);**
>
> **Surface(width, height, color);**
>
> **Surface(font, color, text);**
>
> **Surface(imagePath);**
>
> **SurfaceArray(n, &surface,...);**
>
> **Button(nfSurface, fSurface);**
>
> **ButtonArray(n, &button,...);**

Here are the STBmenu Widgets:

WIcon(font, color, text) and WIcon(imagePath)
   Display a static image created from a constant text string or an image file.

WText(font, color, text)
   Displays a variable text string.

WIconArray(surfaceArray, trackedIndex)
   Displays one of an array of static images, depending on an application index variable.

WButton(button, callback, data)
   Displays a button consisting of one static image when highlighted, and another when not highlighted. When activated, invokes an application callback with specified data.

WButtonArray(buttonArray, trackedIndex, callback, data)

> Displays one of an array of buttons, depending on an application index variable. When activated, invokes an application callback with specified data.

"Hello, world!" with STBmenu

In the remainder of this section, we will demonstrate the STBmenu toolkit by working through a simple example. This example is on the Laddie CD in the directory /Code/src/examples/stb_hello. At this point, we recommend you return to the Laddie CD and exit the Laddie framebuffer UI, if it's still running (remember to switch between consoles with CTRL-ALT-F1 or CTRL-ALT-F7, and use the arrow keys and ENTER to navigate the framebuffer menu). Then change to the stb_hello directory, make and run the example using the following commands.

```
laddie:~# cd /Code/src/examples/stb_hello
laddie:~# make
laddie:~# ./stb_hello
```

You should see the display illustrated in Figure 11-12.

Figure 11-12: "Hello, world!" with STBmenu

This example implements two button widgets. You can select the buttons by pressing the arrow keys on your keyboard, and you can activate them with the ENTER key. When you activate the Hello button, it prints *Hello, world!* to the standard output, which you can verify after closing the UI by activating the Exit button.

In the remainder of this section, we will work through the implementation of the stb_hello example.

Building a UI with STBmenu involves three steps:

1. Define any data structures and callbacks required for monitoring and controlling the application.

2. Build the UI with widgets that point to these data structures and callbacks.

3. Handle events using the STBmenu framework's methods.

We'll demonstrate these steps for the two-button example.

Define Data Structures and Callbacks

In this simple example, there is no data to monitor. Control consists of printing a message or exiting the program, and it requires a single piece of data and two callbacks.

```
int enableQuit = 0;

❶ static void Hello(InputClass* const widget)
   {
     printf("Hello, world!\n");
   }

❷ static void QuitApplication(InputClass* const widget)
   {
❸   enableQuit = 1;
   }
```

The ❶ Hello() callback (invoked by the Hello button) will print a message to the console. The ❷ QuitApplication() callback (invoked by the Exit button) will set ❸ the enableQuit variable to 1. All widget callbacks take a pointer to the widget that invoked them as an argument. All such widgets will have the STBmenu type InputClass and may provide additional data useful to the callback; however, we don't use that capability here.

Build the UI

The first step in building a UI is to declare a menu object.

```
#include "STBmenu.h"

Menu* menu = new Menu(1, 640, 480, 8);
```

This has to be done before any other UI objects are declared, since it initializes the underlying SDL video context. We specify the number of pages (1), the width (640) and height (480) of the UI's screen (in pixels), and the number of bits per pixel (8).

Next, we declare and attach the single page for the menu object.

```
#define BLACK 0x000000

Surface background(640,480,BLACK);
Page page(2, 1, background);
menu->AttachPage(0, page);
```

For a real UI, we would want a more interesting background, but for a quick example, we specify a black, 640-by-480–pixel surface. Then we declare the page, providing the number of rows (2), number of columns (1), and background. We attach the page to the menu object using AttachPage(), specifying a page number.

We can now specify the button widgets. Here is the code for the Test button.

```
#define CYAN      0x00FFFF
#define YELLOW    0xFFFF00

❶ Font font("/usr/local/share/fonts/bitstream/VeraBI.ttf",42);
❷ Surface nfHello(font,CYAN,  "Hello");
❸ Surface fHello (font,YELLOW,"Hello <");
❹ Button helloButton(nfHello,fHello);
❺ WButton wHello(helloButton,Hello,NULL);
```

We declare a TrueType font by ❶ specifying a pathname and a font size. We use that font to construct two surfaces, ❷ one with cyan text for the button when it isn't selected (i.e., doesn't have focus), and ❸ one with yellow text and a < symbol for the button when it is selected. We ❹ construct a button from the two surfaces, specifying the surface without focus first. Finally, we ❺ construct a button widget, specifying the button, the callback, and any data that callback might require (NULL, in this case).

After constructing the button widget, we attach it to the page.

```
page.AttachWidget(0, 0, 250, 200, wHello);
```

Recall that we declared this page to have two rows and one column. When attaching the widgets, we specify their row (0) and column (0) within the page, as well as their absolute x (250) and y (200) pixel positions. The row and column will determine how the Up, Down, Left, and Right cursor inputs will select the various button widgets.

The Exit button is constructed and attached analogously to the Hello widget. You can see the example code on the CD in /Code/src/examples/ stb_hello.

With the menu, pages, and widgets constructed, we can now display the menu.

```
❶ menu->SetCursor(0, 0, 0);
❷ menu->DisplayCurrentPage();
```

Here, the ❶ SetCursor() method specifies a page, row, and column for the initially highlighted widget. In the current case, this is the Hello button. The ❷ DisplayCurrentPage() method produces the screen shown in Figure 11-12.

Handle Events

The rest of our program includes a simple event loop.

```
enableQuit = 0;
while(!enableQuit){
  SDL_WaitEvent(&event);
  switch(event.type){
```

```
      case SDL_KEYDOWN:
        switch(event.key.keysym.sym){
          case SDLK_LEFT:
❶          menu->CursorLeft();
            break;
          case SDLK_RIGHT:
            menu->CursorRight();
            break;
          case SDLK_UP:
            menu->CursorUp();
            break;
          case SDLK_DOWN:
            menu->CursorDown();
            break;
          case SDLK_RETURN:
❷          menu->Activate();
            break;
        }
        break;
    }
❸   menu->Update();
  }
```

When arrow key events are received, the menu's four navigation methods
(❶ CursorLeft(), CursorRight(), etc.) are used to update the highlighted button.
The ENTER key invokes ❷ the Activate() method, which invokes the callback
for the currently highlighted button. We'll learn in the next chapter how to
use an infrared remote control in place of the keyboard, but this segment of
code won't have to change, since we will use the IR interface to produce SDL
keyboard events.

Each time an event occurs, we use ❸ the Update() method to redraw any
widgets that have changed.

The Laddie Framebuffer UI

As we saw in the previous section, an application that uses STBmenu has two
obligations: provide pointers to data to be displayed, and provide callbacks
for UI inputs. Figure 11-13 illustrates how the Laddie framebuffer UI meets
these two obligations.

On the user side, keyboard or remote control events select a widget and
then invoke that widget's Activate method. This action invokes a callback in
the application interface, which controls the alarm daemon via the RTA/
PostgreSQL protocol. On the application side, logmuxd relays events indicating that the Laddie alarm daemon's status has changed. Responding to
these events, the UpdateZoneData code uses the RTA/PostgreSQL protocol
to update a local copy of the alarm daemon's Zone data and invoke the
menu's Update method. This action prompts the menu's widgets to redraw
themselves, based on the new Zone data.

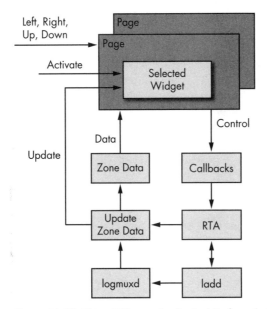

Figure 11-13: Using STBmenu for the Laddie framebuffer UI

NOTE   *If you're reading this book's chapters out of order, please refer to Chapter 3 for a description of the RTA/PostrgeSQL protocol, Chapter 5 to learn about the alarm daemon ladd, and Chapter 6 for an introduction to logmuxd.*

In the "Hello, world!" example, we saw how to build widgets with callbacks. Now, using the Laddie framebuffer UI as an example, we'll demonstrate how to build widgets that display application data.

We start by providing data structures that capture the state of the Laddie alarm daemon.

```
typedef enum{INACTIVE, SAFE, ALARM} AlarmState;

typedef struct
{
  char name[17];      // the alarm name with null-termination
  AlarmState state;   // 0=INACTIVE, 1=SAFE, or 2=ALARM
  int  alarm;         // ==1 if in alarm
  int  enable;        // ==1 if enabled
  int  latch;         // ==1 if the alarm should latch
  int  contact;       // ==1 if alarm on low to high (normally closed)
❶ } LaddZone;

extern LaddZone laddZones[5];
❷ extern int laddAlarm; // Indicates at least one LADD zone is in alarm
```

The fields in ❶ the LaddZone data structure correspond directly to the fields that are displayed on the two menu pages. The ❷ laddAlarm variable is nonzero when at least one zone is in alarm, and it is used to enable the Clear All button.

Recall from Chapter 6 that the event handler logmuxd can be configured to route events through pipes. We configure logmuxd (using the files Filters.sql and FileDest.sql in the directory /opt/laddie/logmuxd) to route all Laddie Alarm events to the pipe /opt/laddie/fbmenu/laddevents. The framebuffer UI's main thread uses a select() system call to wait on messages received via this pipe, then uses the alarm daemon's RTA interface to update the array of LaddZone structures.

For our UI, we will provide several columns of widgets to display the laddZones alarm data. Let's just consider the State column from the Status page. As we saw in Figure 11-10, these widgets display an *Inactive*, *Safe*, or *Alarm* indication, depending on the state of each zone. We use a WIconArray widget, as demonstrated in the following code, to display the alarm states.

```
❶ Surface stateInactive(stateFont,INACTIVE_COLOR,"Inactive");
   Surface stateSafe    (stateFont,SAFE_COLOR,    "Safe");
   Surface stateAlarm   (stateFont,ALARM_COLOR,   "Alarm");

❷ SurfaceArray alarmState(3, &stateInactive,&stateSafe,&stateAlarm);

❸ WIconArray wAlarmState1(alarmState,(int*)&laddZones[0].state);
   WIconArray wAlarmState2(alarmState,(int*)&laddZones[1].state);
   WIconArray wAlarmState3(alarmState,(int*)&laddZones[2].state);
   WIconArray wAlarmState4(alarmState,(int*)&laddZones[3].state);
   WIconArray wAlarmState5(alarmState,(int*)&laddZones[4].state);
```

Here we ❶ declare three surfaces, corresponding to the three alarm states, with appropriate colors. We form ❷ a SurfaceArray from these surfaces and use it to build the alarm state widgets. In declaring ❸ a WIconArray widget, we provide a pointer to an integer value in the application interface's local data structures. Note that the order of the alarmState surfaces corresponds to the possible values for laddZones[N].state.

To complete this UI, we have to define additional widgets to display the remaining data in the laddZones array and, where appropriate, to update the Laddie alarm daemon with callbacks. As in the "Hello, world!" example, we also have to attach the widgets to pages and the pages to the main menu. One item we haven't discussed yet is how to switch between pages. Fortunately, this is straightforward. The STBmenu framework provides a SetCursor function for selecting a page and cursor position. Therefore, we switch pages by providing button widgets on each page with callbacks to set the cursor to the opposite page.

The event handler for the Laddie framebuffer UI is a little different than that of the stb_hello example. Instead of waiting on SDL events, it uses a select system call to wait on Laddie alarm daemon events from logmuxd. It uses a time-out of 100 milliseconds, and when it completes or times out, it uses the function SDL_PollEvent to check for keypresses. As in the stb_hello example, we only need five inputs, so we monitor and respond to the arrow keys and ENTER key. In the next chapter we'll see how to control this UI using a handheld remote.

For the details we've omitted, please see the code on the Laddie CD in the directory /Code/src/fbmenu. The code for STBmenu is included in /Code/src/stbmenu.

Summary

As illustrated in Figure 11-14, building an appliance's GUI requires the use of several layers.

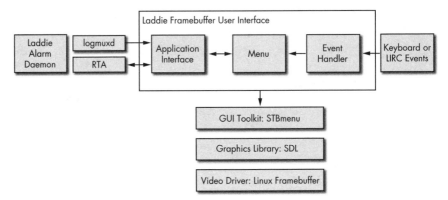

Figure 11-14: The Laddie framebuffer UI and graphics stack

The Linux framebuffer device driver provides an abstraction of video hardware that facilitates configuring the video mode and manipulating pixel memory. Various graphics libraries are available that use this device driver, and these libraries provide support for manipulating graphical objects and text. These libraries typically provide support for event handling, as well. We chose to use the Simple DirectMedia Layer for the Laddie appliance because it is well supported, well documented, and lightweight. GUI toolkits supply the next layer; they provide and manage widgets, objects for which the input events and the graphical display are tightly coupled. For the Laddie appliance, we developed a thin GUI toolkit, STBmenu, which is intended for use with simple, handheld remotes, and which facilitates adding a GUI layer to an existing application with little additional effort. In support of this last point, we also showed how we connected the Laddie framebuffer UI to the Laddie alarm daemon using the RTA/PostgreSQL protocol and the logmuxd event handler. In the next chapter, we will complete the Laddie framebuffer UI by adding support for remote control.

12

INFRARED REMOTE CONTROL

Remotes have become our most natural means of controlling certain appliances, and if you're like us, you'll occasionally spend several minutes trying to locate a remote control rather than trying to engage some device's obscure front panel. In the future, we expect to see more appliances forfeiting the front panel altogether in favor of the keypad of a simple remote. Here's a rule of thumb: If you are building an appliance that might be enjoyed by people while they are sitting on a couch, include a remote control.

In this chapter we will cover the following topics:

- Communicating with infrared light
- Hardware for remote control receivers
- Installing and configuring LIRC for the Laddie appliance

Communicating with Infrared Light

The infrared (IR) light used by remote controls has a wavelength close to, but greater than, visible light. Because it's close to visible light, it travels in straight lines and reflects off of surfaces, but it doesn't go through opaque objects. This limits the applications for which IR is useful. It's good for controlling a set-top box, but not so good for opening a garage door, if there's a solid wall between the transmitter and the receiver.

For the most part, the fact that IR is invisible is a good thing. It may be harder to debug something that's invisible, but when you're watching the late-night movie on your new Linux-based DVR, it's nice to know you can turn down the volume without shining visible light onto the screen.

NOTE   *If you wish you could see the light from a remote control, perhaps to verify that a unit isn't broken, you can look at it using a cell phone camera. These cameras are sensitive to infrared, and on cameras we've experimented with, they display this "color" as bright white.*

Protocols for Encoding Remote Control Commands

In order to transfer information, a remote control transmitter and its receiver must use the same standard or *protocol* for encoding commands. A remote control protocol specifies the following three things:

- How it represents ones and zeros
- How these ones and zeros are combined or *framed* to form messages
- How these different messages are to be interpreted

Companies that build remote-controlled devices don't generally publish their protocols, but it's not hard to reverse engineer the basic commands, and the Internet has plenty of information from people who have done just that. As an example, we'll consider a protocol Sony has used for some of its televisions. If you do some research on the Internet, you might see this protocol referred to as the Sony Integrated Remote Control System (SIRCS) protocol. We chose to use this protocol for the Laddie appliance because the protocol is easy to understand. It is also easy to produce: We purchased a universal remote (RCA RCU410) and programmed it to "Sony TV" (Code 002).

This Sony TV protocol uses pulse-coded data encoding. With this encoding, a bit is represented as a variable-width *pulse*, or presence of light, followed by a constant-width *space*, or absence of light. Based on our own timing measurements with our handheld remote, a zero has a 650-microsecond pulse, a one has a 1,300-microsecond pulse, and each is followed by a 500-microsecond space. These encodings are illustrated in Figure 12-1.

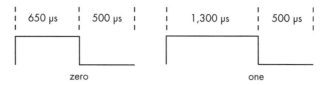

Figure 12-1: Zeros and ones in the Sony TV protocol

A frame in the Sony TV protocol (again, as measured for our particular remote) begins with a header consisting of a single 2,500-microsecond pulse followed by a 500-microsecond space. A seven-bit command immediately follows the header, and a five-bit address follows the command. Both the command and the address are transmitted with the least-significant bit (lsb) first. Figure 12-2 shows the waveform for the TV/Volume– command.

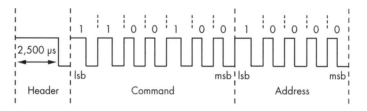

Figure 12-2: The TV/Volume– command in the Sony TV protocol

The address specifies a device (in our case, always 0x01 for TV), and the command specifies the input to that device. Table 12-1 lists some of the command codes for the Sony TV protocol.

Table 12-1: Device Addresses and Command Codes in the Sony TV Protocol

Command code	Command
0x00–0x09	1–9, 0
0x10	Channel+
0x11	Channel–
0x12	Volume+
0x13	Volume–
0x15	Power

For the Laddie appliance, we use the commands Channel+, Channel–, Volume+, Volume–, and Power. Of course, the Laddie appliance doesn't really have channels or volume levels; we have simply chosen these as convenient inputs for the framebuffer menu navigation.

There are many other remote control protocols, and each represents a set of engineering trade-offs. For example, Panasonic's REC-80 protocol uses constant-width pulses and encodes zeros and ones by the length of the space between pulses. This approach can lead to longer battery life because it minimizes the amount of time the remote control spends emitting light. Other protocols save battery life by transmitting a short "Repeat" command when a button is held down, rather than repeatedly transmitting the entire command, as the Sony TV protocol does.

NOTE   *To learn about some of these other protocols, visit http://sbprojects.com/knowledge/ir/ ir.htm.*

Reducing Interference by Modulating the Infrared Signal

So far, we've treated infrared pulses as if they corresponded to steady beams of light. But consider Figure 12-2, and suppose that some flickering light bulb were to generate pulses of IR that overlapped some of the spaces in a message. Clearly, such interference could make it impossible for a receiver to correctly interpret the message. The solution is to modulate the pulses of IR light. In a modulated pulse, the IR light is actually turning on and off at a fixed frequency, typically between 30 and 60 kHz (kilohertz). Like picking out a voice in a crowded room, the receiver can use this frequency as a signature to discriminate the intended signal from the background noise. Because of this modulation, the pulse-coded zeros and ones of the Sony TV protocol are more accurately depicted as in Figure 12-3.

Figure 12-3: Modulated pulses in the Sony TV protocol

We measured the modulation frequency for our remote as roughly 40 kHz. Thus, for our remote, the zero "pulse" in Figure 12-3 actually consists of $40,000 * 0.000650 = 26$ much shorter pulses.

Controlling an Appliance with Infrared Light

Now that we've seen how infrared light can convey information, we can design a system for implementing remote control of an application. Figure 12-4 illustrates such a system.

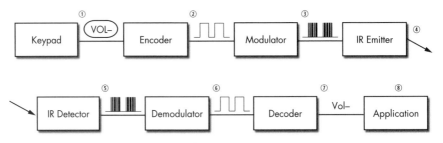

Figure 12-4: A complete remote control system

On the transmitting side, a typical handheld remote control performs the following steps:

1. It scans a *keypad*.
2. It *encodes* the input as a waveform according to some protocol.
3. It *modulates* this encoding with a frequency between 30 and 60 kHz.
4. It *emits* a corresponding pattern of infrared light.

On the receiving side, a typical IR receiver performs the following stages:

5. An infrared *detector* converts the input signal to a voltage waveform.
6. A *demodulator* removes the 30 to 60 kHz modulation.
7. A *decoder* analyzes this waveform and determines the corresponding command.
8. An *application* responds appropriately to this input.

Hardware for Remote Control Receivers

In this section we'll focus on IR receiver hardware. Designing remote control transmitters is beyond the scope of this chapter, but our recommendation is to take the same approach we took with the Laddie appliance: Use an off-the-shelf, universal remote.

Detecting and Demodulating the IR Signal

The two stages of detecting and demodulating an IR input can be handled by a single, commercial, off-the-shelf component. Figure 12-5 shows three examples of this part, all produced by Sharp Microelectronics.

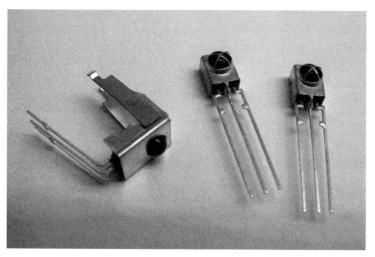

Figure 12-5: Infrared detector/demodulators

For the Laddie appliance, we chose the 40 kHz unit from Sharp's GP1UV70QS series (pictured on the right in Figure 12-5). Also popular is the TSOP17XX series from Vishay. Each of these parts is easy to use with perfboard or solderless breadboard prototyping materials. Each requires a 5V power supply and provides an output corresponding to the demodulated IR waveform (see step 6 in Figure 12-4). When evaluating a particular device, make sure the demodulation frequency is appropriate for your chosen protocol. For low-power applications, you'll also want to compare the power requirements for different devices.

There isn't a standard nomenclature for these devices. When you're searching for information, expect to see names like "IR Remote Receiver," "Photo Module for Remote Control," or "Infrared Detecting Unit for Remote Control." In the remainder of this chapter, we'll refer to them as *infrared detector/demodulators* to emphasize the two functions they provide.

BUILDING A SIMPLE IR DETECTOR

If you have access to an oscilloscope and would like to see a remote control signal *before* it is demodulated, you can build the simple IR detector circuit depicted in Figure 12-6. All you need is a power supply (a 9V battery is fine), an appropriately valued resistor, and a phototransistor.

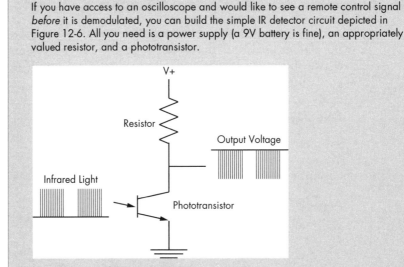

Figure 12-6: A simple IR detector

You'll want to choose the resistor so that the output voltage is about half of the supply voltage when the remote control is off. When we tried this, we used a 100K resistor, and we held the remote control very close to the detector. We had good results both with a Radio Shack infrared phototransistor (catalog number 276-142) and when using another, unidentified, phototransistor we happened to have lying around. The output will be weak, but it should be adequate for an oscilloscope. By the way, this experiment is also useful if you need to determine the modulation frequency for an unfamiliar protocol.

Decoding Remote Control Waveforms

In the previous section we introduced off-the-shelf devices that will respond to a remote control IR signal and produce a demodulated voltage waveform. Before designing a circuit to take advantage of these devices, we need to decide how we will decode that waveform. Decoding can be broken into two steps: *measuring* the timing of the pulses and spaces that comprise a waveform and *interpreting* this sequence of timings to identify the intended message. We have three options for designing a decoder, depending on which of these two tasks we assign to external hardware and which we assign to the appliance's processor. We'll briefly discuss these three options before describing the approach we took for the Laddie appliance.

Measuring and Interpreting in External Hardware

It's possible to build receiver hardware that performs all of the decoding tasks: measuring the waveform, determining the corresponding command, and then transmitting that command as one or more serial bytes to the appliance's processor. Figure 12-7 illustrates this approach. Here, the receiver has recognized the waveform for the Volume– command and has produced the single ASCII character *D* for *down*.

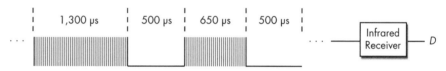

Figure 12-7: Decoding waveforms in external hardware

The website http://linuxtoys.org/xirrc/xirrc.html describes an example of this approach in which a preprogrammed Microchip PIC microcontroller is used to decode Sony remote control commands and transmit command characters to a serial port.

A limitation of this approach is that the receiver supports only one remote control protocol. On the positive side, this approach makes it incredibly easy to add remote control to your appliance. Just plug in the receiver and listen for commands on the serial port.

Measuring in Hardware and Interpreting on the Appliance

In order to accommodate any remote control protocol, we can build receiver hardware that measures waveforms but passes the timing information to the appliance's processor for interpretation. Figure 12-8 illustrates an approach in which the timing of the pulses and spaces is encoded as a series of bytes, each representing time in 50-microsecond increments.

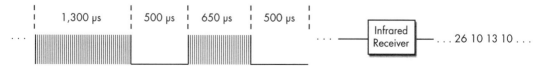

Figure 12-8: Measuring waveform timing in external hardware

Since the appliance is given a complete representation of the input waveform, it can, in theory, decode waveforms for any protocol. The LIRC website provides a link for a protocol called Universal Infrared Remote Transceiver, second version (UIRT2), which works out the details of this approach. It is described at http://users.skynet.be/sky50985.

As a related example, the Irman remote control receiver, available at http://www.evation.com/irman/index.html, takes an innovative approach and encodes any remote control command waveform by creating "pseudo-random" signatures of six bytes. Irman works on the assumption that different waveforms from a given remote will almost invariably have different signatures. Because this technique applies to any waveform, this type of receiver can work with any of the common remote control protocols, but the user has to train it to interpret the signatures it derives.

As a third example, the LIRC website refers to the USB-IR-Boy project. This project uses the inexpensive Freescale MC68HC908JB8 microcontroller with built-in USB support to provide IR waveform timing values. It also includes a Linux device driver to make these timing values available via the /dev/usbirboy device file. Information is available at http://usbirboy .sourceforge.net.

Measuring and Interpreting on the Appliance

The third approach to decoding waveforms is appealing because of its simple hardware requirements. All the hardware has to do is power an infrared detector/demodulator and provide the signal as an input to the appliance's processor. On the negative side, this method does place extra demands on the processor. Specifically, the processor must respond to an interrupt every time the input signal transitions high or low in order to measure timing information. Nevertheless, because of the simple hardware requirements, we have chosen this third approach for the Laddie appliance. In the next section we will work through the details of building this kind of receiver.

Infrared Remote Control Hardware for the Laddie Appliance

If you're not comfortable with building hardware, you might seek out a friend who is, or—this is our recommendation—jump in and build it yourself anyway. It's a good first project and a satisfying one because of the new mode of control it gives you for your Linux projects. You will certainly find the remainder of this chapter more educational if you have hardware to experiment with.

To integrate our simple IR receiver with an appliance, we need two things: a power source for the IR detector/demodulator and an input that generates interrupts. The good news is that a typical serial port satisfies both requirements. The output pins on a serial port provide adequate power, and its Data Carrier Detect (DCD) input pin generates interrupts. The bad news is that the serial port output voltages range from 3.7V to 12V on the positive side and from −3.7V to −12V on the negative side. Moreover, the serial port inputs require a swing between these same positive and negative ranges. An IR detector, however, expects a clean 5V power supply (for some parts, 3.3V); it outputs a 0V to 5V signal (for some parts, 0V to

3.3V). Thus, if you want to use a serial port input, you will need additional circuitry to provide the required voltage for the detector and to shift the detector output to valid serial port levels. Figure 12-9 illustrates this kind of circuit.

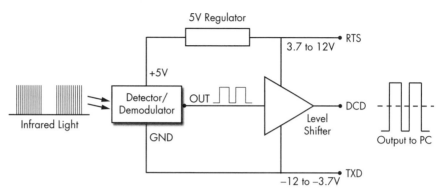

Figure 12-9: A block diagram for a simple IR receiver

Here we assume the serial port has been configured to keep the Request to Send (RTS) output at a high voltage level and the Transmit Data (TXD) output at a low voltage level. The 5V regulator provides the voltage required by the detector. The level shifter provides the correct voltage levels to the DCD input.

NOTE *If you look at IR receiver circuits presented on the Web, you'll find some that take a simpler approach, omitting the level-shifter and providing an output that swings between 0V and 5V. This may work for your computer. If not, or if you want a more robust solution, take the approach we've chosen here.*

Figure 12-10 shows the schematic we chose for the Laddie IR receiver.

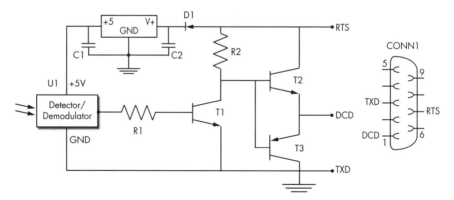

Figure 12-10: The IR receiver schematic used for the Laddie appliance

Here, U1 is an off-the-shelf IR detector/demodulator, U2 is a linear voltage regulator that provides 5V to U1, and the transistor/resistor circuit is the level-shifter that provides an output appropriate for the serial port. The diode, D1, protects the circuit in case the RTS signal is improperly initialized, which may cause it to go negative relative to TXD. Table 12-2 provides the specific parts that we've used, with their approximate costs. Where we've listed multiple parts, you can assume they are interchangeable. Between Digi-Key (http://www.digikey.com) and Jameco Electronics (http://www.jameco.com), you shouldn't have any trouble finding these parts.

Table 12-2: Parts List for the Laddie Appliance's IR Receiver

Ref	Part	Cost	Description
U1	Sharp GP1UV701QS, GP1UV70QS, GP1UW701QS, GP1UW700QS	$1.50	Infrared detector/demodulator
U2	LM78L05, LP2950CZ5	$0.80	5V linear voltage regulator
C1	0.47 uF or higher	$0.15	Electrolytic capacitor
C2	0.47 uF or higher	$0.15	Electrolytic capacitor
D1	1N4148, BAT46	$0.35	Diode
R1	220K, ¼ watt	$0.06	Resistor
R2	100K, ¼ watt	$0.06	Resistor
T1, T2	PN2222A, 2N3904	$0.20	NPN transistor
T3	PN2907A, 2N3906	$0.20	PNP transistor
CONN1	DB9 socket	$0.50	9-pin d-sub serial connector, female

Figure 12-11 shows a few of our prototypes. We recommend starting with a solderless breadboard and 22 AWG solid (non-stranded) wire, as pictured on the left. You'll also need a wire stripper for the 22 AWG wire and a voltmeter for debugging. The one place you'll want to use a soldering iron is to connect wires to the DB9 serial connector. In the left picture, two wires from the DB9 connector provide power and ground to the strips along the edges of the breadboard. The third wire provides the DCD signal back to the computer via the serial cable.

Figure 12-11: Two prototypes for an infrared remote receiver

Once you have a working circuit, you can build something more permanent using perfboard and a plastic enclosure. In the picture on the right, only one side of the enclosure is shown. We drilled a hole at one side for the IR detector/demodulator and cut a hole on the other side for the DB9 connector. A piece of cardboard holds the detector/demodulator in place.

When building your prototype, follow these steps to make sure the circuit is operating properly:

1. Build the circuit, but don't connect the serial port or the IR detector/demodulator. In place of the RTS and TXD pins, use a 9V battery for power. Use the positive battery terminal in place of the RTS input and the negative terminal in place of the TXD input.

2. Verify that the voltage between the regulator output and the negative battery terminal is 5V.

3. Verify that the voltage between the circuit output and the negative battery terminal is at least 8V. (The "circuit output" is the point that you will later connect to the DCD pin of the serial port.)

4. Now connect the open end of R1 to the 5V output of the regulator, and verify that the voltage between the circuit output and the negative battery terminal is zero volts.

5. Finally, complete the circuit by adding the IR detector/demodulator and connecting your computer's serial port.

The remaining tests for your IR receiver hardware require the LIRC software. In the next section, we'll introduce the LIRC software package and describe how we incorporated it into the Laddie appliance.

Installing and Configuring LIRC for the Laddie Appliance

The LIRC software package can be downloaded from http://www.lirc.org; it includes an extensive collection of device drivers, daemons, and tools for controlling user applications with remote control hardware. We don't have room to cover all of these elements here, but we will present the layers that make up this software architecture, and we will describe in detail the particular device driver and daemon that are appropriate for the Laddie appliance. Once you've understood this subset, you should find it easy to master any other parts of the architecture required for your own appliance.

Figure 12-12 provides a high-level view of the LIRC software architecture as it applies to the Laddie appliance. At the right of the diagram, we've shown how elements of the LIRC architecture correspond to our earlier, more general discussion of IR receivers.

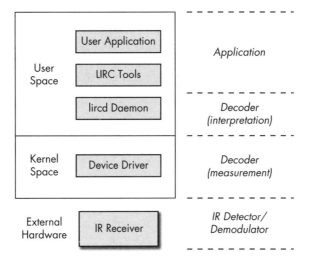

Figure 12-12: The LIRC architecture

In kernel space, a device driver accesses the receiver hardware through an external port. For our appliance, this driver is provided by the LIRC package and uses interrupts to perform waveform timing on the input waveform.

NOTE *As you saw in the section "Decoding Remote Control Waveforms" on page 203, there are some IR receivers that perform the waveform timing and possibly even the waveform interpretation in external hardware. For these receivers, the kernel device driver may be a generic Linux serial driver or a USB driver.*

In user space, for systems such as ours that don't perform interpretation in external hardware, we use the lircd daemon. This daemon accesses a configuration file that characterizes the remote control's command protocol and analyzes the timing information provided by the device driver to generate the corresponding commands. In some cases, the user application will access the output of the lircd daemon directly. The Laddie appliance takes this approach. For applications that were not built with the lircd daemon in mind, several LIRC tools are available to process the output of the lircd daemon and provide program input, execute appropriate commands, or simulate mouse or keyboard events. We'll discuss these tools later in the section "LIRC Tools for Controlling Applications" on page 218.

In the remainder of this chapter, we will describe in detail the elements of the LIRC architecture and show how we configured LIRC for the Laddie appliance.

Installing the LIRC Software

The LIRC package is included on this book's companion CD, and we recommend you use the CD when working through the examples in this chapter. However, if you need to set up your own system in the future, we will describe the steps we took to install the package.

We downloaded version lirc-0.8.1 from http://www.lirc.org and installed it with these commands:

```
./setup.sh
./configure --with-kerneldir=/usr/src/linux-2.6.10 --with-driver=serial
make
make install
```

The setup.sh script asked us to make choices about our installation. Under the Driver Configuration (driver:serial io:0x3f8 irq:4) menu, we chose the **Home-brew (16x50 UART compatible serial port)** driver, selected **COM1 (0x3f8, 4)** for the base address and IRQ, and disabled all driver-specific options. Under the Software Configuration menu, we disabled all options. Then we selected **Save Configuration and exit**.

LIRC is a package that allows you to decode and send IR and other signals of many (but not all) commonly used remote controls. It includes daemons that decode the received signals as well as user space applications that allow controlling a computer with a remote control.

The ./configure --help command provided a long list of driver choices, as well as a dauntingly long list of configuration options. For our appliance, the defaults were generally appropriate. We only needed to provide the location of our Linux kernel source tree using the --with-kerneldir option and to specify the serial driver with the --with-driver option.

Figure 12-13 shows how representative components installed by the LIRC package fit into the LIRC software architecture. Although the LIRC package includes utilities that support the X Window System, we don't show them here, since the Laddie appliance doesn't use X.

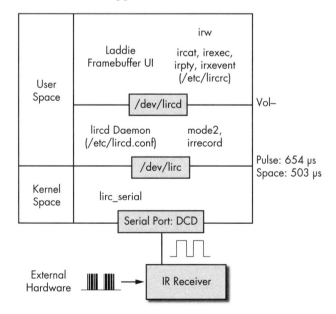

Figure 12-13: Components of the LIRC package

Before we dive into the details, let's start with a quick, bottom-to-top tour and explain how the LIRC receiver controls the Laddie appliance's framebuffer UI, which is described in Chapter 11. The IR receiver external hardware provides the remote control waveform to the DCD pin of a serial port. In kernel space, the lirc_serial device driver (one of many included in the LIRC package) monitors this pin and produces a binary stream of timing data via the device file /dev/lirc. In user space, the lircd daemon analyzes the timing data from the /dev/lirc device file to provide a sequence of command strings on the Unix socket /dev/lircd. The framebuffer UI connects directly to this socket in order to respond to user input.

Now for all the details we left out. In the remainder of this section, we will look more carefully at each of the layers of the LIRC software architecture.

Configuring the lirc_serial Kernel Device Driver

The lirc_serial device driver is actually implemented by two kernel modules, lirc_serial.ko and lirc_dev.ko, which were placed in the directory /lib/modules/2.6.10/misc/ when we installed the software. In order to use these modules, we had to perform three additional steps: free up a serial port, create a device file, and load the modules into the kernel. We created a startup script, lircd, to perform these steps. We will review the steps here; you can see the complete code on the CD in the /etc/rc.d/init.d directory.

Freeing Up a Serial Port

For the Laddie appliance's IR receiver input port, we chose COM1 (/dev/ttyS0). The Linux kernel typically enables COM1 through COM4 as serial ports at startup; thus, we needed to free up COM1 for LIRC. To do this, we used the setserial command:

```
setserial /dev/ttyS0 uart none
```

By setting the type of the hardware (the UART) to *none*, this command disabled the specified port.

NOTE *UART stands for Universal Asynchronous Receiver Transmitter. A UART handles the low-level implementation of a serial link so that the CPU need only be concerned with providing bytes to transmit and processing bytes that are received.*

For the remainder of this chapter, we recommend that you boot the Laddie appliance using the Laddie CD and follow along with the exercises. After booting the CD, exit the framebuffer UI (press ESC), and log in as root with an empty password. Verify that port COM1 was configured properly by executing the following command at the laddie:~# prompt:

```
laddie:~# setserial /dev/ttyS0
```

You should see the following output:

```
/dev/ttyS0, UART: unknown, Port: 0x03f8, IRQ: 4
```

The UART type is unknown, which means the port is available.

Creating a Device File

You may recall from the previous chapter that we used a device file /dev/fb0 to expose the framebuffer functionality. Similarly, we had to provide a device file to expose the lirc_serial functionality. The following code created the character device file /dev/lirc with major number 61 and minor number 0, as required for the lirc driver.

```
mknod /dev/lirc c 61 0
```

With the Laddie CD, verify that the /dev/lirc device file exists by using the command:

```
laddie:~# ls -l /dev/lirc
```

You should see the output:

```
❶crw-------   1 root root ❷61, ❸0 2007-01-27 08:03 /dev/lirc
```

This indicates that the file represents a character device that is ❶ readable and writable by root, ❷ with major number 61, and ❸ with minor number 0.

Loading the lirc_serial Modules into the Kernel

With the serial port available and the device file in place, we were able to load the lirc_serial device driver using the modprobe command:

```
modprobe lirc_serial
```

To verify that the lirc_serial device driver is loaded, execute the following:

```
laddie:~# lsmod | grep lirc
```

You should see output like this:

```
lirc_serial          13152  1
❷lirc_dev             14804  1 ❶lirc_serial
```

The first column shows the loaded modules; the fourth column shows dependencies. Here we see that ❶ the lirc_serial module depends on ❷ the lirc_dev module.

NOTE *If we had wanted to use a different port than COM1 for our IR receiver, we would have provided additional arguments to the lirc_serial driver with the* modprobe *command. To specify COM2, we would have used the command* modprobe lirc_serial irq=3 io=0x2f8. *The default irq and io values for COM3 and COM4 are (4, 0x3e8) and (3, 0x2e8), respectively.*

Testing the lirc_serial Driver

Now that we've verified that the lirc_serial driver is loaded properly, we can use the Laddie CD to test the IR receiver hardware we built earlier. We'll begin by reviewing what we want to test.

Recall that the signal provided by our LIRC receiver looks something like Figure 12-14 (at least in the case of a Sony TV Volume– command).

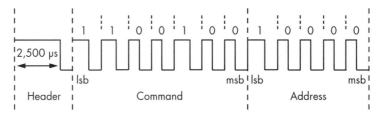

Figure 12-14: Waveform for the Sony TV Volume– command

The job of the lirc_serial kernel device driver is to measure the timing of spaces and pulses in this signal and provide that information via a device file. The particular waveform shown here complies with the Sony TV protocol, but the lirc_serial driver is designed to work with any protocol. The driver includes an interrupt handler that is invoked every time the DCD pin changes state. The handler uses a system timer to measure the pulses and spaces in microseconds, and then it emits this timing information via the /dev/lirc device file as a sequence of 32-bit words. In each word, bits 0 through 23 specify the length of the space or pulse in microseconds (with a maximum value of 0xFF FFFF). Bit 24 is zero for a space and one for a pulse. Bits 25 through 31 are always zero. To test the lirc_serial device driver, we'd like to verify that these values are generated when we press a remote control button.

Before we can access the /dev/lirc device file, we need to make sure it's not already in use by some other process. When the Laddie CD boots, it launches the lircd daemon in order to support the framebuffer UI. Since the lircd daemon accesses /dev/lirc, we prepare for our test by killing that process.

Execute the following commands at the Laddie appliance command prompt:

```
laddie:~# laddie stop
laddie:~# kill $(pidof lircd)
```

After the first command, you will need to wait a few moments for the Laddie application to stop. In the second command, the pidof function outputs the process ID of the lircd process. The $(...) construct provides this output as a parameter to the kill command, which terminates the specified process. We can now access the /dev/lirc device file for our own purposes.

As we saw in the previous chapter, we can use the cat command to access output that is provided via device files. Now we don't want to simply cat the output of /dev/lirc to the console, because some of the output data might be interpreted as control characters and the console could end up in an unusable state. One thing we can do is pipe that output through the hexdump utility, which translates binary data into printable ASCII hexadecimal characters.

Enter the following command:

```
laddie:~# cat /dev/lirc | hexdump
```

Now, any pulses that arrive on the DCD pin of serial port COM1 will be measured by the lirc_serial device driver, read by the cat command via the /dev/lirc device file, and displayed in ASCII hex by hexdump. To generate such pulses, connect your IR receiver to the COM1 port, point your remote control at the IR detector/demodulator, and press a button. (At this point, the particular kind of remote doesn't matter.) If everything is working properly, you should see output like the following:

```
0000000 df67 0061 099d 0100 01fb 0000 04f6 0100
0000010 0216 0000 04fd 0100 01fa 0000 026e 0100
0000020 022d 0000 028a 0100 01fb 0000 04f7 0100
0000030 01fd 0000 02a1 0100 01fa 0000 02a0 0100
0000040 01fb 0000 04fc 0100 01fb 0000 02a0 0100
0000050 01fa 0000 0283 0100 0218 0000 0289 0100
```

This is the output we generated by briefly tapping the Volume– button on the universal remote that we programmed for Sony TV.

If you're not sure your IR receiver hardware is working (or if you don't have an IR receiver at this point), you can still test the lirc_serial device driver by creating random pulses on the DCD pin of the serial port. One way to do this is to intermittently connect pin 1 (DCD) to pin 7 (RTS) of the serial port. If this doesn't produce a result, try intermittently connecting pin 1 to pin 3 (TXD). If your computer's serial port is built to standard specifications, it won't be a problem if you connect the wrong pins by mistake. Still, if you've just purchased a fancy, new laptop, you might want to try this experiment on a friend's Linux box first.

Using the cat /dev/lirc | hexdump command is a good exercise because it demonstrates that the output of /dev/lirc is simply binary data that can be read like a file. Neither cat nor hexdump know anything about infrared, yet they display the data just fine. But the output of hexdump isn't easy to read.

Fortunately, the LIRC package includes a utility, mode2, that does understand the output of the lirc_serial driver and can display it as pulse and space timing data.

Press CTRL-C to terminate the previous command, and execute the following one:

```
laddie:~# mode2
```

Now point an IR remote control at the receiver while pressing buttons. The command mode2 reads the output of /dev/lirc, parses the 23-bit timing data and the one-bit pulse or space indicator, and produces a stream of pulse and space timing information. As an example, we observed the following train of space and pulse timings from mode2 when we stimulated our IR receiver with a single Sony TV Volume– command.

laddie:~# mode2	space 568	pulse 1265
space 5794213	pulse 663	space 517
pulse 2471	space 494	pulse 663
space 496	pulse 1260	space 516
pulse 1282	space 497	pulse 633
space 546	pulse 685	space 546
pulse 1263	space 518	pulse 639
space 517	pulse 661	space 496
pulse 611	space 515	pulse 682

If you refer to "Protocols for Encoding Remote Control Commands" on page 198, you will notice that these timing values are noisier than the idealized waveform would suggest. The first pulse is roughly 2,500 milliseconds and corresponds to the header. The other pulses are roughly 1,300 or 650 milliseconds, corresponding to ones and zeros, respectively. The spaces are roughly 500 milliseconds, but note the large initial space value corresponding to the time between button presses. It is the job of the lircd daemon to reject the pulse trains that do not correspond to valid waveforms and to correctly interpret the ones that do. When you are finished experimenting with mode2, press CTRL-C to terminate the utility.

At this point, we have established that the lirc_serial device driver is working. In the next section we will provide instructions on configuring the lircd daemon, which will use the output of this device driver.

NOTE   *If you would like to write a program that uses the output of the lirc_serial device driver directly, the source code for the mode2 utility provides an example of how to access the /dev/lirc device file. This source is available from http://www.lirc.org and is also provided in the lirc-0.8.1.tar.bz2 tarball in the /usr/src/packages/ directory of this book's companion CD.*

Configuring the lircd Daemon

The cleverest part of the LIRC package is the lircd daemon. This is the part that analyzes the noisy timing values coming from the /dev/lirc device file and produces a sequence of commands that are easily parsed by downstream LIRC tools or user applications.

In order for the lircd daemon to interpret the timing data from /dev/lirc, it has to understand the remote control protocol. The configuration file /etc/lircd.conf captures this protocol information. The following is the lircd.conf file used by the Laddie appliance with comments and a few of the button entries removed to save space.

```
begin remote
  name        SONY-TV
  bits             12
  flags     SPACE_ENC
  eps              30
  aeps            100
  header         2457    525
  one            1269    520
  zero            650    520
  gap           26076
  toggle_bit        0
      begin codes
          POWER                    0xA90
          ENTER                    0xD10
          VOL-                     0xC90
          VOL+                     0x490
          CH-                      0x890
          CH+                      0x090
      end codes
end remote
```

You don't need to understand the entries in this file to use LIRC, but we'll make a few comments here in case you want to edit the file manually. The *name* can be any string you like that describes the remote. The *bits* field is the total number of data bits (in our case, command-code bits plus address bits). The *eps* and *aeps* fields represent relative and absolute error tolerances (in our case, 30 percent and 100 microseconds). The *header, one,* and *zero* fields represent the pulse and space timings (in microseconds) for the header and data bits. There is a *gap* of about 26,000 microseconds between repeated commands, and there is no toggle bit that changes for repeated commands. Note that these fields reflect actual timings measured by the device driver and can vary from the protocol standard. The *codes* are the actual data bit sequences for the various commands. For the additional fields that may apply for other remotes, you can see the details at the WinLIRC web page, http://winlirc.sourceforge.net/technicaldetails.html.

If you have a remote that uses the same protocol as ours, you should be able to control the Laddie appliance without updating the /etc/lircd.conf file. (Again, we are using an RCA RCU410 universal remote, programmed as a Sony TV, code 002.) The LIRC website also provides configuration files for many remotes, but using the LIRC irrecord utility, it's easy enough to generate these files from scratch. The irrecord utility creates configuration files by monitoring the output of /dev/lirc while prompting the user for remote control input.

Now let's create a configuration file for your remote. As we mentioned when we were testing the lirc_serial device driver, we need to kill the lircd daemon before we access /dev/lirc. If you didn't kill lircd earlier, do so now:

```
laddie:~# kill $(pidof lircd)
```

To create a new lircd configuration file, rename or delete the old one, then run the irrecord command:

```
laddie:~# mv /etc/lircd.conf /etc/lircd.conf.bak
laddie:~# irrecord /etc/lircd.conf
```

Read the instructions printed by the irrecord utility carefully. The utility will prompt you to press remote control buttons in a particular sequence, and it will also ask you to assign names for the buttons you choose to program. Since you will be using the remote to control the Laddie framebuffer UI, you will need to provide the button names that the Laddie appliance expects. It doesn't matter how you assign the actual buttons, but you will need to use the following names in uppercase letters: POWER, VOL+, VOL–, CH+, and CH–. If you restart the irrecord utility, be sure to rename or delete the previous /etc/lircd.conf file first. Once you're satisfied with the configuration file, you are ready to test the lircd daemon.

NOTE *If you choose to download a configuration file for your remote from http://www.lirc.org, you will need to edit it to make sure the button names are the ones the Laddie appliance expects. Keep in mind that any updated configuration files will be replaced with the original files when you reboot the Laddie CD.*

Testing the lircd Daemon

To use your new lircd configuration file, start the lircd daemon with the command:

```
laddie:~# lircd
```

This command will complete immediately without printing anything. To verify that the daemon is running, execute the command:

```
laddie:~# pidof lircd
```

and verify that it returns an integer. The lircd daemon will read timing data from the /dev/lirc device file and, using the configuration specified in /etc/lircd.conf, provide button-press information at the Unix socket /dev/lircd in the form of newline-delimited ASCII strings.

Unix sockets are different from regular files or device files. In particular, you can't use the system call open() to access them; you have to use connect() instead. This means that we can't simply use cat to examine the output of /dev/lircd the way we did with /dev/lirc. Let's write a simple program, socket_cat, that does allow us to view this output.

NOTE   *If you are eager to test the lircd daemon and would rather skip this exercise, you can use the LIRC utility irw, with no arguments, to display the output of /dev/lircd. However, the program socket_cat will help you understand how the Laddie appliance works, since it uses the same approach as socket_cat to access remote control button presses.*

If you've programmed with sockets before, the following program will look familiar. We use the function ❶ socket to create an unnamed, Unix internal socket. We use the function ❷ connect to connect to the named socket /dev/lircd. Then we ❸ loop forever, copying all received data to the standard output.

```
#include <unistd.h>        /* read, write */
#include <sys/un.h>        /* sockaddr_un */
#include <sys/types.h>     /* socket, connect */
#include <sys/socket.h>    /* socket, connect */
#include <string.h>        /* strcpy */

int main(int argc,char *argv[])
{
  int fd,i;
  char buf[128];
  struct sockaddr_un address;
  address.sun_family=AF_UNIX;
  if(argc<2){
    printf("Usage: socket_cat <unix socket path>\n");
    return;
  }
  strcpy(address.sun_path,argv[1]);

  fd=socket(AF_UNIX,SOCK_STREAM,0);
  if(connect(fd,(struct sockaddr *)&address,sizeof(address)) == -1){
  perror("Connect");
  exit(1);
  }
  for(;;){
  i=read(fd,buf,128);
  write(STDOUT_FILENO,buf,i);
  };
}
```

This program is on the CD at /Code/src/examples/socket_cat.c. Build and run the program, using the following commands:

```
laddie:~# cd /Code/src/examples/socket_cat
laddie:~# make
laddie:~# ./socket_cat /dev/lircd
```

Then press a few buttons on your remote. You should see output like the following.

```
0000000000000c90 00 VOL- /etc/lircd.conf
0000000000000490 00 VOL+ /etc/lircd.conf
0000000000000890 00 CH- /etc/lircd.conf
0000000000000090 00 CH+ /etc/lircd.conf
0000000000000a90 00 POWER /etc/lircd.conf
0000000000000a90 01 POWER /etc/lircd.conf
0000000000000a90 02 POWER /etc/lircd.conf
```

Each string includes a 16-character hexadecimal command code, a hexadecimal repetition count, a command string, and a name for the remote (which defaults to the name of the lircd config file). Note how, at the end of this sequence, the repetition count increases when the POWER button is held down continually.

The 16-character command codes are generally not useful, since all relevant information is captured by the names of the commands and the remote. However, it is interesting to see how the command code corresponds to the input waveform. Note, for example, that *0xc90* is the hexadecimal representation for the 12 bits (left to right) in the command waveform for the Sony TV Volume– command that we saw in "Protocols for Encoding Remote Control Commands" on page 198. When you are done with socket_cat, press CTRL-C to terminate the program.

NOTE   *When a remote control button is pushed, depending on the button and the protocol, the commands can repeat pretty quickly. For the Laddie framebuffer UI, we took advantage of the repetition count associated with the lircd output to ignore all but the first command associated with each button press.*

LIRC Tools for Controlling Applications

As you saw in the previous section, it is simple to write a program that responds to remote control commands via the /dev/lircd socket. But what if you want to use a remote to control a program that already exists, but was designed, say, for keyboard input rather than remote control input? In fact, the LIRC package addresses this need with tools that connect to the /dev/lircd socket and produce the kinds of output that many programs do expect.

The ircat tool is a good example because it is the simplest; it prints user-specifiable, newline-delimited strings to the standard output when remote control buttons are pressed. If you have a program that takes commands from standard input, you can control it with LIRC by piping the output of ircat to your program. To map remote control buttons to appropriate output, configure the file /etc/lircrc. The HTML documentation provided with the LIRC package provides details on the format of this file.

Similarly, the LIRC package provides an irpty utility for simulating keyboard input, an irexec utility for invoking system calls, and an irxevent utility that generates X events (for systems running X). Again, these actions are mapped to remote control buttons according to the /etc/lircrc file. All of these utilities use an API called the lirc_client library to access the /dev/lircd socket. The source code for the ircat tool provides a simple example of how to use this library.

Finally, the LIRC package contains a daemon lircmd that uses remote control input to emulate a mouse. This daemon connects to the /dev/lircd socket and produces mouse events on the pipe /dev/lircm. The configuration file /etc/lircmd.conf selects the protocol for X mouse events (e.g., IntelliMouse) and specifies how remote commands map to mouse movements and button presses. The XF86Config file must be updated to include /dev/lircm as an input device. Again, the LIRC HTML documentation provides details.

Controlling the Laddie Appliance

For the Laddie appliance, we installed the LIRC package and configured the lirc_serial driver and lircd daemon as described in the previous sections. Since we built the Laddie appliance from scratch, we did not need to use LIRC tools like ircat or irpty; instead, we wrote code similar to the socket_cat example, which accessed the /dev/lircd socket directly.

As discussed in the previous chapter, Laddie's framebuffer user interface is built on the Simple DirectMedia Layer (SDL) library. Since SDL includes its own event handler which, in particular, handles keyboard presses, it was a simple matter to incorporate remote control events. We created a separate lircHandler() thread to read commands from the /dev/lircd socket, parse these commands, and then push appropriate keyboard events onto the SDL event queue. Specifically, we responded to the Channel+/− and Volume+/− remote control commands by simulating the SDL keypress events for the Up, Down, Right, and Left arrow keys, respectively. We responded to the remote control Power command with the SDL Enter keypress event. In Laddie's SDL event handler, we responded to these keypress events by calling navigation commands in Laddie's menu object. This use of the /dev/lircd output to control Laddie's framebuffer menu is illustrated in Figure 12-15.

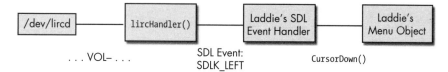

Figure 12-15: Controlling the Laddie framebuffer UI

If you would like to see the details of the lircHandler() thread, you can take a look at the /Code/src/fbmenu/lirc_if.cc file on the CD.

If you have built the IR receiver we described in this chapter and successfully worked through the exercises, you should be able to use it to control the Laddie framebuffer UI. We had stopped the Laddie appliance daemons in order to do the exercises; you will need to restart them now. Do this with the following command:

```
laddie:~# laddie start
```

This will take a few moments, after which you should see the framebuffer UI. Now experiment with the buttons you programmed when you used irrecord to create the lircd.conf file. You should be able to navigate through the menu buttons and switch menu pages.

Summary

Infrared light is a useful means for controlling an appliance when the appliance is in the line of sight. To be effective, infrared light must be modulated by the transmitter with a signature frequency, and this modulation must be removed by the receiver. Fortunately, there are commercial devices that make it easy to meet these requirements. For IR receivers, we introduced infrared detector/demodulators and showed how to use them in simple IR receiver circuits. For IR transmitters, we recommended using universal remotes.

We also described the Linux Infrared Remote Control (LIRC) package as a useful tool for controlling appliances. This package provides device drivers and daemons for measuring and interpreting infrared waveforms, as well as utilities for controlling appliances. Although we didn't discuss the entire LIRC package, we did describe those elements of the package that we used for the Laddie appliance. We hope this overview of infrared communications and this example application of the LIRC software package will be a useful starting point if you decide to use infrared remote control for your own appliance.

13

HANDS-ON INTRODUCTION TO SNMP

We like to say that the difference between a hobby and a commercial network appliance is SNMP. Any corporation with a large network will use Simple Network Management Protocol (SNMP) as part of its network- and system-management solution. You simply cannot sell into the large enterprise and telecommunications carrier markets without SNMP support on your appliance.

If your target market includes companies with large networks and you are not confident in your knowledge of SNMP, this chapter is for you. If, however, you will be targeting the home or small business market (or your appliance will not be networked at all), you can safely skip this and the SNMP chapters that follow.

This chapter will introduce SNMP and provide you with an appreciation of some of the things SNMP can do. The topics covered in this chapter are:

- A brief introduction to SNMP terminology
- Finding the software

- Installing the software
- Starting the agent
- Exploring with SNMP
- Writing values with SNMP
- SNMP traps

A Quick Note on Terminology

Here is a quick tour of the most basic concepts and terms you will need in order to understand the material in this chapter. For a complete introduction to SNMP concepts and terminology, see Appendix B.

SNMP is a protocol designed to facilitate the reading and writing of small amounts of information over a network, like single numbers and character strings. You would not use SNMP for large volumes of data, like file transfer.

A read operation in SNMP is called a GET, while a write is called a SET. The target of a SET or GET operation is called an object. An *object* is like a field in a database record.

SNMP treats objects as if they were organized into a single large database called the *Management Information Base (MIB)*. It may be helpful to think of SNMP as an API to the information on a device. It hides the details of object retrieval beneath an organized hierarchical namespace. An SNMP agent on each system provides this API. The *agent* is a background (daemon) process listening for SNMP requests on UDP port 161. Beneath the API, the agent may interact with the kernel or some application process running on the system; it may also read several pieces of information from different sources and apply a mathematical formula to furnish the value defined in a MIB. An object in the MIB may also represent functionality rather than data; for example, setting a MIB object to a particular value might trigger a reboot or the restarting of a service.

The MIB hierarchical namespace is much like the Unix filesystem, but it uses numbers instead of directory and filenames, and it uses the . character instead of the / directory separator. So, whereas a file path may look like this:

```
/usr/sbin/ifconfig
```

the name (called an *Object Identifier*, or *OID*) for an object in the MIB might look like this:

```
.1.3.6.1.2.1.1.1
```

MIB files describe portions of the complete MIB database. Typically, each MIB file describes a *MIB module*, which is a subtree of the overall database. MIB files are both human readable and program readable. They document the MIB for humans, and they provide a means for programs to translate between these number strings and their human-readable names. Although we have talked about *the MIB* as the SNMP-addressable universe, the more common use of the term *MIB* is for one of these named subtrees.

For example, you will hear talk of the *Host Resources MIB*, or the *HP Printer MIB*, or *MIB-2*. These are all subtrees, but they are also all addressable within the overall namespace.

First and foremost among MIBs is the cryptically named *MIB-II*. When SNMP was first created, the SNMP working group of the IETF[1] defined a core set of information. This was the first MIB, or *MIB-I*. A few years later, the SNMP WG revised this core set and it became *MIB-II*. We use *MIB-2*, rather than MIB-II, in this chapter to match the name used in the MIB file that defines this MIB.

Once you have the right MIB files installed (you'll see how to do this later), you can use the snmptranslate command to give you the human-readable names for a numeric ID (more on this later, too). For example:

```
$snmptranslate -Of .1.3.6.1.2.1.1.1
.iso.org.dod.internet.mgmt.mib-2.system.sysDescr
$
```

This should be enough terminology to get started.

The Software

The Net-SNMP is an excellent free package containing all you'll need to follow along in this chapter. Net-SNMP will provide you with commands (snmpget, snmpset, snmpwalk, snmptrap), an SNMP agent, and the standard MIB files. Normally, the commands and agent would be running on different systems, but for simplicity you'll be running both on the same system. If you have two systems available, you can perform the full installation on both systems; then you can run snmpget, for example, on one system, and talk to the agent on the other. If you use two systems, remember to change all instances of localhost or 127.0.0.1 in this chapter's code to the name or address of the system running the SNMP agent.

Installing SNMP

Before installing, check to see if Net-SNMP is already installed on your system—many common Linux distributions provide some version of it. If you have a very old Linux distribution (like Red Hat 7.*x*) you may find UCD-SNMP instead; this is an older version—or parent—of Net-SNMP. Although its behavior is very similar to that of Net-SNMP, there are enough differences to confuse someone trying to follow this tutorial; you should remove it, and follow the instructions here to install Net-SNMP. If you find some other package installed, definitely remove it before continuing.

---

[1] The Internet Engineering Task Force (IETF), started in 1986, is the principle standards organization for the Internet. Participation is voluntary and open to anyone. Most of its work is performed in *working groups (WGs)*, which are ad hoc groups composed of parties interested in some specific topic.

Even if Net-SNMP is not currently installed on your system, it may be packaged with your Linux distribution, so check your CDs. Be aware, though, that various Linux distributions may have modified Net-SNMP to comply with their own ideas of default file locations and it may include different patches. Naturally, the closer your version of Net-SNMP is to the one used in this chapter (version 5.2.1), the closer your results will be to the ones shown here.

Download and Install

If Net-SNMP is not included with your Linux distribution, you can download it from http://net-snmp.sourceforge.net. You can install either from RPM (assuming you are running an RPM-based distribution like Fedora) or source, but for now let's install the binary RPM. (By the way, if rpm complains about missing dependencies, you may have to take care of them first and then retry this command.)

```
$ rpm -Uvh net-snmp-5.2.1.fc4.i686.rpm
Preparing...        ######################################### [100%]
   1:net-snmp       ######################################### [100%]
$
```

Check the Installation

Now test that it worked. First, test the agent.

```
$ /usr/sbin/snmpd --version

NET-SNMP version:  5.2.1
Web:               http://www.net-snmp.org/
Email:             net-snmp-coders@lists.sourceforge.net

$
```

Now check the tools. Use which to find out where they were installed, then list all the commands in that directory that start with *snmp*.

```
$ which snmpwalk
/usr/bin/snmpwalk

$ ls /usr/bin/snmp*
/usr/bin/snmpbulkget    /usr/bin/snmpdf         /usr/bin/snmpstatus
/usr/bin/snmpusm        /usr/bin/snmpbulkwalk   /usr/bin/snmpget
/usr/bin/snmptable      /usr/bin/snmpvacm       /usr/bin/snmpcheck
/usr/bin/snmpgetnext    /usr/bin/snmptest       /usr/bin/snmpwalk
/usr/bin/snmpconf       /usr/bin/snmpnetstat    /usr/bin/snmptranslate
/usr/bin/snmpdelta      /usr/bin/snmpset        /usr/bin/snmptrap
```

We'll only use a handful of these commands, but feel free to explore others once you've mastered the basics.

Now let's check the version to make sure it is what we just installed and not some older version that's lurking on your path.

```
$ snmpwalk --version
NET-SNMP version: 5.2.1
$
```

Configure the Agent

So far, so good—you have the client-side programs. Now you need to get the agent running so these programs have something to query.

The agent runs as a daemon and listens for incoming SNMP requests on UDP port 161, by default. It requires some configuration information that it normally picks up from the file snmpd.conf in the directory /etc/snmp. (Note the *d* in snmpd.conf; it indicates *daemon*—our agent. Do not confuse this with snmp.conf, which we will introduce later on.) Snmpd.conf tells the agent how to authenticate incoming requests, where to send traps (which are SNMP alarm notifications), and so forth.

Net-SNMP provides a program called snmpconf[2] that generates the snmpd.conf file from the answers to a series of questions, but because your needs here are pretty simple, you can generate the configuration by hand. Your snmpd.conf file should contain:

```
rocommunity  public
syslocation  "my den"
syscontact   me@myaddr.com
```

The rocommunity macro sets your read-only community string, which for now you can think of as something like a password. Net-SNMP gives you much more precise access control than this, but that's beyond our needs right now.

The syslocation and syscontact lines set the values for the sysLocation and sysContact objects in the MIB-2 system group. When you are managing only a small set of systems all in one location, this information may not be very interesting, but in a large corporate network with multiple sites, it may be invaluable to know how to locate a system and find out who is in charge of it. (A little later in this chapter, you'll see how to access this information across the network with SNMP queries.)

Place this snmpd.conf file into the /etc/snmp directory. The three lines above are all you'll need to get started.

Start the Agent

Start the agent, and put it into the background. The agent listens on port 161, so you'll need to be logged in as root to issue this command:

```
/usr/sbin/snmpd -c /etc/snmp/snmpd.conf -C &
```

---

[2] In the parlance of the CLI chapter, snmpconf would be called a *wizard*.

The `-c /etc/snmp/snmpd.conf` tells the agent to use the given configuration file, and `-C` tells the agent to use only this configuration file.

For now, you can just type the above command (as root), but on your appliance you'll want the SNMP agent to start up with the system.

Exploring with SNMP

Now let's turn our attention to the client side. The commands `snmpget`, `snmpwalk`, and `snmpset` are all SNMP client commands, or *SNMP management applications*, in SNMP-speak. SNMP uses the term *manager* or *management application* for the client side and *agent* for the server side. The agent serves up the data on the appliance, and the SNMP manager is the client requesting the appliance's information. You won't need to be logged in as root to use these client commands.

Let's use `snmpget` to test our agent install.

```
$ snmpget -v2c -c public localhost sysLocation.0
SNMPv2-MIB::sysLocation.0 = STRING: "my den"3
$
```

You've told `snmpget` to use SNMPv2c (community-based[4] SNMP version 2) and the community string `public` to send a query to the local machine asking for the value of the `sysLocation` variable, which you configured in your snmpd.conf file.[5] The `.0` appended to the `sysLocation` name is SNMP's way of indicating that you want the *instance* of this variable. In object-oriented language, think of `sysLocation` as a class that has one instance. If this were an array (table) of locations, the `.0` would be replaced by the row number of the variable (.1, .2, .3, and so on). Row numbers always start with 1, so there is no confusion between a row index and a scalar indicator.

You need to tell the `snmpget` command to use SNMPv2c, because it defaults to SNMPv3; you can change that by generating an snmp.conf file with a different default. You could use `snmpconf` to generate the file, this time selecting snmp.conf (no *d*), but you can also just create the snmp.conf file by hand with this single command (run as root).

```
echo "defversion 2c" > /etc/snmp/snmp.conf
```

Now you can stop typing the `-v2c` with each command.

---

[3] If you get the message `Timeout: No Response from localhost` instead, you may have something blocking UDP requests to port 161. Check your firewall settings and your /etc/hosts.deny file. If you find `ALL:ALL` in your hosts.deny file, comment it out and try the `snmpget` again.

[4] SNMPv2c is called "community-based" because it retains the use of SNMPv1 community strings (think of these as passwords) for authentication. There was disagreement about the new security framework that was intended for SNMPv2, so SNMPv2c was released without it. When it was ready, the new security framework was released in SNMPv3.

[5] Notice that the MIB object is `sysLocation`, but the command in the snmpd.conf file is `syslocation`. There is no significance to this; it was just the implementer's design choice to use all lowercase letters for the key words in the configuration file.

If you have access to any other networked devices, you might try querying them. For example, here's the snmpwalk command run against an Apple AirPort Base Station:

```
$ snmpwalk -c public 10.0.1.1
SNMPv2-MIB::sysDescr.0 = STRING: Apple Base Station V3.84 Compatible
SNMPv2-MIB::sysObjectID.0 = OID: SNMPv2-SMI::zeroDotZero
DISMAN-EVENT-MIB::sysUpTimeInstance = Timeticks: (4971188) 13:48:31.88
SNMPv2-MIB::sysContact.0 = STRING: me@myaddr.com
SNMPv2-MIB::sysName.0 = STRING: MyAirport
SNMPv2-MIB::sysLocation.0 = STRING: my den
SNMPv2-MIB::sysServices.0 = INTEGER: 79
SNMPv2-MIB::sysServices.0 = No more variables left in this MIB View (It is
past the end of the MIB tree)
$
```

Clearly, the device's sysDescr.0 (system description) identifies this as an Apple Base Station. You'll also recognize the sysLocation and sysContact information for this device. This device doesn't offer up a lot of information, but there is enough to identify what it is, where it is, and who to contact about any issues you have with this box, should you discover that it's misbehaving. Of course, the availability of the system contact and location both rely on the administrator of that system, who is configuring these values on the target device. An inattentive system administrator may leave you little to work with.

Notice that for this query we used snmpwalk instead of snmpget because we wanted to see what other information might be furnished by this device. The snmpget command retrieves a single object instance using an SNMP GET protocol data unit, while snmpwalk uses multiple SNMP GETNEXT PDUs to "walk" an entire MIB. You pick a starting point, and snmpwalk asks for the lexically next object instance; the agent returns that object and its OID, and snmpwalk asks for the next object instance after the new OID. Eventually, the agent responds that there is nothing more to return, and the walk terminates.

MIB Files for Readable Names

The display of nice, readable names for OIDs—like *sysDescr* and *sysLocation*—depends on having the right MIB files registered on your client system. In the case of Net-SNMP, *registration* simply means putting these files in the right directory and telling the SNMP commands (like snmpget and snmpwalk) to use them. You can set a few environment variables to do this job for you. Just put these lines in your shell startup file (e.g., .bashrc):

```
export MIBS=ALL
export MIBDIRS=/usr/share/snmp/mibs
```

When you installed Net-SNMP, it placed a set of standard MIB files in /usr/share/snmp/mibs, as you can see in the list below. These are all plain-text files written using a human-readable and machine-parseable syntax.

Some of these actually describe MIBs. Others are support files that define information needed by the files that describe the MIBs, just as header files are used in the C language.

```
$ ls /usr/share/snmp/mibs
AGENTX-MIB.txt                              RFC1155-SMI.txt
DISMAN-EVENT-MIB.txt                        RFC1213-MIB.txt
DISMAN-SCHEDULE-MIB.txt                     RFC-1215.txt
DISMAN-SCRIPT-MIB.txt                       RMON-MIB.txt
EtherLike-MIB.txt                           SMUX-MIB.txt
HCNUM-TC.txt                                SNMP-COMMUNITY-MIB.txt
HOST-RESOURCES-MIB.txt                      SNMP-FRAMEWORK-MIB.txt
HOST-RESOURCES-TYPES.txt                    SNMP-MPD-MIB.txt
IANA-ADDRESS-FAMILY-NUMBERS-MIB.txt         SNMP-NOTIFICATION-MIB.txt
IANAifType-MIB.txt                          SNMP-PROXY-MIB.txt
IANA-LANGUAGE-MIB.txt                       SNMP-TARGET-MIB.txt
IF-INVERTED-STACK-MIB.txt                   SNMP-USER-BASED-SM-MIB.txt
IF-MIB.txt                                  SNMPv2-CONF.txt
INET-ADDRESS-MIB.txt                        SNMPv2-MIB.txt
IP-FORWARD-MIB.txt                          SNMPv2-SMI.txt
IP-MIB.txt                                  SNMPv2-TC.txt
IPV6-ICMP-MIB.txt                           SNMPv2-TM.txt
IPV6-MIB.txt                                SNMP-VIEW-BASED-ACM-MIB.txt
IPV6-TCP-MIB.txt                            TCP-MIB.txt
IPV6-TC.txt                                 UCD-DEMO-MIB.txt
IPV6-UDP-MIB.txt                            UCD-DISKIO-MIB.txt
NET-SNMP-AGENT-MIB.txt                      UCD-DLMOD-MIB.txt
NET-SNMP-EXAMPLES-MIB.txt                   UCD-IPFWACC-MIB.txt
NET-SNMP-MIB.txt                            UCD-SNMP-MIB.txt
NET-SNMP-TC.txt                             UDP-MIB.txt
NOTIFICATION-LOG-MIB.txt
$
```

Without these MIB files, the display of the Apple Base Station system group would have looked like this:

```
$ snmpwalk -On -v2c -c public 10.0.1.1 system
.1.3.6.1.2.1.1.1.0 = STRING: Apple Base Station V3.84 Compatible
.1.3.6.1.2.1.1.2.0 = OID: .0.0
.1.3.6.1.2.1.1.3.0 = Timeticks: (629726) 1:44:57.26
.1.3.6.1.2.1.1.4.0 = STRING: me@myaddr.com
.1.3.6.1.2.1.1.5.0 = STRING: MyAirport
.1.3.6.1.2.1.1.6.0 = STRING: my den
.1.3.6.1.2.1.1.7.0 = INTEGER: 79
.1.3.6.1.2.1.1.7.0 = No more variables left in this MIB View (It is past the
end of the MIB tree)
$
```

You can still tell a lot about the device just from examining the responses, but it's nice to know what the OIDs mean.

A Networked Printer

Let's try another query against a different kind of device:

```
$snmpwalk -c public 10.0.1.9
SNMPv2-MIB::sysDescr.0 = STRING: HP ETHERNET MULTI-ENVIRONMENT,ROM
L.20.07,JETDIRECT,JD84,EEPROM L.20.24
SNMPv2-MIB::sysObjectID.0 = OID: SNMPv2-SMI::enterprises.11.2.3.9.1
SNMPv2-MIB::sysUpTime.0 = Timeticks: (354480750) 41 days, 0:40:07.50
SNMPv2-MIB::sysContact.0 = STRING:
SNMPv2-MIB::sysName.0 = STRING: BW2
SNMPv2-MIB::sysLocation.0 = STRING:
SNMPv2-MIB::sysServices.0 = INTEGER: 79
$
```

This time, the administrator has not set sysContact and sysLocation. However, we can at least determine the type of device being used. One clue is in the sysDescr field: *HP ETHERNET . . . JETDIRECT.* . . . This is a networked HPJetdirect printer.

Another clue, though one much harder for a novice to read, is in the *sysObjectID*—the OID in this field indicates the type of device. This OID starts with enterprises, indicating that the next number (11) is the enterprise number of the manufacturer; you can find a list of manufacturers' enterprise numbers at http://www.iana.org/assignments/enterprise-numbers. Here you will find that 11 is registered to Hewlett Packard. The rest of the OID (.2.3.9.1) would identify the type of device, if you had the right MIB file on your system.

The snmptable Command

This printer's SNMP agent offers much more information than just the system group, giving us a chance to illustrate another command, snmptable. This command behaves much like snmpwalk, but it formats the output differently. We use it here to look at the TCP Connection Table on the same HP Jetdirect printer.

```
$ snmptable  -v1 -c public 10.0.0.183 tcpConnTable
SNMP table: TCP-MIB::tcpConnTable
```

tcpConnState	tcpConnLocalAddress	tcpConnLocalPort	tcpConnRemAddress	tcpConnRemPort
listen	0.0.0.0	21	0.0.0.0	0
listen	0.0.0.0	23	0.0.0.0	0
listen	0.0.0.0	80	0.0.0.0	0
listen	0.0.0.0	280	0.0.0.0	0
listen	0.0.0.0	515	0.0.0.0	0
listen	0.0.0.0	631	0.0.0.0	0
listen	0.0.0.0	1782	0.0.0.0	0
listen	0.0.0.0	9100	0.0.0.0	0
timeWait	10.0.0.183	80	10.0.1.3	1933
timeWait	127.0.0.1	2872	127.0.0.1	8000
listen	127.0.0.1	8000	0.0.0.0	0

```
$
```

From this table you can see the TCP ports on which the printer is listening. You can also see that two connections are in *timeWait* state, one between the printer (10.0.0.183, port 80) and a remote system (10.0.1.3, port 19333), and another between two TCP ports on the local system itself.

MIB-2: The TCP Connection Table

Now we'll take a look at our own system. Here is the TCP Connection Table from our local system:

```
$ snmptable -c public localhost tcpConnTable
SNMP table: TCP-MIB::tcpConnTable

tcpConnState tcpConnLocalAddress tcpConnLocalPort tcpConnRemAddress tcpConnRemPort
      listen             0.0.0.0               22           0.0.0.0              0
      listen             0.0.0.0              111           0.0.0.0              0
      listen             0.0.0.0              199           0.0.0.0              0
      listen             0.0.0.0            32770           0.0.0.0              0
      listen           127.0.0.1               25           0.0.0.0              0
      listen           127.0.0.1              631           0.0.0.0              0
      listen           127.0.0.1            32771           0.0.0.0              0
$
```

Compare this to the information about our TCP listening habits from the output of netstat:

```
$ netstat -tlp

tcp   0   0 0.0.0.0:32770     0.0.0.0:*     LISTEN   1789/rpc.statd
tcp   0   0 127.0.0.1:32771   0.0.0.0:*     LISTEN   1955/xinetd
tcp   0   0 0.0.0.0:199       0.0.0.0:*     LISTEN   9828/snmpd
tcp   0   0 0.0.0.0:111       0.0.0.0:*     LISTEN   1769/portmap
tcp   0   0 0.0.0.0:22        0.0.0.0:*     LISTEN   1939/sshd
tcp   0   0 127.0.0.1:631     0.0.0.0:*     LISTEN   3633/cupsd
tcp   0   0 127.0.0.1:25      0.0.0.0:*     LISTEN   2000/sendmail: acce
```

It is clearly the same information, right? SNMP lets you access this information not only on your local system, but on other systems across the network, as well.

Now open Firefox, point your browser to http://www.cnn.com, and then look at the TCP Connection Table again:

```
      State LocalAddress LocalPort     RemAddress  RemPort
     listen      0.0.0.0        22        0.0.0.0        0
     listen      0.0.0.0       111        0.0.0.0        0
     listen      0.0.0.0       199        0.0.0.0        0
     listen      0.0.0.0     32770        0.0.0.0        0
established     10.0.1.5     32852    64.236.24.4       80
established     10.0.1.5     32853  64.236.16.137       80
established     10.0.1.5     32854  64.12.174.121       80
established     10.0.1.5     32855  64.236.16.137       80
```

established	10.0.1.5	32856	64.236.44.88	80
established	10.0.1.5	32857	64.236.44.88	80
timeWait	10.0.1.5	32859	64.70.10.83	80
listen	127.0.0.1	25	0.0.0.0	0
listen	127.0.0.1	631	0.0.0.0	0
listen	127.0.0.1	32771	0.0.0.0	0

Several connections have been added to the table, all from ephemeral ports on your local system to port 80 on several remote systems. These are the connections used by the browser to fetch the various parts of the CNN main page.

MIB-2: The UDP Table

Another table from MIB-2 that might be of interest is the UDP table.

```
$ snmptable -c public localhost udpTable
SNMP table: UDP-MIB::udpTable

udpLocalAddress udpLocalPort
       0.0.0.0           68
       0.0.0.0          111
       0.0.0.0          123
       0.0.0.0          161
       0.0.0.0          631
       0.0.0.0          691
       0.0.0.0        32768
       0.0.0.0        32769
     127.0.0.1          123
      10.0.1.5          123
```

This table shows the open UDP ports on your system, that is, the ports where some application on your system is listening. (The SNMP agent itself is listening on port 161.) For reference, the address of *this* system is 10.0.1.5.

Compare this with the netstat output. You'll have to run netstat as root to get the program names.

```
# netstat -ulp
Active Internet connections (only servers)
Proto Recv-Q Send-Q Local Address Foreign Address  State PID/Program name
udp        0      0 *:32768              *:*               1787/rpc.statd
udp        0      0 *:snmp               *:*               2553/snmpd
udp        0      0 *:691                *:*               1787/rpc.statd
udp        0      0 *:bootpc             *:*               1694/dhclient
udp        0      0 *:sunrpc             *:*               1767/portmap
udp        0      0 *:ipp                *:*               2656/cupsd
udp        0      0 10.0.1.5:ntp         *:*               1977/ntpd
udp        0      0 localhost.localdoma:ntp *:*            1977/ntpd
udp        0      0 *:ntp                *:*               1977/ntpd
#
```

MIB-2 Contents

In SNMP, the term *group* refers to a subdivision of a MIB consisting of a collection of objects or tables that are related in some way. For example, MIB-2's UPD and TCP groups are all about UDP and TCP traffic, respectively. The Net-SNMP agent can be built to support a variety of MIBs, but you can always expect to find the MIB-2 groups system, interfaces, ip, icmp, tcp, udp, and snmp. These are not all of the groups defined in MIB-2, but they are the ones most likely to be supported by any SNMP agent. Figure 13-1 shows the location of MIB-2 in the overall MIB address space and breaks out some of the groups that comprise MIB-2. Also notice the location of the private.enterprises branch. That's where you can find the HP Printer MIB objects you saw earlier.

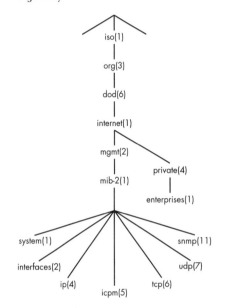

Figure 13-1: MIB-2

Try walking these groups:

```
snmpwalk -c public localhost system
snmpwalk -c public localhost interfaces
snmpwalk -c public localhost ip
snmpwalk -c public localhost icmp
snmpwalk -c public localhost tcp
snmpwalk -c public localhost udp
snmpwalk -c public localhost snmp
```

If you feel up to a challenge, try comparing the output of the above commands with the contents of the MIB files.[6] The output of the snmpwalk

---

[6] In case you've forgotten, the MIB files are in the directory /usr/share/snmp/mibs.

commands listed here will indicate, at the beginning of each output line, the MIB file where you can find the definition of the object displayed.

```
SNMPv2-MIB::snmpInPkts.0 = Counter32: 5998
SNMPv2-MIB::snmpOutPkts.0 = Counter32: 5998
SNMPv2-MIB::snmpInBadVersions.0 = Counter32: 0
```

These lines indicate that you can find these definitions in the MIB file SNMPv2-MIB.txt. For help interpreting what you find in the MIB file, you can read Appendix B.

You are also likely to find that your SNMP agent has been built to include the Host Resources MIB, the UCDavis MIB, and the newer Net-SNMP MIB. Try walking these with the following commands:

```
snmpwalk -c public localhost enterprises ucdavis
snmpwalk -c public localhost enterprises netSnmp
```

One of the objects that might interest you is the version of your own agent.

```
$snmpget -c public localhost versionTag.0
UCD-SNMP-MIB::versionTag.0 = STRING: 5.2.1
```

Writing Values with SNMP

As well as reading information from an agent, SNMP can be used to set the values of objects on a remote system. Let's pick an object that is defined to have read-write access and experiment with it a little.

Setting sysContact

Look through the MIB defining the system group in MIB-2. Remember that when we accessed the system group, the resulting display contained lines that looked like this:

```
SNMPv2-MIB::sysContact.0 = STRING: me@myaddr.com
SNMPv2-MIB::sysName.0 = STRING: localhost.localdomain
SNMPv2-MIB::sysLocation.0 = STRING: "the den"
```

See the SNMPV2-MIB at the start of each line? That indicates that these objects are defined in the file SNMPv2-MIB.txt. If you look at the definitions of these objects in that file, you'll see this snippet:

```
sysContact OBJECT-TYPE
    SYNTAX      DisplayString (SIZE (0..255))
    MAX-ACCESS  read-write
    STATUS      current
    DESCRIPTION
            "The textual identification of the contact person for
            this managed node, together with information on how
```

```
          to contact this person. If no contact information is
          known, the value is the zero-length string."
    ::= { system 4 }

sysName OBJECT-TYPE
    SYNTAX      DisplayString (SIZE (0..255))
    MAX-ACCESS  read-write
    STATUS      current
    DESCRIPTION
          "An administratively-assigned name for this managed
          node. By convention, this is the node's fully-qualified
          domain name. If the name is unknown, the value is
          the zero-length string."
    ::= { system 5 }

sysLocation OBJECT-TYPE
    SYNTAX      DisplayString (SIZE (0..255))
    MAX-ACCESS  read-write
    STATUS      current
    DESCRIPTION
          "The physical location of this node (e.g., 'telephone
          closet, 3rd floor'). If the location is unknown, the
          value is the zero-length string."
    ::= { system 6 }
```

You can see from this snippet that the MIB file defines the three objects we read the values of above: sysContact, sysName, and sysLocation. Each of these is described as an OBJECT-TYPE with a syntax of DisplayString, read-write access, and a status of current.[7] Each object has a description and a line starting with ::=, meaning *is defined as*. *System* is a group in MIB-2 that has an OID of { .1.3.6.1.2.1.1 }. These lines in the MIB file indicate that these three object types are defined as objects 4, 5, and 6 following system (.1.3.6.1.2.1.1), so their OIDs are:

```
sysContact   OID = .1.3.6.1.2.1.1.4
sysName      OID = .1.3.6.1.2.1.1.5
sysLocation  OID = .1.3.6.1.2.1.1.6
```

Notice that these are OIDs of the OBJECT-TYPE definitions, not their instances. Remember, if you want to use snmpget to read the value of the instance, you need to add a .0 to the end of the type OID.

Enough of reading MIBs—we just want to find a read-write type so we can try a SET. Let's try setting sysContact.

```
$ snmpset -c public localhost sysContact.0 s "me@myself.com"
snmpset: Unknown host (Permission denied)[8]
$
```

---

[7] The term *current* means that it's an active type in the MIB, and you can expect to get a value back for it.

[8] Your error message may be different depending on your version of Net-SNMP and whether you are using SNMPv1 or SNMPv2, but you will get an error in any case.

The agent refused the request. Why? Remember your configuration file?

```
rocommunity  public
syslocation  "the den"
syscontact   me@myaddr.com
```

You set a read-only community string, but not a read-write one, so you don't have permission to set any values. You'll have to configure a read-write community name. Add the following line to your snmpd.conf file to configure a read-write community string writer:

```
rwcommunity writer
```

Now you'll need to bring this change to the attention of the SNMP agent. Send the agent a SIGHUP signal to make it re-read its configuration. You will have to do this as root:

```
killall -s HUP snmpd
```

Now try snmpset again.

```
$ snmpset -c writer localhost sysContact.0 s "me@myself.com"
Error in packet.
Reason: notWritable (that object does not support modification)
Failed object: SNMPv2-MIB::sysContact.0
```

The agent refused again! This time, the reason is a little less obvious. The Net-SNMP agent will refuse requests to set new values if the object's value has been configured in the snmpd.conf file. This is not part of the SNMP standard, it's just how Net-SNMP works. It presumes that since you configured these values through the snmpd.conf file, you probably don't want someone else changing them remotely. If you want these values to be writable, you need to set their values using local snmpset commands, rather than by using the configuration file.

NOTE   *Apologies for leading you astray here. Our intent was to highlight this non-obvious behavior of Net-SNMP and possibly save you some time later.*

Setting sysName

Now that you know sysContact and sysLocation are not writable for you because of their definitions in the configuration file, try sysName. You haven't configured a value for that.

```
$ snmpset -c writer localhost sysName.0 s "NewName"
SNMPv2-MIB::sysName.0 = STRING: NewName
```

The snmpset command requires that you use the read-write community string and that you specify the name of the object instance, the type, and the new value. The s indicates that you are writing a string value. This tells the snmpset command how to format the SET packet. Had you written an integer variable, the type would have been i. For a full list of types, read the man page for snmpset. The type of the value you set, of course, must match the type of the object you are setting.

Here's what sysContact, sysName, and sysLocation look like now:

```
$ snmpget -c public localhost sysContact.0 sysName.0 sysLocation.0
SNMPv2-MIB::sysContact.0 = STRING: me@myaddr.com
SNMPv2-MIB::sysName.0 = STRING: NewName
SNMPv2-MIB::sysLocation.0 = STRING: "the den"
$
```

SNMP Traps

As well as responding to SNMP requests like SET and GET, SNMP-enabled devices in the network can send out spontaneous notifications of local events. These notifications are sent either as SNMP traps or informs. *Traps* are datagrams sent without the expectation of a response. *Informs* are an improvement over traps because they expect a confirmation response and are re-sent when the trap receiver does not confirm them in a timely fashion. The time-out and the number of retries can be set by the trap sender as parameters to the snmptrap command.

Receiving Traps with snmptrapd

You can use snmptrapd to receive traps. In the 5.2.1 release of Net-SNMP, which we have been using in this chapter, all you have to do is open a separate terminal window and execute the following command as root:

```
snmptrapd -Os -Le -f
```

As of the 5.3 release, however, the security of snmptrapd was tightened so that it no longer defaults to accepting traps with any community name. In later versions, you need to create an snmptrapd.conf file in the /etc/snmp directory and include a line telling it which communities to accept. We will be using *public*, so our snmptrapd.conf file would contain the following:

```
authCommunity log public
```

Now you can issue the snmptrapd command described above to view the traps you receive.

This command normally runs in the background where it can receive traps, format them, and write them to a log file. However, you are using the -f parameter here to tell snmptrapd to stay in the foreground and the -Le parameter to send its output to stderr. You can also use the -Os parameter to tell snmptrapd to print only the last symbolic part of the OID, which will save space and make the output more readable.

Use a separate command window for sending traps using the snmptrap command. You'll need to run snmptrapd as root, because it wants to listen on UDP port 162. To give it a quick try, run either of the following as root:[9]

```
snmptrap -c public localhost "" coldStart
```

or

```
snmptrap -c public localhost "" .1.3.6.1.6.3.1.1.5.1
```

You can change the format of the output to be much more readable than we show below, but that would require formatting instructions that are beyond what you need here. The default format for output from snmptrapd looks like this:

```
2007-02-14 20:43:26 localhost.localdomain [127.0.0.1]:
sysUpTimeInstance = Timeticks: (4694125) 13:02:21.25
snmpTrapOID.0 = OID: cold Start
```

Keep in mind that you are using SNMPv2. The format for sending an SNMPv1 trap is different and a bit more complicated.

A coldStart trap technically means the network management software has restarted with no change in configuration. Typically, this only happens when the system running the agent has rebooted, so many users think of coldStart as a reboot indicator; however, it will also be sent any time the agent restarts. If you configure a trap target in the snmpd.conf file and restart the agent, your snmptrapd will receive a trap from it. Give it a try—add the following line to your snmpd.conf file:

```
trap2sink  localhost  public
```

Now kill the agent and restart it, or send it another SIGHUP; snmptrapd will indicate that it has received a coldStart trap. Now that the agent has the trap target configured, restart it again. Here's what snmptrapd will display this time:

```
2007-02-14 12:06:17 localhost.localdomain [127.0.0.1]:
sysUpTimeInstance = Timeticks: (33324) 0:05:33.24      snmpTrapOID.0 = OID:
nsNotifyShutdown
2007-02-14 12:06:37 localhost.localdomain [127.0.0.1]:
sysUpTimeInstance = Timeticks: (36) 0:00:00.36 snmpTrapOID.0 = OID: coldStart
snmpTrapEnterprise.0 = OID: netSnmpAgentOIDs.10
```

This is a bit of a jumble, but you can find the beginning of each trap by looking for the time stamp. You will have received two traps: nsNotifyShutdown and coldStart. The agent had the trap target configured

---

[9]You need to be logged in as root because the command will want to write to /var/net-snmp/ snmpapp.conf, which is the persistent data storage. As of Net-SNMP 5.3, it appears to want to write an SNMPv3 engine ID there, even though we are not using SNMPv3 here. (SNMPv3 is not covered in this book.)

at the time it was shut down, so it sent out a trap indicating it was going away. When we started it again (20 seconds later, by the time stamp in this example) it sent a coldStart.

Unlike the coldStart, nsNotifyShutdown is not a trap defined in the SNMP specification, but rather in the NET-SNMP-AGENT-MIB.txt file. It is one of the Net-SNMP enterprise traps, meaning it has OIDs under the private.enterprises section of the MIB tree. This is where you will define your traps when you develop your own MIB in the next chapter.

Traps That Carry Data: linkUp and linkDown

The traps you've seen here, coldStart and nsNotifyShutdown, do not carry any extra data. They only tell you that a shutdown or startup happened. The generic traps linkDown and linkUp are different; they contain extra information as specified in the OBJECTS line of their definitions:

```
linkDown NOTIFICATION-TYPE
    OBJECTS { ifIndex, ifAdminStatus, ifOperStatus }
    STATUS  current
    DESCRIPTION
            "A linkDown trap signifies that the SNMP entity, acting
            in an agent role, has detected that the ifOperStatus
            object for one of its communication links is about to
            enter the down state from some other state (but not
            from the notPresent state). This other state is
            indicated by the included value of ifOperStatus."
    ::= { snmpTraps 3 }

linkUp NOTIFICATION-TYPE
    OBJECTS { ifIndex, ifAdminStatus, ifOperStatus }
    STATUS  current
    DESCRIPTION
            "A linkUp trap signifies that the SNMP entity, acting in an
            agent role, has detected that the ifOperStatus object for
            one of its communication links left the down state and
            transitioned into some other state (but not into the
            notPresent state). This other state is indicated by the
            included value of ifOperStatus."
    ::= { snmpTraps 4 }
```

The OBJECTS line in each trap definition is the list of parameters that will be sent in the trap. The first is ifIndex, which is the index into the interface table in the interfaces section under MIB-2. The others define the administrative and operational status of the interface. Try viewing this table on your own system. It is a little wide to display with the snmptable command, so here's an snmpwalk of ifTable.

```
$ snmpwalk -c public localhost ifTable
IF-MIB::ifIndex.1 = INTEGER: 1
IF-MIB::ifIndex.2 = INTEGER: 2
```

```
IF-MIB::ifDescr.1 = STRING: lo
IF-MIB::ifDescr.2 = STRING: eth0
IF-MIB::ifType.1 = INTEGER: softwareLoopback(24)
IF-MIB::ifType.2 = INTEGER: ethernetCsmacd(6)
IF-MIB::ifMtu.1 = INTEGER: 16436
IF-MIB::ifMtu.2 = INTEGER: 1500
IF-MIB::ifSpeed.1 = Gauge32: 10000000
IF-MIB::ifSpeed.2 = Gauge32: 0
IF-MIB::ifPhysAddress.1 = STRING:
IF-MIB::ifPhysAddress.2 = STRING: 0:10:5a:ce:72:c3
IF-MIB::ifAdminStatus.1 = INTEGER: up(1)
IF-MIB::ifAdminStatus.2 = INTEGER: up(1)
IF-MIB::ifOperStatus.1 = INTEGER: up(1)
IF-MIB::ifOperStatus.2 = INTEGER: down(2)
IF-MIB::ifInOctets.1 = Counter32: 4501945
IF-MIB::ifInOctets.2 = Counter32: 312184
IF-MIB::ifInUcastPkts.1 = Counter32: 21113
IF-MIB::ifInUcastPkts.2 = Counter32: 2865
IF-MIB::ifInDiscards.1 = Counter32: 0
IF-MIB::ifInDiscards.2 = Counter32: 0
IF-MIB::ifInErrors.1 = Counter32: 0
IF-MIB::ifInErrors.2 = Counter32: 0
IF-MIB::ifOutOctets.1 = Counter32: 4503127
IF-MIB::ifOutOctets.2 = Counter32: 312697
IF-MIB::ifOutUcastPkts.1 = Counter32: 21129
IF-MIB::ifOutUcastPkts.2 = Counter32: 3471
IF-MIB::ifOutDiscards.1 = Counter32: 0
IF-MIB::ifOutDiscards.2 = Counter32: 0
IF-MIB::ifOutErrors.1 = Counter32: 0
IF-MIB::ifOutErrors.2 = Counter32: 0
IF-MIB::ifOutQLen.1 = Gauge32: 0
IF-MIB::ifOutQLen.2 = Gauge32: 0
IF-MIB::ifSpecific.1 = OID: SNMPv2-SMI::zeroDotZero
IF-MIB::ifSpecific.2 = OID: SNMPv2-SMI::zeroDotZero
$
```

Try sending a linkDown trap like this:

```
snmptrap -c public localhost "" linkDown \
    ifIndex i 2                           \
    ifAdminStatus i 1                     \
    ifOperStatus i 2
```

This is what snmptrapd displays:

```
2007-02-14 12:48:15 localhost.localdomain [127.0.0.1]:
sysUpTimeInstance = Timeticks: (10483057) 1 day, 5:07:10.57     snmpTrapOID.0
= OID: linkDown    ifIndex = INTEGER: 2        ifAdminStatus = INTEGER: up(1)
ifOperStatus = INTEGER: down(2)
```

This trap shows that interface 2 (which you can see is eth0, from the walk of ifTable above) is administratively up but operationally down. Since this machine only has a single Ethernet interface, you're unlikely to see any traps of this kind (you can't send a trap from an interface that's offline), but you would see the linkUp trap when the interface comes back up.

```
2007-02-14 12:52:15 localhost.localdomain [127.0.0.1]:
sysUpTimeInstance = Timeticks: (10507037) 1 day, 5:11:10.37      snmpTrapOID.0
= OID: linkUp      ifIndex = INTEGER: 2        ifAdminStatus = INTEGER: up(1)
ifOperStatus = INTEGER: up(1)
```

By this time, you should be able to figure out how to send the trap that generated this output. Give it a try.

Summary

This chapter has given you a taste of what SNMP can do. You have installed, configured, and started the Net-SNMP agent on your own computer. You have explored what SNMP can tell you about a networked machine using the snmpget, snmpwalk, and snmptable commands provided by Net-SNMP. You have modified one of the settings on your system (sysName) with SNMP. You have also sent and received some traps. Except for the brief probes of a wireless access point and networked printer, we have limited ourselves to the local machine so that even readers not currently on a network can still have some fun exploring.

We have also limited our tools to those which come with the Net-SNMP package. The nice thing about standard protocols is that software from multiple sources can interoperate. You might try taking a look at a MIB browser from another source. MIB browsers walk a MIB for you and give you a graphical view of the MIB tree offered by the target system. You can find one such browser at http://www.mibble.org.

We hope this chapter has given you a taste for how useful SNMP can be to a network manager or IT professional. SNMP can be used to discover devices on a network, identify the type of device based on its IP address, or even reconfigure options on a device. This perspective will be helpful when it comes to designing your own MIB in the next chapter.

14

DESIGNING AN SNMP MIB

If you read the previous chapter, you already have some idea of why you may need an SNMP interface and how it can be useful. In this chapter and the next, you'll see how the information specific to an appliance can be added to this interface. Like the web, LCD, and CLI interfaces, the SNMP interface will also be based on the information available from RTA tables within the Laddie application itself.

This chapter is concerned primarily with the design of the MIB and creation of a valid MIB file. The topics covered here are:

- Applying for an enterprise number
- Designing the MIB
- Creating the MIB file
- Validating the MIB

You will learn how to implement the agent in the next chapter.

Our Goal

In Chapter 5 you saw several of the Laddie application's user interfaces to the ZONE structure: framebuffer, CLI, and web. Here's the ZONE struct from the Laddie source:

```
typedef struct
{
    int    id;           // ID number of alarm [1-5]
    char   name[ZONE_NAME_LEN]; // the alarm name
    int    enabled;      // 1 if enabled
    int    edge;         // 1 if alarm on low to high transition
    int    latching;     // 1 if should latch the alarm
    int    input;        // is the latest raw input from the alarm
    int    alarm;        // 1 if in alarm
    int    count;        // count of alarms on this pin
}
ZONE;
```

Figure 14-1 shows how this looked in the RTA table editor.

Zone

id	name	enabled	edge	latching	input	alarm	count	
1	Garage Door	1	0	0	1	0	7	(edit)
2	Motion Detector	1	1	0	0	0	2281	(edit)
3	Front Door	1	0	0	1	0	0	(edit)
4	Kitchen Window	1	1	0	1	0	0	(edit)
5	Refrigerator	1	1	1	0	0	0	(edit)

Figure 14-1: The ZONE struct in the RTA table editor

Jumping ahead a bit, this is how the same information will look in our SNMP interface when we're done designing and implementing our MIB.

```
$ snmptable -c public -v2c myappliance ladAlarmTable
SNMP table: LAD-MIB::ladAlarmTable

ladAlarmZoneName ladAlarmEnable ladAlarmLatching ladAlarmState ladAlarmCount
     Garage Door           true                0             0             7
 Motion Detector           true                0             0          2281
      Front Door           true                0             0             0
  Kitchen Window           true                0             0             0
    Refrigerator           true             true             0             0
```

Our task in this chapter and the next is to show you how to go from the ZONE struct to the above SNMP interface, step by step. When we are done, you should understand how to do the same thing in your own application, doing a fair amount of cutting and pasting from this MIB.

You may have noticed that we did not include the *id*, *edge*, and *input* columns in our SNMP view of this table. This was not an oversight. It is up to the MIB designer (or any interface designer, for that matter) to decide what makes sense in light of the intended use of the interface. In our case, we decided that the *edge* and *input* information was too hardware specific to be necessary in this interface. The *id* column is not returned by our SNMP agent, but will be used as an index into the alarm table whenever access to a specific row is necessary.

Your Enterprise Number

Now that your interest is piqued, we'll build suspense by taking a little detour for those of you actually in the process of starting a small company to sell your appliance. You may remember the brief discussion about enterprise numbers in the last chapter when we were identifying a printer using SNMP. Every MIB needs to be anchored to the overall namespace, and if you are designing a private MIB, you need an enterprise number of your own. These are assigned by IANA (Internet Assigned Numbers Authority). Each company or organization only needs one enterprise number because IANA grants you the authority to manage the tree beneath your number.

Obtaining an enterprise number from IANA may take awhile, so you should get the ball rolling early. Once you apply, IANA will tell you to expect the process to take about a month. You can design and implement your MIB while IANA is processing your request.

The process itself is pretty easy. Just use your favorite web browser to navigate to the IANA website (http://www.iana.org) and click **Application Forms** in the menu. On the next page, select **Private Enterprise Numbers (SNMP)**. You'll be presented with an online form to fill out.

At the bottom of the web page, there's a link to the current list of registered numbers. You might want to check it out just to see who's on the list. You'll notice some pretty recognizable names near the beginning; these companies have been in the SNMP game since the beginning. IBM's number is 2. Cisco has 9. Hewlett Packard has 11. You can scroll down to the bottom to see what the current high number is. You might also recognize the entry at number 23528. It is the start of the subtree where we will anchor the Laddie MIB we will develop in this chapter.

When you start your application, you will be asked to provide the following information:

- Your company or organization name
- The company's address
- The company's phone number
- The name of the contact person
- The contact person's address
- The contact person's phone number
- The contact person's email address
- A fax number

As you may have noticed when looking at the current list, only the enterprise number, company name, contact person's name, and contact's email address are listed online. It's a good idea to use something other than your general email address here, since it's likely that spambots will harvest it. It's handy to have a separate address for this purpose, something generic you can forward to whomever is responsible for your SNMP work in the future.

Just enter your information in the form and click the **Submit Application** button.

The MIB Files

IANA grants you the authority to manage your own subtree, but it's up to you to do a good job of it. Plan for success and don't think of this appliance as the end of the line—leave room for expansion. You might want to define your enterprise number in a separate file where you can put information common to all your MIBs. (By the way, reading other people's MIBs is a very good idea. You'll find out what is common usage and you may pick up styles you find attractive along the way.)

Here are the two files we'll be creating in this chapter:

LADDIE-GROUP-SMI.txt

This is the file where we'll define the Laddie Group enterprise number and our product identification OIDs.[1]

LAD-MIB.txt

This file will hold the Laddie product MIB. This MIB will be anchored under an OID defined in the LADDIE-GROUP-SMI.txt file.

We'll run these files through a utility supplied by Net-SNMP to produce skeleton code for our MIB implementation. You'll also want these files on any system that will be running the management applications (snmpget, snmpset, snmpwalk, and so on) or interpreting traps and informs.

The network management system you are using will define where you place these files. The Net-SNMP management applications tend to want them in the directory /usr/local/share/snmp/mibs, though you can modify this, and it's subject to the preferences of the OS distribution you are using. For our appliance we will place them in /opt/snmp/share/snmp/mibs.

LADDIE-GROUP-SMI

This is the file that describes the top-level structure we will be using to organize our Laddie enterprise subtree. It holds our enterprise number and product identification OID. This file is small, so let's look at the whole thing and then discuss its structure. (The address, phone number, and fax number are bogus to protect Bob's privacy, but you'll get the general idea.)

---

[1] OIDs used to identify products are returned as the value of sysObjectId in MIB-2.

```
LADDIE-GROUP-SMI DEFINITIONS ::= BEGIN

IMPORTS
    MODULE-IDENTITY,
    enterprises
        FROM SNMPv2-SMI
;

laddieGroup MODULE-IDENTITY
    LAST-UPDATED  "200502220000Z"
    ORGANIZATION  "The Laddie Group"
    CONTACT-INFO
        "Contact:  Bob Smith

        Postal:  221B Baker Street
                 Santa Clara, California, USA 12345

        Phone:  408-555-1138
        FAX:    408-555-1234

        Web:    www.runtimeaccess.com

        Email:  bsmith@linuxtoys.org"

    DESCRIPTION
        "The Laddie Group MIB.

        Copyright 2005 The Laddie Group
        All rights reserved.

        This MIB module specifies the anchor point of the
        Laddie Group MIBs and definitions common to these MIBs."

    REVISION  "200502220000Z"
        DESCRIPTION
            " 1.0  - Initial Document."
      ::= { enterprises 23528 }


-- MIBs are defined here:
laddieMgmt      OBJECT IDENTIFIER ::= { laddieGroup 1 }

-- Products are registered here:
laddieProducts  OBJECT IDENTIFIER ::= { laddieGroup 2 }
laddieAppliance OBJECT IDENTIFIER ::= { laddieProducts 1 }
END
```

Now let's go through this file again in more detail. We'll show you a section of the MIB file first and then discuss it. The best way to read this is to scan the MIB text briefly, then read the description while referring to the MIB text.

```
LADDIE-GROUP-SMI DEFINITIONS ::= BEGIN
```

This line gives the MIB a name and tells the reader (human or program) that this is the beginning of our definitions for this MIB. Look for a matching END at the bottom of the file to tell the reader when all definitions are complete.

```
    IMPORTS
❶       MODULE-IDENTITY,
❷       enterprises
            FROM SNMPv2-SMI
    ;
```

The IMPORTS section is like the #include section in a C program—it tells where to find the terms used in this MIB but not defined here. We included ❶ the MODULE-IDENTITY macro and ❷ the enterprises for use below.

Next, we defined the laddieGroup module:

```
❶ laddieGroup MODULE-IDENTITY
❷     LAST-UPDATED  "200502220000Z"
      ORGANIZATION  "The Laddie Group"
      CONTACT-INFO
          "Here is where you tell your users who you are and
          how to contact you."

      DESCRIPTION
          "Here is where you describe the general purpose of
          this MIB. This is also where you will want to put
          a copyright notice."

      REVISION "200502220000Z"
          DESCRIPTION
              " 1.0 - Initial Document."
❸     ::= { enterprises 23528 }
```

We'll give ❶ the name laddieGroup to this module and define it as having ❸ the value of 23528 under enterprises, so the full OID looks like this:

```
.1.3.6.1.4.1.23528
```

The funny-looking string in the LAST-UPDATED and REVISION lines is a time stamp specifying the year, month, day, hour, and minute of the last change or revision. The *Z* stands for GMT (Greenwich Mean Time), sometimes called *Zulu Time*. The hours and minutes are generally zeros, because no one really cares what hour and minute a revision was made. The ❷ number "200702220000Z" means February 22, 2007. With separators, it would look like this: 2007-02-22 00:00.

```
-- MIBs are defined here:
laddieMgmt      OBJECT IDENTIFIER ::= { laddieGroup 1 }
```

This is where we'll anchor the LAD-MIB we'll be defining in the next section.

```
-- Products are registered here:
laddieProducts  OBJECT IDENTIFIER ::= { laddieGroup 2 }
laddieAppliance  OBJECT IDENTIFIER ::= { laddieProducts 1 }
```

The laddieProducts section is where we defined the OIDs that identify our products (or entire product lines, if you're thinking really big). We have defined an OID for our Laddie appliance here, and we'll be setting sysObjectID in MIB-2[2] to this value on our appliances. This will allow someone polling the box with an SNMP utility like snmpget to determine that this box is a Laddie appliance. Large corporations may put the OIDs that identify all their products into a single file. Cisco, for example, has a CISCO-PRODUCTS file where it gathers all these OIDs. For now, Laddie only has a single product OID, so we won't go to this trouble.

```
END
```

Here's that END we were looking for. This is the end of the LADDIE-SMI-MIB.txt file and wraps up our discussion of it.

Creating the LAD-MIB

In this section, we'll create our appliance MIB. Refer to the illustration of the LAD-MIB structure in Figure 14-2 for a better idea of how the MIB components interrelate. It may be helpful to refer to this picture as you follow along with the development of the MIB file.

The LAD-MIB is divided into three main sections:

- ladTraps, containing definitions of traps
- ladTrapInfo, containing definitions of information objects sent in traps
- ladSystem, containing definitions of pollable objects

Let's start the detailed walk-through. Again, we'll be showing one or more lines followed by a discussion of what we've shown.

We'll start with the BEGIN statement and the definition of our MIB name:

```
LAD-MIB DEFINITIONS ::= BEGIN
```

Hopefully this looks familiar. If not, take another look at the beginning of the LADDIE-GROUP-SMI.txt file. The BEGIN line says we are starting the definition of the LAD-MIB, which is the name we gave the MIB for our appliance.

---

[2] You can find sysObjectID defined in the SNMPv2-MIB.txt file, which is included with the Net-SNMP package.

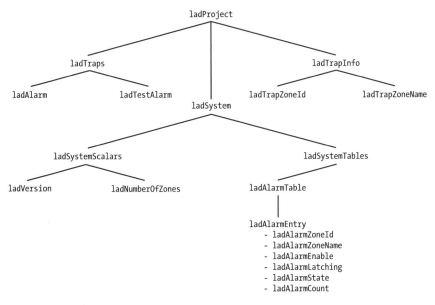

Figure 14-2: LAD-MIB Structure

Next, we'll import the externally defined types and macros that we will be using from other files:

```
IMPORTS
    NOTIFICATION-TYPE,
    MODULE-IDENTITY,
    OBJECT-TYPE,
    Counter32,
    Integer32,
    Gauge32
❶       FROM SNMPv2-SMI
    DisplayString,
    TruthValue
❷       FROM SNMPv2-TC
❸   laddieMgmt
        FROM LADDIE-GROUP-SMI
;
```

The first set comes from ❶ SNMPv2-SMI just like in the LADDIE-GROUP-SMI.txt file we covered in the previous section.

The next set comes from ❷ SNMPv2-TC. The letters *TC* stand for *textual conventions*. SNMPv2-TC is basically a file that defines new, commonly used object types.

The ❸ laddieMgmt OID from the LADDIE-GROUP-SMI.txt file will be our starting point in the overall namespace for our appliance MIB. We'll use laddieMgmt as our link to the overall namespace by defining the module in this group below laddieMgmt in the code portion of the "Module Definition" section next.

The SNMPv2-SMI and SNMPv2-TC MIB definitions are supplied with the Net-SNMP package. When you installed Net-SNMP on your system in the Chapter 13, these files were probably put into either /usr/share/snmp/mibs or /usr/local/share/snmp/mibs. Look for the files SNMPv2-SMI.txt and SNMPv2-TC.txt there.

Module Definition

We start by defining a module, ladProject, to contain our appliance MIB. This is where we put the copyright, revision history, contact information, and a general description of what the module contains.

```
ladProject MODULE-IDENTITY
    LAST-UPDATED  "200505280000Z"
    ORGANIZATION  "The Laddie Group"
    CONTACT-INFO
        "Here we put contact information."

    DESCRIPTION
        "The LAD MIB.

        Copyright 2005 Laddie Group
        All rights reserved.

        This MIB module specifies the pollable and set-able
        objects in the Linux Appliance Design demonstration
        application: an alarm system monitor. This MIB also
        describes traps associated with this demo appliance."

❶   REVISION  "200505280000Z"
        DESCRIPTION
            " 1.1  - Traps added along with trapInfo section."

❷   REVISION  "200502220000Z"
        DESCRIPTION
            " 1.0  - Initial Document."

    ::= { laddieMgmt❸ 1 }
```

The MODULE-IDENTITY section is like one long sentence. The first and last lines, taken together, say that ladProject is a module defined directly below ❸ laddieMgmt in the namespace and that its OID is laddieMgmt.1. Here's the OID in numeric form:

```
.1.3.6.1.4.1.3382.1
```

The rest of the MODULE-IDENTITY section should be fairly clear after our discussion of the LADDIE-SMI in the previous section. You may notice that we have two REVISION clauses listed at lines ❶ and ❷. If you make changes to your MIB in the future, you will need to add revision clauses to explain what you did. The convention is to keep revision clauses in reverse-chronological order (that is, the most recent change appears at the top). This does not mean you should feel free to make any changes you want to your MIB; you will just be creating confusion for your customers if you change anything (names, OIDs, and so on) that is already defined in your MIB. You may, however, find it necessary to enhance your MIB with new information required by customer demand or to help manage new features you'll be adding to your appliance. You may add new structure, but do not change existing structure!

Clearly your LAST-UPDATED time stamp will match that of your most recent revision clause, as ours does above.

The next set of lines defines the sections we will be fleshing out later:

```
-- top level MIB headings of the LAD MIB
❶ ladTraps     OBJECT IDENTIFIER  ::= { ladProject 0 }
  ladSystem    OBJECT IDENTIFIER  ::= { ladProject 1 }
  ladTrapInfo  OBJECT IDENTIFIER  ::= { ladProject 2 }
```

Putting all of the section heading OIDs together at the top, as we have done here, is a stylistic choice we feel can help communicate the structure of the rest of the MIB. We're making it clear that there will be a section for defining traps, one for system information (where we will be putting our Alarm Table), and another section for the non-pollable information we will only send along with traps.

Numbering in SNMP usually begins with 1, not zero, but you may have noticed that we gave ❶ the ladTraps section above the OID of ladProject.0. Our reason for doing this dates back to the early days of SNMPv2 (SNMP version 2), when compatibility with SNMPv1 (SNMP version 1) was being crafted. For more details, you may want to read *RFC 1908: Coexistence between Version 1 and Version 2 of the Internet-Standard Network Management Framework.*

We'll continue our review of our MIB with the ladSystem section and leave the traps for later. That will allow us to immediately follow our discussion of the trap with the ladTrapInfo section.

```
-- LAD System Information
ladSystemScalars  OBJECT IDENTIFIER  ::= { ladSystem 1 }
ladSystemTables   OBJECT IDENTIFIER  ::= { ladSystem 2 }
```

Here we further subdivide the ladSystem section into a section for scalars and another for tables. *Scalars* are just objects that are not columns in tables. Experience has taught us to keep scalars and tables separate to avoid having scalars sprinkled around between tables as the MIB evolves over time.

Version and Number of Zones

Next, we'll define some scalars in our ladSystemScalars section.

```
-- ----------------------------------------
-- LAD System Scalars
-- ----------------------------------------

ladVersion OBJECT-TYPE
    SYNTAX        DisplayString
    MAX-ACCESS    read-only
    STATUS        current
    DESCRIPTION
        "This string represents the version of the LAD Alarm
         appliance software."
    ::= { ladSystemScalars 1 }

ladNumberOfZones OBJECT-TYPE
    SYNTAX        Integer32 (1..128)
    MAX-ACCESS    read-only
    STATUS        current
    DESCRIPTION
        "The number of alarm zones, therefore the number of rows
         in the ladAlarmTable."
    ::= { ladSystemScalars 2 }
```

Here we have defined two objects (note the OBJECT-TYPE keyword): ladVersion and ladNumberOfZones. The SYNTAX clause tells us that ladVersion is a DisplayString, meaning it is represented as a string of displayable (printable) characters, and ladNumberOfZones is a 32-bit integer with values ranging from 1 through 128. If you refer back to our IMPORT section at the start of this MIB, you will see that both of these syntaxes were imported from SNMPv2-TC, the textual conventions file.

The MAX-ACCESS clause tells us that each of these objects is read-only. Some objects we will encounter later in this MIB will have read-write, not-accessible, or accessible-for-notify access. *Read-write* just means you can read the object's value as well as write a new value. You can't read or write objects defined as *not-accessible*, but you might use one as an index into a table. *Accessible-for-notify* is how we define information sent with a trap but that otherwise is not pollable.

One point to keep in mind here is that the MAX-ACCESS clause defines *maximum* access, not *actual* access. You will never be able to write an object that has max-access read-only, but you may not be able to write to an object whose max-access is read-write, either. The ability to write to the object may be restricted by other factors. For example, in Net-SNMP, you may not write to any object that has a value set in the snmpd.conf file, regardless of what the MAX-ACCESS clause indicates in the MIB file.

The STATUS clause indicates that both objects are current, that is, they are are valid objects in this version of the MIB. To remove an object from a MIB, you would make its status deprecated. This is a brand new MIB, so nothing is deprecated.

The DESCRIPTION clause is intended specifically for the human reader of the MIB, rather than a computer program. It should contain a brief description of the object. It might also contain possible uses of the value and any caveats the reader may need to know.

The last line of each section defines the OID. The ::= means *is defined as.* Each OID is described as appending to a previous OID. The `ladNumberOfZones` object's OID is the same as `ladSystemScalars` with a *2* appended to the end. Its whole numeric OID looks like this:

```
.1.3.6.1.4.1.23528.1.1.1.1.2
```

The first six numbers in this string are from standard MIBs and can be read like this:

```
.iso(1).org(3).dod(6).internet(1).private(4).enterprises(1)
```

The next number is where IANA gave us our own enterprise number, 23528. So after enterprises, the rest of the OID continues

```
laddieGroup.laddieMgmt.ladProject.ladSystem.ladSystemScalars.ladNumberOfZones
```

See Figure 14-3 for the correspondence between each number in the OID and its descriptive name.

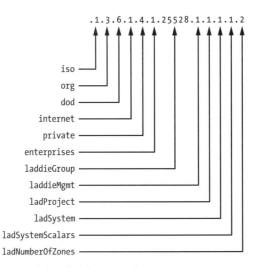

Figure 14-3: OID for `ladNumberOfZones`

The Alarm Table

Now for the core of our MIB: the Alarm Table. This is the table we displayed at the beginning of this chapter, showing the zones and alarm states. Here is how we define this table in our MIB:

```
-- ----------------------------------------
-- LAD Alarm Table
-- ----------------------------------------

ladAlarmTable OBJECT-TYPE
    SYNTAX      SEQUENCE OF LadAlarmEntry
    MAX-ACCESS  not-accessible
    STATUS      current
    DESCRIPTION
        "A table of alarms."
    ::= { ladSystemTables 1 }

ladAlarmEntry OBJECT-TYPE
    SYNTAX      LadAlarmEntry
    MAX-ACCESS  not-accessible
    STATUS      current
    DESCRIPTION
        "An entry in the Alarm Table."
    INDEX { ladAlarmZoneId }
    ::= { ladAlarmTable 1 }

LadAlarmEntry ::=
    SEQUENCE {
        ladAlarmZoneId   Integer32,
        ladAlarmZoneName DisplayString,
        ladAlarmEnable   TruthValue,
        ladAlarmLatching TruthValue,
        ladAlarmState    TruthValue,
        ladAlarmCount    Counter32
    }
```

Notice that we have three blocks of definition above: ladAlarmTable, ladAlarmEntry, and LadAlarmEntry. SNMP requires that all object names begin with a lowercase letter (hence, ladAlarmTable, ladAlarmEntry). However, LadAlarmEntry is not an object, but rather a definition of the syntax of the table entry. It is common practice to define the *syntax* of a table with the same name as the table entry, but starting with an uppercase letter (ladAlarmEntry versus LadAlarmEntry). The syntax of ladAlarmTableEntry is a sequence (list or array) of other object types which are the columns in the table.

After the definition of the table entry syntax, we'll list the detailed definitions of each of the columns listed in the SEQUENCE clause:

```
ladAlarmZoneId     OBJECT-TYPE
    SYNTAX      Integer32 (1..128)
    MAX-ACCESS  not-accessible
```

```
STATUS      current
DESCRIPTION
    "The index (table row number) of this zone."
::= { ladAlarmEntry 1 }


ladAlarmZoneName   OBJECT-TYPE
    SYNTAX      DisplayString
    MAX-ACCESS  read-only
    STATUS      current
    DESCRIPTION
        "A user-configured name for this zone."
    ::= { ladAlarmEntry 2 }


ladAlarmEnable OBJECT-TYPE
    SYNTAX      TruthValue
    MAX-ACCESS  read-write
    STATUS      current
    DESCRIPTION
        "Set to true to enable this alarm input.
         Set to false to disable this alarm input."
    ::= { ladAlarmEntry 3 }


ladAlarmLatching OBJECT-TYPE
    SYNTAX      TruthValue
    MAX-ACCESS  read-write
    STATUS      current
    DESCRIPTION
        "If set to to True, this alarm will persist after
         the alarm pin returns to its normal state. Latching
         alarms must be reset by clearing the alarm state."
    ::= { ladAlarmEntry 4 }


ladAlarmState  OBJECT-TYPE
    SYNTAX      TruthValue
    MAX-ACCESS  read-write
    STATUS      current
    DESCRIPTION
        "Alarm state. The (possibly latched) state of the
         alarm for this input. The user sets this field
         to false to clear a latched alarm."
    ::= { ladAlarmEntry 5 }


ladAlarmCount  OBJECT-TYPE
    SYNTAX      Counter32
    MAX-ACCESS  read-only
    STATUS      current
    DESCRIPTION
        "A count of the number of times the
         alarm has triggered."
    ::= { ladAlarmEntry 6 }
```

The MAX-ACCESS clause in each of these objects defines how it may be used. We have made ladAlarmZoneId not-accessible because we will only be using it to index into the table to read or write the other values. Notice that ladAlarmEnable, ladAlarmLatching, and ladAlarmState are read-write, but ladAlarmZoneName is read-only. We wanted to be able to use SNMP commands to enable or disable alarms, change whether or not they latch, and clear alarms by setting their state to false. We felt, however, that changing the name of a zone is a static configuration that should be done through another interface, like the web interface or the CLI. The ladAlarmCount is a history of the number of times the alarm has triggered, so we have made this read-only.

There is nothing mandatory about the MAX-ACCESS choices we have made here. You might well disagree with some of these choices and design your MIB differently. Look at the SNMP display of the Zone structure in the section "Our Goal" on page 244. Had we defined our ladAlarmZoneId as readable, you would see the row number at the start of each row right before the zone name. We also could have defined the count field as writable so you could reset it to zero periodically; this would allow you to see how many times the alarm has triggered over a period without having to save the old value and subtract it from the new one. These choices belong to the designer.

The Traps

Now let's leave the Alarm Table and move on to our traps:

```
-- ----------------------------------------
-- LAD traps
-- ----------------------------------------

ladAlarm NOTIFICATION-TYPE
    OBJECTS     { ladTrapZoneId, ladTrapZoneName }
    STATUS      current
    DESCRIPTION
    " Trap issued when an alarm is triggered. "
    ::= { ladTraps 1 }

ladAlarmClear NOTIFICATION-TYPE
    STATUS      current
    DESCRIPTION
    " Trap issued when last raised alarm returns to normal state. "
    ::= { ladTraps 2 }
```

We have included two traps: one to raise a red flag when an intrusion has been detected and the other to let you know when everything has returned to normal. These look a lot like the OBJECT-TYPE definitions above, but we use NOTIFICATION-TYPE for traps.

The OBJECTS clause in the `ladAlarm` trap definition tells what other information will accompany the trap. This is often called the varbind list, for *var*iable *bind*ings. These variables, which explain why the trap was sent, are bound to the trap when it is sent.

```
-- ------------------------------------------
-- LAD Trap Info: varbinds sent with traps
-- ------------------------------------------

ladTrapZoneId OBJECT-TYPE
    SYNTAX      Integer32
    MAX-ACCESS  accessible-for-notify
    STATUS      current
    DESCRIPTION
        "This is the ID (row number in the ladAlarmTable) of the
        zone generating the alarm."
    ::= { ladTrapInfo 1 }

ladTrapZoneName OBJECT-TYPE
    SYNTAX      DisplayString
    MAX-ACCESS  accessible-for-notify
    STATUS      current
    DESCRIPTION
        "This is the name of the zone generating the alarm."
    ::= { ladTrapInfo 2 }
```

These are the definitions of the objects in our varbind list. The MAX-ACCESS of these is set to accessible-for-notify, meaning they cannot be polled; they merely define the objects for the benefit of the trap receiver. These objects only have meaning when attached to a trap.

Early SNMP documents (RFCs) were created with concern for keeping SNMP traffic to a minimum to prevent burdening networks with extra traffic. Traps were intended just to draw attention to a possible problem; you were supposed to poll the device for specifics about what was wrong. Today, however, some network administrators use trap logs as a history of what's been happening on the device. They want all pertinent information sent with the trap and logged by the trap-receiving software.

You'll also want to take care that your device doesn't become too chatty with its traps. Laddie is unlikely to have this problem, but if you are building an appliance intended to sit on a major corporate, ISP, or carrier network, you had better consider this. If you check for error conditions every minute and generate a trap each time some measure is over an acceptable threshold, an appliance that notices an error on Friday night will be able to send about 3,500 traps by Monday morning, all reporting the same problem. Any other problem from a different device will be lost in the jabber. You may want to just report the problem once when it is first noticed, then send another trap to indicate when the problem is corrected.

The argument in favor of sending lots of traps is that SNMP is unreliable by design. It uses UDP packets to report problems with the assumption that any problem of importance will be noticed more than once, so the loss of a single trap will not be a problem. If you can't be sure your trap was received, you had better keep sending it until someone notices, right? Well, that's one approach. Another is just to use informs instead of traps. *Informs* became available with SNMPv2 and are essentially traps with some built-in reliability. Informs expect a confirmation message from the receiver and will retry some number of times if they don't see the confirm. If this isn't good enough for you, then you might want to consider some reduced frequency schedule for resending your trap if your device has not received some attention.

END

Last but not least, there's the END marker that signals the end of the MIB.

Validating Your MIB

Now that the MIB has been written, we need to test it for validity. The MIB must be not only human-readable, but machine parse-able. The syntax of a MIB must be as correct as the syntax of a computer program, or the applications using the MIB will be unable to interpret it. Lucky for us, multiple free MIB validators are available online. All you need is a browser and your MIB files. There's always the risk that any online resources discussed here may be unavailable by the time you read this book, but the one we will be using here is on the SimpleWeb website, shown in Figure 14-4. You can find it at http://wwwsnmp.cs.utwente.nl/ietf/mibs/validate. It has been around since 1997 and is run by the Universiteit Twente in the Netherlands.

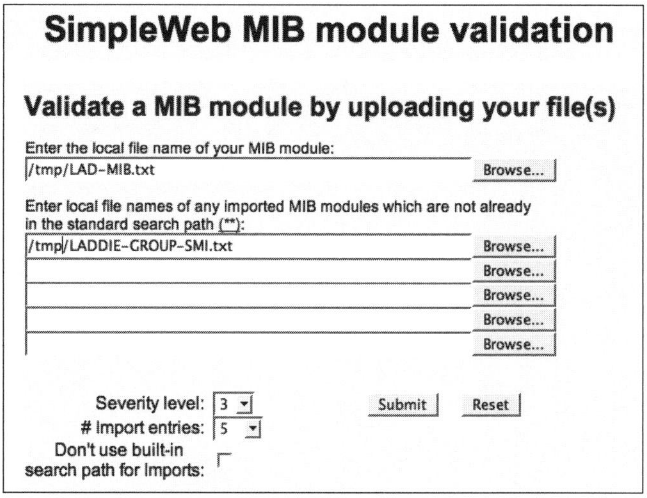

SimpleWeb MIB module validation

Validate a MIB module by uploading your file(s)

Enter the local file name of your MIB module:

/tmp/LAD-MIB.txt   Browse...

Enter local file names of any imported MIB modules which are not already in the standard search path (**):

/tmp/LADDIE-GROUP-SMI.txt   Browse...
          Browse...
          Browse...
          Browse...
          Browse...

Severity level: 3 ▾   Submit   Reset
Import entries: 5 ▾
Don't use built-in
search path for Imports: ☐

Figure 14-4: The SimpleWeb MIB validator

Another free validator we have used is the one provided by Muonics at http://www.muonics.com/Tools/smicheck.php.

Make sure you do not skip the validation step! If you don't get the syntax of your MIB exactly right, nothing will work for you from here on.

Summary

In this chapter you have seen how to apply for an enterprise number, develop an MIB, and validate that MIB. The hard part is trying to design the MIB structure to accommodate future changes. Our task for Laddie has been fairly simple because our whole MIB revolves around a simple RTA table, and the MIB is unlikely to evolve much over time. A designer working on a MIB for a real appliance doesn't have it so easy. We suggest thinking about the basic types of information you may need to have, regardless of what direction your product takes in the future. For example, you may have:

- Configuration information
- Statistics
- Historical information
- Miscellaneous run-time states
- Performance measures
- Usage levels
- Service or resource saturation levels

This may guide you in structuring your MIB to make your life easier as future demands are made on you and your MIB.

15

IMPLEMENTING YOUR SNMP MIB

In this chapter we will implement the MIB we developed in Chapter 14 by writing an extension to the Net-SNMP agent to add support for the LAD-MIB. We'll cover the following topics:

- The Net-SNMP Agent
- The MIB skeleton: mib2c
- The header file: ladProject.h
- The code file: ladProject.c
- Makefile revisited
- Debugging
- Traps

Remember that our goal is to implement a working SNMP agent that supports our MIB. When queried for the objects we have defined, the agent will respond with the current values of those objects. We will also be able to assign values to the objects we defined with read-write access. For example, we will be able to use the `snmptable` command to retrieve values from the Alarm table, as shown below. Don't be too concerned with the format of this command (though if you read Chapter 13, you should be familiar with it). The `snmptable` command retrieves the ladAlarmTable from a system called myappliance using SNMPv2 and the community name *public*; then it displays the table row by row to make it easy to read.

```
$ snmptable -c public -v2c myappliance ladAlarmTable
SNMP table: LAD-MIB::ladAlarmTable

ladAlarmZoneName ladAlarmEnable ladAlarmLatching ladAlarmState ladAlarmCount
     Garage Door           true                0             0             7
 Motion Detector           true                0             0          2281
      Front Door           true                0             0             0
  Kitchen Window           true                0             0             0
    Refrigerator           true             true             0             0
```

The SNMP commands will allow remote access to information kept within the ladd daemon's internal data structures. As shown in Figure 15-1, SNMP is used between the remote system and the SNMP agent. The agent then uses PostgreSQL to request the information from RTA running within the ladd daemon.

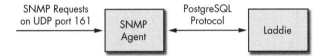

Figure 15-1: SNMP agent as go-between

NOTE *You will notice some differences in file placement in this chapter compared with Chapter 13, because here we are designing the agent for the appliance itself. For clarity, we will be keeping our files under /opt rather than distributing them around the filesystem in their normal default locations.*

The Net-SNMP Agent

We'll be extending the Net-SNMP agent, so we'll need to download the source tarball, which we can find at http://net-snmp.sourceforge.net. As of this writing, version 5.2.1 is current, so we'll retrieve net-snmp-5.2.1.tar.gz. No doubt by the time you read this, Net-SNMP will be several releases ahead, but you can just grab the most current version. The process for extending the agent that we will be describing in this chapter hasn't changed significantly in all the time the we have been working with it (that is, since at least UCD-SNMP 4.1).

Our goal is to set up a way of building our agent that will make it easy to download a new release of Net-SNMP in the future and just drop it into a build. The plan is to create a Makefile that will untar Net-SNMP, copy the agent extensions into the right location in the build tree, configure the Net-SNMP agent to include the extensions, and then build it. To upgrade to a newer version of Net-SNMP, all you need to do is drop a new version of the Net-SNMP source tarball into the directory and change the one line of the Makefile that defines the Net-SNMP version. We don't have our extension ready yet, so let's just start by untarring and building the vanilla agent. This will allow us to test the process before we complicate things with our MIB. The following is a simplified version of the Makefile you'll find on the CD that comes with this book:

```
❶ NETSNMP_VERSION = 5.2.1
  BUILD_DIR     = ./net-snmp-$(NETSNMP_VERSION)

  #
  # Targets
  #
  all:  clean setup config build

  clean:
          rm -rf $(BUILD_DIR)
          rm -rf /oft/snmp/*

  setup:
          tar zxf net-snmp-$(NETSNMP_VERSION).tar.gz

  config:
          cd $(BUILD_DIR); \
          ./configure --prefix=/opt/snmp <../configure.input; \
          cd ..

  build:
          cd $(BUILD_DIR); \
          make

  install:
          cd $(BUILD_DIR); \
          install
```

If you are using a newer version of Net-SNMP, just drop your tarball into the same directory as the Makefile, change ❶ the NETSNMP_VERSION line to match your version, and continue with the instructions below.

We'll put the Makefile and configure.input files into the same directory as the tarball we just downloaded. Configure.input contains the interactive answers expected by the configure step. The -prefix option tells configure to use the /opt/snmp prefix to our file locations. Installation of Net-SNMP follows the familiar

```
./configure
make
make install
```

steps of most Linux source packages, though we will let the Makefile do this for us.

Here's what our configure.input looks like:

```
<blank line>
2
Not Set
Not Set
/var/log/snmpd.log
/var/net-snmp
```

The first line must be blank because the configure script asks us to hit ENTER when we are ready to enter the input.

The 2 selects SNMPv2 as our default version of SNMP. This doesn't really apply to the agent because it takes its cue from the requests received, but the Net-SNMP package contains the source for management applications like snmpget and snmpwalk, as well.

The two Not Set lines are for system contact and system location (objects available in MIB-2). We will be overriding these values in our agent configuration file, so we'll just set these objects to the string Not Set.

The next two lines are the default log file and persistent storage locations.

Give this a try by typing **make**. It will build the Net-SNMP applications (snmpget, snmpwalk, etc.), the libraries, and the agent. If it doesn't work, try executing the steps by hand, without the Makefile. First untar the tarball and drop down into the directory it generates. Then run **./configure** and answer the questions as we have laid them out in configure.input, above. Check the output from configure to see if you are missing something, like a library you need to install. If you don't see anything wrong, type **make** (in the net-snmp.5.2.1 directory) and watch for errors. You can't move on until this works.

Once you get make working, install Net-SNMP onto your development system. As root, type

```
make install
```

This will install files in several directories under /opt/snmp.

```
$ ls /opt/snmp
bin/   include/   lib/   man/   sbin/   share/
```

The /opt/snmp directory tree is our staging area for the files we will need to copy to our appliance to get the agent working there. We won't need the include or man directories on our appliance.

We may also decide to remove client applications like snmpget and snmpset from the bin directory on our appliance, but be sure *not* to remove snmptrap, since we will be using that to send traps from our appliance. The other commands may come in handy if we ever need to log in to the box for debugging or if we want to invoke them from the CLI or web interface for diagnostic purposes, but they are not necessary for the functioning of the agent or the sending of traps.

The agent itself, snmpd, will be in the /opt/snmp/sbin directory, along with snmptrapd. We can remove snmptrapd, because it will not be needed on our appliance. You should keep it on your development system, though—it will come in handy when you want to test your ability to send traps.

MIB files reside in /opt/snmp/share/snmp/mibs. They are not strictly necessary for the appliance, but there are reasons we may want to include them. First, we may want to simplify creation of the filters used to send traps (see the example on logmuxd and SNMP traps in Chapter 7). Second, we may want to deliver them on the appliance for use by the customer's network management software.

If we want to use the human-readable names for numeric object identifiers (OIDs) in logmuxd filters, we will have to tell the snmptrap command where to find these MIB files. We can either add these options to the command line used to invoke snmptrap:

```
-m ALL -M /opt/snmp/share/snmp/mibs
```

or make these environment variables available to it:

```
export MIBS=ALL
export MIBDIRS=/opt/snmp/share/snmp/mibs
```

This tells the SNMP commands (snmpget, snmpset, snmpwalk, snmptrap, and so on) to use all the MIB files found in the /opt/snmp/share/snmp/mibs directory.

Although you may be removing things from this staging area before installing the software on your appliance, let's not do that quite yet. We'll need some of what's there for creating our MIB extension. In fact, you should add /opt/snmp/bin to your environment variable, like so:

```
export PATH=/opt/snmp/bin:$PATH
```

Now it's time to move on and create the agent extension and implement the MIB.

The MIB Skeleton: mib2c

Net-SNMP kindly provides a utility that can read an MIB file and produce skeleton code for an agent extension. Later in this chapter, we'll show you how to flesh out this skeleton into a complete implementation of your MIB.

NOTE   *Net-SNMP provides multiple output code styles for mib2c; we will be using the older UCD-SNMP code style. The newer, so-called "MIB for Dummies" style is not what this chapter describes. We have chosen to use the older style because it's sufficient for our needs (and it's also where our experience lies).*

Before we can run mib2c, you'll need to install the SNMP Perl module, which is provided in the Net-SNMP tarball. When you ran make earlier, it decompressed this tarball and created the directory net-snmp-5.2.1 (or whatever version you used). Drop down into this directory and then to perl/SNMP.

There you'll find a README file to explain how to build and install the SNMP Perl module. Alternatively, you can install the libsnmp-perl package if one is provided by your Linux distribution.

We also need to make our MIB files (LADDIE-GROUP-SMI.txt and LAD-MIB.txt, which we created in Chapter 12) available to mib2c by copying them into the directory containing our other MIBs (/opt/snmp/share/snmp/mibs). Or, if you prefer, you can add a period (.) to your MIBDIRS list like this:

```
export MIBDIRS=.:/opt/snmp/share/snmp/mibs
```

Now let's run mib2c to generate the skeleton code. You'll want to be in the same directory as your MIB files if you added the . to your directory path. Please note that we provide mib2c with a MIB module or OID, not the name of the MIB file.

```
$ mib2c LAD-MIB:ladProject
writing to -
mib2c has multiple configuration files depending on the type of
code you need to write.  You must pick one depending on your need.

You requested mib2c to be run on the following part of the MIB tree:
  OID:                        ladProject
    numeric translation:      .1.3.6.1.4.1.23528.1.1
    number of scalars within: 4
    number of tables within:  1
    number of notifications within:  2

First, do you want to generate code that is compatible with the
ucd-snmp 4.X line of code, or code for the newer Net-SNMP 5.X code
base (which provides a much greater choice of APIs to pick from):
```
❶
```
    1) ucd-snmp style code
    2) Net-SNMP style code

Select your choice : 1
**********************************************************************
    GENERATING CODE FOR THE 4.X LINE OF CODE (THE OLDER API)
**********************************************************************


    using the mib2c.old-api.conf configuration file to generate your code.
writing to ladProject.h
writing to ladProject.c


**********************************************************************
* NOTE WELL: The code generated by mib2c is only a template.  *YOU* *
* must fill in the code before it'll work most of the time.  In many *
* cases, spots that MUST be edited within the files are marked with  *
* /* XXX */ or /* TODO */ comments.                                  *
**********************************************************************
running indent on ladProject.c
running indent on ladProject.h
```

In the middle of all this, you will see the following at line ❶:

```
1) ucd-snmp style code
2) Net-SNMP style code

Select your choice : 1
```

We use option one because that's where we have experience. You may want to try the newer and more flexible Net-SNMP type, but we don't need that flexibility for what we're doing here.

The Header File: ladProject.h

Two files have been generated for us: ladProject.c and ladProject.h. The header file, ladProject.h, is short and sweet, and we won't need to bother ourselves with it further. Here's what it looks like:

```
/*
 * Note: this file originally auto-generated by mib2c using
 *       : mib2c.old-api.conf,v 1.4 2004/07/28 08:04:58 dts12 Exp $
 */
#ifndef LADPROJECT_H
#define LADPROJECT_H

/*
 * function declarations
 */
void            init_ladProject(void);
FindVarMethod   var_ladProject;
FindVarMethod   var_ladAlarmTable;
WriteMethod     write_ladAlarmEnable;
WriteMethod     write_ladAlarmLatching;
WriteMethod     write_ladAlarmState;

#endif                          /* LADPROJECT_H */
```

These are prototypes for routines generated for us in the code file, ladProject.c.

The Code File: ladProject.c

The ladProject.c file is the one we'll be modifying. Rather than describing the generated code and then making a second pass through it to add our modifications, we'll just step through it, making our changes as we go. We'll distinguish the code we add from what mib2c generated using bold text. Specifically, we need to make the following modifications to the generated skeleton code:

1. Include the header for libpq (the PostgreSQL library).
2. Provide a function to connect to RTA in the ladd daemon.

3. Provide functions to read and write RTA tables over the connection to the ladd daemon.

4. Provide code to read each scalar in the MIB.

5. Provide code to read each table object in the ladAlarmTable.

6. Provide a write function for each writable object in the MIB.

Includes

We begin by including the necessary header files. Remember, we will be marking our additions and modifications in bold.

```
/*
 * Note: this file originally auto-generated by mib2c using
 *       : mib2c.old-api.conf,v 1.4 2004/07/28 08:04:58 dts12 Exp $
 */

#include <net-snmp/net-snmp-config.h>
#include <net-snmp/net-snmp-includes.h>
#include <net-snmp/agent/net-snmp-agent-includes.h>

❶ #include "pgsql/libpq-fe.h"        /* libpq header file */
#include "ladProject.h"
```

Here we have accomplished our first goal by including ❶ the header file that defines the libpq PostgreSQL API.

The Base OID

In this code, the comment generated by mib2c basically says it all. This is the base OID for all the objects defined in our MIB.

```
/*
 * ladProject_variables_oid:
 *   this is the top level oid that we want to register under.  This
 *   is essentially a prefix, with the suffix appearing in the
 *   variable below.
 */

oid             ladProject_variables_oid[] =
    { 1, 3, 6, 1, 4, 1, 23528, 1, 1 };
```

MIB Objects Definitions

The next bit of code defines all the *leaf objects* in our MIB, by which we mean all the objects for which we will be returning values. A define is generated for each of these leaf objects to give a unique number to each object we will be processing. The name of the define is an all-uppercase version of the object name from the MIB file; for example, ladVersion becomes LADVERSION.

Each object also has its own entry in the ladProject_variables table (shown below), which provides the following information for the object:

- A unique identifier to be used later in our case statements (the define name we just discussed)
- The data type
- Whether it is read-only or read-write
- The function that will be called to read the object's value
- The OID suffix, which, when appended to the base OID, will give the complete OID of the object

We find the raw output of mib2c to be a little hard to read because the defines for the unique identifier values are mixed in with the table row definitions. In an attempt to make this more accessible, we have rearranged it a bit to put all the defines together and line everything up in columns. Unfortunately, mib2c has not generated perfect code for us, but we'll take advantage of this to give a lesson on what should have been generated. Tools like mib2c are great time savers, but you should always be aware of what should have been generated and remember to check the output. Ultimately, you will be responsible for the code working properly. First, let's take a look at the code, and then we'll discuss the problems we see.

```
#define LADVERSION          1
#define LADNUMBEROFZONES    2
#define LADTRAPZONEID       3
#define LADTRAPZONENAME     4
#define LADALARMZONEID      5
#define LADALARMZONENAME    6
#define LADALARMENABLE      7
#define LADALARMLATCHING    8
#define LADALARMSTATE       9
#define LADALARMCOUNT       10

/*
 * variable4 ladProject_variables:
 *   this variable defines function callbacks and type return information
 *   for the  mib section
 */

struct variable4 ladProject_variables[] = {
  /*
   * magic number,    variable type, ro/rw , callback fn,      L, oidsuffix
   */
  {LADVERSION,        ASN_OCTET_STR, RONLY, var_ladProject,    1, {1}},
  {LADNUMBEROFZONES, ASN_INTEGER,    RONLY, var_ladProject,    1, {2}},
❶ {LADTRAPZONEID,     ASN_INTEGER,    RONLY, var_ladProject,    1, {1}},
❷ {LADTRAPZONENAME,  ASN_OCTET_STR, RONLY, var_ladProject,    1, {2}},

  {LADALARMZONEID,    ASN_INTEGER,   RONLY, var_ladAlarmTable, 3, {1, 1, 1}},
  {LADALARMZONENAME, ASN_OCTET_STR, RONLY, var_ladAlarmTable, 3, {1, 1, 2}},
  {LADALARMENABLE,    ASN_INTEGER,   RWRITE, var_ladAlarmTable, 3, {1, 1, 3}},
```

```
    {LADALARMLATCHING, ASN_INTEGER,   RWRITE, var_ladAlarmTable, 3, {1, 1, 4}},
    {LADALARMSTATE,    ASN_INTEGER,   RWRITE, var_ladAlarmTable, 3, {1, 1, 5}},
    {LADALARMCOUNT,    ASN_COUNTER,   RONLY,  var_ladAlarmTable, 3, {1, 1, 6}},
};

/*
 * (L = length of the oidsuffix)
 */
```

The first problem above is that the generated code includes ❶ ladTrapZoneId and ❷ ladTrapZoneName as readable objects, but it shouldn't. These objects are only used in traps, and they are not readable or writable by the agent, so we have no code to write for them and will not need to indicate a callback for them here. We should remove these two lines.

Second, the OID suffix field is wrong for every object here. You append this suffix to the base OID (ladProject_variables_oid, defined in the previous section) to get the OID of the individual object. This is how we defined the base OID:

```
oid            ladProject_variables_oid[] =
    { 1, 3, 6, 1, 4, 1, 23528, 1, 1 };
```

So, for example, the OID for ladAlarmState in the generated code should be:

```
    { 1, 3, 6, 1, 4, 1, 23528, 1, 1, 1, 1, 5 };
```

Let's see if this is right. We can check it by running snmptranslate.

```
$ snmptranslate -On LAD-MIB:ladAlarmState
.1.3.6.1.4.1.23528.1.1.1.2.1.1.5
```

That's certainly not right. We're missing two nodes from our OID hierarchy. If you perform this snmptranslate test on each of the scalars in the LAD-MIB, you'll find they are all missing the numbers for ladSystem (1) and ladSystemScalars (1). If you repeat the test for the table columns, you'll see that they are missing ladSystem (1) and ladSystemTables (2). This is like missing a few directory levels from a file pathname.

Let's fix this table before we move on. Here is the corrected code, with the added numbers in bold:

```
struct variable7 ladProject_variables[] = {
    /*
     * magic number,    variable type, ro/rw , callback fn,      L, oidsuffix
     */

    {LADVERSION,       ASN_OCTET_STR, RONLY, var_ladProject,    3, {1, 1, 1}},
    {LADNUMBEROFZONES, ASN_INTEGER,   RONLY, var_ladProject,    3, {1, 1, 2}},
```

```
{LADALARMZONEID,   ASN_INTEGER,   RONLY,  var_ladAlarmTable, 5, {1, 2, 1, 1, 1}},
{LADALARMZONENAME, ASN_OCTET_STR, RONLY,  var_ladAlarmTable, 5, {1, 2, 1, 1, 2}},
{LADALARMENABLE,   ASN_INTEGER,   RWRITE, var_ladAlarmTable, 5, {1, 2, 1, 1, 3}},
{LADALARMLATCHING, ASN_INTEGER,   RWRITE, var_ladAlarmTable, 5, {1, 2, 1, 1, 4}},
{LADALARMSTATE,    ASN_INTEGER,   RWRITE, var_ladAlarmTable, 5, {1, 2, 1, 1, 5}},
{LADALARMCOUNT,    ASN_COUNTER,   RONLY,  var_ladAlarmTable, 5, {1, 2, 1, 1, 6}},
};
```

That's better. We've removed the objects from the trapInfo section, corrected the OIDs, and corrected the length of the suffix. Note also that we had to change the struct type we are using as a template for this array from variable4 to variable7, because our OIDs are now longer. A few different structs are provided by the Net-SNMP headers for different lengths of OIDs. You don't want to use excess memory, but you do need a struct long enough for the longest suffix you will be defining. When we increased our suffix length from three to five for our table objects, we exceeded the length of variable4, and the next longer one is variable7. You can find these structures defined in var_struct.h in the directory include/net-snmp/agent, under the net-snmp-5.2.1 directory. You can look here for what's available in case you need an even longer struct. See how variable7 is defined:

```
struct variable7 {
    u_char        magic;        /* passed to function as a hint */
    u_char        type;         /* type of variable */
    u_short       acl;          /* access control list for variable */
    FindVarMethod *findVar;      /* function that finds variable */
    u_char        namelen;      /* length of name below */
❶   oid           name[7];      /* object identifier of variable */
};
```

Notice the length of ❶ the name field.

RTA Access Routines

Now we need to insert the functions we'll be using to connect and communicate with the ladd daemon: lad_connect(), query(), and update().

```
/* LAD-specific variables */
❶ PGconn     *conn;                  /* holds database connection */

/*************************************************
 * Connect to the application
 *************************************************/
static
❷ int lad_connect (void)
{
    conn = PQconnectdb("host=localhost port=8888");
    if (PQstatus(conn) == CONNECTION_BAD)          {
        DEBUGMSGTL(("LAD", "Connection to application failed.\n"));
        DEBUGMSGTL(("LAD", "%s", PQerrorMessage(conn)));
        PQfinish(conn);
```

```
        return (-1);
    }
    DEBUGMSGTL(("LAD", "Connection to application succeeded.\n"));
    return (0);
}
```

We have defined ❶ a global variable to hold the handle for our connection to Laddie and ❷ the function to establish this connection, lad_connect. Notice the use of PQconnectdb, PQStatus, PQerrorMessage, and PQfinish. These are functions provided in libpq; you can read more about them in the documentation PostgreSQL provides for this library. Basically, we are attempting a connection to port 8888 (the port the ladd daemon decided to use) on localhost. If we fail, we return resources (PQfinish), log an error message using the DEBUGMSGTL macro we saw earlier, and return an error. Otherwise, we return success. Take note that DEBUGMSGTL takes a format statement and parameters like printf, but it requires an extra set of parentheses. We have replaced the default ladProject strings in the DEBUGMSGTL calls with the shorter LAD, just to save some horizontal space in our examples. The unchanged generated code you will see below uses ladProject by default. You should make these consistent in your code; that is, if you add new DEBUGMSGTL statements, use the same value mib2c generated. You are not required to keep the DEBUGMSGTL strings consistent with your project name, but it avoids confusion to do so. We only make the change in these examples to prevent line wrap, due to the limited horizontal space on a book's printed page. You won't need to do this in your code.

We follow this with our function to read values from RTA tables. You pass it the table and field names, a filter string (you might use this to select a table row), options, a buffer to return the value from the table, and the length of that buffer. We haven't made any provisions for querying more than a single field from an RTA table at one time. (This isn't really a problem, since Net-SNMP will only pass us one MIB object at a time to read.) While it's true that a single MIB object could require reading multiple RTA tables—that is, there needn't be a one-to-one correspondence between RTA fields and MIB objects—our MIB for Laddie does not require this.

```
/*************************************************
 * query() - request a value from a table.
 *************************************************/
static
int query(char *table, char *field, char *filter, char* options, char
*output_str, int output_len)
{
    char          query_string[256];  /* holds constructed SQL query */
    PGresult      *result;            /* holds query result */
    ExecStatusType status;            /* return type from PQresultStatus */
    char          *errMsg;

❶  /* check connection to LAD application */
    if (PQstatus(conn) != CONNECTION_OK) {
```

```
                /* try to re-connect */
                if (0 != lad_connect()) {
                    return(-1);    /* fail the query */
                }
            }

            /* Construct query string */
            if (strlen(filter) > 0) {
                sprintf (query_string, "select %s from %s where %s %s;",
                        field, table, filter, options);
            } else {
                sprintf (query_string, "select %s from %s %s;", field, table, options);
            }
            DEBUGMSGTL(("LAD", "sending query '%s'\n", query_string));

❷          result = PQexec(conn, query_string);    /* send the query */
            if ((status = PQresultStatus(result)) != PGRES_TUPLES_OK) {
                DEBUGMSGTL(("LAD", "query failed:  PQresultStatus returned %d; %s",
                        status, PQerrorMessage(conn)));
                printf ("%s", errMsg);
                PQclear(result);
                PQfinish(conn);
❸              return (-1);
            }
            DEBUGMSGTL(("LAD", "success! result = %d\n", status));
            strncpy (output_str, PQgetvalue(result, 0, 0), output_len);
            DEBUGMSGTL(("LAD", "query suceeded; returning '%s'\n", output_str));
❹      return (0);
    }
```

We start by checking that ❶ our connection to Laddie is still valid. If it is
not, we reconnect by calling lad_connect(). Then we construct our query string
and ❷ execute the query using Pqexec(). The application programming interface (API) of the PostreSQL library allows you to request multiple values in a
single query, which is why the result is returned as a list of tuples. We check
that our tuples are okay. If they aren't, we clean up, return resources, and ❸
return an error to our caller. Otherwise, we extract the first value returned
(there should only be one, in our case), return it in the buffer provided to
us, then ❹ return success.

The code below is very similar to the query routine above, but it builds
an update request for writing to the field, then passes it to libpq. This is the
routine our MIB write routines will call.

```
/************************************************
 * update() - update a value in a table.
 ************************************************/
static
int update(char *table, char *field, char *filter, char *newval_str)
{
    char            update_string[256];  /* holds constructed SQL update */
    PGresult        *result;             /* holds update result */
    ExecStatusType status;               /* return type from PQresultStatus */
    char            *errMsg;
```

```
/* check connection to LAD application */
if (PQstatus(conn) != CONNECTION_OK) {
    /* try to re-connect */
    if (0 != lad_connect()) {
        return(-1);   /* fail the update */
    }
}

sprintf (update_string, "update %s SET %s=%s where %s;",
        table, field, newval_str, filter);
DEBUGMSGTL(("LAD", "sending update '%s'\n", update_string));

result = PQexec(conn, update_string);   /* send the update */
if ((status = PQresultStatus(result)) != PGRES_COMMAND_OK) {
    DEBUGMSGTL(("LAD", "update failed:  PQresultStatus returned %d; %s",
                status, PQerrorMessage(conn)));
    printf ("%s", errMsg);
    PQclear(result);
    PQfinish(conn);
    return (-1);
}
DEBUGMSGTL(("LAD", "success! result = %d\n", status));
return (0);
}
```

We should point out that these are just simple, generic routines for reading from and writing to a PostgreSQL database and, thus, RTA tables. There is nothing SNMP-specific or Laddie-specific about them. You could use them in any application written in C that needs to access RTA tables from another application on the same system—the only thing you'd need to change is the port number.

The Initialization Routine

Now we come to the fairly simple initialization routine that mib2c generated for us. Notice that we made no changes to the generated code. We could have put a call to lad_connect() here, but we refrained, for the sake of simplicity. Our first call to the query() or update() routines we defined above will detect that the connection does not exist and then create it for us.

```
/** Initializes the ladProject module */
void
init_ladProject(void)
{

    DEBUGMSGTL(("LAD", "Initializing\n"));

    /*
     * register ourselves with the agent to handle our mib tree
     */
❶   REGISTER_MIB("ladProject", ladProject_variables, variable7,
                ladProject_variables_oid);
```

```
    /*
     * place any other initialization junk you need here
     */
}
```

The ❶ REGISTER_MIB line will register your OID subtree with the central agent code so it will know to call you to read and write the objects in this subtree. Notice that we had to change the variable4 to variable7 here, as well.

The Scalars

The next routine is where all reads of scalars are processed. *Scalars* are leaf objects in the MIB (that is, they are not accessed by indexing into a table).

Before we dive into this function, let's take a moment to look at the input parameters. They are described quite nicely in the AGENT.txt file that is provided with the Net-SNMP package (highly recommended reading, by the way), but we'll summarize them here:

- vp is a pointer to the relevant entry in the ladProject_variables array we discussed in the section "MIB Objects Definitions" on page 268.

- name is the OID from the request, and length is the length of this OID.

- exact indicates whether you are processing a request for the exact OID passed to you, like a GET or SET, or one that requires you to find the OID to process, like a GETNEXT. (GETNEXT is why name and length are also output parameters. You have to set them appropriately for GETNEXT requests to indicate the OID for which you are returning a value.)

- var_len is an output parameter that the function must set to the length of the data being returned.

- write_method is also an output parameter and is used to point to the function that will handle a SET for any of the OIDs you have made SET-able.

- The function returns the value of the data requested, or a NULL if the data is not available.

Now let's tackle the body of the function. We have reformatted some of the lines to better fit the printed page, but otherwise, most of this routine remains as it was generated. We have highlighted the few lines that needed to be added or changed to retrieve the values from the RTA tables in the Laddie daemon. As you can see, very little work needs to be done in the SNMP agent to retrieve the readable values in our MIB. Each object requires a single access of a field in Laddie's RTA-accessible tables.

```
/*
 * var_ladProject():
 *   This function is called every time the agent gets a request for
 *   a scalar variable that might be found within your mib section
 *   registered above.  It is up to you to do the right thing and
 *   return the correct value.
 *     You should also correct the value of "var_len" if necessary.
 *
```

```
 *    Please see the documentation for more information about writing
 *    module extensions, and check out the examples in the examples
 *    and mibII directories.
 */
unsigned char *
var_ladProject(struct variable *vp,
                 oid      *name,
                 size_t   *length,
                 int      exact,
                 size_t   *var_len,
                 WriteMethod **write_method)
{
    /* variables we may use later */
    static long          long_ret;
    static u_long        ulong_ret;
    static unsigned char string[SPRINT_MAX_LEN];
    static oid           objid[MAX_OID_LEN];
    static struct        counter64 c64;

    if (header_generic(vp,name,length,exact,var_len,write_method)
                                == MATCH_FAILED )
    return NULL;

  /*
   * this is where we do the value assignments for the mib results.
   */
    switch(vp->magic) {
    case LADVERSION:
        if (0 == query("Config",
                       "version",
                       "",
❶                     "LIMIT 1 OFFSET 1",
                       string,
                       SPRINT_MAX_LEN)) {
        *var_len = strlen(string);
        return (u_char*) &string;
        }
        break;

    case LADNUMBEROFZONES:
❷       if (0 == query("rta_tables",
❸                      "nrows",
❹                      "name=Zone",
                       "",
                       string,
                       SPRINT_MAX_LEN)) {
            long_ret = atol(string);
            return (u_char*) &long_ret;
        }
        break;

    default:
      ERROR_MSG("");
    }
    return NULL;
}
```

Our only changes are in the switch statement. We call our query() routine to retrieve values from RTA tables in Laddie to fulfill the request. The value of ladVersion comes from the version field of Laddie's Config table. We added ❶ the options LIMIT 1 OFFSET 1 because the Config table has multiple rows for different purposes. Each row has a version field, but we only want one answer to our request, so we use the option LIMIT 1. We also want the second row of the table, so we add the option OFFSET 1.

We don't have any such problem with the number of zones, which we take simply from ❸ the nrows (number of rows) field in ❷ the rta_tables table, but we do have to use the filter parameter to query() and select the row for which ❹ the name field is Zone. The rta_tables table has a row for every RTA table in the ladd daemon, so we can just go to the row describing the Zone table to find the number of rows.

Reading the Alarm Table

The var_ladAlarmTable() function processes reads of objects in the ladAlarmTable. Again, most of our work will be to add code to the switch statement. The main difference in routines for reading tables is the need to handle the index to the table row and the determination of the table size.

```
/*
 * var_ladAlarmTable():
 *   Handle this table separately from the scalar value case.
 *   The workings of this are basically the same as for var_ above.
 */
unsigned char *
var_ladAlarmTable(struct variable *vp,
            oid      *name,
            size_t   *length,
            int      exact,
            size_t   *var_len,
            WriteMethod **write_method)
{
    /* variables we may use later */
    static long           long_ret;
    static u_long         ulong_ret;
❶   static u_long         table_size;
❷   static u_long         table_index;
    static unsigned char  string[SPRINT_MAX_LEN];
❸   static unsigned char  filter[SPRINT_MAX_LEN];
    static oid            objid[MAX_OID_LEN];
    static struct counter64 c64;
```

The beginning of var_ladAlarmTable looks a lot like var_ladProject, where we implemented our scalars. All we've done so far is add a few local variables, specifically:

❶ table_size, which will hold the number of rows in our table.

❷ table_index, which shows the table row we want to retrieve.

❸ filter, which is what we will pass to query() to tell it which row we want.

```
    if (0 == query("rta_tables", "nrows", "name=Zone", "", string, SPRINT_MAX_LEN)) {
        table_size = atol(string);
    } else {
        /* This shouldn't fail, but if it does just return an error */
❶       return NULL;
    }
```

This should be familiar from our discussion of LADNUMBEROFZONES in the section "The Scalars" on page 275. We need the length of the table for our processing below. Notice that the reaction to a failure to retrieve the table length is ❶ returning NULL. This should never fail, but we still need to cover this case. If we fail to get the length of the table, the agent will just bypass this table as if it didn't exist when someone walks our MIB.

```
    /*
     * This assumes that the table is a 'simple' table.
     *     See the implementation documentation for the meaning of this.
     *     You will need to provide the correct value for the TABLE_SIZE
     *     parameter
     *
     * If this table does not meet the requirements for a simple table,
     *     you will need to provide the replacement code yourself.
     *     Mib2c is not smart enough to write this for you.
     *     Again, see the implementation documentation for what is required.
     */
❶       if (header_simple_table(vp,
                            name,
                            length,
                            exact,
                            var_len,
                            write_method,
                            table_size)
                                        == MATCH_FAILED )
        return NULL;
```

In the code above we take advantage of ❶ the header_simple_table() function provided by Net-SNMP. The AGENT.txt file defines a *simple table* as one that is singly indexed by an integer running from 1 to some determinable maximum value; all rows within that range are valid (no holes) and the data can be retrieved directly—for example, by indexing into an underlying data structure, such as our RTA Zone table.

The comment block was generated by mib2c, and it includes a constant called TABLE_SIZE that we have replaced with the variable table_size, as we discussed earlier.

```
❶       table_index = name[*length-1];
❷       sprintf(filter, "id=%d", table_index);
```

We simply ❶ take our table index from the end of our OID. The OID of the *instance* of an object is the OID of the *object definition*, suffixed by the instance index. In the case of any simple table, as defined above, the instance index will be the table row number (the first row starting with row 1, not row 0). We then use this to create the filter string for our calls to query the Zone table. We are getting all of our values for the objects in the ladAlarmTable from the Zone table, so we can just ❷ create this filter once and use it in all of our queries.

The rest of the routine (below) is a switch statement indexed by the object requested.

```
/*
 * this is where we do the value assignments for the mib results.
 */
 switch(vp->magic) {

 case LADALARMZONENAME:
     DEBUGMSGTL(("LAD", "reading ladAlarmZoneName\n"));
     if (0 == query("Zone", "name", filter, "", string, SPRINT_MAX_LEN)) {
         DEBUGMSGTL(("LAD", "ladAlarmZoneName[%d]=%s\n", table_index, string));
         *var_len = strlen(string);
         return (u_char*) &string;
     }
     break;

 case LADALARMENABLE:
     DEBUGMSGTL(("LAD", "reading ladAlarmEnable\n"));
     if (0 == query("Zone", "enabled", filter, "", string, SPRINT_MAX_LEN)) {
         DEBUGMSGTL(("LAD", "ladAlarmZoneEnable[%d]=%s\n", table_index, string));
         *write_method = write_ladAlarmEnable;
         long_ret = atol(string);
         return (u_char*) &long_ret;
     }
     break;

 case LADALARMLATCHING:
     DEBUGMSGTL(("LAD", "reading ladAlarmLatching\n"));
     if (0 == query("Zone", "latching", filter, "", string, SPRINT_MAX_LEN)) {
         DEBUGMSGTL(("LAD", "ladAlarmZoneLatching[%d]=%s\n", table_index, string));
         *write_method = write_ladAlarmLatching;
         long_ret = atol(string);
         return (u_char*) &long_ret;
     }
     break;

 case LADALARMSTATE:
     DEBUGMSGTL(("LAD", "reading ladAlarmState\n"));
     if (0 == query("Zone", "alarm", filter, "", string, SPRINT_MAX_LEN)) {
         DEBUGMSGTL(("LAD", "ladAlarmZoneState[%d]=%s\n", table_index, string));
         *write_method = write_ladAlarmState;
         long_ret = atol(string);
         return (u_char*) &long_ret;
     }
     break;
```

```
case LADALARMCOUNT:
    DEBUGMSGTL(("LAD", "reading ladAlarmCount\n"));
    if (0 == query("Zone", "count", filter, "", string, SPRINT_MAX_LEN)) {
        DEBUGMSGTL(("LAD", "ladAlarmZoneCount[%d]=%s\n", table_index, string));
        long_ret = atol(string);
        return (u_char*) &long_ret;
    }
    break;

default:
  ERROR_MSG("");
}
return NULL;
}
```

In each of the cases, we query some field in the Zone table to get the value in our switch statement. If the query fails, we break out of the switch and return NULL, which tells the agent this value is not retrievable.

Another thing to notice here is that we have to return a write_method for each of the objects we have defined as having read-write access. Each writable object has its own write method—that is, a pointer to the routine called to handle SETs. Whenever a write (snmpset) is done, the main agent code first calls the read routine to find the appropriate write routine.

Writing the Alarm Table

Each of the write routines for writable objects looks basically the same, so we'll just take the ladAlarmEnable object as an example.

The write routines all center around a switch statement selecting between different processing based on the action parameter. The cases in the switch will always be as follows:

- RESERVE1
- RESERVE2
- FREE
- ACTION
- UNDO
- COMMIT

Writing is much more complex than reading. When the agent receives an SNMPSET command for one of your objects, the read code we discussed above will be called to return the write_method (a pointer to the write routine for the specific object). This write function will then be called repeatedly with a different action parameter each time. If everything goes without a hitch, the write method will be called for RESERVE1, RESERVE2, ACTION, and COMMIT, in succession. The second RESERVE is to allow for dependencies between objects when a write is received for more than one object. If there is a failure returned from either RESERVE, you will be called with FREE to allow any allocated resources to be released. UNDO is provided for cases that fail further into the process.

You have to promise (cross your heart and hope to die) that UNDO cannot fail, so your settings do not become inconsistent—or at least do your best, and keep this in mind. More information on this subject is provided with the Net-SNMP package in the AGENT.txt file in the top directory. Here is the code we have modified for Laddie's agent.

```
int
write_ladAlarmEnable(int      action,
                     u_char   *var_val,
                     u_char   var_val_type,
                     size_t   var_val_len,
                     u_char   *statP,
                     oid      *name,
                     size_t   name_len)
{
    static long value;
    int         size;
    static int  saved_value;
```

We have changed the code generated by mib2c to make value static and to add another static variable to hold a saved value. This function will be called repeatedly with a sequence of action parameters, so we can save some information from call to call.

```
/* variables we will need for query and update calls */
static u_long          table_index;
static unsigned char   string[SPRINT_MAX_LEN];
static unsigned char   filter[SPRINT_MAX_LEN];
```

These should look familiar from our scalar and ladAlarmTable queries, above. Here, we'll be using them for both queries and updates.

```
table_index = name[name_len-1];
```

This should look familiar, too. We're grabbing the table index from the end of the OID.

```
switch ( action ) {
  case RESERVE1:
    if (var_val_type != ASN_INTEGER) {
        DEBUGMSGTL(("LAD", "write to ladAlarmEnable - not ASN_INTEGER\n"));
        return SNMP_ERR_WRONGTYPE;
    }
    if (var_val_len > sizeof(long)) {
        DEBUGMSGTL(("LAD","write to ladAlarmEnable -  bad length\n"));
        return SNMP_ERR_WRONGLENGTH;
    }
    value = *((long *) var_val);
❶   if (value > 1) {
        DEBUGMSGTL(("LAD", "write to ladAlarmEnable - wrong value %x\n", value));
        return SNMP_ERR_WRONGVALUE;
```

```
    }
    DEBUGMSGTL(("LAD", "\nRESERVE1 ok; value is %d\n", value));
    break;
```

The `RESERVE1` action checks the value type and length for accuracy. The code to check for wrong type and wrong length was generated for us, but we've changed it a bit, replacing the printfs with `DEBUGMSGTL` macros. We've also added ❶ a range check for the value being written. The enable value should always be either 0 or 1.

```
case RESERVE2:
    size  = var_val_len;
    value = * (long *) var_val;

    DEBUGMSGTL(("LAD", "\nRESERVE2 ok; value is %d\n", value));
    break;

case FREE:
    /* Release any resources that have been allocated */
    DEBUGMSGTL(("LAD", "\nFREE ok; value is %d\n", value));
    break;
```

In Laddie we don't have any use for `RESERVE2` and `FREE`. Normally, `RESERVE2` would be used for checking interdependencies between the objects in the varbind list of the SNMP SET, and `FREE` would be used to free any resources we tied up temporarily, but neither of these apply to our Laddie MIB. No code is highlighted in `RESERVE2` because we didn't add anything. Even the comments were generated for us by mib2c.

```
case ACTION:
    /*
     * The variable has been stored in 'value' for you to use,
     * and you have just been asked to do something with it.
     * Note that anything done here must be reversable in the UNDO case
     */
    DEBUGMSGTL(("LAD", "\nACTION; value is %d\n", value));
    DEBUGMSGTL(("LAD", "writing ladAlarmEnable in row %d\n", table_index));
    sprintf(filter, "id=%d", table_index);
    if (0 != query("Zone", "enabled", filter, "", string, SPRINT_MAX_LEN)) {
        saved_value = -1;  /* ... so we can tell the query failed */
        return SNMP_ERR_RESOURCEUNAVAILABLE;
    }
    saved_value = atol(string);  /* save current value in case of undo later */

    sprintf(filter, "id=%d", table_index);
    sprintf(string, "%d", value);
    if (0 != update("Zone", "enabled", filter, string)) {
        return SNMP_ERR_RESOURCEUNAVAILABLE;
    }
    break;
```

In ACTION, we are retrieving the current value and saving it in saved_value before we write the new value to the RTA Zone table. If we run into trouble, we return an error. The value we save may be used in the UNDO case.

```
case UNDO:
    /* Back out any changes made in the ACTION case */
    sprintf(filter, "id=%d", table_index);
    sprintf(string, "%d", saved_value);
    if (saved_value != -1) {
        /* if we have a saved_value, write it back */
        if (0 != update("Zone", "enabled", filter, string)) {
            return SNMP_ERR_RESOURCEUNAVAILABLE;
        }
    }
    break;
```

We UNDO by writing the saved value back, but only if ACTION got as far as retrieving the old value.

```
case COMMIT:
    /*
     * Things are working well, so it's now safe to make the change
     * permanently.  Make sure that anything done here can't fail!
     */

    /* Can't fail here.  There's nothing left to do! */
    break;
```

We have nothing to do in the COMMIT case. ACTION already wrote the value to the RTA table in the Laddie daemon.

```
    }
    return SNMP_ERR_NOERROR;
}
```

If we didn't return an error before this point, we return a successful completion.

All of the other write routines look just like this, so that wraps up our discussion of the LAD-MIB implementation. The next step is to build it.

Makefile Revisited

In "The Net-SNMP Agent" on page 262, we used a Makefile to generate our agent. Now we just have to modify this Makefile to include our LAD-MIB code.

```
NETSNMP_VERSION = 5.2.1
BUILD_DIR       = ./net-snmp-$(NETSNMP_VERSION)

#
```

```
# Targets
#
all:  clean setup config build

clean:
        rm -rf $(BUILD_DIR)
        rm -rf /opt/snmp/*

setup:
        tar zxvf net-snmp-$(NETSNMP_VERSION).tar.gz; \
❶      mkdir $(BUILD_DIR)/agent/mibgroup/lad; \
❷      cp ladProject.[ch] $(BUILD_DIR)/agent/mibgroup/lad

config:
        cd $(BUILD_DIR); \
❸      export LDFLAGS="-lpq"; \
        ./configure --prefix=/opt/snmp \
❹              --with-mib-modules="lad/ladProject"<../configure.input; \
        cd ..

build:
        cd $(BUILD_DIR); \
        make
install:
        cd $(BUILD_DIR); \
        install
```

The changes are fairly minor. We've added two lines to the setup case to ❶ create the lad directory under agent/mibgroup and ❷ copy our ladProject header and C file there.

The config case ❸ adds "-lpq" to LDFLAGS to tell the linker to include libpq for the PostgreSQL code used by our update and query routines. We also ❹ tell configure to include our MIB in the build.

That's it! If Net-SNMP releases new security improvements, bug fixes, or new features, all we have to do is drop a new source tarball into the build directory, change the NETSNMP_VERSION line in the Makefile, and rebuild. Each Net-SNMP release has maintained backward compatibility since we started using it, when Net-SNMP was still UCD-SNMP, and it has been blissfully easy to roll a new Net-SNMP version into new releases of our appliance software. For this (among other things) we are eternally grateful to the maintainers of UCD/NET-SNMP.

In Chapter 14 we mentioned that our SNMP agent uses the old style, non-RTA configuration method (that is, a .conf file somewhere under /etc). You may have wondered why we didn't discuss how to RTA-ize the SNMP agent so we could change its configuration on the fly, as we can with Laddie. Well, this is the reason. We don't want to customize the basic agent because that would complicate rolling in new releases as they become available. Right now it's simple—we don't have changes to port to the agent each time we update, and all of our customizations are localized in our MIB extension.

All we need to do now is build and install it.

```
make
make install
```

You'll also need to copy the files you need from /opt/snmp into your appliance build, but that's beyond the scope of this chapter.

Debugging

Thanks to the DEBUGMSGTL macros, we have dropped in our MIB extension as we wrote it, and we are all set to trace the flow of control in our agent, should this become necessary. Just shut down the agent running in the background

```
/etc/rc.d/init.d/snmpd  stop
```

and run your own copy from the command line:

```
/opt/snmp/sbin/snmpd -D "LAD" -Le -f  -c /opt/snmp/etc/snmp/snmpd.conf -C
```

The -c <path to config file> -C is from the normal command string to run the agent. We discussed this in Chapter 14. What's new are the first three options.

The -D "LAD" activates our DEBUGMSGTL statements, which specified "LAD". Here's one taken from the code we discussed above:

```
DEBUGMSGTL(("LAD", "reading ladAlarmState\n"));
```

The -Le tells the agent to send the output to stderr. Other options are stdout, syslog, or a file. See the man page for snmpd for more information.

The -f tells the agent not to fork and go into the background. This keeps it tied to our current terminal window so we can see the output.

Now query the agent using snmpget, snmpset, or snmpwalk from another terminal window and watch the output, or capture it to a file.

Traps

We have defined two traps in our MIB, but we will not be discussing how to send these traps in this chapter. In Chapter 14 we discussed the use of the snmptrap utility to send traps for us, and in Chapter 7 we explained how to use a log event to trigger an SNMP trap. Just keep in mind that the traps we have defined in our LAD-MIB are not generated by the SNMP agent. They are generated through the logging subsystem from events recorded by the ladd daemon, itself.

Summary

In Chapter 14 you learned how to create a MIB to match an application, and in this chapter you learned how to create a MIB extension for the Net-SNMP agent to implement that MIB, as well as how to use the PostgreSQL interface library and RTA to retrieve the MIB data values from another daemon process. At this point you should feel comfortable that you could do this yourself from scratch.

You should also feel familiar enough with the structure of MIB and a Net-SNMP agent extension to hack new objects into the MIB and the code. There is no need to go back through generating skeleton code with mib2c. All you have to do is add the new objects to the MIB file (mostly cut-and-paste work), define new numbers for these variables in the list of defines, add the appropriate rows to the ladProject_variables array, and then add cases to the to the appropriate switch statements. Just keep in mind that while you can add things to a MIB, you cannot reassign OIDs. If you always add to the end of a branch, you should be in good shape.

In Chapter 14 we mentioned that we had neglected to include the edge and input columns from our Laddie table in our MIB. A good test of your understanding of these two chapters would be to go back and add one or both of these fields to the MIB and agent yourself.

A

RTA REFERENCE

Run Time Access (RTA) is a library that displays your program's internal structures and arrays as database tables. RTA uses a subset of the PostgreSQL protocol and is compatible with the PostgreSQL bindings for C and PHP, as well as for the PostgreSQL command-line tool, psql. This appendix contains the definitions, data structures, and function prototypes for the RTA package.

The contents of this appendix that are taken from the RTA include excerpts from the file rta.h. We use the exact text of rta.h wherever possible. A less technical description of the material in this appendix is given in Chapters 2 and 3.

This appendix covers:

- Overview of RTA
- RTA constants
- Data structures

- API subroutines
- SELECT and UPDATE syntax
- Internal RTA tables
- Debug configuration
- Error messages
- Callback routines

Linux appliances lack real-time access to status and statistics, as well as the ability to configure a service once it has started. As Linux users, we assume that to configure an application we will be able to use SSH or telnet to gain access to the service, use an editor to modify the /etc configuration file, and use the kill -1 command to terminate the process—so real-time status and statistics are features Linux programmers don't even think to request. The lack of run-time access poses a particular challenge for network appliances where SSH is unavailable, either because it is not installed or it is not allowed.

Another challenge for appliance designers is that more than one type of user interface may be required. Many appliances have some combination of web, command-line, SNMP agent, front panel, and framebuffer interfaces. It is a nontrivial task to give the end user a consistent view regardless of the UI.

Overview of RTA

The RTA package addresses the challenges described above by giving real-time access to the data structures and arrays inside a running program. With minimal effort, we can use RTA to make a program's data structures appear as PostgreSQL tables in a PostgreSQL database.

Using RTA, a structure definition is also the definition for a table row, and an array of structures will appear as a table. For example, the code below shows a definition of a data structure for TCP connection information.

```
struct tcpconn {
        int    fd;         // conn's file descriptor
        int    lport;      // local port number
        int    dport;      // destination port number
        long   nsbytes;    // number of sent bytes
        long   nrbytes;    // number of received bytes
        long   nread;      // number of reads on the socket
        long   nwrite;     // number of writes on the socket
};
```

The tcpconn structure describes a single connection. An array of these structures is needed if there's more than one connection. This array might be allocated with

```
struct tcpconn Conns[10];
```

The above array of structures could be considered a database table, with each structure in the array as a row and each member in the structure as a column. RTA allows you to use any programming language with a PostgreSQL binding to query this table of TCP connections. Here are two sample SQL statements to manipulate the data in the Conns table:

```
SELECT lport, dport FROM Conns WHERE fd != -1;
UPDATE Conns SET dport = 0 WHERE fd = -1;
```

Don't worry if the above statements do not make sense; there is a short tutorial on SQL later in this appendix.

The addition of a database API offers several advantages. For one, debugging is made easier because you can use simple PostgreSQL tools to view much of your program's state. The PostgreSQL database API also makes it easier to build UI programs, since it includes bindings for PHP, Tcl/Tk, Perl, C, Java, Visual C++, and many other programming languages.

A database API can also help speed up development. When the tables used by the UI programs are carefully defined, the core application team can build the application while the UI developers work on the web pages, wizards, and MIBs of the various UI programs.

In order to make your arrays and structures available to the database API, you must tell RTA about the tables (including things like the name, start address, number of rows, and length of each row) and columns (including things like the associate table name, column name, column's data type, and whether special functions called *callbacks* are to be called when the column is read or written).

RTA Constants

Here is an excerpt from the rta.h file showing the constants that describe the internal size limits for the RTA package. You can change these limits, but if you do, be sure to recompile the RTA package using your new settings.

```
#include <limits.h>              /* for PATH_MAX */

       /** Maximum number of tables allowed in the system.
        * Your database may not contain more than this number
        * of tables. */
#define MX_TBL       (500)

       /** Maximum number of columns allowed in the system.
        * Your database may not contain more than this number
        * of columns. */
#define MX_COL       (2500)

       /** Maximum number of characters in a column name, table
        * name, and in help. See TBLDEF and COLDEF below. */
#define MXCOLNAME    (30)
#define MXTBLNAME    (30)
#define MXHELPSTR    (1000)
```

```
#define MXFILENAME      (300)

        /** Maximum number of characters in the 'ident' field of
         * the openlog() call. See the rta_dbg table below. */
#define MXDBGIDENT      (20)

        /** Maximum line size. SQL commands in save files may
         * contain no more than MX_LN_SZ characters.  Lines with
         * more than MX_LN_SZ characters are silently truncated
         * to MX_LN_SZ characters. */
#define MX_LN_SZ        (1500)

        /* Maximum number of columns allowed in a single table */
#define NCMDCOLS        (40)
```

Data Structures

Recall that each column in a table corresponds to a structure member, and each row in a table corresponds to an array element. In order for RTA to treat your arrays of structures as tables, you have the tell RTA about the tables. You describe each column by filling in a COLDEF structure, and you describe each table by filling in a TBLDEF structure. Here is an excerpt from rta.h that completely defines the data structures and constants associated with tables and columns.

```
        /** The column definition (COLDEF) structure describes
         * one column of a table. A table description has an
         * array of COLDEFs to describe the columns in the
         * table. */

typedef struct
{
        /** The name of the table that has this column. */
  char    *table;

        /** The name of the column. This must be at most MXCOLNAME
         * characters in length and unique within a
         * table. The same column name may be used in more
         * than one table. */
  char    *name;

        /** The data type of the column. This must be int, long,
         * string, pointer to void, pointer to int, pointer
         * to long, or pointer to string. The DB types are
         * defined immediately following this structure. */
  int     type;

        /** The number of bytes in the string if the above
         * type is RTA_STR or RTA_PSTR. The length includes
         * the null at the end of the string.  */
  int     length;
```

```
          /** Number of bytes from the start of the structure to
           * this column. For example, a structure with an int,
           * a 20 character string, and a long, would have the
           * offset of the long set to 24. Use of the function
           * offsetof() is encouraged. If you have structure
           * members that do not start on word boundaries and
           * you do not want to use offsetof(), then consider
           * using -fpack-struct with gcc. */
int       offset;

          /** Boolean flags which describe attributes of the
           * columns. The flags are defined after this
           * structure and include a "read-only" flag and a
           * flag to indicate that UPDATEs to this column
           * should cause a table save. (See table savefile
           * described below.)  */
int       flags;

          /** Read callback. This routine is called before the
           * column value is used. Input values include the
           * table name, the column name, the input SQL command,
           * a pointer to the row affected, and the (zero indexed)
           * row number for the row that is being read.
           * This routine is called *each* time the column is
           * read so the following would produce two calls:
           *     SELECT intime FROM inns WHERE intime >= 100;
           * The callback returns zero on success and nonzero on
           * failure. */
int       (*readcb) (char *tbl, char *column, char *SQL, void *pr,
                    int row_num);

          /** Write callback. This routine is called after an
           * UPDATE in which the column is written. Input values
           * include the table name, the column name, the SQL
           * command, a pointer to the row affected, the (zero
           * indexed) row number of the modified row, and a pointer
           * to a copy of the row before any modifications.  See the
           * callback section below.
           * This routine is called only once after all column
           * UPDATEs have occurred. For example, if there were
           * a write callback attached to the addr column, the
           * following SQL statement would cause the execution
           * of the write callback after both mask and addr
           * have been written:
           * UPDATE ethers SET mask="255.255.255.0", addr = \
           *     "192.168.1.10" WHERE name = "eth1";
           * The callback is called once for each row modified.

           * The callback returns zero on success and nonzero on
           * failure. On failure, the table's row is restored
           * to it's initial values and an SQL error is returned
           * to the client. The error is TRIGGERED ACTION EXCEPTION
           */
int       (*writecb) (char *tbl, char *column, char *SQL, void *pr,
```

```
                          int row_num,  void *poldrow);

            /** A brief description of the column. This should
             * include the meaning of the data in the column, the
             * limits, if any, and the default values. Include
             * a brief description of the side effects of changes.
             * This field is particularly important for tables
             * which are part of the "boundary" between the UI
             * developers and the application programmers.  */
  char    *help;
}
COLDEF;

            /** The data types.
             * String refers to an array of char. The 'length' of
             * column must contain the number of bytes in the array.
             */
#define RTA_STR         0

            /** Pointer to void. Use for generic pointers */
#define RTA_PTR         1

            /** Integer. This is the compiler/architecture native
             * integer. On Linux/gcc/Pentium an integer is 32 bits.
             */
#define RTA_INT         2

            /** Long. This is the compiler/architecture native
             * long long. On Linux/gcc/Pentium a long long is 64
             * bits.  */
#define RTA_LONG        3

            /** Pointer to string. Pointer to an array of char, or
             * a (**char). Note that the column length should be
             * the number of bytes in the string, not sizeof(char *).
             */
#define RTA_PSTR        4

            /** Pointers to int and long.  */
#define RTA_PINT        5
#define RTA_PLONG       6

            /** Float and pointer to float */
#define RTA_FLOAT       7
#define RTA_PFLOAT      8
#define MXCOLTYPE       (RTA_PFLOAT)

            /** The boolean flags.
             * If the disksave bit is set, any writes to the column
             * causes the table to be saved to the "savefile". (See
             * savefile described in the TBLDEF section below.) */
#define RTA_DISKSAVE    (1<<0)

            /** If the readonly flag is set, any writes to the
             * column will fail and a debug log message will be
```

```
                  * sent. (For unit test you may find it very handy to
                  * leave this bit clear to get better test coverage of
                  * the corner cases.)    */
#define RTA_READONLY     (1<<1)


                  /** The table definition (TBLDEF) structure describes
                  * a table and is passed into the DB system by the
                  * rta_add_table() subroutine.  */
typedef struct
{
                  /** The name of the table. This name must be less than
                  * MXTLBNAME characters in length and must be unique
                  * within the DB.  */
    char    *name;

                  /** The address of the first element of the first row of
                  * the array of structs that make up the table.  */
    void    *address;

                  /** The number of bytes in each row of the table.
                  * This is usually a sizeof() of the structure
                  * associated with the table. (The idea is that we
                  * can get to data element E in row R with ...
                  *     data = *(address + (R * rowlen) + offset(E)) */
    int     rowlen;

                  /** The number of rows in the table.    */
    int     nrows;

                  /** An 'iterator' on the rows of the data. This is
                  * useful if you want to have a linked list (or other
                  * arrangement) instead of a linear array of struct.
                  * Your iterator should return a pointer to the first
                  * row when the input is NULL and return a NULL
                  * when asked for the row after the last row. The rowid
                  * is the zero-indexed number of the row desired.  */
    void    *(*iterator) (void *cur_row, void *it_info, int rowid);

                  /** This is a pointer to any kind of information that the
                  * caller wants passed into each iterator call.
                  * For example, to have one iterator for all of your
                  * linked lists you could pass in a unique identifier
                  * for each table for the function to handle each one
                  * as appropriate. */
    void    *it_info;

                  /** An array of COLDEF structures which describe each
                  * column in the table. These must be in statically
                  * allocated memory since the rta system references
                  * them while running.  */
    COLDEF  *cols;

                  /** The number of columns in the table which is the
                  * number of COLDEFs defined by 'cols'.  */
```

```
int     ncol;

        /** Save file.  Path and name of a file which stores
         * the non-volatile part of the table.  The file has
         * all of the UPDATE statements needed to rebuild the
         * table.  The file is rewritten in its entirety each
         * time a 'savetodisk' column is UPDATEd.  No file
         * save is attempted if savefile is blank. */
char    *savefile;

        /** Help text.  A description of the table, how it is
         * used, and what its intent is.  A brief note to
         * describe how it relates to other parts of the system
         * and description of important callbacks is a nice
         * thing to include here.  */
char    *help;
}
TBLDEF;
```

API Subroutines

There are only six subroutines in the RTA API. Table A-1 summarizes them.

Table A-1: Subroutines for the RTA PostgreSQL API

Subroutine	Description
dbcommand()	Provides an interface to PostgreSQL clients
rta_add_table()	Adds a table and its columns to the RTA database
SQL_string()	Executes an SQL statement in the RTA database
rta_config_dir()	Sets the default path to the savefiles directory
rta_save()	Saves a table to a file
rta_load()	Loads a table from a file

The subroutines in the RTA libraries usually return one of the following values.

```
        /* successfully executed request or command */
    #define RTA_SUCCESS    (0)

        /* input did not have a full command */
    #define RTA_NOCMD      (1)

        /* encountered an internal error */
    #define RTA_ERROR      (2)

        /* DB client requests a session close */
    #define RTA_CLOSE      (3)

        /* Insufficient output buffer space */
    #define RTA_NOBUF      (4)
```

The dbcommand() Subroutine

The main application in your appliance accepts TCP connections from PostgreSQL clients and passes the stream of bytes (encoded SQL requests) from the client into RTA via the dbcommand() subroutine. In turn, dbcommand() writes the stream of bytes to an input buffer to be parsed for an SQL command.

If the input buffer contains a complete command, the command will be executed, the number-of-characters-in (nin) variable will be decreased by the number of bytes consumed, and RTA_SUCCESS will be returned. If there is not a complete command in the input buffer, RTA_NOCMD will be returned and no bytes will be removed from the input buffer.

If a command is executed, the results will be encoded into the PostgreSQL protocol and placed in the output buffer (out). When the subroutine is called, the input variable, number-of-characters-out (nout), has the number of free bytes available in the output buffer. When the subroutine returns, the nout variable will be decremented by the size of the response placed in the output buffer. An error message is generated if the number of available bytes in the output buffer is too small to hold the response from the SQL command.

The list below summarizes the input buffers and bytes for the dbcommand() subroutine.

Buffer/Bytes	Description
cmd	The buffer with PostgreSQL packets
nin	On entry, the number of bytes in the cmd buffer; on exit, the number of bytes remaining in the cmd buffer
out	The buffer that holds responses back to the client
nout	On entry, the number of free bytes in the out buffer; on exit, the number of remaining free bytes in the out buffer

The list below summarizes the returns for the dbcommand() subroutine.

Returns	Description
RTA_SUCCESS	One command was executed.
RTA_NOCMD	The input was not a complete command.
RTA_CLOSE	The client requested an orderly close.
RTA_NOBUF	There was insufficient space in the output buffer.

The prototype for the dbcommand() subroutine is shown below.

```
int     dbcommand(char *cmd, int *nin, char *out, int *nout);
```

The rta_add_table() Subroutine

The rta_add_table() subroutine registers a table for inclusion in the database interface, which gives external PostgreSQL clients access to the contents of the table. You need to call rta_add_table() for each of your tables.

Note that the TBLDEF structure must be statically allocated. RTA keeps only the pointer to the table and does not copy the information. This means that you can change the contents of the table definition by changing the contents of the TBLDEF structure, which is useful if you need to allocate more memory for the table and change its row count and address.

When you add an RTA table, you will see an error message if another table with the same name already exists in the database or if the table is defined without any columns.

If you specify a savefile, the SQL commands in the savefile will be loaded as part of the rta_add_table() call. See "The rta_load() Subroutine" on page 300 for more details.

This list summarizes the input for the rta_add_table() subroutine.

Input	Description
ptbl	A pointer to the TBLDEF structure to add a table

This list summarizes the returns for the rta_add_table() subroutine.

Returns	Description
RTA_SUCCESS	One table was successfully added.
RTA_ERROR	A table was not added due to an error.

The prototype of the rta_add_table() subroutine is shown below.

```
int     rta_add_table(TBLDEF *ptbl);
```

The SQL_string() Subroutine

The SQL_string() subroutine executes the SQL command placed in the null-terminated input string, cmd. The results are encoded into the PostgreSQL protocol and placed in the output buffer, out. When the subroutine is called, the input variable, nout, has the number of free bytes available in the output buffer, out. When the subroutine returns, nout has been decremented by the size of the response placed in the output buffer. An error message is generated if the number of available bytes in the output buffer is too small to hold the response from the SQL command.

This subroutine may be most useful when updating a table value in order to invoke the write callbacks. (The output buffer has the results encoded in the PostgreSQL protocol and might not be too useful directly.)

The list below summarizes the input for the SQL_string() subroutine.

Input	Description
cmd	The buffer with the SQL command
out	The buffer that holds responses back to client
nout	On entry, the number of free bytes in the out buffer; on exit, the number of remaining free bytes in the out buffer

The SQL_string() subroutine returns nothing.

The prototype for the SQL_string() subroutine is shown below.

```
void     SQL_string(char *cmd, char *out, int *nout);
```

The rta_config_dir() Subroutine

The rta_config_dir() subroutine sets the default path to the savefile directory. The string that the input parameter, configdir, points to is saved and prepended to the savefile names for tables with savefiles.

You should call the rta_config_dir() subroutine before you load your application tables. This subroutine is intended to simplify applications that let the user specify a configuration directory on the command line.

If the savefile uses an absolute path (starting with /), it is not prepended with the configuration directory.

This list summarizes the input for the rta_config_dir() subroutine.

Input	Description
configdir	The target configuration directory

This list summarizes the return values for the rta_config_dir() subroutine.

Returns	Description
RTA_SUCCESS	The configuration path was set correctly.
RTA_ERROR	No path was set due to an error, such as an invalid directory.

The prototype of the rta_config_dir() subroutine is shown below.

```
int rta_config_dir(char *configdir);
```

The rta_save() Subroutine

The rta_save() subroutine saves a table to a file, including all savetodisk columns to the path and file specified. Only savetodisk columns are saved.

The resulting file is a list of UPDATE commands containing the desired data. There is one UPDATE command for each row in a table.

The rta_save() subroutine tries to prevent corrupted save files by opening a temporary (temp) file in the same directory as the target file. The subroutine saves the data in the temp file and then automatically calls the rename() subroutine to atomically move the temp file to the savefile. The rta_save() subroutine generates errors if it cannot open the temp file or if it is unable to rename the temp file with rename().

NOTE   *As a general warning, keep in mind that any disk I/O can cause a program to block briefly. Therefore, saving and loading tables can cause your program to block for a moment.*

This list summarizes the input for the rta_save() subroutine.

Input	Description
ptbl	A pointer to the TBLDEF structure for the table to save
fname	A null-terminated string with the path and filename for the stored data

This list summarizes the return values for the rta_save() subroutine.

Returns	Description
RTA_SUCCESS	One table was successfully saved.
RTA_ERROR	No table was saved due to an error.

The prototype of the rta_save() subroutine is shown below.

```
int     rta_save(TBLDEF *ptbl, char *fname);
```

The rta_load() Subroutine

The rta_load() subroutine loads a table from a file of UPDATE commands. The file format is a series of UPDATE commands with one command per line. Any write callbacks are executed as each UPDATE occurs. Note that a call to rta_load() occurs automatically when you add the table using rta_add_table().

This list summarizes the input for the rta_load() subroutine.

Input	Description
ptbl	A pointer to the table to be loaded
fname	A string with name of the load file

This list summarizes the return values for the rta_load() subroutine.

Returns	Description
RTA_SUCCESS	One table was successfully loaded.
RTA_ERROR	RTA could not open the file specified.

The prototype of the rta_save() subroutine is shown below.

```
int     rta_load(TBLDEF *ptbl, char *fname);
```

SELECT and UPDATE Syntax

The next two sections give a brief introduction to the two SQL commands implemented by the RTA API. Neither the RTA UPDATE command nor the RTA SELECT command adhere strictly to their PostgreSQL equivalents. RTA does not allow JOIN clauses, and the WHERE clause supports only the boolean AND operator. There are no locks or transactions.

The SELECT Command

The prototype for the RTA SELECT command is shown below.

```
SELECT column_list FROM table [where_clause] [limit_clause]
```

Most NCMDCOLS (defined above) columns can be specified in the column_list or in the WHERE clause. The reserved word *LIMIT* restricts the number of rows returned to the number specified. The reserved word *OFFSET* skips the number of rows specified and begins output with the next row.

A column_list can contain * (a wild card character that represents all columns), a single column name, or a comma-separated list of column names.

A sample of the where_clause syntax is shown below:

```
col_name = value [AND col_name = value ..]
```

In this example, all the col_name = value pairs must match for a row to match. Note that you can use five other comparison operators in addition to equality. The list below shows the six available comparison operators.

Operator	Description
=	Is equal to
!=	Is not equal to
>	Is greater than
<	Is less than
>=	Is greater than or equal to
<=	Is less than or equal to

A sample of the limit_clause syntax is shown below:

```
LIMIT 5
```

You will find the LIMIT and OFFSET columns to be very useful because they prevent a buffer overflow on the output buffer of dbcommand(). They are also useful for web-based UIs in which users want to be able to view data one page at a time.

There are eight reserved words that can not be used as column or table names. The reserved words are *AND*, *FROM*, *LIMIT*, *OFFSET*, *SELECT*, *SET*, *UPDATE*, and *WHERE*. These are not case sensitive.

Strings may contain any of the following characters:

```
! @ # $ % ^ & * ( ) _ + - = { } [ ] \ | : ; < > ? , . / ~ `
```

If a string contains a double quote, use a single quote to wrap it. The string below is enclosed in single quotes since the string contains double quotes surrounding the *Hi mom!* substring.

```
'The sign says "Hi mom!"'
```

Use double quotes to wrap strings with embedded single quotes. Examples of the SELECT command are shown below.

```
SELECT * FROM rta_tables

SELECT destIP FROM conns WHERE fd != 0

SELECT destIP FROM conns WHERE fd != 0 AND lport = 80

SELECT destIP, destPort FROM conns \
    WHERE fd != 0 \
    LIMIT 100 OFFSET 0

SELECT destIP, destPort FROM conns \
    WHERE fd != 0 \
    LIMIT 100 OFFSET 0
```

The UPDATE Command

The UPDATE command writes values into a table. The prototype for the RTA UPDATE command is shown below.

```
UPDATE table SET UPDATE_list [where_clause] [limit_clause]
```

The format of `UPDATE_list` looks like this:

```
col_name = val [, col_name = val ...]
```

The `where_clause` syntax is:

```
col_name = value [AND col_name = value ..]
```

The `limit_clause` syntax is:

```
LIMIT n
```

An UPDATE invokes write callbacks on the affected columns. All data in the UPDATE_list is written before the callbacks are invoked.

The LIMIT clause for UPDATE is not standard PostgreSQL, but this clause can be useful for stepping through a table one row at a time. To change only the *n*th row of a table, use a limit clause like the one below. Note that *n* is zero indexed.

```
LIMIT 1 OFFSET n
```

See the examples of the UPDATE command below.

```
UPDATE conn SET lport = 0

UPDATE ethers SET mask = "255.255.255.0", addr = "192.168.1.10"   \

    WHERE name = "eth0"

UPDATE conn SET usecount = 0 WHERE fd != 0 AND lport = 21
```

Internal RTA Tables

When you use the RTA library, your application will include the following four RTA tables.

Table Name	Description
rta_tables	A table of all tables
rta_columns	A table of all columns
rta_dbg	A table of logging control variables
rta_stats	A table of usage and error statistics

The rta_tables Table

The rta_tables table gives SQL access to all internal and registered tables. The data in the table is exactly the same as the data in the TBLDEF structures registered with the rta_add_table() subroutine. This table is the generic table editor, which is used for application debugging. The columns in the rta_tables table are shown below and correspond to the fields in the RTA_TABLE data structure described above.

Column Name	Description
name	The name of the table
address	The start address of the table in memory
rowlen	The number of bytes in each row of the table
nrows	The number of rows in the table
iterator	A subroutine to advance from one row to next
it_info	Transparent data for the iterator

(continued)

Column Name	Description
cols	A pointer to the array of column definitions
ncol	The number of columns in the table
savefile	The file used to store non-volatile columns
help	A description of the table

The rta_columns Table

The rta_columns table lists the column definitions for all the columns in the database. The data in the table is exactly the same as the data in the COLDEF structures registered with the rta_add_table() subroutine. This table is used for the generic table viewer and table editor applications, which are used mostly for application debugging.

The columns in the rta_columns table are shown below.

Column Name	Description
table	The name of the column's table
name	The name of the column.
type	The column data type
length	The number of bytes in the column's data type
offset	The number of bytes from the start of the structure
flags	A bit field for read-only and save-to-disk
readcb	A pointer to the subroutine called before reads
writecb	A pointer to the subroutine called after writes
help	A description of the column

Debug Configuration

The RTA package does not generates any user-level log messages, only debug messages. The rta_dbgconfig table specifies the handling of these debug log messages. All of the fields in this table are volatile. You need to set the values in your main program to make them seem persistent. See the sample SQL string subroutine below.

```
SQL_string("UPDATE rta_dbgconfig SET target = 3")
```

The columns in the rta_dbgconfig table are shown below.

Column Name	Description
syserr	Integer. Zero means no log; 1 means log. Logs OS call errors such as malloc() failures. The default is 1.
rtaerr	Integer. Zero means no log; 1 means log. Enables logging of errors internal to the RTA package itself. The default is 1.

(continued)

Column Name	Description
sqlerr	Integer. Zero means no log; 1 means log. Logs the SQL request that generates an error reply. An error reply occurs if an SQL request is malformed or if it requests a non-existent table or column. The default is 1. (SQL errors are usually client programming errors.)
trace	Integer. Zero means no log; 1 means log all SQL requests. The default is 0.
target	0: Disable all debug logging 1: Log debug messages to syslog() 2: Log debug messages to stderr 3: Log to both syslog() and stderr
level	Integer. Syslog() requires a priority as part of all log messages. The integer specifies the log level to use when sending rta debug messages. Changes to this do not take effect until dbg_target is UPDATEd. 0: LOG_EMERG 1: LOG_ALERT 2: LOG_CRIT 3: LOG_ERR 4: LOG_WARNING 5: LOG_NOTICE 6: LOG_INFO 7: LOG_DEBUG The default is 3.
facility	Integer. Syslog() requires a facility as part of all log messages. This specifies the facility to use when sending rta debug messages. It is best to use the defines in .../sys/syslog.h to set this. The default is LOG_USER. Changes to this do not take effect until dbg_target is UPDATEd.
ident	String. Syslog() requires an ident string as part of all log messages. This specifies the ident string to use when sending rta debug messages. This is normally set to the process or command name. The default is rta. Changes to this do not take effect until dbg_target is UPDATEd. This can be, at most, MXDBGIDENT characters in length.

Error Messages

There are two types of error messages available in the RTA package: SQL request messages and internal debug messages.

SQL Request Errors

SQL request messages include the error messages returned as part of an SQL request. The six messages of this type are listed below.

```
ERROR:  Relation '%s' does not exist
```

This reply indicates that a table requested in a SELECT or UPDATE statement does not exist. The %s is replaced by the name of the requested table.

```
ERROR:  Attribute '%s' not found
```

This reply indicates that a column requested in a SELECT or UPDATE statement does not exist. The %s is replaced by the name of the requested column.

ERROR: SQL parse error

This reply indicates a malformed SQL request or a mismatch in the types of data in a where clause or in an UPDATE list.

ERROR: Output buffer full

This reply indicates that the size of the response to a request exceeds the size of the output buffer. (See dbcommand() and the out and nout parameters.) This error can be avoided with a large enough output buffer, or, preferably, with the use of LIMIT and OFFSET.

ERROR: String too long for '%s'

This reply indicates that an UPDATE to a column of type string or pointer to string would have exceeded the width of the column. The %s is replaced by the column name.

ERROR: Can not UPDATE read-only column '%s'

This reply indicates an attempt to UPDATE a column marked as read-only. The %s is replaced by the column name.

Internal Debug Messages

The RTA program logs internal errors using the standard syslog() facility, which is available on all Linux systems. The default syslog() facility is LOG_USER, but you can change the default by setting facility in the rta_dbg table.

You can modify syslogd in order to do post-processing, such as generating SNMP traps from these debug messages. The RTA program sends all internal debug error messages to syslog() in this format:

---
rta[PID]: FILE LINE#: error_message

The RTA program will replace PID, FILE, and LINE# with the process ID, the source filename, and the line number where the error was detected.

Here are the definitions used to generate debug and error messages. The RTA program will replace %s %d at the start of each error string with the filename and line number where the error was detected.

System Errors

```
#define Er_No_Mem    "%s %d: Cannot allocate memory"
#define Er_No_Save   "%s %d: Table '%s' save failure.  Cannot open %s"
#define Er_No_Load   "%s %d: Table '%s' load failure.  Cannot open %s"
```

RTA Errors

```
#define Er_Max_Tbls   "%s %d: Too many tables in DB"
#define Er_Max_Cols   "%s %d: Too many columns in DB"
#define Er_Tname_Big  "%s %d: Too many characters in table name: %s"
#define Er_Cname_Big  "%s %d: Too many characters in column name: %s"
#define Er_Hname_Big  "%s %d: Too many characters in help text: %s"
#define Er_Tbl_Dup    "%s %d: DB already has table named: %s"
#define Er_Col_Dup    "%s %d: Table '%s' already has column named: %s"
#define Er_Col_Type   "%s %d: Column contains an unknown data type: %s"
#define Er_Col_Flag   "%s %d: Column contains unknown flag data: %s"
#define Er_Col_Name   "%s %d: Incorrect table in column definition: %s"
#define Er_Cmd_Cols   "%s %d: Too many columns in table: %s"
#define Er_No_Space   "%s %d: Not enough buffer space"
#define Er_Reserved   "%s %d: Table or column is a reserved word: %s"
```

SQL Errors

```
#define Er_Bad_SQL    "%s %d: SQL parse error: %s"
#define Er_Readonly   "%s %d: Attempt to UPDATE readonly column: %s"
```

Trace Messages

```
#define Er_Trace_SQL "%s %d: SQL command: %s  (%s)"
```

Callback Routines

As mentioned above, read callbacks are executed before a column value is used, and write callbacks are called after all columns have been UPDATEd. Both read and write callbacks return zero on success and nonzero on error.

Read Callbacks

Read callbacks have the following calling parameters:

Read Callback		Description
char	*tblname:	The name of the table referenced
char	*colname:	The name of the column referenced
char	*sqlcmd:	The text of the SQL command
void	*pr;	A pointer to the affected row in the table
int	rowid:	The zero-indexed row number of the row being read or written

Read callbacks are particularly useful for computing values like sums and averages. These values are not worth the effort to compute continuously if it's possible to compute them only when the values are required.

Write Callbacks

Write callbacks are most applicable when tied to configuration changes. As such, a write callback is also a good place to log configuration changes.

Write callbacks have the same parameters as read callbacks, with the addition of a pointer to a copy of the row before it was modified. Access to a copy of the unmodified row is useful to detect changes in the row's data. This is useful since some UIs can generate an UPDATE even if nothing actually changed.

The callback returns zero on success and nonzero on failure. On failure, the table's row is restored to its initial values and an SQL error is returned to the client. The returned error is TRIGGERED ACTION EXCEPTION.

Write callbacks have the following calling parameters:

Write Callback	Description
char *tblname:	The name of the table referenced
char *colname:	The name of the column referenced
char *sqlcmd:	The text of the SQL command
void *pr;	Pointer to affected row in table
int rowid:	The zero-indexed row number of the row being read or written
void *poldrow;	Pointer to a copy of the row before any changes were made

B

REVIEW OF SNMP

This appendix is supplied for those who would like additional details or background information on SNMP.

In this appendix, we will cover the following topics:

- Why SNMP
- Agents and managers
- Namespace, grammar, and protocol
- The MIB
- The OID
- MIB-2
- The SMI
- The SNMP protocol
- SNMPv1, SNMPv2, and SNMPv3
- SNMP data types
- Defining new types
- Structure of an MIB file

Why SNMP?

In the early 1970s, computers and their I/O devices were large enough to need air-conditioned rooms of their own. Most large companies performed their computing tasks on stand-alone systems. It wasn't hard to tell when something went wrong—an error would print on the system console, and the front panel lights would stop blinking.

Today, even small technology companies have a server room with racks of computers and network appliances from multiple vendors, including switches, routers, print servers, webservers, RAID servers, and so forth. Network printers are distributed at convenient locations around the site, and each desk has a desktop or laptop computer. In fact, high-tech firms typically have more computers than employees.

Unlike those large computers of yore, the failure of any single component in this network of devices is not so easy to detect. IT managers need some form of automation to help them manage all these devices.

The automation may be as simple as a roll-your-own script that performs periodic ping sweeps, but larger networks are likely to rely on a Network Management System (NMS) that uses SNMP, such as Hewlett Packard's OpenView. Such a system can tell much more than when a device breaks down. It can record performance statistics, keep a restart history, and maintain a log of notifications sent from the devices themselves about impending problems. Devices may report excessive packet drops or retransmissions; connectivity failures; a fan running slowly or a CPU running too hot; excessive CPU, memory, or disk utilization; as well as system restarts.

Agents and Managers

The managed devices (routers, switches, web hosts, desktop computers, network printers, and so on) each run a server process (daemon) called an SNMP agent. This *agent* listens on a particular UDP port (usually, but not always, port 161) for read (GET) and write (SET) commands. It's the agent's responsibility to fetch the requested data and return it. This agent, as well as other monitoring software on the device, may also send spontaneous notifications called *traps* or *informs* to one or more configured target systems.

Management applications (*managers*) poll the agents for information. They may keep historical information, generate reports, or create graphical maps of the devices in your network. Some management applications are just simple command-line tools (like the snmpwalk, snmpget, and snmpset commands supplied with Net-SNMP).

Namespace, Grammar, and Protocol

SNMP stands for Simple Network Management Protocol, but it is actually more than just a protocol—it's a way of naming data, a grammar for describing data, and a protocol for exchanging data over a network. These components are called the *MIB* (the naming scheme), *SMI* (the grammar) and the *SNMP protocol*. The RFCs that describe SNMP include a common set of information useful in managing networked devices. This is called called *MIB-2* (it took two tries to get it right). We'll be discussing more about MIB-2 later.

The MIB

MIB stands for *Management Information Base.* That's a mouthful, but you can just think of it as a hierarchical naming scheme for a virtual database. This is a "virtual" database because the data may not exist anywhere in storage until the agent receives a request to read the data. When asked for an object (think of this as a field in a record in the database) the agent retrieves the information and returns it in a process that may involve getting multiple pieces of information from the managed system and computing the value to be returned. (You might think of this as a just-in-time database.) The very act of requesting a piece of information may trigger the creation of the value.

Although there is one universal addressing scheme, we break it down into subdivisions, which we also call MIBs. Normally, when people use the word *MIB*, they are referring not to the overall namespace, but to one of these subdivisions. MIB-2 is one of them, and many others are defined by different groups for different purposes. Some are produced by standards groups, while others are defined by private companies to describe proprietary data furnished by their networked products. (In Chapter 14 we describe how you can define a private MIB for your own appliance and find a place for it in the namespace.)

The OID

Every object in every MIB has an object identifier (OID). An *OID* is a unique name consisting of a sequence of decimal digits separated by periods, or dots, like this:

```
.1.3.6.1.2.1.1.2.0
```

This name represents the object's location in the namespace. The first dot represents the root of the tree, and each number represents a *node* (the base of a branch) in the tree. Everything nameable in SNMP is located somewhere in this OID tree, and every name (OID) contains the entire path to that object from the root of the tree.

This may look strange at first, but it works in the same way as the Unix filesystem, with which you should be familiar. Paths to files start at root, indicated by an initial slash (/), proceed through a number of named nodes (*directories*) separated by more slashes, and end with the name of the file itself.

Let's take the example of a file on a Unix filesystem:

```
/usr/local/bin/myprog
```

If we use a dot to separate directories instead of a slash, the path to the file would look like this:

```
.usr.local.bin.myprog
```

Suppose the following table defined a map between the directory names and a set of numbers:

Directory	No.
usr	1
local	3
bin	6
myprog	1

If we use the numbers in place of the names, the path would look like this:

```
.1.3.6.1
```

Figure B-1 shows part of the OID tree (or namespace). Note that some nodes in the tree are named for organizations: ISO is the International Standards Organization, and DOD is the US Department of Defense. (The DOD is in this structure because it was instrumental in the creation of DARPANet, which originally consisted of a four-computer network. By 1972, DARPANet had grown to a network of 37 computers and was renamed ARPANet, which led to today's Internet. End of history lesson.)

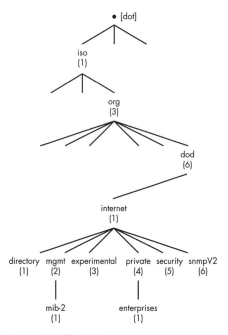

Figure B-1: The OID tree

The Internet Assigned Numbers Authority (IANA) is responsible for assigning numbers to companies and organizations under the *enterprises node*, giving the company or organization the authority to administer the OIDs in their own subtrees.

The part of the tree that we're most interested in is under .1.3.6.1 (.iso.org .dod.internet). Beneath this node are the mgmt.mib-2 (.1.3.6.1.2.1) subtree and the private.enterprises (.1.3.6.1.4.1) subtree. MIB-2 is the common set of objects that we mentioned earlier; it is supported by all networked devices that are manageable by SNMP. The enterprises OID is where organizations register their private MIBs. (For more on this topic, see Chapter 14.)

MIB-2

MIB-2, defined in RFC 1213,[1] describes a core set of information that is helpful for managing networked devices. MIB-2 is organized into the ten groups shown below. Not all groups are supported on all networked devices, but you can generally expect to find most of them.

System

This group contains objects such as sysDescr (a printable description of the operating system, hardware, networking software, etc.), sysContact (typically the email address of the person administering this system), sysLocation (a printable description of where the system is located), and sysObjectID (an OID that can be used to determine the type of device).

Interfaces

This group is a table describing the network interfaces available on the system. The interfaces table contains information on the speed of each interface and the activity on the interface (octets in and out). By polling the in and out octets periodically, you can tell what percent of the bandwidth available in the interface is being used. This can help you monitor the capacity of routers in a network.

AT

This is the Address Translation group. MIB-2 deprecates this group and includes it only for compatibility with devices implementing MIB-1. You should ignore this group unless you have a particular interest in SNMP history.

IP

This group includes information related to the IP (network) layer, including ipAddrTable (IP Address Table), which describes the IP address of the interfaces available on the system.

ICMP

This group includes various Internet Control Message Protocol (ICMP) statistics.

TCP

This group includes various TCP layer statistics, including the tcpConnTable (TCP Connection Table) describing the current TCP connections between this and other systems in the network. This table is often used in network discovery. Once you have the address of this system, you can find out the addresses of other systems that are in contact with it.

---

[1] Network Working Group, Request For Comments: 1213. *Management Information Base for Network Management of TCP/IP-based internets: MIB-II.* K. McCloghrie and M. Rose, March 1991.

UDP

This group includes various User Datagram Protocol (UDP) datagram statistics.

EGP

This group contains Exterior Gateway Protocol (EGP) statistics for those systems supporting the EGP protocol.

Transmission

This group contains information related to managing transmission media.

SNMP

This group includes various statistics related to the SNMP protocol, itself.

The SMI

MIBs are described using a grammar defined by the Structure of Management Information (SMI), which is a subset of Abstract Syntax Notation One (ASN.1). ASN.1 was created to allow description of data in a way independent of machine architecture (for example, no assumptions about endian-ness or word size). The SNMP SMI adopted a subset of the object types definable under ASN.1 and then simplified the notation.

All you really need to know about all this is how to read and write the notation used to describe a MIB. This is best accomplished with minimal notation definitions illustrated by examples. You can create a new MIB largely by cutting and pasting from other MIBs.

NOTE   *We've attempted to keep our discussion of MIBs as simple as possible. For more in-depth coverage, pick up a copy of* Understanding SNMP MIBs *by David Perkins and Evan McGinnis (Prentice Hall, 1996).*

Here is an example of an object definition using the grammar described in the SMI:

```
system      OBJECT IDENTIFIER ::= { mib-2 1 }

sysDescr OBJECT-TYPE
            SYNTAX  DisplayString (SIZE (0..255))
            ACCESS  read-only
            STATUS  mandatory
            DESCRIPTION
                    "A textual description of the entity. This value
                    should include the full name and version
                    identification of the system's hardware type,
                    software operating-system, and networking
                    software. It is mandatory that this only contain
                    printable ASCII characters."
            ::= { system 1 }
```

The ::= reads *is defined as*, and {mib-2 1} means that if mib-2 is .1.3.6.1.2.1, then system is .1.3.6.1.2.1.1. Therefore, sysDescr is .1.3.6.1.2.1.1.1. Each definition describes a single step in the OID tree.

Note that some object identifiers simply describe nodes in the tree structure and others describe objects you may actually read (leaf nodes). These are like directories and files in a filesystem. In fact, when you try to read sysDescr, you must ask for .1.3.6.1.4.1.1.1.0. This is where we diverge a bit from the filesystem analogy. The ending zero says you are retrieving an *instance* of the object. Scalar object instances (scalars are just stand-alone objects not in a table) are always .0 (dot zero). In object-oriented terminology, it's like .1.3.6.1.2.1.1.1 is the *class*, while .0 describes an object that is an instance of the class.

This may make more sense if you think of objects as fields in a table structure that must be retrieved by a row index. The table row number would replace the zero. For example, ifDescr is a field in a table whose rows each describe information about a particular network interface on the machine. Another node under mib-2, interfaces, is described as

---

```
interfaces    OBJECT IDENTIFIER ::= { mib-2 2 }
```

If you retrieved the ifDescr field for the first two interfaces on a system, you might get this:

```
interfaces.ifTable.ifEntry.ifDescr.1 = lo
interfaces.ifTable.ifEntry.ifDescr.2 = eth0
```

Contrast this with what you might retrieve when asking for sysDescr:

```
system.sysDescr.0 = Linux localhost.localdomain 2.4.18-27.8.0 #1 Fri Mar 14 06:45:49 EST 2003 i686
```

The .1 and .2 at the end of the ifDescr OIDs indicate the table row from which they were retrieved. In SNMP table rows are numbered from 1, which leaves 0 to indicate a scalar.

The SMI description of a MIB is normally distributed in a *MIB file*. This is a text file containing the unambiguous description of a portion of the universal MIB.

Sometimes descriptions of individual tables are placed in separate files. Other files just contain common objects or definitions, such as textual conventions, used by a set of other MIB files. Generally, a private MIB for a particular product is described in a single file or a small set of files, importing types and conventions as needed from other files, much like the use of the #include statement in the C language.

The MIB file is used as a formal definition of the MIB for humans, but it is also used programmatically to interpret SNMP responses for display to human beings. (We'll see this below.) MIB files, therefore, must be as syntactically correct as any computer program. There are MIB compilers and checkers (the equivalent of the lint program for C) to help verify the correctness of a MIB file. (We discuss this further in Chapter 14, where we cover the creation and validation of our own MIB.)

The SNMP Protocol

Although worthy of a chapter all its own, we can understand most of what we need to know about the SNMP protocol from the Protocol Data Units (PDUs) it defines and their uses.

The Basic Commands: GET, SET, GETNEXT

The SNMP protocol is used to exchange information between managed systems and the applications written to manage them. Managed systems host a daemon called an *agent*, usually named snmpd, which provides the ability to read information from or write information to one or more MIBs. The GET, SET, and GETNEXT PDUs are used to read from, write to, and walk a MIB.

Walking a MIB with GETNEXT

GETNEXT allows you to name one object and ask the agent to return the OID and value of the next object in the MIB tree. *Walking a MIB* means starting at some point in the OID tree and traversing the entire subtree below it with repeated use of the GETNEXT command. The walk is finished when the OID returned is not within the subtree defined by the first OID. An application can find out which MIBs are supported on a managed system by walking the entire MIB tree in this way.

Traps and Informs

Managed systems can also spontaneously send information to a configured target-management node, a process called sending an SNMP *trap* or *inform*. A trap is sent toward a target system, but the sender never knows if it got there. An inform is an improvement over a trap because it expects a reply from the receiver; it can be retried if the reply is not received in a reasonable amount of time.

Command-Line Tools: Examples

Let's look at some examples of using command-line tools that use the SNMP PDUs we have just discussed to achieve their function. These commands are supplied as part of the Net-SNMP package (http://net-snmp.sourceforge.net), which we use throughout the SNMP chapters in this book.

To retrieve the sysDescr field shown in the previous section, you might issue the command

```
snmpget -c public 10.1.1.21 .1.3.6.1.2.1.1.1.0
```

This asks for the instance of the sysDescr object from the system whose IP address is 10.1.1.21, using the community name public (think of this as a password). As you can guess from its name, the snmpget command generates an SNMP GET PDU.

Now let's walk a subtree. The snmpwalk command uses a series of GETNEXT PDUs. If you issue the following command to retrieve the interface table from a system:

```
snmpwalk -c public 10.1.1.21 .1.3.6.1.2.1.2
```

This is what you might get back:

```
interfaces.ifNumber.0 = 2
interfaces.ifTable.ifEntry.ifIndex.1 = 1
interfaces.ifTable.ifEntry.ifIndex.2 = 2
interfaces.ifTable.ifEntry.ifDescr.1 = lo
interfaces.ifTable.ifEntry.ifDescr.2 = eth0
interfaces.ifTable.ifEntry.ifType.1 = softwareLoopback(24)
interfaces.ifTable.ifEntry.ifType.2 = ethernetCsmacd(6)
interfaces.ifTable.ifEntry.ifMtu.1 = 16436
interfaces.ifTable.ifEntry.ifMtu.2 = 1500
interfaces.ifTable.ifEntry.ifSpeed.1 = Gauge32: 10000000
interfaces.ifTable.ifEntry.ifSpeed.2 = Gauge32: 100000000
interfaces.ifTable.ifEntry.ifPhysAddress.1 =
interfaces.ifTable.ifEntry.ifPhysAddress.2 = 0:8:74:93:4d:29
interfaces.ifTable.ifEntry.ifAdminStatus.1 = up(1)
interfaces.ifTable.ifEntry.ifAdminStatus.2 = up(1)
interfaces.ifTable.ifEntry.ifOperStatus.1 = up(1)
interfaces.ifTable.ifEntry.ifOperStatus.2 = up(1)
interfaces.ifTable.ifEntry.ifInOctets.1 = Counter32: 199082
interfaces.ifTable.ifEntry.ifInOctets.2 = Counter32: 291688668
interfaces.ifTable.ifEntry.ifInUcastPkts.1 = Counter32: 3380
interfaces.ifTable.ifEntry.ifInUcastPkts.2 = Counter32: 1579204
interfaces.ifTable.ifEntry.ifInDiscards.1 = Counter32: 0
interfaces.ifTable.ifEntry.ifInDiscards.2 = Counter32: 0
interfaces.ifTable.ifEntry.ifInErrors.1 = Counter32: 0
interfaces.ifTable.ifEntry.ifInErrors.2 = Counter32: 0
interfaces.ifTable.ifEntry.ifOutOctets.1 = Counter32: 199082
interfaces.ifTable.ifEntry.ifOutOctets.2 = Counter32: 61187262
interfaces.ifTable.ifEntry.ifOutUcastPkts.1 = Counter32: 3380
interfaces.ifTable.ifEntry.ifOutUcastPkts.2 = Counter32: 682356
interfaces.ifTable.ifEntry.ifOutDiscards.1 = Counter32: 0
interfaces.ifTable.ifEntry.ifOutDiscards.2 = Counter32: 0
interfaces.ifTable.ifEntry.ifOutErrors.1 = Counter32: 0
interfaces.ifTable.ifEntry.ifOutErrors.2 = Counter32: 0
interfaces.ifTable.ifEntry.ifOutQLen.1 = Gauge32: 0
interfaces.ifTable.ifEntry.ifOutQLen.2 = Gauge32: 0
interfaces.ifTable.ifEntry.ifSpecific.1 = OID: .ccitt.zeroDotZero
interfaces.ifTable.ifEntry.ifSpecific.2 = OID: .ccitt.zeroDotZero
```

This output is a little awkward to read because it is a depth-first walk; that is, it walks down each column before going back to row one and starting down the next column. This is a result of the lexical ordering of the OIDs. For example, since ifDescr is ifEntry.1 and ifType is ifEntry.2, you see all ifDescr fields before any ifType fields.

KNOWING AN APPLIANCE BY ITS MIBS

Walking can often identify the type of a machine by the MIBs it supports. For example, one of the authors was once assigned an IP address for a new workstation and found that someone else was already using this address. Since he had been assigned this address through proper channels, he assumed someone else was invalidly using it. He turned off his system and used another system to read system.sysContact from the offending system; this should have been set to the contact information for the administrator for that node, but it was not. He then tried walking all the MIBs supported by that system and found that it supported the printer MIB. Hmm . . . As it turned out, he had been incorrectly given the IP address of the department's printer!

SNMPv1, SNMPv2, and SNMPv3

There are three main variants of SNMP. The original, SNMPv1 (version 1), is the simplest, but it has some drawbacks that newer versions seek to remedy. Its shortcomings include:

- No support for integers larger than 32 bits.
- No means to ask for bulk data (each object must be asked for by name).
- No mechanism to ensure that a trap reaches its destination.
- Security/authentication is accomplished using community names, which are like passwords, but are transmitted on the network in the clear (that is, unencrypted).

SNMPv2c (community-based SNMPv2) addressed the first three of these problems, but reaching an agreement on a new security mechanism proved more difficult, so SNMPv2c still relies on community names for authentication. SNMPv2c includes 64-bit integers, the GETBULK command, and introduces informs, which are confirmed traps.

SNMPv3 replaces the community-name authentication mechanism with more secure authentication and encryption, but in-depth discussion of it is beyond the scope of this book.

NOTE *SNMPv1 has been moved to "historical" status, but many applications used by IT organizations still use it. Your network appliance may need to speak SNMPv1 for compatibility with these older applications. Expect, however, that in the not-too-distant future, some of your customers will want to disable the older, less secure versions of SNMP.*

SNMP Data Types

SNMP data types are a subset of ASN.1 types. A complete description of the SNMP data types and their uses is beyond the scope of this brief introduction, but this section is a summary of the major types. SNMP defines three kinds of data types: primitive, defined, and constructor. We won't dwell on the differences here, other than to say primitives are the basic types, defined types have special meanings but have underlying primitive types, and constructor types are the tables we will discuss below. Although it may look a little strange, we'll try to stay consistent here with SNMP's standard of using all capital letters in the names of primitive types, but just initial capitals for the defined types.

INTEGER

An `INTEGER` may be positive or negative. Its values may be enumerated, a range of legal values specified in the form of (`lowValue..highValue`), or a fixed size (e.g., `Size(4)`). In SNMPv2 `INTEGER` becomes `Integer32`, explicitly indicating the size as 32 bits. SNMPv2 also adds an `Unsigned32` type for a 32-bit integer of only positive values.

Gauge

Gauges are integers that take only non-negative values and whose values rise or fall within a specified range (e.g., between 0 and 100 percent, or between 0 and some maximum capacity). SNMPv2 redefines this as `Gauge32`.

Counter

Like `Gauge`, `Counter` is an integer that takes only non-negative values. Unlike `Gauge`, the value of a counter only increases until it wraps back to zero at its maximum limit. SNMPv2 replaced `Counter` with `Counter32` and `Counter64`.

TimeTicks

`TimeTicks` are integers describing time in 1/100ths of a second. They are generally used to describe the time since some significant event or starting point, such as system boot or last configuration change.

OCTET STRING

An `OCTET STRING` is a string of eight-bit bytes. It is not necessarily a null-terminated C string; each octet can contain any value (`0..255`) at any position (i.e., there may be nulls in the middle). SNMPv2 added the restriction that an `OCTET STRING` may be no longer than 65,535 (i.e., its length must be expressible in 16 bits).

OBJECT IDENTIFIER

This is used to contain SNMP OID values. SNMPv2 added the restriction that an `OBJECT IDENTIFIER` may contain no more than 128 components, each of which must be expressible in a maximum of 32 bits.

IpAddress

The `IpAddress` string is an octet string of length four. (Note that this allows expression only of Ipv4 addresses.)

Opaque

This type is much like OCTET STRING in that it is a string of octets with similar restrictions. Opaque was defined to allow extensions of the SMI. Defining new types based on the Opaque type is strongly discouraged.

BITS

BITS was added in SNMPv2 to provide a way to express bit fields of labeled bits (i.e., where each bit has a separate meaning).

NOTE *Types that have been removed from the later revisions of SNMP are not shown in the above list.*

SNMP Tables

In addition to the simple types described above, tables may be described using SEQUENCE and SEQUENCE OF. A table in a MIB is described as a SEQUENCE OF a type that describes the entry. The table entry is then described as a SEQUENCE containing the individual fields of the entry. The entry type describes the columns that constitute each row in the table, while the table itself is described as an array of these entry structures.

For example, here's the definition of the interfaces table from MIB-2:

```
ifTable OBJECT-TYPE
    SYNTAX      SEQUENCE OF IfEntry
    MAX-ACCESS  not-accessible
    STATUS      current
    DESCRIPTION
            "A list of interface entries. The number of entries is
            given by the value of ifNumber."
    ::= { interfaces 2 }

ifEntry OBJECT-TYPE
    SYNTAX      IfEntry
    MAX-ACCESS  not-accessible
    STATUS      current
    DESCRIPTION
            "An entry containing management information applicable to a
            particular interface."
    INDEX   { ifIndex }
    ::= { ifTable 1 }

IfEntry ::=
    SEQUENCE {
            ifIndex                 InterfaceIndex,
            ifDescr                 DisplayString,
            ifType                  IANAifType,
            ifMtu                   Integer32,
            ifSpeed                 Gauge32,
            ifPhysAddress           PhysAddress,
            ifAdminStatus           INTEGER,
            ifOperStatus            INTEGER,
            ifLastChange            TimeTicks,
```

```
ifInOctets              Counter32,
ifInUcastPkts           Counter32,
ifInNUcastPkts          Counter32,   -- deprecated
ifInDiscards            Counter32,
ifInErrors              Counter32,
ifInUnknownProtos       Counter32,
ifOutOctets             Counter32,
ifOutUcastPkts          Counter32,
ifOutNUcastPkts         Counter32,   -- deprecated
ifOutDiscards           Counter32,
ifOutErrors             Counter32,
ifOutQLen               Gauge32,     -- deprecated
ifSpecific              OBJECT IDENTIFIER -- deprecated
}
```

Note the use of both ifEntry and IfEntry, one initial-capped and the other not. All object names start with lowercase; for example, ifTable and ifEntry. Because IfEntry is initial-capped, we know that it describes a type, rather than an object.

The IfEntry type is like a struct in C; it describes the layout of each table row. The lowercase ifEntry is a node in the OID tree beneath which the column objects will be defined. Thus, the description of a particular interface will have an OID like this:

```
ifTable.ifEntry.ifDescr.x
```

where *x* is the row index.

Following the definition of the entry type will be the definitions of each of the objects that make up the entry sequence. You will see this format again and again in MIB definitions; much MIB information is organized into tables.

Defining New Types

Although the data types defined in the SMI are sufficient, it is sometimes convenient to be a bit more specific. For example, you may want to restrict the possible values in an OCTET STRING or the range covered by an Integer32; if your MIB uses the same restricted values repeatedly, it will become tedious to describe these same restrictions repeatedly.

RFC 1903 describes the *textual convention*, a macro that allows you to bind your clarifications together into a new type. The following textual convention is taken from the file SNMPv2-TC.txt distributed with Net-SNMP (version 5.0.8).

```
DisplayString ::= TEXTUAL-CONVENTION
    DISPLAY-HINT "255a"
    STATUS      current
    DESCRIPTION
            "Represents textual information taken from the NVT ASCII
            character set, as defined in pages 4, 10-11 of RFC 854.
```

To summarize RFC 854, the NVT ASCII repertoire specifies:

- the use of character codes 0-127 (decimal)

- the graphics characters (32-126) are interpreted as
  US ASCII

- NUL, LF, CR, BEL, BS, HT, VT and FF have the special
  meanings specified in RFC 854

- the other 25 codes have no standard interpretation

- the sequence 'CR LF' means newline

- the sequence 'CR NUL' means carriage-return

- an 'LF' not preceded by a 'CR' means moving to the
  same column on the next line.

- the sequence 'CR x' for any x other than LF or NUL is
  illegal. (Note that this also means that a string may
  end with either 'CR LF' or 'CR NUL', but not with CR.)

```
            Any object defined using this syntax may not exceed 255
            characters in length."
SYNTAX      OCTET STRING (SIZE (0..255))
```

This describes a type called DisplayString that can take up to 255 octets whose values are restricted to those that correspond to displayable characters. The DISPLAY-HINT clause shows how a DisplayString may appear. *255a* means it can take the form of up to 255 ASCII characters. RFC 1903 describes the complete syntax for the display hint.

Structure of a MIB File

When you read a MIB file, you will notice that it is named and defined between BEGIN and END statements. It will describe what it includes from other MIB files, and it will name the module being defined in this MIB file, the contact information for the person responsible for the MIB, and the revision history. Next you will see the definition of the objects in the MIB.

If you look at the IF-MIB, again distributed with the Net-SNMP package, you can see all of these parts. The MIB is enclosed within these lines

```
IF-MIB DEFINITIONS ::= BEGIN

END
```

The first section states the external dependencies.

```
IMPORTS
    MODULE-IDENTITY, OBJECT-TYPE, Counter32, Gauge32, Counter64,
    Integer32, TimeTicks, mib-2,
```

```
NOTIFICATION-TYPE                           FROM SNMPv2-SMI
TEXTUAL-CONVENTION, DisplayString,
PhysAddress, TruthValue, RowStatus,
TimeStamp, AutonomousType, TestAndIncr      FROM SNMPv2-TC
MODULE-COMPLIANCE, OBJECT-GROUP,
NOTIFICATION-GROUP                          FROM SNMPv2-CONF
snmpTraps                                   FROM SNMPv2-MIB
IANAifType                                  FROM IANAifType-MIB;
```

Then comes the definition of the module.

```
ifMIB MODULE-IDENTITY
    LAST-UPDATED "200006140000Z"
    ORGANIZATION "IETF Interfaces MIB Working Group"
    CONTACT-INFO
            "   Keith McCloghrie
                Cisco Systems, Inc.
                170 West Tasman Drive
                San Jose, CA  95134-1706
                US

                408-526-5260
                kzm@cisco.com"
    DESCRIPTION
            "The MIB module to describe generic objects for
            network interface sub-layers. This MIB is an
            updated version of MIB-II's ifTable, and incorporates
            the extensions defined in RFC 1229."

    REVISION      "200006140000Z"
    DESCRIPTION
            "Clarifications agreed upon by the Interfaces MIB WG,
            and published as RFC 2863."
    REVISION      "199602282155Z"
    DESCRIPTION
            "Revisions made by the Interfaces MIB WG, and
            published in RFC 2233."
    REVISION      "199311082155Z"
    DESCRIPTION
            "Initial revision, published as part of RFC 1573."
    ::= { mib-2 31 }
```

This describes the module ifMib, which takes the location { mib-2 31 } in the overall MIB address space. The organization and contact information are clearly identifiable, followed by the descriptions of the various revisions of this MIB in reverse chronological order. The time and date look pretty cryptic, but they are just a concatenation of year, month, day, hour, and minute in GMT (indicated by the Z for Zulu Time). Therefore, the most recent revision (200006140000Z) was made on June 14, 2000.

Next, you'll see the definition of the actual structure of the MIB objects, along with any textual conventions new to this MIB.

Summary

This has been a whirlwind tour of SNMP. We've covered the basic parts of SNMP: the protocol, the grammar, and the first group of managed objects. You should now understand the acronyms *SMI*, *MIB*, and *OID*, and the terms *object* and *trap*. You should also be familiar with the term MIB-2 and have an idea of what it contains. We have discussed the various data types, both scalars and tables. At this point, you should be able to take an unfamiliar MIB and read through it, understanding its basic structure and what it is trying to describe. We have also touched on a couple of the command-line utilities you may find useful to probe an SNMP-enabled device: `snmpwalk` and `snmpget`.

With a little cut and paste and some judicious modifications, you may now be able to develop a simple MIB.

C

INSTALLING A FRAMEBUFFER DEVICE DRIVER

The Laddie CD was designed to work with as many video cards as possible. To accomplish this, it defaults to a framebuffer device driver for a widely adopted video standard and configures it for a low-resolution display with only eight bits per pixel. If this driver fails, the system then attempts to find a hardware-specific driver for your video card and loads that driver with its default configuration. This approach will provide a minimal, working framebuffer for most systems. However, if you would like to take better advantage of your particular hardware, you will need to take some additional steps.

In this appendix, we will cover the following topics:

- Finding framebuffer device drivers for your video card
- Configuring the framebuffer device driver

Finding Framebuffer Device Drivers for Your Video Card

To find available device drivers for your video card, boot your PC with the Laddie CD.

If the Laddie CD succeeds in finding a driver for your video card, it will launch the Laddie framebuffer UI, shown in Figure C-1. Otherwise, it will display the message *The framebuffer (/dev/fb0) is unavailable* before the login prompt.

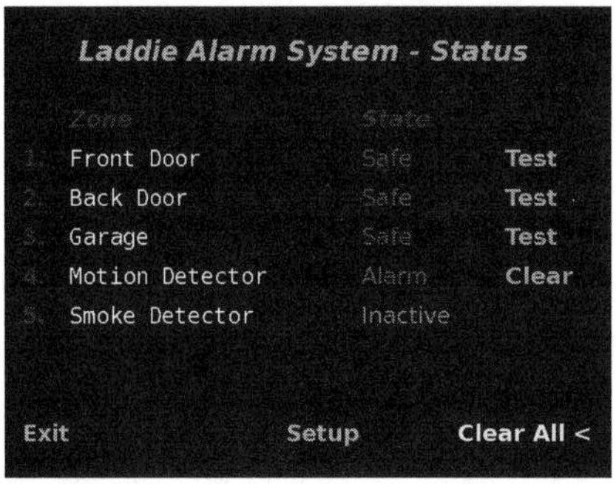

Figure C-1: The Laddie framebuffer UI

For now, we'll assume that a framebuffer driver loaded successfully. To determine which driver was loaded, first exit the framebuffer UI by pressing ESC. Then type the following at the command prompt:

```
laddie:~# dmesg | grep fb
```

The dmesg command displays the buffer of messages produced by the kernel since startup, and the grep command selects those that might have something to do with framebuffers.

The vesafb Driver

The Laddie CD first attempts to load the vesfab video driver, since this is the most likely candidate for an unknown graphics card. The vesafb driver supports an interface developed by the Video Electronics Standards Association (VESA) known as VESA BIOS Extensions (VBE). The driver relies on the BIOS and must therefore be configured at system startup. This means that the vesafb driver has to be compiled into the kernel, rather than be supplied as a separate module. The Laddie appliance configures the driver using a boot prompt command, which we will describe later.

Here is example output from one of our systems on which a vesafb driver installed successfully:

```
vesafb: framebuffer at 0xd8000000, mapped to 0xf8880000, using 600k, total 32768k
vesafb: mode is 640x480x8, linelength=640, pages=11
vesafb: protected mode interface info at c000:0f03
vesafb: scrolling: redraw
```

```
vesafb: Pseudocolor: size=8:8:8:8, shift=0:0:0:0
vesafb: Mode is VGA compatible
fb0: VESA VGA frame buffer device
```

Hardware-Specific Drivers

If your system successfully loaded the vesafb driver, you will need to disable
that driver at boot time in order to check for other drivers. To do this, reboot
the Laddie CD. When you see the boot prompt, type **novesa** and press ENTER.
If the framebuffer UI launches, that means the system found an appropriate
driver. Exit the framebuffer UI, and type the command **dmesg | grep fb**. When
we did this for one of our systems, the command produced the following:

```
vesafb: probe of vesafb0 failed with error -6
rivafb: nVidia device/chipset 10DE002D
rivafb: nVidia Corporation NV5M64 [RIVA TNT2 Model 64/Model 64 Pro]
rivafb: RIVA MTRR set to ON
rivafb: could not retrieve EDID from DDC/I2C
rivafb: setting virtual Y resolution to 52428
rivafb: PCI nVidia NV4 framebuffer ver 0.9.5b (32MB @ 0xF8000000)
[additional lines omitted...]
```

Here we see that the vesafb driver failed to load, and a device-specific
driver succeeded. The rivafb is a video driver for NVIDIA graphics cards.

You can also check which hardware-specific framebuffer driver your
system loaded with the lsmod command. Execute the following at the console:

```
lsmod | grep  fb
```

The lsmod command lists all the modules currently loaded by the kernel;
framebuffer names typically include the letters *fb*, for example *nvidiafb*,
radeonfb, *savagefb*, or *matroxfb_g450*. By the way, the lsmod command won't
work for the vesafb driver, since the vesafb driver isn't a module—it's compiled
into the kernel.

Drivers Not Included on the Laddie CD

If the Laddie CD did not find a driver for your graphics card, it is possible
that a newer kernel will support it. In this case, use the lspci command to
identify your graphics card. If your card is AGP, PCI, or PCI-Express, this command will report it. The following is one of several lines produced when
running the lspci command on one of our development machines.

```
01:00.0 VGA compatible controller: nVidia Corporation NV15 [GeForce2 GTS/Pro] (rev a4)
```

This output shows us that we have an NVIDIA VGA-compatible controller
(VGA stands for *Video Graphics Array*). At this point, you may need to spend
some time on the Internet finding a driver for your graphics card. Also keep
in mind that Linux doesn't support all graphics cards, so you may have to
install a different card in order to use the Linux framebuffer.

Configuring the Framebuffer Device Driver

Once you've found the right video driver for your hardware, you'll need to configure it for your desired video mode.

The vesafb Driver

Since the vesafb driver relies on real-mode BIOS functions for initialization, it must be built into the kernel and configured at boot time. This configuration is specified at the kernel command line and may be provided at the boot prompt or in the bootloader's configuration file. For the vesafb driver, the kernel command line should include the following:

```
video=vesafb vga=<Linux video mode>
```

The `Linux video mode` is a number that specifies a particular resolution and number of bits per pixel. This number is formed by adding *0x200* to the video mode numbers specified by the VESA BIOS Extensions standard. These Linux video modes are summarized in Table C-1.

Table C-1: Linux Video Mode Numbers

Bits per pixel	320x200	640x400	640x480	800x600	1024x768	1280x1024
4	-	-	-	0x302	0x304	0x306
8	-	0x300	0x301	0x303	0x305	0x307
15 (1:5:5:5)	0x30d	-	0x310	0x313	0x316	0x319
16 (5:6:5)	0x30e	-	0x311	0x314	0x317	0x31a
24 (8:8:8)	0x30f	-	0x312	0x315	0x318	0x31b

Choose an Appropriate Video Mode

A typical VBE-compliant graphics card will not support all of these modes, so you may need to experiment to find one that works. The easiest way to do this is to specify

```
video=vesafb vga=ask
```

at the Linux boot prompt. (If you are experimenting with the Laddie CD, the complete boot prompt line would be linux vga=ask.) The kernel initialization code will display a list of modes and ask for a mode number. You can ignore the ones it presents, since these are for text-only consoles.

Also, don't bother to choose the scan option. At best, this will provide a longer list of text modes; at worst, it will hang the system and you will have to reboot. In fact, whenever you enter an unsupported number, the kernel responds immediately with *Unknown mode ID. Try again*, so it doesn't take long to find one that works. When entering a mode, just provide the hex digits without the leading *0x*.

Update the Kernel Command Line

Once you have found a VBE video mode that works, you can update the kernel command line in your bootloader configuration file. In this case, you do need to use the leading *0x*. For example, the command

```
video=vesafb vga=0x311 3
```

would be appropriate for a VBE-compatible video card that supports a resolution of 640 by 480 with 16 bits per pixel. The final *3* specifies runlevel 3 to prevent the X display manager from loading a separate video driver.

NOTE   *The vesafb driver does accept optional parameters for features like efficient scrolling. See /usr/src/linux/Documentation/fb/vesafb.txt for details.*

Hardware-Specific Drivers

If you booted the Laddie CD with the novesa option and if the system was able to find a hardware-specific video driver, it will have come up with default settings for the video mode.

In this section, we will describe how you can experiment with those settings using the Laddie CD, and then how you can select your preferred settings at boot time for your own system. These comments also apply to video drivers that the Laddie CD doesn't support, though you will have to use your own system to experiment with them.

Experiment with Different Video Modes

Unlike the vesafb driver, non-VBE drivers can change modes after startup. To change video mode, use the fbset utility. This utility accesses the file /etc/fb.modes to associate mode names with geometry and timing parameters. For example, the command

```
fbset 640x480-60
```

will find the geometry and timing parameters associated with the string 640x480-60 and use these to switch the framebuffer to a resolution of 640 by 480 at 60 Hz. If this command is successful, you will probably see the console screen change (e.g., to a larger font) as it switches to a different graphics mode.

If the fbset utility is not available on your distribution, you can download it from http://packages.debian.org/stable/admin/fbset. If you install it yourself, be sure to install an appropriate fb.modes file in /etc. You can use one of the fb.modes files provided with the fbset package (which is what we did), but do so with caution, because incorrect timing values can damage some monitors.

Select the Desired Video Mode at Startup

The Laddie CD maintains hardware-specific video drivers as modules, but once you've found the appropriate framebuffer device driver for your system, you may want to build it into the kernel. This is not an option with the Laddie CD, of course, but if you rebuild the kernel for your own system, you will need to configure the driver at the kernel boot prompt. Many non-VBE framebuffer device drivers now support a common syntax for providing the video mode on the kernel command line. Following this syntax, the examplefb driver would be selected at boot time with the following command:

```
video=examplefb:1024x768-24@76
```

This specifies a width of 1,024 pixels, a height of 768 pixels, 24 bits per pixel, and a refresh rate of 76 Hz.

NOTE *No timing information has been provided except for the refresh rate. The kernel includes a database of timing parameters (see the file /usr/src/linux/drivers/video/modedb.c for details) and will search for an entry that matches the provided resolution and refresh rate. If it fails to find a match, it will use a default video mode, and if that fails, it will attempt all modes in the database.*

In general, the following format is used to specify the video mode:

```
<xres>x<yres>[M][R][-<bpp>][@<refresh>][i][m]
```

Here, an optional M requests the use of *VESA Coordinated Video Timings*, a systematic method for determining appropriate timings based on resolution, refresh rate, the type of monitor (CRT or digital display), and interlacing. The optional R specifies reduced blanking for digital displays. The optional i specifies an interlaced mode, and the optional m requests an additional 1.8 percent margin in the timing calculations.

Besides the common syntax outlined here, specific drivers may support other options, such as disabling acceleration. There is little commonality among drivers; you may need to consult your driver's source code to find these options.

Verify the Settings for Your Framebuffer Driver

If you have successfully loaded a framebuffer driver and would like to learn more about its configuration, you can use the fbset -i command to report your framebuffer's geometry, timings, and various other parameters.

To see configuration data on a loaded framebuffer driver, try using cat to examine the contents of /proc/fb and the files in the /sys/class/graphics/fb0 directory. Not all drivers update the /sys directory, but when they do, these files provide a convenient way to access framebuffer parameters such as bits_per_pixel and color_map.

For more information on the Linux framebuffer, see the (somewhat dated) HOWTO at http://tldp.org/HOWTO/Framebuffer-HOWTO.html. The VBE 3.0 specification is available at http://www.vesa.org/public/VBE/vbe3.pdf.

D

A DB-TO-FILE UTILITY

This appendix describes tbl2filed, a daemon that allows you to use SQL to read and write values in Linux configuration files as if those values were in a database instead of a file. This utility is convenient if you want to use RTA for new daemons and want to keep the same database metaphor for reading and writing values into traditional, non-RTA configuration files. Topics discussed in this appendix include:

- Overview
- Table definitions
- Usage and API
- Security notes

Overview

The goal of the tbl2filed daemon is to allow your UI programs to use a PostgreSQL library to read or write (SELECT or UPDATE) an RTA table and have an underlying system configuration file scanned or modified as part of the SELECT or UPDATE. This utility tries to mimic the common tasks of:

- Viewing values in a configuration file (SELECT value . . .)
- Editing the values in a configuration file (UPDATE value . . .)
- Atomically writing a file to disk (UPDATE tbl2file SET do_commit . . .)
- Restarting a service if necessary (UPDATE tbl2file SET do_script . . .)

The tbl2filed daemon allows you to read and write configuration files by using PostgreSQL commands on two RTA tables. The first table, tbl2file, describes the files managed by the daemon, and the second table, tbl2field, describes the managed fields.

Figure D-1 illustrates how this utility maps two tables into text fields inside of disk files.

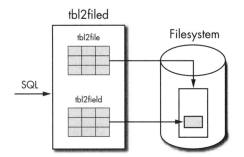

Figure D-1: Use SQL to access data in files.

This daemon also lets us put all of the restart scripts for system services in a single file and use a single method (a write callback) to invoke them. This approach might help security because it allows a non-privileged UI program to safely change the system configuration files.

Table Definitions

An example is given later in this appendix, but for that example to make sense, you need some understanding of the contents of the two tbl2filed tables. Laddie uses tbl2filed to help with the networking configuration, and you may find the tables easier to understand by looking at them in a running Laddie system. Boot the Laddie CD and follow the tbl2filed link at http://192.168.1.11/table_editor/rta/rta_apps.html.

The tbl2file Table

The table of managed file information, tbl2file, has the following columns:

```
name            // name of the file
path            // full path to the file
do_commit       // flush values to the file on 0->1
timestamp       // time we last read/parsed file
do_script       // run script on 0->1 transition
script_parms    // the parameters passed to the script
```

The name of the file is the name as seen by the UI. It is also used as part of the index into tbl2field table. This can just be shorthand or a mnemonic for the file, for example, *resolv*.

The path is the full path to the file, including the filename. For example, the name field might be *resolv*, while the path might be */etc/resolv.conf*.

Writing a 1 to the do_commit flag causes the managed file's values to be written back to the disk file. The file is written to a temporary file first and then rename() is called to move the temporary file to the destination file. This mechanism helps maintain consistency in the system by trying to make a write of the entire file as atomic as possible. A SELECT on do_commit always returns a zero.

Reading and parsing the values from a file is expensive in terms of time and CPU cycles. Since the files won't change often, we can improve the system's responsiveness by caching the file's values in the tbl2field table and only rereading the file if it has been modified since the last time we read it. The timestamp marks the last time we read and parsed the file; time is measured as the number of seconds since the last write. When a UI asks for a value, our daemon compares the mtime (time of last modification) in the file's inode to our time stamp, and either rescans the file if necessary or returns the values directly from the fields table, if the cached values are still valid.

Setting do_script to 1 starts the script /usr/local/tbl2filed/tbl2script.sh. (The script location is set in the tbl2filed Makefile.) The script_parms field has a set of space-separated parameters that are passed to the script. The parameters are not passed on the command line; rather, they are passed in on standard input and parsed into parameters using a cut command. This script is spawned and forgotten—that is, we ignore any return value from it. The script is only run by an explicit write of 1 to the do_script column, and the column is only used for its write callback. A SELECT on this column will always return a zero. Laddie uses this script, for example, to restart networking when the user changes the appliance's IP address.

The tbl2field Table

The tbl2field table that holds the values for the individual fields and has the following columns:

```
name       // name of the file, e.g., "resolv"
field      // field name, e.g., "search_domain"
pattern    // regex to extract value from line
regerr     // nonzero if any errors in the pattern string
skip       // skip this many patterns to target
format     // printf format to replace line
value      // current value of field
```

The name is the name of the file and must match the name column in the tbl2file table.

The field is the name of the field as seen by all of the UI programs. This is always used in a WHERE clause to identify the exact field to read and update.

The pattern is a regular expression that, in combination with the skip count, uniquely identifies the field in the file. The pattern should include exactly one set of parentheses to extract the value from the text of the line. For example, to get the first DNS name server from the resolv.conf file, we might use the following regular expression:

```
^nameserver[ \t]+([0-9\.]+)
```

The regerr field is nonzero if the pattern can not be parsed as a regular expression. It should be necessary to examine regerr only during development.

The skip column tells the daemon how many of the above patterns to skip before selecting a line as the source of the value. For example, we'd use a skip value of 1 to read the second DNS nameserver from resolv.conf. This would skip over one nameserver and read the second one.

The format field is used to reproduce the line of configuration data in the target file. We could get this from the regular expression, but having a printf format string is a lot easier. If this column is left blank, the field is considered a read-only field. Any of the read-only values in /proc or /sys should have a blank format field. You can see a good example of a read-only value by looking at the uptime field in tbl2field table. For a nameserver line in resolv.conf, the format string would be nameserver %s. There's no need for a \n in the format string, since it is added automatically by the print statement.

The value is the current value of the field as a string. Doing a SELECT on this column will cause the file to be read and parsed if necessary (see timestamp in tbl2file above). If the cached value is still valid, the value is taken directly from the table. A write on this column saves the value in the table but does not actually write the value to the file; writing a 1 to do_commit does that.

A tbl2filed Example

Let's look at a complete example by continuing with the nameserver configuration for Laddie. The /etc/resolv.conf file on a running Laddie system looks like this:

```
nameserver 204.117.214.10
nameserver 199.2.252.10
nameserver 65.173.40.10
```

Our goal is to be able to read the first DNS nameserver with a SELECT statement as follows:

```
psql -h localhost -p 8885
> SELECT * FROM tbl2field where name = "nameserver_1";
> \q
```

Similarly, to modify the second DNS server, Laddie uses the following UPDATE statement:

```
psql -h localhost -p 8885
> UPDATE tbl2field SET value="192.168.1.1"
>    WHERE name=resolv AND field="nameserver_2";
> \q
```

You can verify the above by booting the Laddie CD, exiting from the framebuffer menu, logging in as root, and executing the commands given above. Be sure to verify that the file has been modified after the UPDATE command.

Now let's look at the tbl2file and tbl2field configuration that gives us the ability to read and write the nameserver IP addresses as if they were in a PostgreSQL database. We'll start by listing the file we want to manage in the tbl2file table:

```
UPDATE tbl2file SET name=resolv, path=/etc/resolv.conf,
      script_parms="" LIMIT 1 OFFSET 0
```

We don't need to run a script after editing the resolv.conf file, so we can leave script_parms blank. You can use either full or relative path names, but as a security precaution, it is a good idea to use the full path name.

In this example, we want to manage the three DNS nameservers. The SQL for this is taken from tbl2field.sql (perhaps use the full path, i.e., /opt/laddie/tbl2filed/...) and is as follows:

```
UPDATE tbl2field SET name="resolv", field="nameserver_1", skip=0,
   pattern="^nameserver[ \t]+([0-9\.]+)" LIMIT 1 OFFSET 1
UPDATE tbl2field SET name="resolv", field="nameserver_2", skip=1,
   pattern="^nameserver[ \t]+([0-9\.]+)" LIMIT 1 OFFSET 2
UPDATE tbl2field SET name="resolv", field="nameserver_3", skip=2,
   pattern="^nameserver[ \t]+([0-9\.]+)" LIMIT 1 OFFSET 3
```

The pattern recognizes the line with the parameter, and the single set of parentheses in the pattern extracts the actual field value. In the above examples, the value of a nameserver field must have only the digits zero through nine and/or decimal points. The parentheses are not part of the recognition—they are only used to extract the field value.

One nice feature of the tbl2filed daemon is that when you write a value to a field, the daemon uses the format string to build a copy of what the new configuration line will look like. Then it runs the pattern against the new line and rejects the update if the pattern doesn't recognize the new line. In this example, an update for a nameserver of 11.22.33.44 would succeed, since it contains the required digits and decimal points; however a nameserver update of Bob's fun house would fail, since it does not contain the required digits and decimals.

The nameserver example also illustrates the use of the skip column. The primary nameserver has skip set to zero, meaning that we use the first line with a matching pattern. The secondary nameserver is specified with skip set to 1, meaning we skip one matching line and use the second matching line.[1]

Security Notes

Depending on how you use it, this daemon can either enhance or hurt your system security. At first glance, having a daemon that runs with root privileges and accepts database connections seems like a bad idea. On the other hand, this might allow you to improve security by running only *one* daemon as root and running each of the UI programs as a non-root user. This way, if an attacker breaks into one of your UI programs, he or she only gains the privileges of that non-root user. Compare this to most Linux appliances, in which a UI needs to run as root in order to make system changes.

The daemon reads tbl2file.sql and tbl2field.sql when it starts, and then marks all of its configuration columns as read-only. Not allowing updates to the managed files or script parameters helps security, but it also means that you cannot update any part of the configuration after the program starts. You must edit the tbl2file.sql and tbl2field.sql files directly before starting the tbl2filed daemon. If you must mark any column as read-write to make development easier, be sure to change it back to read-only before you ship your product. Also, be sure to protect the write privileges on the directory and files with the daemon's initial configuration.

---

[1] The resolv.conf file is different from most Linux configuration files in that switching to or from DHCP as the boot configuration protocol can completely destroy any values you've previously written into it. The simple solution to this problem is to keep a template file and copy it to /etc/resolv.conf when necessary.

E

THE LADDIE APPLIANCE BOOTABLE CD

The CD accompanying this book serves two purposes. First, it allows you to demonstrate the techniques described in this book by turning your x86 PC into a working appliance. Second, it allows you to study, in as much detail as you care to, the source code that implements this appliance. In this appendix, we show you how to boot and run the Laddie appliance CD, and we provide a tour of the CD's contents. We also provide a simple example of how the CD supports modifying, rebuilding, and reinstalling the appliance.

Running the Laddie Appliance

The Laddie CD doesn't require that your machine be running a specific operating system, you don't need to install anything, and the CD won't place anything on your hard drive. In fact, you don't even need a hard drive. The CD creates a ramdisk for the root filesystem with links back to the CD, and in this context it runs the Laddie appliance. When you're finished using the CD, simply remove it and reboot your original operating system. You'll find that nothing has changed.

What you do need in order to run the Laddie appliance is an x86-based PC with at least 64 megabytes of system memory, a VESA-compliant video card (if you wish to run the framebuffer user interface), and a BIOS that is configured to boot from a CD-ROM.

In this section we'll explain how to boot the CD, show you how to verify that the framebuffer and web interfaces are working, and then explain how to access the other user interfaces. We'll also explain how to shut down the appliance.

Booting the CD

With the Laddie CD in the drive, reboot your computer. If the CD boots successfully, you'll be greeted with a message like the following:

```
ISOLINUX 2.08 0x4072248c Copyright (C) 1994-2003 H. Peter Anvin
Welcome to LAD distro 2007.02.25
*** To abort, hit <SPACE>, then eject the CD. ***
Select "linux", "svga", "novesa", or "shell"
Booting default (linux) in 6 seconds...
boot:
```

At this point, you should press ENTER or wait six seconds to continue the boot sequence.

A commercial appliance would typically hide boot messages from the user. Since this is an educational system, we want you to see them. A commercial appliance designed for a specific hardware configuration would also boot up more quickly. But this CD is designed to work with a broad range of hardware configurations and provide a flexible environment for users to experiment with and build from, so the process takes a little longer. In particular, the startup scripts load drivers for any hardware the system recognizes, even hardware that isn't required for the Laddie appliance.

Navigating the Framebuffer User Interface

Once the CD boots successfully, the system will present you with the main screen for the Laddie framebuffer user interface (see Figure E-1). If you see this screen, you've succeeded in running the appliance and you should now be able to use your keyboard's arrow keys and ENTER key to navigate the Laddie framebuffer user interface. (If your keyboard doesn't have arrow keys, use **i** for up, **j** for left, **k** for down, and **l** for right.)

NOTE   *If the boot up process completes and a login prompt appears instead of the screen shown in Figure E-1, your video card is probably not VESA-compliant. In that case, the Laddie appliance will still run, but you won't be able to experiment with the framebuffer interface.*

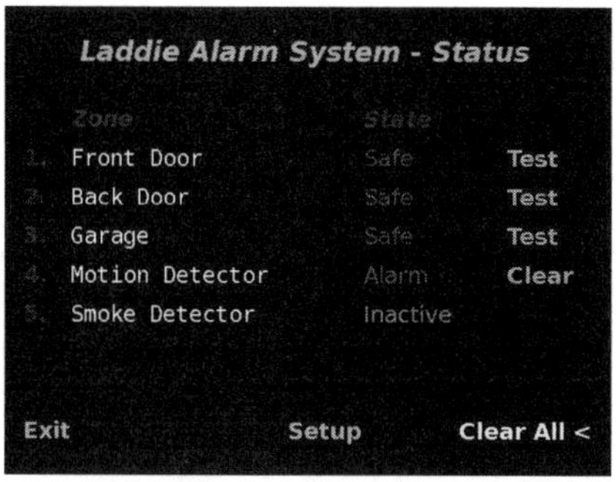

Figure E-1: The Laddie framebuffer user interface

Accessing the Web Interface

The Laddie appliance boots up with the static IP address 192.168.1.11. If your PC is connected to a local area network with an Ethernet card recognized by Laddie's operating system, the appliance will serve web pages that allow you to monitor and control the appliance (see Figure E-2). You can access this web interface with a browser on the local network by using the URL http://192.168.1.11.

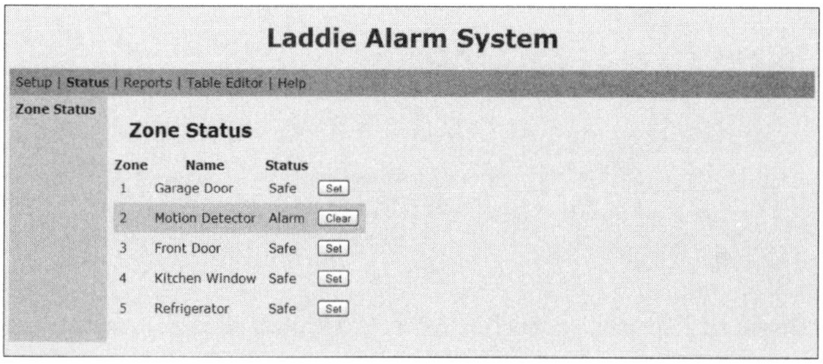

Figure E-2: The Laddie web interface

NOTE   *You can also use the text-based web browser Lynx to access the Laddie web pages. Type **lynx** at a command prompt, and then navigate by following the instructions at the bottom of the display.*

Experimenting with the Linux Shell and Other User Interfaces

In addition to the framebuffer and web interfaces, the Laddie appliance supports a command line interface, a front panel interface, and an SNMP interface. When experimenting with these other interfaces, you will find it useful to have a Linux shell so that you can interact directly with the operating system. If the Laddie appliance is on a network, you can access a login shell using telnet (i.e., telnet 192.168.1.11). To log in, enter the username root and an empty password. You can also switch from the framebuffer user interface to a login prompt by pressing CTRL-ALT-F1. (If you want to return to the framebuffer interface later, press CTRL-ALT-F7.)

Please see the appropriate chapters for instructions on accessing the CLI, front panel, and SNMP interfaces.

Shutting Down the Laddie Appliance

The Laddie operating system will not eject the CD while the system is running because it relies on the CD for necessary system files. To eject the CD and return to your original operating system, reboot your computer by typing reboot in a Linux shell. When you see the Laddie boot prompt (as shown in "Booting the CD" on page 338), press the spacebar to interrupt the automatic boot, eject the CD, then press CTRL-ALT-DEL to reboot your computer with your original operating system.

Exploring the CD Contents

If you boot the Laddie appliance and then explore the root filesystem from a Linux shell, you'll find that most of the top-level directories exist in the ramdisk, and only the /bin, /lib, /sbin, and /usr directories are linked back to the CD. In particular, all the directories related to the Laddie appliance are read-write, so you can use the CD to experiment with, rebuild, and reinstall the appliance.

Laddie Appliance Source Code

The Laddie Appliance software is provided in /Code/src and is partitioned into packages corresponding to the various user interfaces and services. The binaries and related files are installed in /opt/laddie. Table E-1 identifies the source and install directories for each of the Laddie appliance components.

Table E-1: Source and Install Directories for Laddie Appliance Components

Component	Source (in /Code/src)	Install Directories
Command line interface	cli	/opt/laddie/{cli,bin}
Empty daemon (used by other components)	empd	n/a
Framebuffer user interface	fbmenu	/opt/laddie/{fbmenu,bin}
Front panel	front_panel	/opt/laddie/bin, /opt/laddie/htdocs/front_panel
Laddie alarm daemon	ladd	/opt/laddie/{ladd,bin}
System logger	logmuxd	/opt/laddie/{logmuxd,bin}
Network daemon	network	/opt/laddie/{networkd,bin}
SNMP agent and MIB	snmpapp	/opt/snmp/sbin, /opt/snmp/share/snmp/mibs
STBmenu	stbmenu	/usr/local/{include,lib}
DB-to-file utility	tbl2filed	/opt/laddie/{tbl2filed,bin}
Web interface	web	/opt/laddie/htdocs/web

In addition to these components, the /Code/src directory contains the buildapp subdirectory, which contains scripts and files that support building the appliance. This subdirectory also contains an examples subdirectory that includes the example programs we discuss in the text.

Where appropriate, component subdirectories include Makefiles. There is also a top-level Makefile in /Code/src that allows you to build and re-install the entire appliance with these commands:

```
laddie:~# make
laddie:~# rm -rf /opt/laddie
laddie:~# make install
```

If you'd like to study the source code, a good place to start is the alarm code in the /Code/src/ladd subdirectory. This is a simple application, but it demonstrates both the empty daemon and the RTA library. The entry point for this service is in /Code/src/empd/main.c. The function main calls appInit in ladd.c, which uses RTA to publish a table of alarm zones.

Laddie Appliance Libraries

The Laddie appliance uses several libraries. The RTA library source is provided in the /usr/src/packages/rta-0.7.5.tgz tarball, and it is installed in /usr/local/lib and /usr/local/include.

The PostgreSQL client, the lighttpd daemon, and the SNMP utilities are well-documented open-source projects that we have compiled and installed without patches. The source code for the versions we use is provided in /usr/src/packages:

- postgresql-base-8.0.1.tar.bz2
- lighttpd-1.4.10.tar.gz
- net-snmp-5.1.3.1.tar.gz

The RTA library and PostgreSQL client do not have configuration files. The lighttpd daemon uses the configuration file /etc/lighttpd.conf. PHP's configuration file is in /etc/php.ini.

Startup Scripts

In order to launch the appliance at system startup, we add scripts to the /etc/rc.d/init.d directory. We also provide links from /etc/rc.d/rc3.d so that these scripts will be invoked in runlevel 3. The Laddie startup scripts include ladd, logmuxd, networkd, snmpd, and tbl2filed. Each of these scripts also provides for the graceful termination of the appliance when the operating system shuts down. The framebuffer user interface is launched at startup using the fbmenuctl script, but because the console must be launched first, we invoke it from the /etc/inittab file.

For convenience when testing, we provide the laddie script in /opt/laddie/bin. This script invokes all of the startup scripts specific to the appliance.

The Linux From-Scratch Distribution and Additional Packages

Had this been a real Linux appliance, we might have opted for a simpler Linux environment. We might have used a smaller kernel, BusyBox utilities, and uclibc libraries, for example. But our emphasis is not embedded Linux, and we feel a more generic Linux environment keeps the focus on the appliance architecture.

As a starting point, we used Linux From Scratch (http://www .linuxfromscratch.org), a distribution that includes most of the tools we needed to build our appliance, and does not include the X Window System (which we didn't need). All the packages required to rebuild the Laddie appliance are included in the /usr/src/packages directory. Most of these packages were installed according to instructions from the Linux From Scratch documentation, which is also included in the usr/src/packages directory as LFS-BOOK-6.0.pdf. Additional packages include the following:

PostgreSQL	FreeType2 and Bitstream fonts	SNMP
PHP	utelnetd	net-tools, libnet, libcap, and arping
SNMP	gdbserver	lynx
dhcpcd	dialog	pciutils
fbset	setserial	lighttpd
SDL and SDL_ttf	LIRC	fanout
Pure-FTPd		

See the file /usr/src/packages/HISTORY for detailed installation notes for these additional packages.

Rebuilding the Laddie Appliance

As a quick illustration of the CD's filesystem structure, let's modify and reinstall a portion of the Laddie appliance. This won't be permanent; we won't create a new CD. We'll just add a line to a .c file in the alarm daemon, recompile it at the Linux shell prompt, reinstall it, and run it.

If you'd like to follow along, boot up an x86 PC using the Laddie CD and bring up a shell console. See "Booting the CD" on page 338 for instructions.

NOTE *This exercise assumes you can use the vi editor. If you're not familiar with vi, you can get up to speed quickly with vimtutor, which is also provided on the CD.*

1. Since the alarm daemon will already be running, kill it with this command:

```
laddie:~# laddie stop
```

2. Then use the following commands to enter the alarm daemon source directory and open the ladd.c file for editing:

```
laddie:~# cd /Code/src/ladd
laddie:~# vi ladd.c
```

3. In the function user_update() at the end of the file, find the following lines:

```
syslog(LOG_ALERT, "User set alarm on zone %d, %s",
Zone[rowid].id, Zone[rowid].name);
```

4. Immediately after these lines, insert the following:

```
syslog(LOG_ALERT, "Hello, world! I've modified the alarm daemon!");
```

5. Save the file and then quit vi. Build and reinstall ladd with the commands:

```
laddie:~# export DEF_APPDIR=/opt/laddie
laddie:~# make -e
laddie:~# make -e install
```

NOTE   *The Laddie appliance components use the environment variable DEF_APPDIR to specify the install location. The default is the more conventional location /usr/local, but we use /opt/laddie instead to make it easier for you to identify the components that are specific to the appliance. The -e option tells the make utility to let environment variables override variables that occur in the Makefiles.*

This will create a new executable and install it in /opt/laddie/bin. Then start the alarm daemon by entering this command:

```
laddie:~# laddie start
```

6. Press ESC to exit the framebuffer user interface. Then monitor the system logs with this command:

```
laddie:~# cat /var/log/messages
```

Log messages are routed to the pipe /var/log/messages by the logmuxd event handler. Using cat, we can display these messages at the console. The command will do nothing until an event occurs.

7. To create a user update event, use CTRL-ALT-F2 to switch to console 2, and then run the command line interface:

```
laddie:~# cli
```

8. Create an update event with the following commands:

```
clear all
test 1
quit
```

9. Now use CTRL-ALT-F1 to switch back to the original console. If your reinstall worked, the displayed log messages will contain a time-stamped entry with your new "Hello, world!" message.

10. Use CTRL-C to terminate the logging display.

INDEX

G

GET request, 106
GetCurrentStatus() function, 128–129
GETNEXT, walking an MIB with, 316
Gnome, 186
GoAhead, 108, 111
graceful degradation, 130–131
grammar using yacc, 144–145
graphical user interface. *See* GUI (graphical user interface) toolkits
graphics libraries
    SDL, 182–185
    Xlib, 181–182
    with X Window System, 181–182
group IDs and daemons, 49–50
GTK+, 186
GUI (graphical user interface) toolkits
    FLTK, 186
    Gnome, 186
    GTK+, 186
    KDE, 186
    licenses for, 186
    Qt, 186
    STBmenu. *See* STBmenu
    widgets, 186

H

hardware monitor, defined, 3
hazy_moon program, 177
"Hello, world!" with STBmenu, 190
help command, 143
HD44780 display controller, 160–163
HTTP (HyperText Transfer Protocol), 106
    and CGI, 107
    and DNS and TCP, 107
    GET request, 106
    httperf testing tool, 112
    and JavaScript, 107
    performance testing tool (httperf), 112
    and telnet, 106
    web basics, 106–107
    webservers, 107. *See also* webservers
httperf tool, 112

I

IANA (Internet Assigned Numbers Authority), 245
infrared remote control
    appliance control, 200–201
    building a simple IR detector, 202
    building a simple IR receiver, 204–205
    communicating with infrared light, 198
    control command protocols, 198–200
    decoding remote control waveforms, 203–204
    detecting/demodulating IR signals, 201–202
    detector, 202, 204–205
    /dev/lirc, 210
    /dev/lircd, 210
    hardware for, 201–207
    interference, 200
    and Laddie appliance, 198–220
    LIRC software package. *See* Linux Infrared Remote Control (LIRC) software package
    receiver
        parts list, 206
        schematics, 205
    signal modulation, 200
    Sony
        command codes, 199
        device addresses, 199
        TV protocol, 198–200
Internet Assigned Numbers Authority (IANA), 245
ioctl command, 175–176
IPC (interprocess communication), 4
irrecord utility, 209, 216, 220
iterator function, 25

video card, finding drivers, 326
video memory
    interpreting bytes, 170–172
    mapping to display, 172–173
virtual terminal, 177–178
vocabulary, using lex, 144

W

web basics, 106–107
web interface for Laddie. *See* Laddie
        web interface
webservers
    Apache, 108, 110, 114
    Boa, 110
    BusyBox httpd, 110
    Cherokee, 110
    choosing, 108–109
    comparisons of, 110–113
    executable size, 111
    GoAhead, 108
    lighttpd, 108
    Linksys wireless router, 109
    memory requirements, 113
    and PHP. *See* PHP
    response time, 112, 113
    thttpd, 111
    TUX, 110
    virtual memory consumed, 111

WHERE clauses, 36
widgets, 186
wireless routers,109
wizards, 139
working directory, setting on a
        daemon, 47
write system call, 174
WRT54G wireless router,
        Linksys, 109

X

Xlib graphics library, 181–182
XML (Extensible Markup
        Language), 14, 118
    alarm status, 129
    SAX, 14
X Window System, 181–182

Y

yacc, 144–145

Z

zalarm, 26
zcount, 26
zname, 26
Zone table, in ladd, 65–67

Electronic Frontier Foundation
Defending Freedom in the Digital World

Free Speech. Privacy. Innovation. Fair Use. Reverse Engineering. **If you care about these rights in the digital world, then you should join the Electronic Frontier Foundation (EFF). EFF was founded in 1990 to protect the rights of users and developers of technology. EFF is the first to identify threats to basic rights online and to advocate on behalf of free expression in the digital age.**

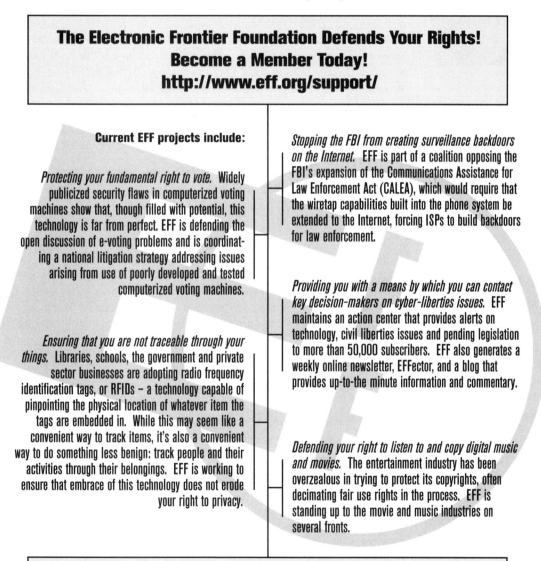

The Electronic Frontier Foundation Defends Your Rights!
Become a Member Today!
http://www.eff.org/support/

Current EFF projects include:

Protecting your fundamental right to vote. Widely publicized security flaws in computerized voting machines show that, though filled with potential, this technology is far from perfect. EFF is defending the open discussion of e-voting problems and is coordinating a national litigation strategy addressing issues arising from use of poorly developed and tested computerized voting machines.

Ensuring that you are not traceable through your things. Libraries, schools, the government and private sector businesses are adopting radio frequency identification tags, or RFIDs – a technology capable of pinpointing the physical location of whatever item the tags are embedded in. While this may seem like a convenient way to track items, it's also a convenient way to do something less benign: track people and their activities through their belongings. EFF is working to ensure that embrace of this technology does not erode your right to privacy.

Stopping the FBI from creating surveillance backdoors on the Internet. EFF is part of a coalition opposing the FBI's expansion of the Communications Assistance for Law Enforcement Act (CALEA), which would require that the wiretap capabilities built into the phone system be extended to the Internet, forcing ISPs to build backdoors for law enforcement.

Providing you with a means by which you can contact key decision-makers on cyber-liberties issues. EFF maintains an action center that provides alerts on technology, civil liberties issues and pending legislation to more than 50,000 subscribers. EFF also generates a weekly online newsletter, EFFector, and a blog that provides up-to-the minute information and commentary.

Defending your right to listen to and copy digital music and movies. The entertainment industry has been overzealous in trying to protect its copyrights, often decimating fair use rights in the process. EFF is standing up to the movie and music industries on several fronts.

Check out all of the things we're working on at http://www.eff.org and join today or make a donation to support the fight to defend freedom online.

ELECTRONIC FRONTIER FOUNDATION · 454 SHOTWELL STREET · SAN FRANCISCO, CA 94110 · 415.436.9333

More No-Nonsense Books from  **NO STARCH PRESS**

HOW LINUX WORKS
What Every Superuser Should Know

by BRIAN WARD

How Linux Works describes the inside of the Linux system for systems adminis-trators, whether they maintain an extensive network in the office or one Linux box at home. After a guided tour of filesystems, the boot sequence, system management basics, and networking, author Brian Ward delves into topics such as development tools, custom kernels, and buying hardware. With a mixture of background theory and real-world examples, this book shows both how to administer Linux, and why each particular technique works, so that you will know how to make Linux work for you.

MAY 2004, 368 PP., $37.95 ($55.95 CDN)
ISBN 978-1-59327-035-3

THE LINUX ENTERPRISE CLUSTER
Build a Highly Available Cluster with Commodity Hardware and Free Software

by KARL KOPPER

The Linux Enterprise Cluster shows how to turn a number of inexpensive net-worked computers into one powerful server. Learn how to: build a high-availability server pair using Heartbeat, use the Linux Virtual Server load balancing software, configure a reliable printing system in a Linux cluster environment, and build a job scheduling system in Linux with no single point of failure. The CD includes the Linux kernel, ldirectord, Mon, Ganglia, OpenSSH, rsync, SystemImager, Heartbeat, and all figures and illustrations used in the book.

MAY 2005, 464 PP., $49.95 ($67.95 CDN)
ISBN 978-1-59327-036-0

THE LINUX COOKBOOK, 2ND EDITION
Tips and Techniques for Everyday Use

by MICHAEL STUTZ

Linux is cool, but it's not always well documented. There are tons of incon-sistent HOWTO files, out-of-date FAQs, and programs scattered everywhere. Whenever you want to do anything with Linux, you usually have to read every piece of documentation out there and basically reverse engineer a solution. Many Linux books for non-geeks are organized by major system, with a chapter on installation, one for video, one for sound, one for networking, and so on. But what if you want to write a book? Or record an album? If you can't dig around on the Web to find someone else doing the same thing, you are out of luck. Unless, that is, you have *The Linux Cookbook*.

AUGUST 2004, 824 PP., $39.95 ($55.95 CDN)
ISBN 978-1-59327-031-5

INSIDE THE MACHINE

An Illustrated Introduction to Microprocessors and Computer Architecture

by JON STOKES

Inside the Machine explains how microprocessors operate—what they do, and how they do it. Written by the co-founder of the highly respected Ars Technica site, the book begins with the fundamentals of computing, defining what a computer is and using analogies, numerous 4-color diagrams, and clear explanations to communicate the concepts that form the basis of modern computing. After discussing computers in the abstract, the book goes on to cover specific microprocessors, discussing in detail how they work and how they differ.

DECEMBER 2006, 320 PP., $49.95 ($61.95 CDN)
ISBN 978-159327-104-6

BUILDING A SERVER WITH FREEBSD

by BRYAN J. HONG

The most difficult aspect of building a server (to act as a file server, web server, or mail server) is the initial software installation and configuration. Getting your hands on the software is one thing; getting it all to function is another thing entirely. For many people, the only option is to hire an expensive consultant. *Building a Server with FreeBSD* tackles the problem systematically, so readers can accomplish the task themselves efficiently and affordably using the freely licensed FreeBSD operating system. Instructions are very clear and straightforward, so the reader need only read and follow the directions. In addition to explaining how to install FreeBSD for the first time, this guide covers configuration of popular third-party software using the ports collection. It takes the pain out of assembling the pieces and putting them all together so the reader can build a server that just works.

AUGUST 2007, 256 PP., $29.95 ($37.95 CDN)
ISBN 978-1-59327-145-9

PHONE:
800.420.7240 OR
415.863.9900
MONDAY THROUGH FRIDAY,
9 A.M. TO 5 P.M. (PST)

FAX:
415.863.9950
24 HOURS A DAY,
7 DAYS A WEEK

EMAIL:
SALES@NOSTARCH.COM

WEB:
WWW.NOSTARCH.COM

MAIL:
NO STARCH PRESS
555 DE HARO ST, SUITE 250
SAN FRANCISCO, CA 94107
USA

COLOPHON

Linux Appliance Design was laid out in Adobe FrameMaker. The font families used are New Baskerville for body text, Futura for headings and tables, and Dogma for titles.

The book was printed and bound at Malloy Incorporated in Ann Arbor, Michigan. The paper is Glatfelter Thor 60# Antique, which is made from 50 percent recycled materials, including 30 percent postconsumer content. The book uses a RepKover binding, which allows it to lay flat when open.

UPDATES

Visit **www.nostarch.com/appliance.htm** for updates, errata, and other information.